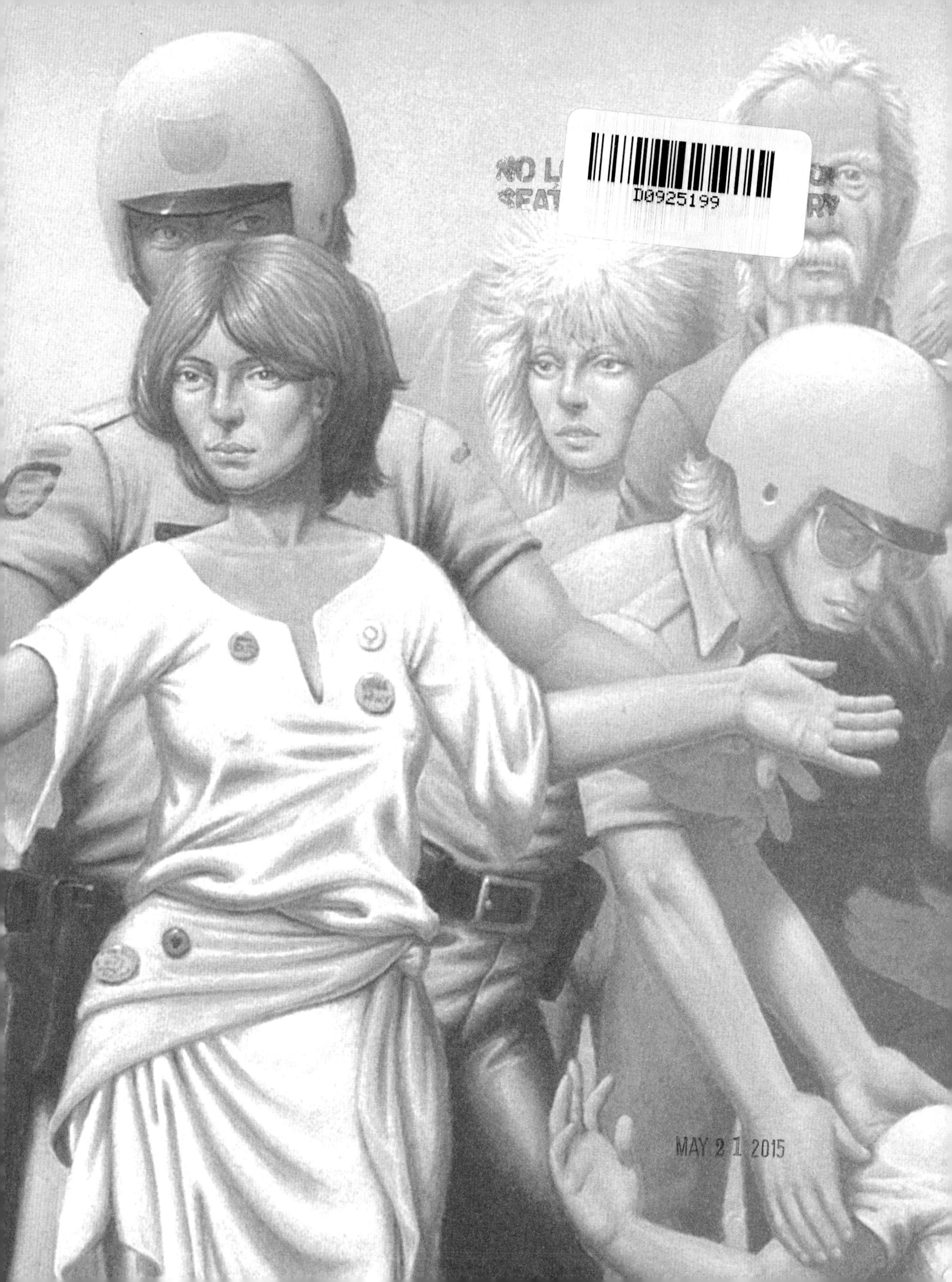

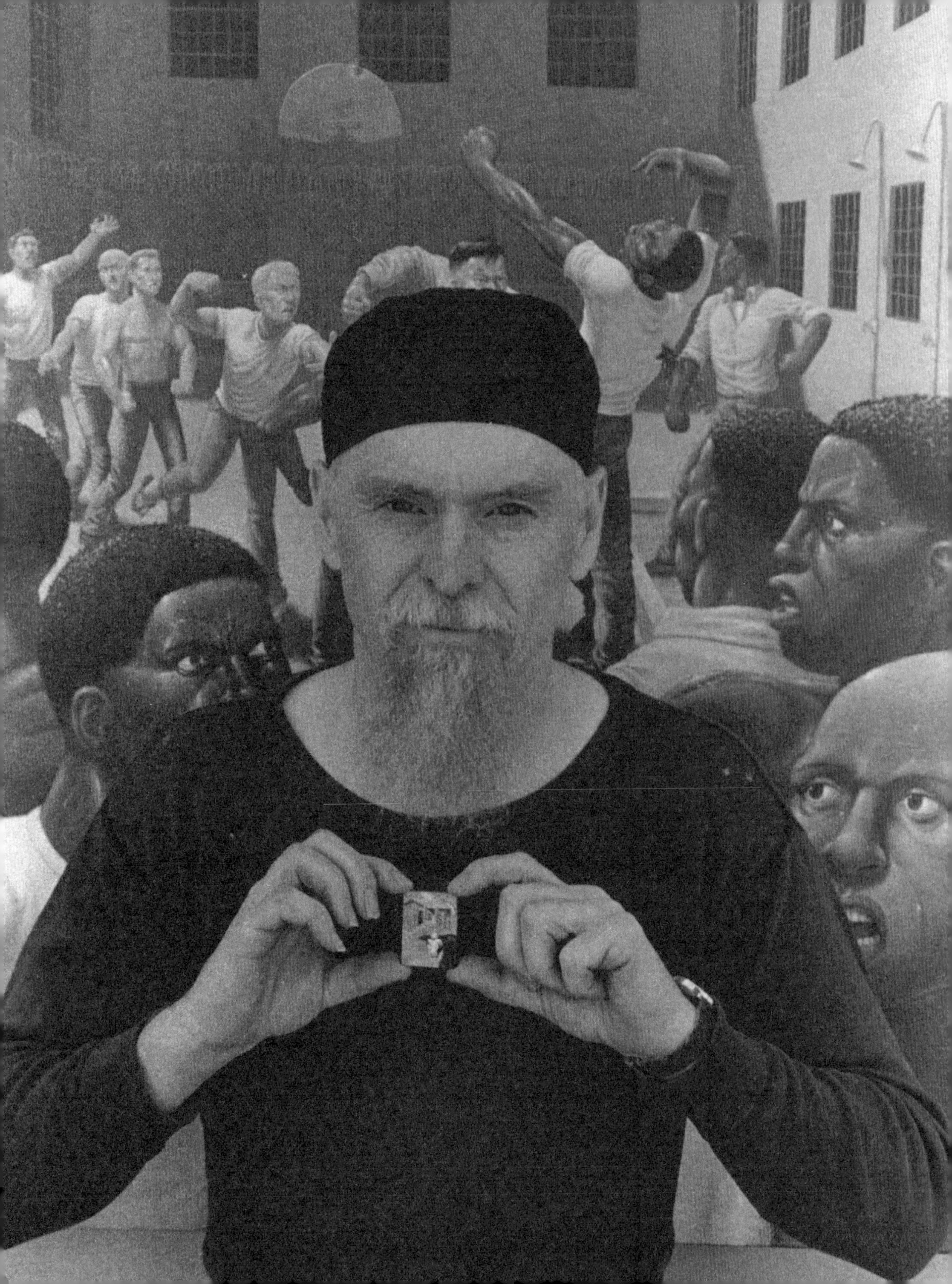

GUY COLWELL

INNER CITY ROMANCE

FANTAGRAPHICS BOOKS, INC.
SEATTLE, WA

Publisher and Executive Editor: GARY GROTH
Senior Editor: J. MICHAEL CATRON
Production: PRESTON WHITE
Associate Publisher: ERIC REYNOLDS

Fantagraphics Books, Inc.
7563 Lake City Way NE
Seattle, WA 98115

Thanks to: Patrick Rosenkranz, Scott Rush, Colin Day, and Lydia Gans.

The comics stories in this book were originally published as follows:
"Choices" in *Inner City Romance* #1, 1972
"Radical Rock" in *Inner City Romance* #2, 1972
"Inner City Romance 3" in *Inner City Romance* #3, 1977
"Ramps" in *Inner City Romance* #4, 1977
"Good for You" in *Inner City Romance* #5, 1978
"Down Up" in *Inner City Romance* #5, 1978
"Interkids" in *Inner City Romance* #5, 1978
"Sex Crime" in *Inner City Romance* #5, 1978
"All Over the Clover" in *Inner City Romance* #5, 1978

Front cover: A detail from Colwell's oil painting *Litter Beach*, 1995–2001.
Back cover: *Bread Line*, acrylic on canvas, 2008. Contrasts wealth and poverty, a prominent theme in Colwell's work since the economic turmoil of recent years.
Inside front cover/page 1 and page 208/inside back cover: A detail from Colwell's *Blockade: Ritual of Non-Violence*, oil on canvas, 1989.
Frontispiece: Guy Colwell with two of his paintings. Behind him is *Death on the Yard*, an oil painting of an actual prison-yard shooting. In his hands, Colwell holds *Cow*, one of his many natural history acrylic miniatures. Photo by Lydia Gans, 1995.

To receive a free catalog of more books like this, as well as an amazing variety of cutting-edge graphic novels, classic comic book and newspaper strip collections, eclectic prose novels, uniquely insightful cultural criticism, and other fine works of artistry, call (800) 657-1100 or visit fantagraphics.com. • Twitter: @fantagraphics • facebook.com/fantagraphics

To dig deeper into Guy Colwell's large body of work, visit his website: www.atelier9.com.

First Fantagraphics Books edition: March 2015
ISBN 978-1-60699-813-7
Printed in Singapore

CONTENTS

All comics stories written and drawn by Guy Colwell

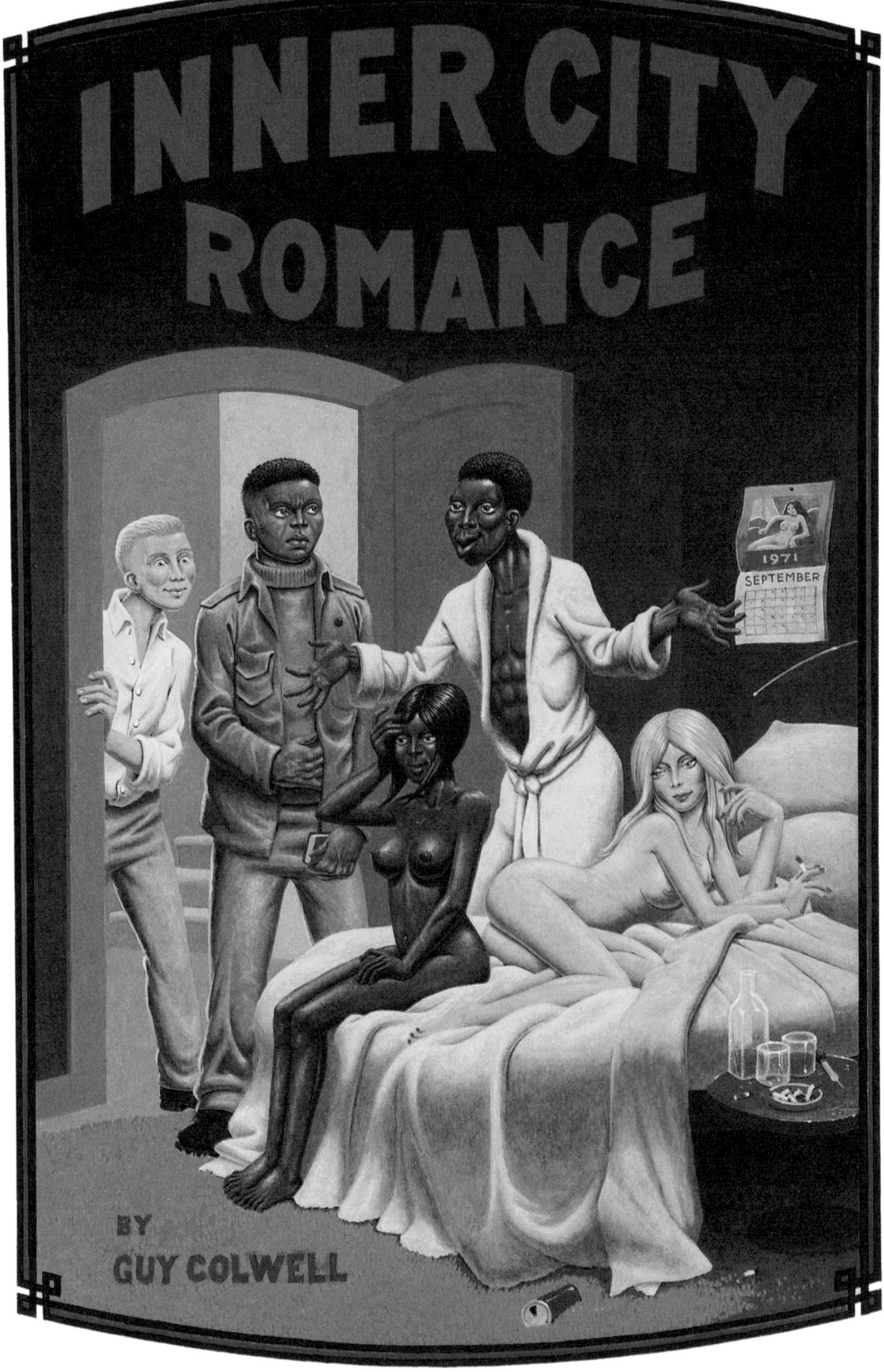
INNER CITY
ROMANCE
1971
SEPTEMBER
BY
GUY COLWELL

Inner City Romance Faux Cover, acrylic on paper, 2010. An imagined version of a cover for a proposed 1980 *Inner City Romance* anthology that never came about.

Good Times and Bad: The Evolution of Revolution

by Patrick Rosenkranz

When Guy Colwell's *Inner City Romance* #1 was cast upon the waters during the high tide of underground comix in 1972, several factors made it stand out from the rapidly inflating field of counterculture funny books. The best-known cartoonists in San Francisco's comics renaissance were telling tales of hippie hijinks, or highly personal stories about childhood traumas and sexual fantasies, or revolutionary fantasies, or satiric send-ups of society. *Inner City Romance* trod new territory. It was about prison, black culture, ghetto life, the sex trade, and radical activism. It portrayed the unpleasant realities of life in the inner city, where opportunities were limited and the American dream was more about survival than lifestyle choices.

Guy Colwell came out of left field as well. He'd been painting for two decades but had never been a cartoonist except for a fleeting aspiration to do animation in junior high school. *Inner City Romance* was overtly political and didn't relate funny stories or develop trademark characters to take the readers on wacky adventures. He portrayed minority culture in such authentic terms that it led to questions about his own racial identity. People wondered who he was, whether he was black or white, and how he knew so much about prison.

"I suppose it was natural to think I was black because so few white creators would touch subjects like I did," suggested Colwell. "Black concerns, issues, stories, would be left to black authors/artists to deal with. A natural assumption, I guess. And I suppose some readers would decide that only a black artist was 'qualified' to do what I was doing. But prison and life in the inner city afterwards gave me enough creds, I believe, to tell these stories because they were derived from my own direct experience and social consciousness. The African-American cartoonist Grass Green told me at a convention that he lost a bet with someone when he, Green, insisted, with money on the table, that Colwell must be black."

Colwell's comic book enjoyed good reviews and the praise of his fellow cartoonists in the underground community.

"I was stunned by the response I got from other artists I admired," he said. "Greg Irons sought me out at a convention and praised *Inner City Romance* #1 as a great and innovative book. Robert Crumb told me he considered it a

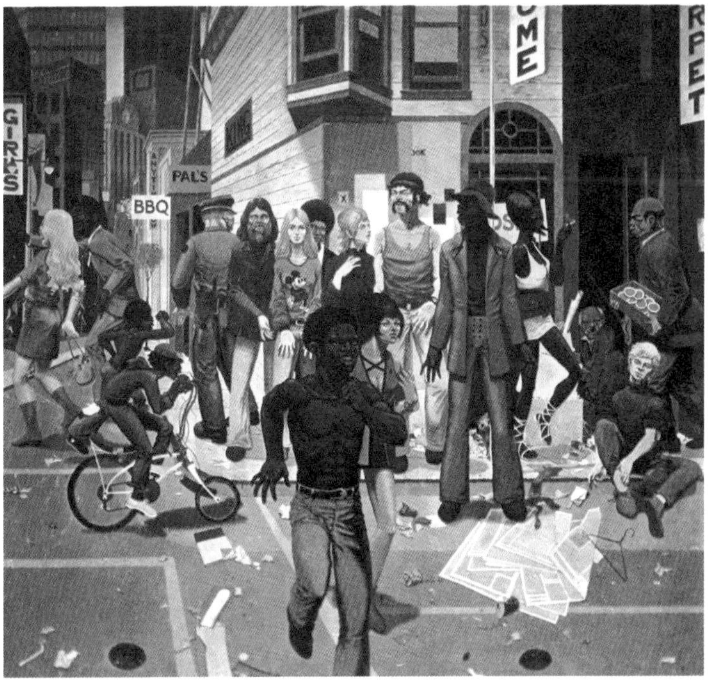
GIRLS
PAL'S
BBQ

Divisadero, oil on canvas, 1970. Colwell completed this large oil painting in San Francisco just prior to beginning the *Inner City Romance* series. This is the environment in which Colwell conceived and executed his first comic book.

masterpiece. British publisher Felix Dennis liked it so much he reprinted pages in *Oz* magazine, though without asking my permission. My comics impressed the staff of the *San Francisco Good Times* enough to let me start a comic strip and edit a page of comics. It was a delight to be suddenly included in the community of underground cartoonists in San Francisco. A lot of professional identity and feeling of self-worth came out of this association."

That level of understanding for his subject matter was the result of a school-of-hard-knocks education, courtesy of the military industrial complex. When he turned 18, Colwell registered with the Selective Service System but then decided he would not cooperate with them or join the military.

"I considered applying as a conscientious objector. By age 18 in 1963 I had read some works on non-violence, especially Gandhi, and I was aware of Martin Luther King Jr.'s efforts to non-violently overcome segregation in the South. It began seeming obvious to me that this tactic could be the answer to achieving social justice and even resisting tyranny without war. I started reading the *Handbook for Conscientious Objectors* by Arlo Tatum. But as I tried to prepare myself for making this application, the Vietnam War started and becoming a C.O. didn't seem strong enough. I wanted to resist the war. So I sent back my draft card and became a non-cooperator. From this point, in 1964, I knew I would end up in prison, though it took four more years to get there. When I was indicted, I went to trial in San Francisco in early 1968. The court sentenced me to two years."

Colwell was sent to the federal McNeil Island Penitentiary (later the Washington State McNeil Island Corrections Center, now closed).

"McNeil was a federal prison that consisted of a big max house and a minimum-security camp on an island in Puget Sound near Tacoma, Washington. The camp, where

Woman on the Line, opaque watercolor, 1969. Painted while Colwell was incarcerated for draft resistance at the McNeil Island Penitentiary. This piece shows the first inkling of the representational social surrealism that would dominate Colwell's work after years of decorative abstraction.

I was sent after a few harrowing days in the max unit, included a 40-acre vegetable garden and facilities where inmates raised livestock, cut lumber, and processed apples from an extensive orchard. The farm produced food for the main maximum-security facility on the island. The dormitories were crowded, and the prison population included the whole range of federal lawbreakers.

"Even a minimum-security prison is a pretty crazy and scary place," said Colwell. "There was always an undercurrent of threat and restrained aggression that would break out from time to time. There were occasional violent altercations between inmates, and there was one killing of a man in my dormitory, who slept not four feet from where I did. But in many ways it was way more relaxed than it would have been in the max unit. There were no walls or fences surrounding the facility. Any inmate could walk away from

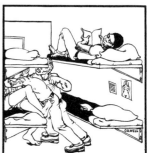

Four Cells, brush and ink, 1972. Colwell's recollections of prison were still strong when he created this illustration for the *San Francisco Good Times* alternative newspaper.

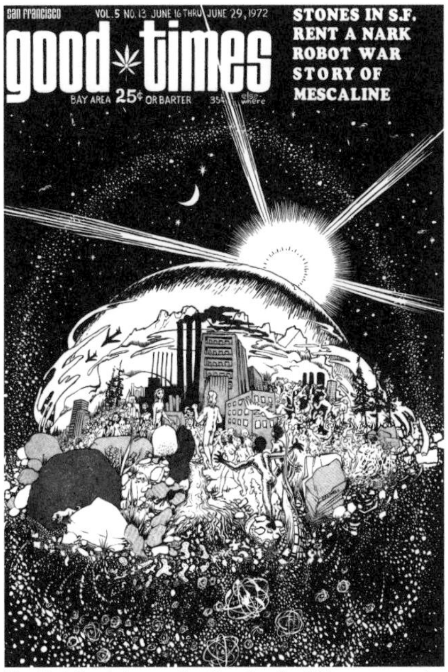
san francisco
VOL.5 NO.13 JUNE 16 THRU JUNE 29, 1972
good times
STONES IN S.F.
RENT A NARK
ROBOT WAR
STORY OF
MESCALINE
BAY AREA 25¢ OR BARTER

Untitled Earth image, *San Francisco Good Times* cover, vol. 5 #13, June 16–June 29, 1972.

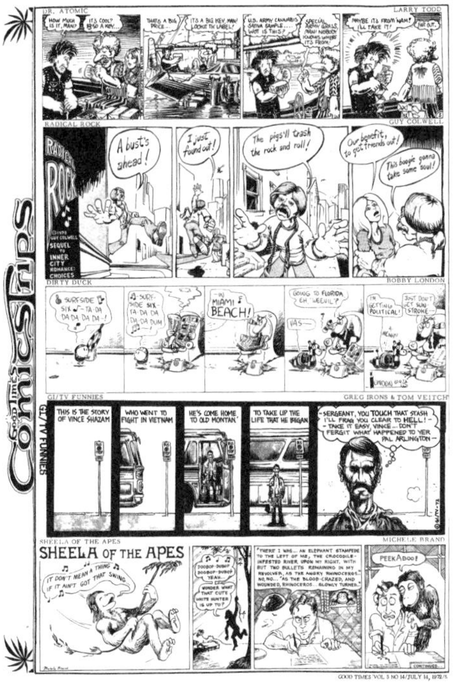
Good Times Comics Trips
DR. ATOMIC
LARRY TODD
HOW MUCH IS IT, MAN?
IT'S COOL? $150 A KEY...
THAT'S A BIG PRICE...
IT'S A BIG KEY, MAN! LOOKIT TH' LABEL!
U.S. ARMY CANNABIS SATIVA SAMPLE.... WOT IS THIS?
SPECIAL ARMY GRASS, MAN! NOBODY KNOWS WHERE IT'S FROM!
MAYBE IT'S FROM 'NAM! I'LL TAKE IT!
FAR OUT.
RADICAL ROCK
GUY COLWELL
RADICAL ROCK
SEQUEL TO INNER CITY ROMANCE: CHOICES
A bust's ahead!
I just found out!
The pigs'll trash the rock and roll!
Our benefit, to get friends out!
This boogie gonna take some soul!
DIRTY DUCK
BOBBY LONDON
SURFSIDE SIX — TA-DA DA-DA DA DA—!
SURF-SIDE SIX—TA-DA DA DA-DA DUM—!
—IN MIAMI BEACH!
GOING TO FLORIDA, EH, WEEVIL?
YAS—
I'M GETTING POLITICAL!
JUST DON'T GET SUN-STROKE—
GI/TV FUNNIES
GREG IRONS & TOM VEITCH
GI/TV FUNNIES
THIS IS THE STORY OF VINCE SHAZAM
WHO WENT TO FIGHT IN VIETNAM
HE'S COME HOME TO OLD MONTAN'
TO TAKE UP THE LIFE THAT HE BEGAN
—SERGEANT, YOU TOUCH THAT STASH I'LL FRAG YOU CLEAR TO HELL!—
—TAKE IT EASY, VINCE... DON'T FERGIT WHAT HAPPENED TO YER PAL ARLINGTON—
SHEELA OF THE APES
MICHELE BRAND
SHEELA OF THE APES
IT DON'T MEAN A THING IF IT AIN'T GOT THAT SWING...
DOOBOP-DUBOP DOOBOP-DUBOP YEAH...
WONDER WHAT THAT CUTE WHITE HUNTER IS UP TO?
"THERE I WAS... AN ELEPHANT STAMPEDE TO THE LEFT OF ME, THE CROCODILE-INFESTED RIVER UPON MY RIGHT, WITH BUT TWO BULLETS REMAINING IN MY REVOLVER, AS THE ANGRY RHINOCEROS." NO, NO... "AS THE BLOOD-CRAZED, AND WOUNDED, RHINOCEROS... SLOWLY TURNED."
PEEKABOO!
CONTINUED...
GOOD TIMES VOL 5 NO 14/JULY 14, 1972/5

Comics Trips, *San Francisco Good Times*, vol. 5 #14, June 30–July 14, 1972. 1972 was a busy year of anti-war and counterculture activism for Colwell, who lived and worked with the *San Francisco Good Times* newspaper commune. This is the first appearance of *Comics Trips*, a full page of episodic strips, including "Radical Rock," which became *Inner City Romance* #2. The other artists include Larry Todd, Bobby London, Greg Irons, and Michelle Brand. Gary Hallgren designed the logo. These strips ended when the paper folded in August 1972.

the farm anytime except when locked down at night. But it was an island, so you couldn't get anywhere if you tried without taking a swim. My assigned jobs included vegetable gardening, driving the swill truck, care and feeding of pigs, harvesting apples, and cutting lawns. When I was in the vegetable garden, I would risk punishment or a longer sentence by slipping out of the compound and taking walks through the beautiful forested areas that surrounded the camp. These little escapes helped me keep my head together while I was getting used to being there."

Racial segregation and prison gang conflicts were not so prevalent at the McNeil camp when he was there, he noted.

"There were some groups of white guys who would have nothing to do with the blacks and some blacks who tried not to interact with any whites. The same dynamic with the Latinos. But in the less-pressurized environment of the minimum-security camp, there were no real harsh consequences for fraternization between the groups. I was so personally willing to be open and friendly enough with anyone that I remember being called a 'nigger lover' behind my back once or twice. But even though there was some racial tension flowing below the surface, no one ever came to me and said 'you gotta get with the Aryan Brotherhood.' Of course, the draft resisters had their own 'gang,' so to speak. Some of the draft people were pretty hardcore rebel guys, more revolutionary than pacifist, and could bad-talk the 'pigs' as hard as any convict. So it got to be that we were all just prisoners of the Man. When I first arrived at the camp, there were only two other draft resisters there, but probably 50 or more by the time I left."

Another prisoner had a subscription to the *East Village Other*, and Colwell usually got a chance to read it, too. The strip *Trashman: Agent of the Sixth International* drawn by Spain Rodriguez was a big hit with the inmates.

"After more than a year in prison with some pretty radical resistors, the vision of armed revolution in the strip was speaking to me in a way that was new. I would never give up the ideal of non-violence, but it began to feel more and more like I was becoming a 'militant' non-violent anti-war activist. *Trashman* helped infuse some of that flavor into my thinking."

McNeil was where the focus of Colwell's art changed as well. He had come of age in Berkeley and eagerly embraced the counterculture revolution when it began to coalesce during his college years. The hedonistic elements that initially fueled his artistic inspirations were gradually replaced by harsh reality in the dangerous environment of incarceration, where he had to keep his eyes wide open to survive.

"When I first started taking marijuana and LSD, it seemed like everyone else was taking them too. There was a great swirling flood of drug-triggered creativity in every artistic field: music, movies, graphic arts, and fine arts. Some books were the rage: *Stranger in a Strange Land*, *The Psychedelic Experience*, *The Doors of Perception*, *Lord of the Rings*, *Naked Lunch* — a lot of the popular stuff among the druggy, hippie crowd. For me, before prison at least, this exposure translated into a lot of experiments in making visual the psychedelic experience in paint like some artists were doing with the dance posters. I produced many paintings of an abstract, drug-inspired nature from 1964 to 1968 of which remarkably few still exist. But after going to prison, I was more drawn to the social and political movements, which influenced my art more than the fantasy and escapist aspects. The hippie thing blended into the political activist thing in activities like anti-war demonstrations and urban realist art."

He spent time painting small abstract watercolors at his bunk. Prisoners who saw him at work often asked him to do portraits of them, so realistic figure drawings also became part of his repertoire. Psychedelic explorations didn't seem so appropriate anymore.

"A lot of serious stuff was going on — war, various liberation struggles, civil rights movements, a world divided between capitalism and communism, lots of injustice, poverty, inequality of wealth and rights. After the education I got in prison, I couldn't see myself going back to being a happy hippie abstract paint dabbler. I had to make my art a vehicle of serious thought, social commentary, and political action. I was bound, after my refusal to join in the military madness, not to live a trivial life but to do something that would add my voice to all those calling for justice, fairness, and peace. Resisting the war and supporting the concept of non-violence as a superior method for making social progress were the most overt motivators toward becoming more and more political in my thinking and in my art."

Colwell was released after 17 months and three days and made plans to buy a bicycle and ride it back to the Bay Area, but prison officials nixed this unconventional transport and told him to take the bus. He had already arranged for gainful employment at his former art school.

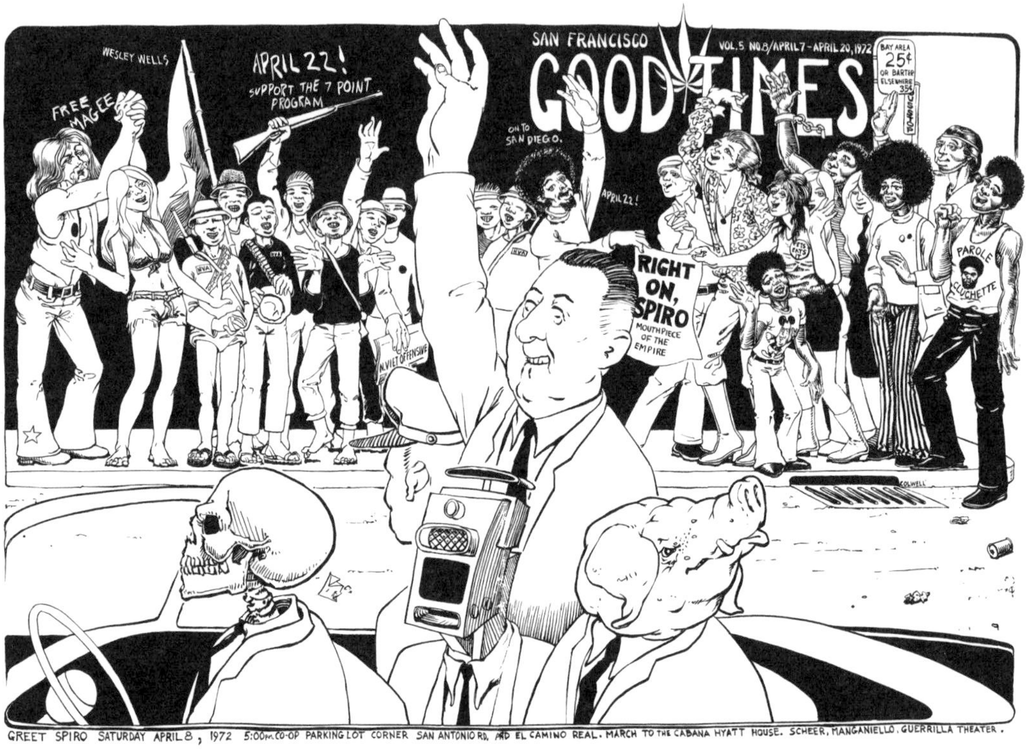

SAN FRANCISCO
GOOD TIMES
VOL. 5 NO. 8/APRIL 7 - APRIL 20, 1972
BAY AREA 25¢ OR BARTER ELSEWHERE 35¢
WESLEY WELLS
FREE MAGEE
APRIL 22! SUPPORT THE 7 POINT PROGRAM
ON TO SAN DIEGO.
APRIL 22!
RIGHT ON, SPIRO
MOUTHPIECE OF THE EMPIRE
PAROLE
COLWELL
GREET SPIRO SATURDAY APRIL 8, 1972 5:00pm. CO-OP PARKING LOT CORNER SAN ANTONIO RD. AND EL CAMINO REAL. MARCH TO THE CABANA HYATT HOUSE. SCHEER, MANGANIELLO, GUERRILLA THEATER.

Spiro Agnew front and back covers, *San Francisco Good Times*, vol. 5 #8, April 7–April 20, 1972. A visit by the vice president to San Francisco in 1972 presented a highly visible opportunity to protest the Vietnam War. This wraparound front/back cover illustration was designed to be a pullout poster announcing the time and place of the demonstration.

"In September 1969 when I was released, I went directly to Oakland, where I had a job lined up doing custodial and maintenance work at the California College of Arts and Crafts. I had to stay at that job for about a year as a requirement of my parole. After that time, I quit the job but hung out in Oakland for another year or so making the transition to figurative social surrealism in a flood of new paintings. My *Self-Portrait With Creature* was done in this period and really made me turn the corner and leave abstraction behind. I got so much more satisfaction from working in a style more derived from classical painting. I also did *Race Street*, which was such a monstrosity of violence in oil that I later [1993] destroyed it in a publicity stunt."

In 1971 he moved across the Bay in hopes of kick-starting his career as a painter and graphic artist in a place where he could find more opportunities. Painting in oils was his preferred medium, but he also liked what he saw in the expanding underground comix scene and considered joining in the fun.

"These underground comics, drawn by people such as Moscoso, Shelton, Crumb, Spain, Griffith, Irons, Beck, and other talented folks really inspired my admiration. They seemed to touch me on all sorts of levels, reviving some of the enjoyment I'd felt reading comics as a child, yet earning my respect as an artist for their creative skill while entering into stunning areas that had been unexplored by comics before then. It was a fairly natural progression for me to begin thinking I could do something like that myself."

Like many American kids of his generation, Colwell learned to read by reading comics.

"Donald Duck, Uncle Scrooge, Little Lulu, Casper, Sad Sack, Mighty Mouse, Bugs Bunny — I preferred comics for bedtime reading. At first my mother read them to me, then I gradually learned to follow the short bits of dialogue as she read.

Guy Colwell's short career as a courtroom sketch artist brought him into direct contact with many of the intense political dramas of the 1970s. Using Prismacolor pencils, he drew Patty Hearst (top) at her arraignment for bank robbery in 1975, White Panthers Tom Stevens and Terry Phillips (middle) on trial in 1974 for a shootout with police, and the San Quentin Six (bottom) on trial in 1972 for their role in a prison revolt that left six people dead.

Portobello, oil on canvas, 1979. Colwell again looks at the reality of urban life at street level, this time in London, England, where he stayed for a few months after living in Paris for a year. This was after the final *Inner City Romance* had been published. In 1980 he returned to San Francisco and was soon back on the fine art track.

Empty Lot, oil on canvas, 1977. This depiction of a city garden is quintessential Colwell, from a period when the central focus of his work was urban reality. This painting, showing processes of nurturing and decay, was used for the cover of a French edition of *Inner City Romance* published by Artefact in 1980.

Eventually I was reading them myself. I moved on to reading a lot of *Classics Illustrated*, which taught me comics could also be a medium for more serious stories, not just jokey stuff. Then, of course, along came *Mad* magazine, which showed me comics could have biting satire and social commentary mixed in with great humor."

Maybe he could recapture some of the excitement he remembered from engaging with his favorite comic books.

Prison had made him a different person, he realized — more burned out and less innocent.

"I was living by myself in a funky room on Divisadero Street in San Francisco, needing to come up with some income, so I decided it was finally time to do a comic book of my own," said Colwell. "I may have been a little crazy to start in on a whole book without figuring the problems I might have getting it published, but I was a little crazy at the time and caught up in a need to say something about my life."

Reading *Legion of Charlies* by Greg Irons and Tom Veitch, which drew parallels between the lives of cult leader Charlie Manson (convicted of 27 counts of murder in January 1971) and Charlie Company leader Lieutenant William "Rusty" Calley (convicted in March 1971 and later pardoned) for the murder of 22 Vietnamese civilians in the Mỹ Lai massacre, convinced him that comic books were now wide open for strong and challenging content.

"I was surprised one day to discover that around the corner from me resided an African-American man who had been in the same prison dormitory as me at McNeil. Our shared experience made it natural for us to do a bit of hanging out together and reminiscing about prison and other inmates we knew, some of whom also turned up in this scene. This person was, however, entangled in heroin addiction, and knowing him managed to bring me into an underclass network that included addicts, prostitutes, dealers, as well as musicians, artists, and politicos. It was a remarkable and memorable year that could have been the basis for many stories. I was able to wander through the hard-drug, black-music, sex-for-sale, and radical-political underground and take in a lot of information that would inform my art and my life from then on. I was more of an observer than a participant. While I could sit and watch the addicts shooting up, watch drug deals go down, or help out when someone overdosed, I never took any drugs myself other than weed and LSD. I didn't get physically involved with any of the women I thought might be prostitutes except to do some portrait sketches. I was careful during this intense and dangerous time to keep my eye

on the really important things — living simply, keeping my health, and doing my fine art. Taken all together, the expression that needed to come out of this year-unlike-any-other was so large and unusual that I had to find something other than a painting to contain it. It needed to be a story, not just an image, though I tried at first to put it into an image in the painting *Divisadero*. But when I finally decided to do a comic book, I set in motion a tale of men rediscovering the world after being in prison, wove these familiar elements into it, and the result was a little book about the inner city that I'm pleased to say has received a lot of praise from comics fans, cartoonists, and reviewers over the years and might have even had its small influence in the underground comics movement."

Last Gasp went through four printings of *Inner City Romance* #1 and eventually sold 50,000 copies. Colwell started on *Inner City Romance* #2 while working at the *San Francisco Good Times* newspaper, where he serialized the first 13 episodes of *Radical Rock* on their "Comics Trips" page. When the paper folded in August 1972 he continued his episodic storyline into a full comic book, which Last Gasp published later that year. Things moved quickly in those heady days when comix publishers had a hard time keeping up with buyer demand.

Explicit sex scenes came with the territory in underground comix, and Colwell had no reluctance in depicting naked males and females doing what comes naturally. Readers appreciated these scenes as well, and Last Gasp's Ron Turner was happy to supply what the customers wanted.

"Well, of course, sex sells," admitted Colwell. "It may be cynical, but I wonder if I had brought a book like *Inner City Romance* #1 to Last Gasp and it had no sex in it whether it would have gotten published. Maybe I was selling the social criticism by using sex and nudity just like a car salesman. Though doing sexual or erotic art has a frivolous or self-indulgent flavor to it, there was a strong prevailing attitude in those years between the introduction of effective birth control and the emergence of AIDS that it was time to loosen up on the traditional morality around sex. So we were tempted to think that sexual themes performed outwardly in cultural productions like films, books, and comics were actually political in nature. This

Clean Up, watercolor, 1979. This is Colwell's appreciation of a small triangular patch of green nature, which attracted garbage like a magnet. People would come from far and wide to throw their refuse on the one place that was not already covered with concrete. Colwell entertained idealistic images of community action for this spot next to his apartment in San Francisco, but in reality, he often cleaned up by himself.

Playground, watercolor, 1984. This bleak big-city street scene represents Colwell's documentation of an urban underclass, composed from life sketches done on the streets of San Francisco throughout the 1970s. It shows an actual playground made inaccessible to children after being occupied by numerous homeless men.

call to create a new way of thinking about love, this surging free love revolution, seemed at the time like an important movement that was intimately connected with the creation of a new, happier world.

"Well, that was our idealistic excuse. But in my comic books, the sex turned out not to be sweet, innocent, spiritual hippie sex. It was not even a declaration of grown-up liberated sex. For the purpose of the stories, I explored a darker side, probably because I had a dark side myself after all the time in prison listening to endless, relentless talk about cocks and pussies and bitches and sadistic desires, that sex couldn't be free to be just sweet anymore. I brought to the comics a sense that I was dealing not just with happy and healthy things but with primitive impulses and powerful, obsessive, dangerous forces that, more than we wish to admit, control us, distract us, and so often muddle our thinking. I also love the human figure as a subject for artwork and have studied the nude in art over the centuries and participated in many figure drawing classes and workshops. So any excuse I could

find to draw naked bodies in my comic books was good enough for me. All these threads got woven together in the comic books."

He didn't know all that much about making comic books when he started. None of his training at Berkeley High School or the California College of Arts and Crafts included cartooning classes, so he approached the project based on what he did know.

"I think I invented my own way of doing comics," said Colwell. "I didn't have a teacher or mentor. In fact, because I so much identified myself first as a painter, when I started my first comic I tried to keep it connected in various ways to painting. The figurative realism of the drawing was a direct extension of the realism I was going for in my paintings. I did not try to do that much 'cartooning' of the figures except to keep them simple enough that I could work quickly. I always figured I would get through a comic book fast and go back to my canvases. *Inner City Romance* #1, #2, and #3 were done entirely with small sable brushes so

I could feel like I was 'painting' them. I added Zip-A-Tone to the pages of *Inner City Romance* #2 after the brushwork. I learned quickly to hate Zip-A-Tone, and I never used it again. *Inner City Romance* #4 and a lot of #5 were done with Rapidograph pens, and I finally made the transition to crow quill pens. I think as I progressed my style became more and more realistic rather than more cartoony. There are also deeper, older artistic influences that perhaps, while more evident in my paintings, do also inform my comic

Race Street was a large oil painting begun in 1969 and finished in 1971 — while Colwell was in the thrall of Hieronymus Bosch, wrestling with the aftereffects of prison, and in need of a challenging project to get his interrupted career moving forward. However, he was always uncomfortable with the shocking violence in this picture, so in 1993 he destroyed it as a publicity stunt.

book work. Very strong inspiration comes from Renaissance painting, especially Northern Renaissance. Van Eyck, Bruegel, and Bosch had a very strong hold on my mind and my direction of development. Then also a lot of American painters — Grant Wood, Thomas Hart Benton, Andrew Wyeth, Edward Hopper, and yes, even Norman Rockwell — with their secular realism and historical consciousness, contributed to my formation both as a painter and comic book author. While I deeply studied, enjoyed, and practiced 20th century abstract art up through art school and on until prison, it did not put so strong a hold on me or prove to be as satisfying to do as the social realism that has asserted dominance throughout most of my life."

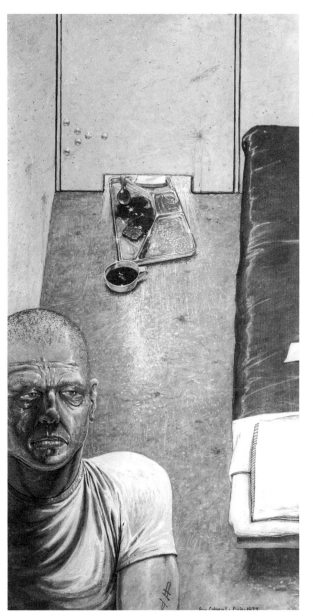

Free Lunch, opaque watercolor, 1977. Here, Colwell returns to a prison environment, in a play on the phrase "There's no such thing as a free lunch."

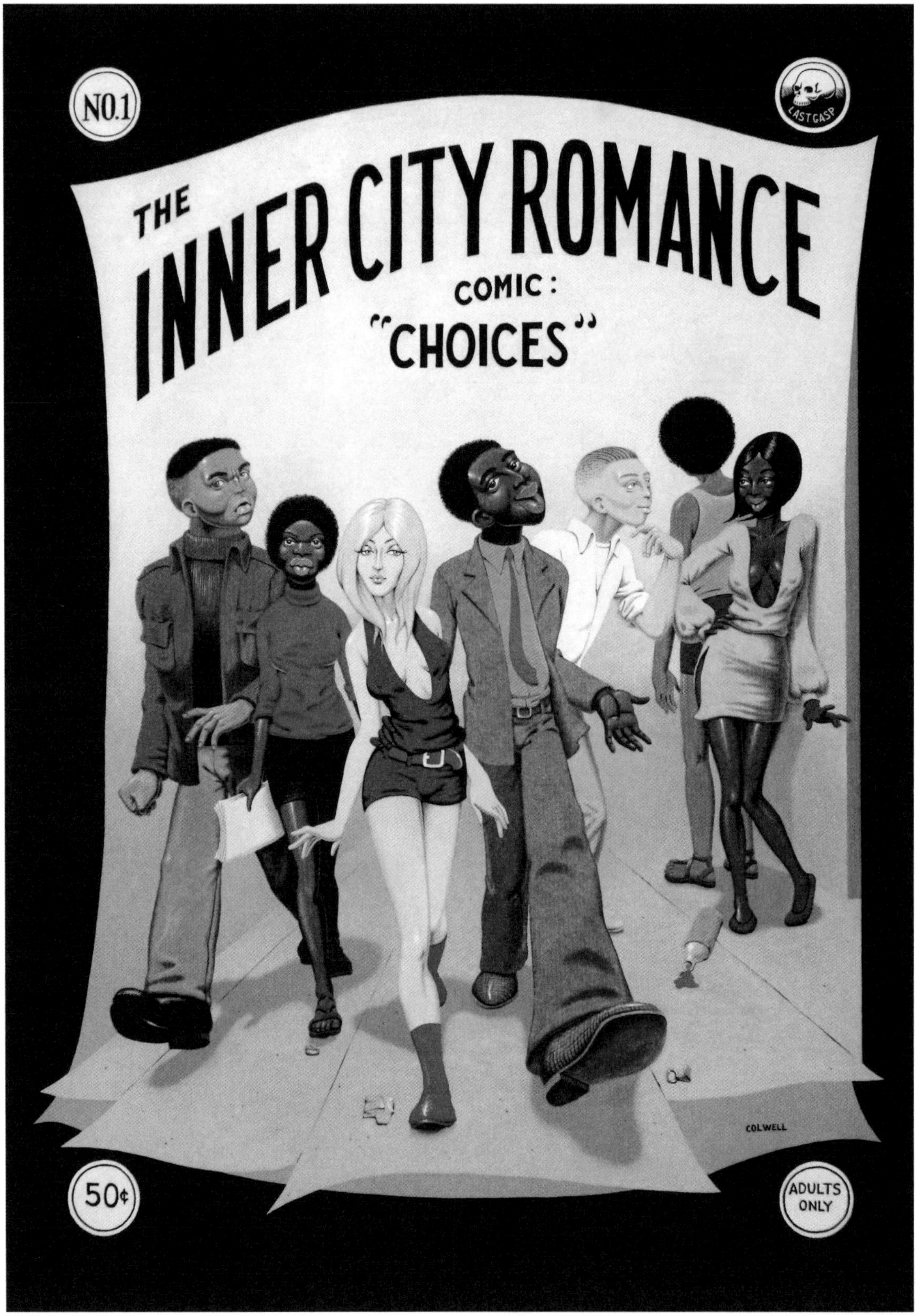
NO.1
LAST GASP
THE
INNER CITY ROMANCE
COMIC:
"CHOICES"
COLWELL
50¢
ADULTS ONLY

Inner City Romance #1 cover re-creation, acrylic on canvas, 2011. This large version of Colwell's first comic book cover was commissioned by a fan.

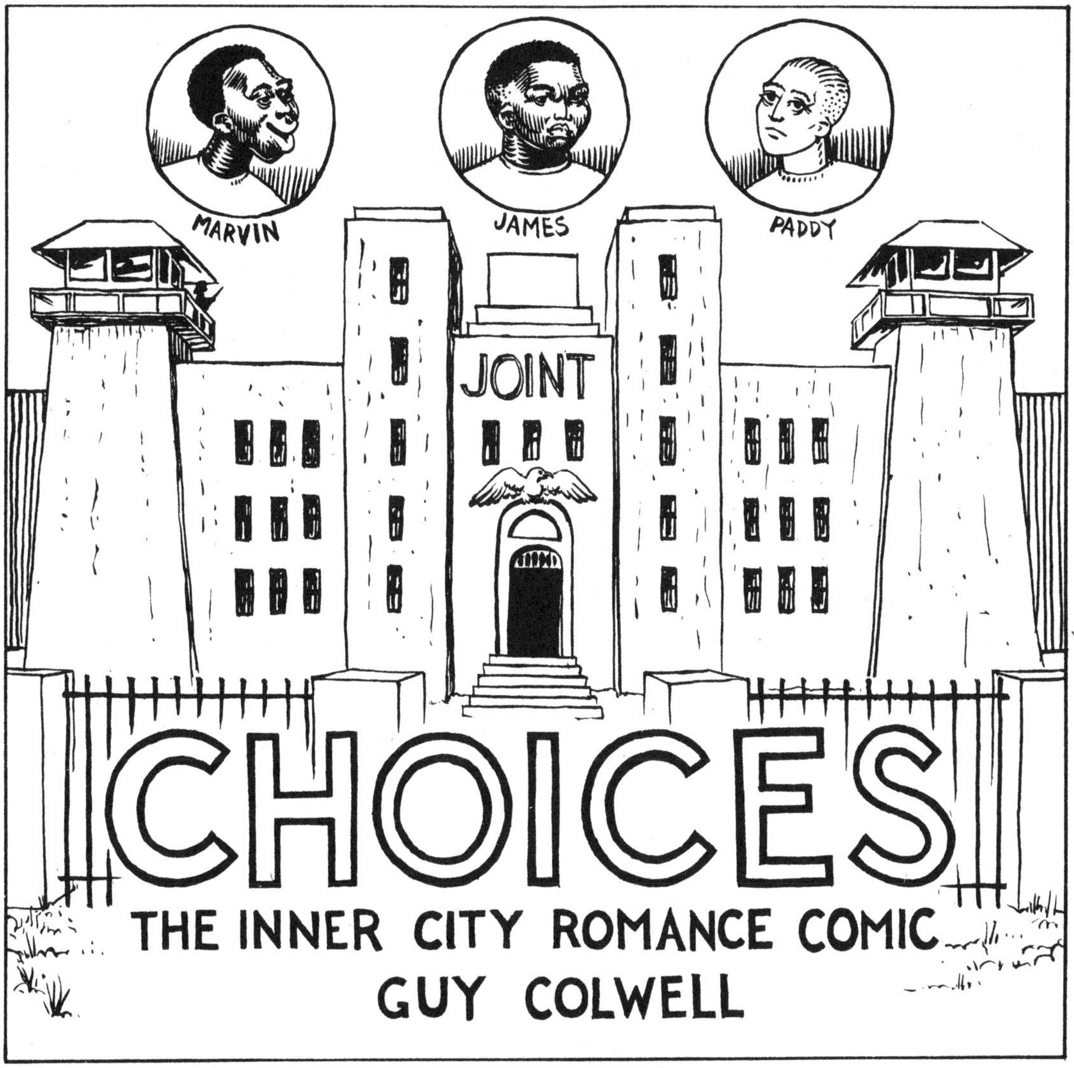
MARVIN
JAMES
PADDY
JOINT
CHOICES
THE INNER CITY ROMANCE COMIC
GUY COLWELL

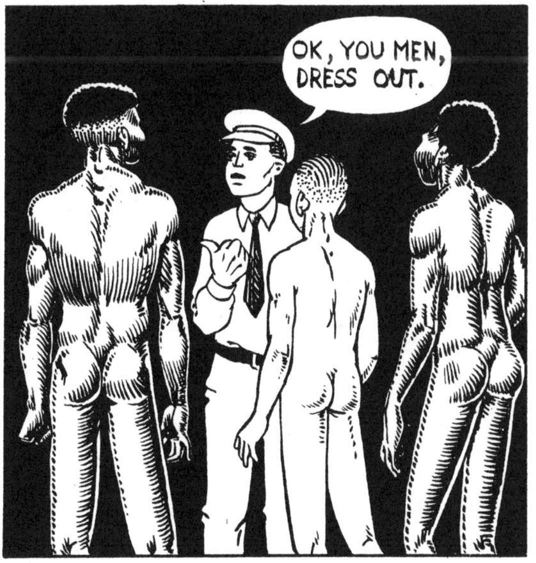
OK, YOU MEN, DRESS OUT.

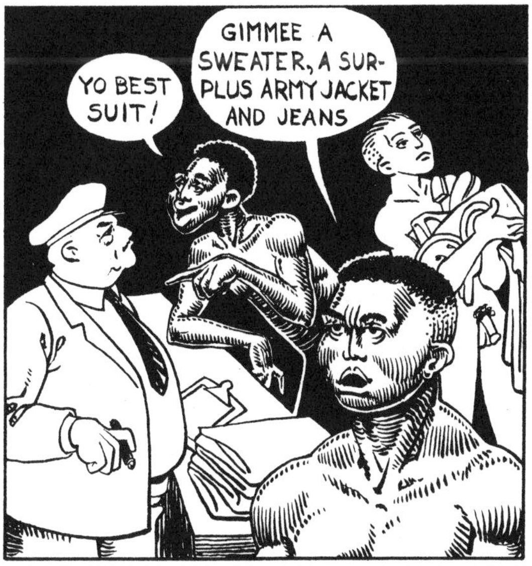
YO BEST SUIT!
GIMMEE A SWEATER, A SURPLUS ARMY JACKET AND JEANS

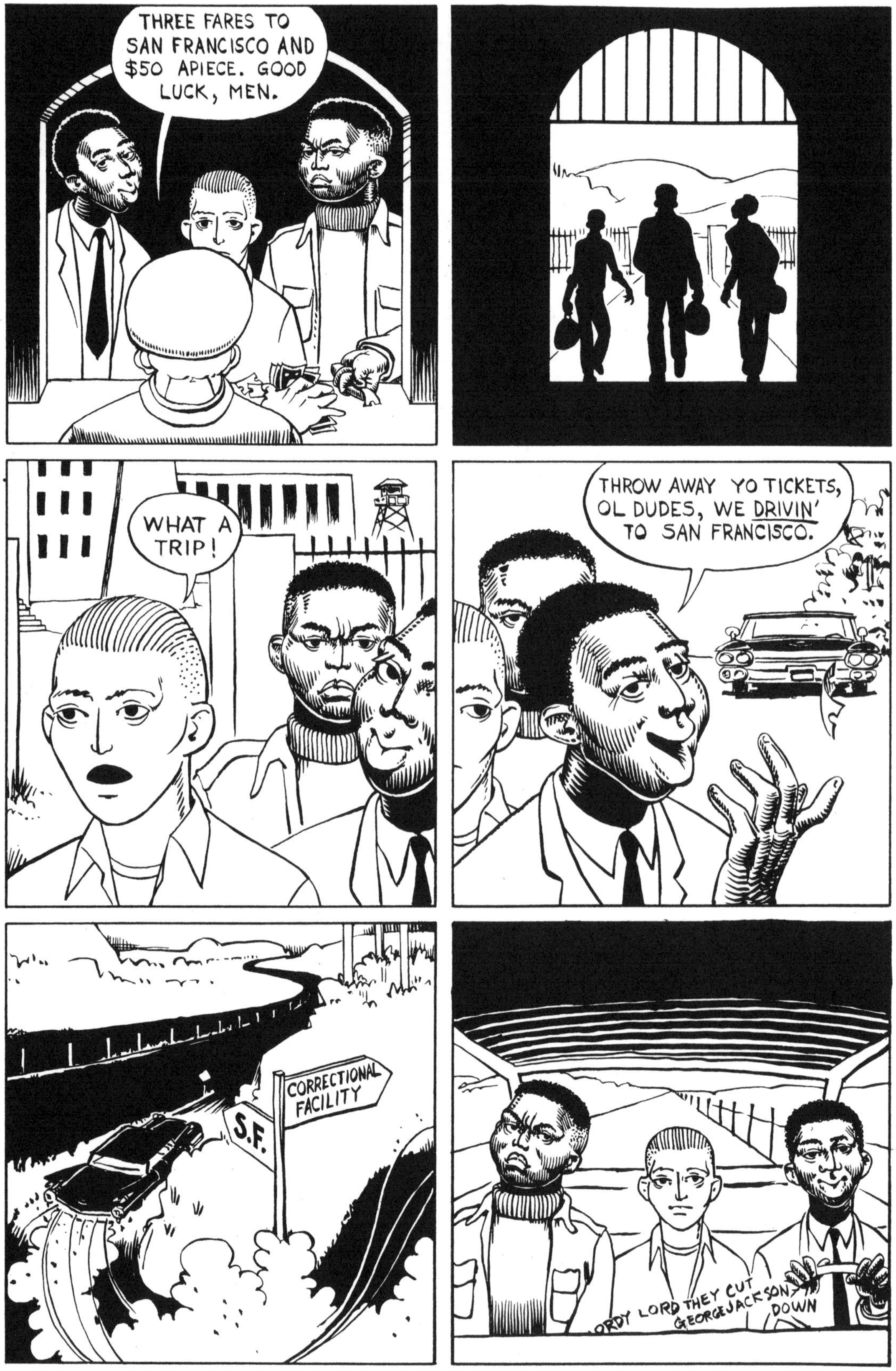
THREE FARES TO SAN FRANCISCO AND $50 APIECE. GOOD LUCK, MEN.
WHAT A TRIP!
THROW AWAY YO TICKETS, OL DUDES, WE DRIVIN' TO SAN FRANCISCO.
CORRECTIONAL FACILITY
S.F.
ORDY LORD THEY CUT GEORGEJACKSON DOWN

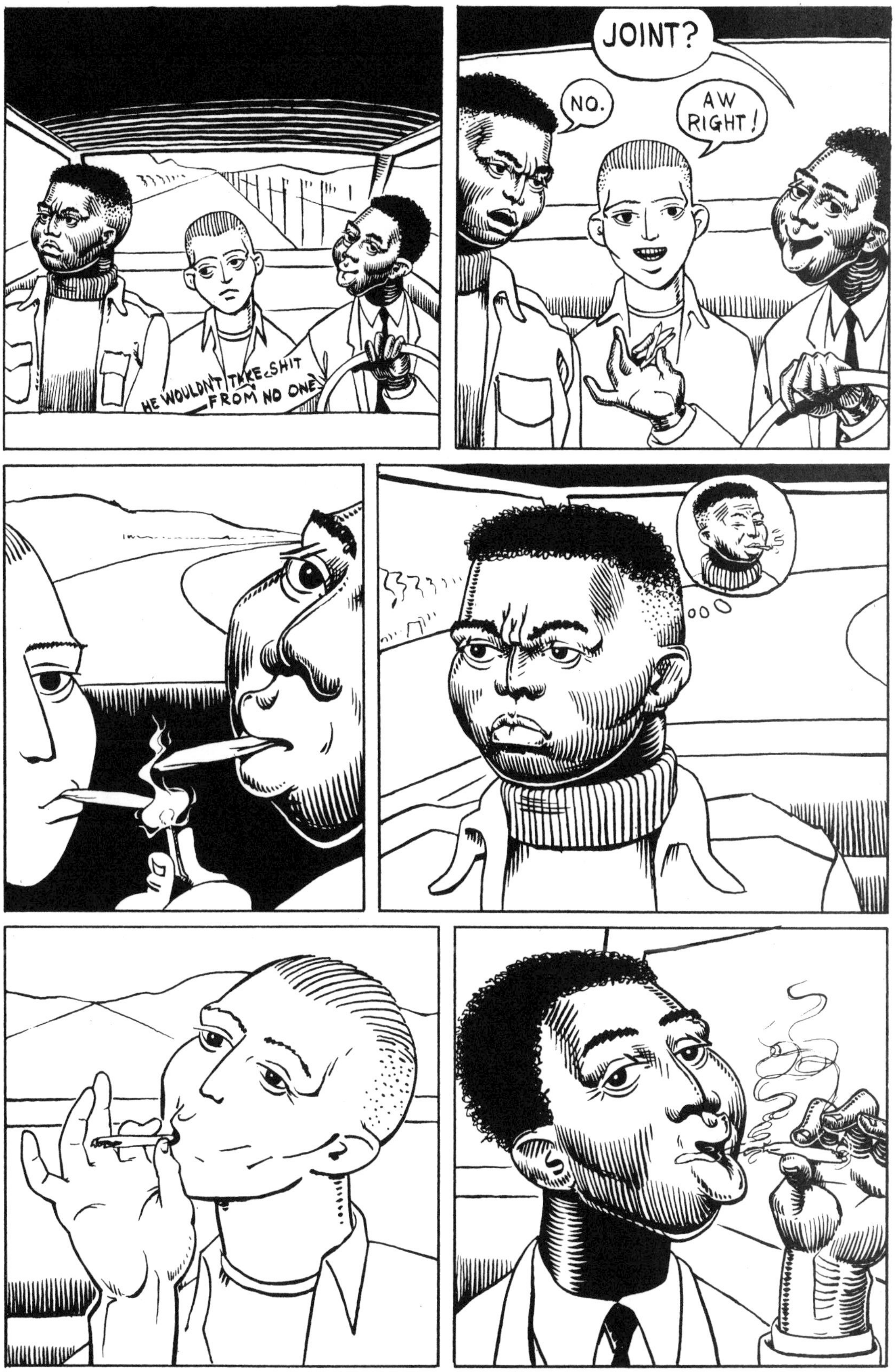
HE WOULDN'T TAKE SHIT FROM NO ONE
JOINT?
NO.
AW RIGHT!

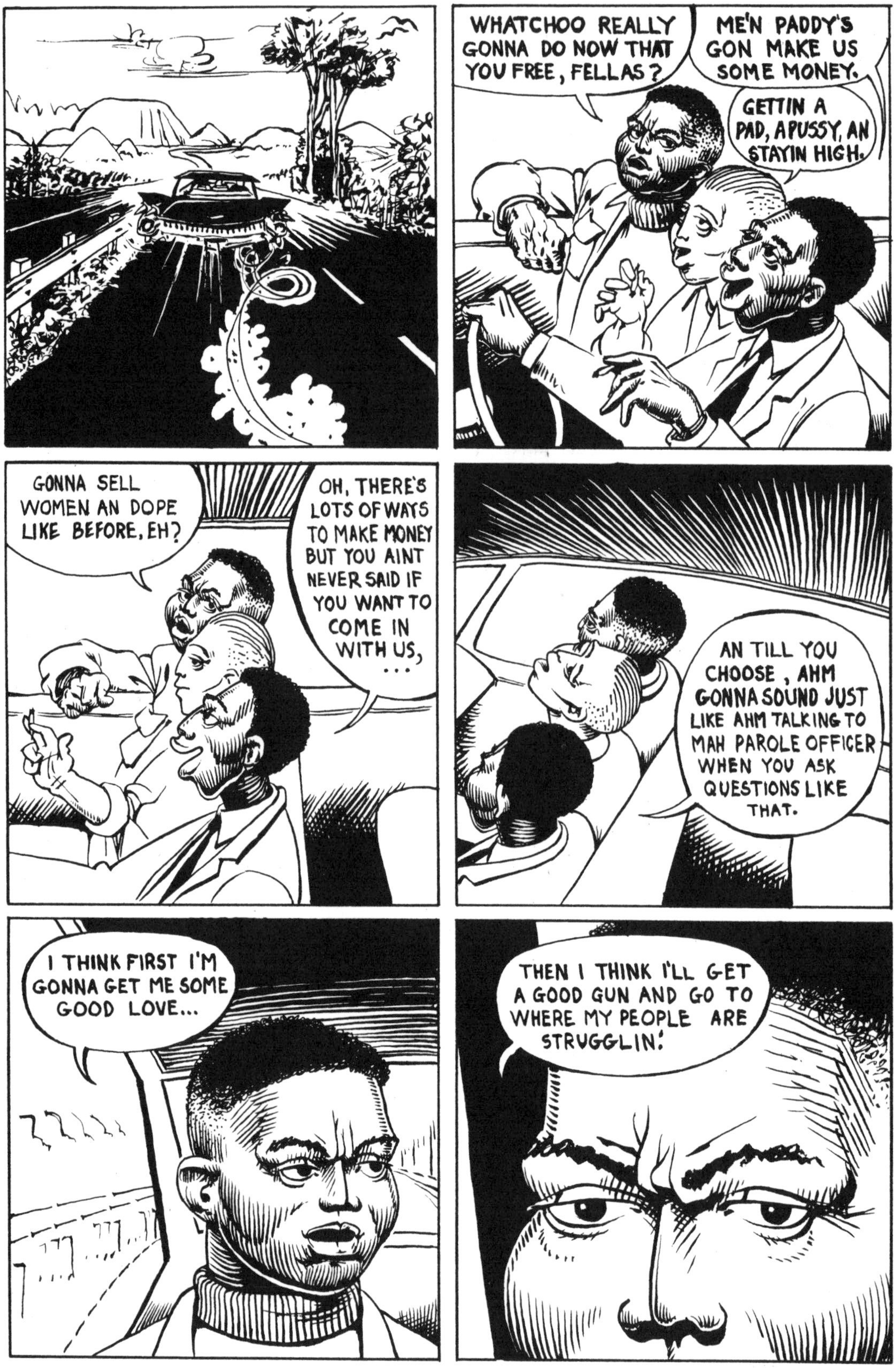
WHATCHOO REALLY GONNA DO NOW THAT YOU FREE, FELLAS?
ME'N PADDY'S GON MAKE US SOME MONEY.
GETTIN A PAD, A PUSSY, AN STAYIN HIGH.
GONNA SELL WOMEN AN DOPE LIKE BEFORE, EH?
OH, THERE'S LOTS OF WAYS TO MAKE MONEY BUT YOU AINT NEVER SAID IF YOU WANT TO COME IN WITH US, ...
AN TILL YOU CHOOSE, AHM GONNA SOUND JUST LIKE AHM TALKING TO MAH PAROLE OFFICER WHEN YOU ASK QUESTIONS LIKE THAT.
I THINK FIRST I'M GONNA GET ME SOME GOOD LOVE...
THEN I THINK I'LL GET A GOOD GUN AND GO TO WHERE MY PEOPLE ARE STRUGGLIN'.

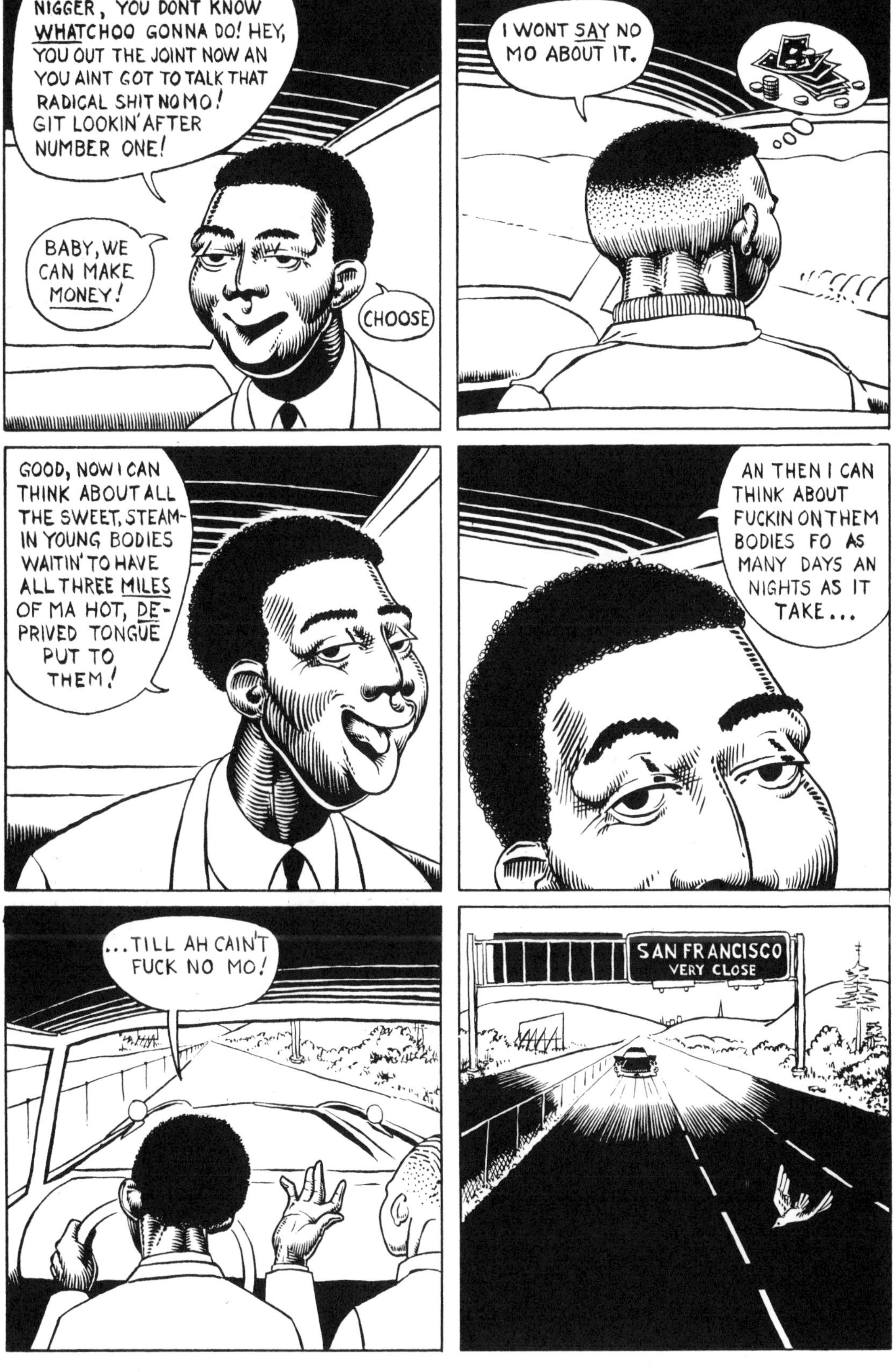
NIGGER, YOU DONT KNOW WHATCHOO GONNA DO! HEY, YOU OUT THE JOINT NOW AN YOU AINT GOT TO TALK THAT RADICAL SHIT NO MO! GIT LOOKIN' AFTER NUMBER ONE!
BABY, WE CAN MAKE MONEY!
CHOOSE
I WONT SAY NO MO ABOUT IT.
GOOD, NOW I CAN THINK ABOUT ALL THE SWEET, STEAMIN YOUNG BODIES WAITIN' TO HAVE ALL THREE MILES OF MA HOT, DEPRIVED TONGUE PUT TO THEM!
AN THEN I CAN THINK ABOUT FUCKIN ON THEM BODIES FO AS MANY DAYS AN NIGHTS AS IT TAKE...
...TILL AH CAIN'T FUCK NO MO!
SAN FRANCISCO
VERY CLOSE

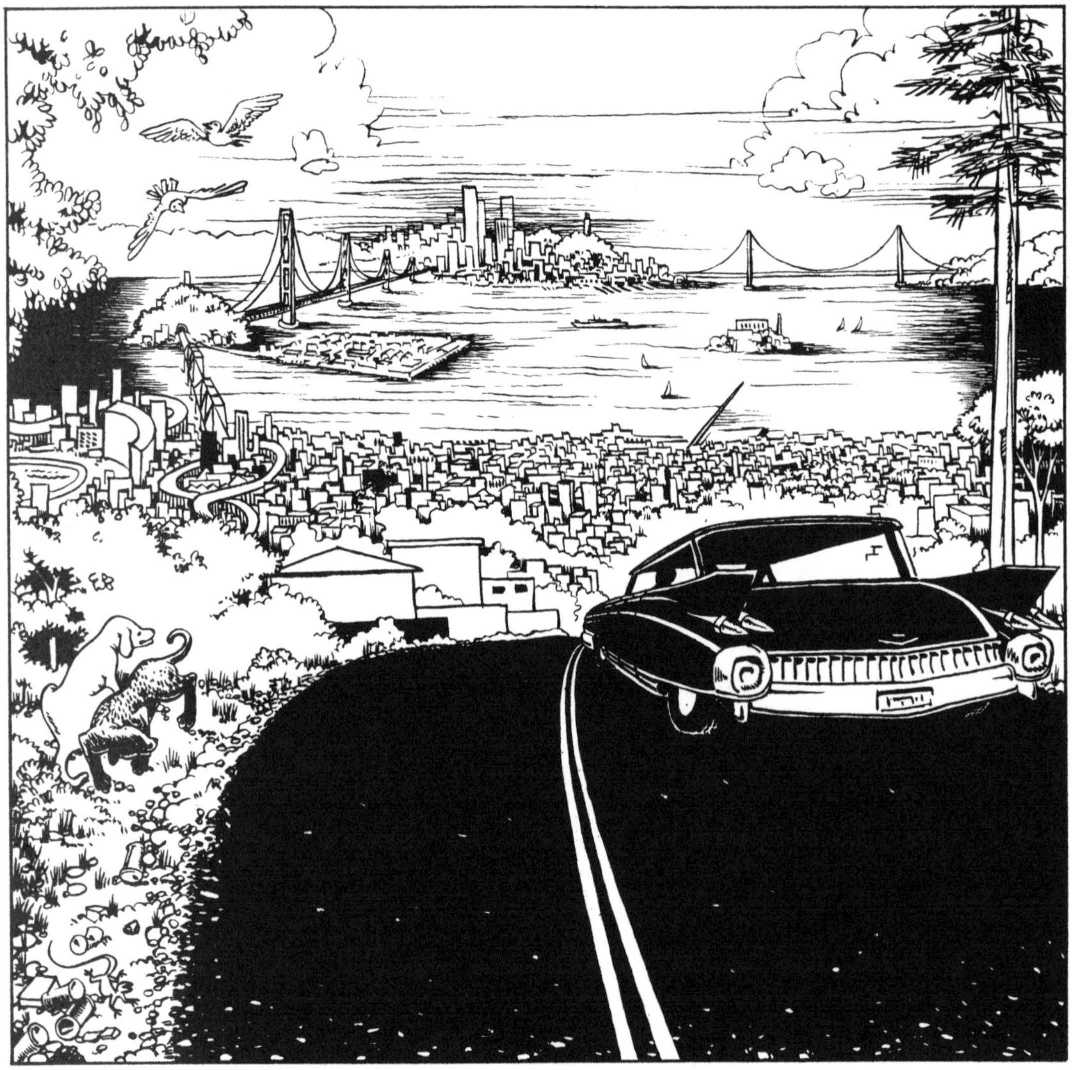

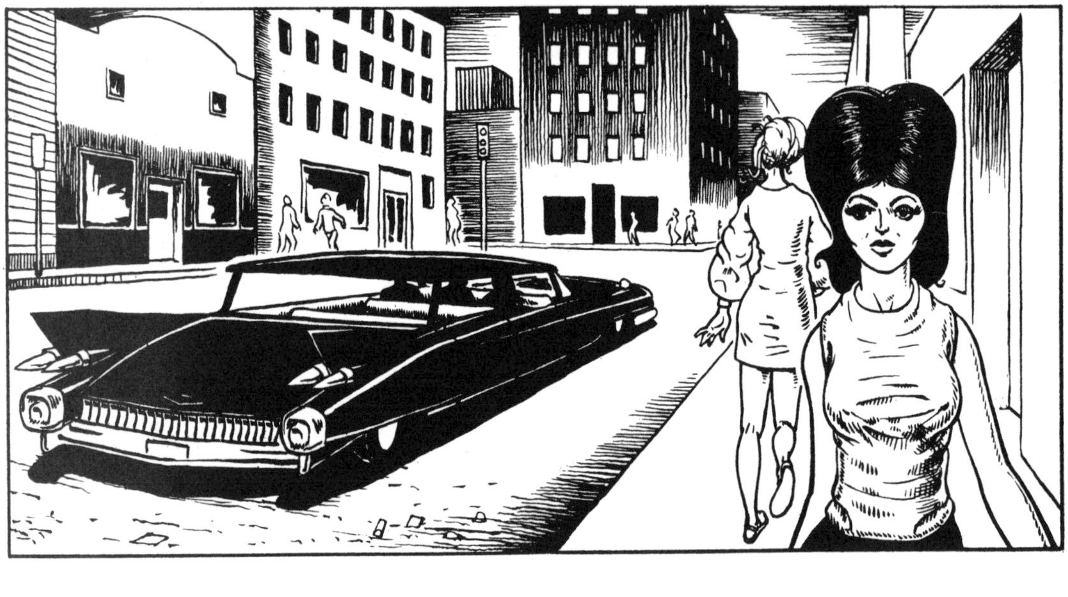

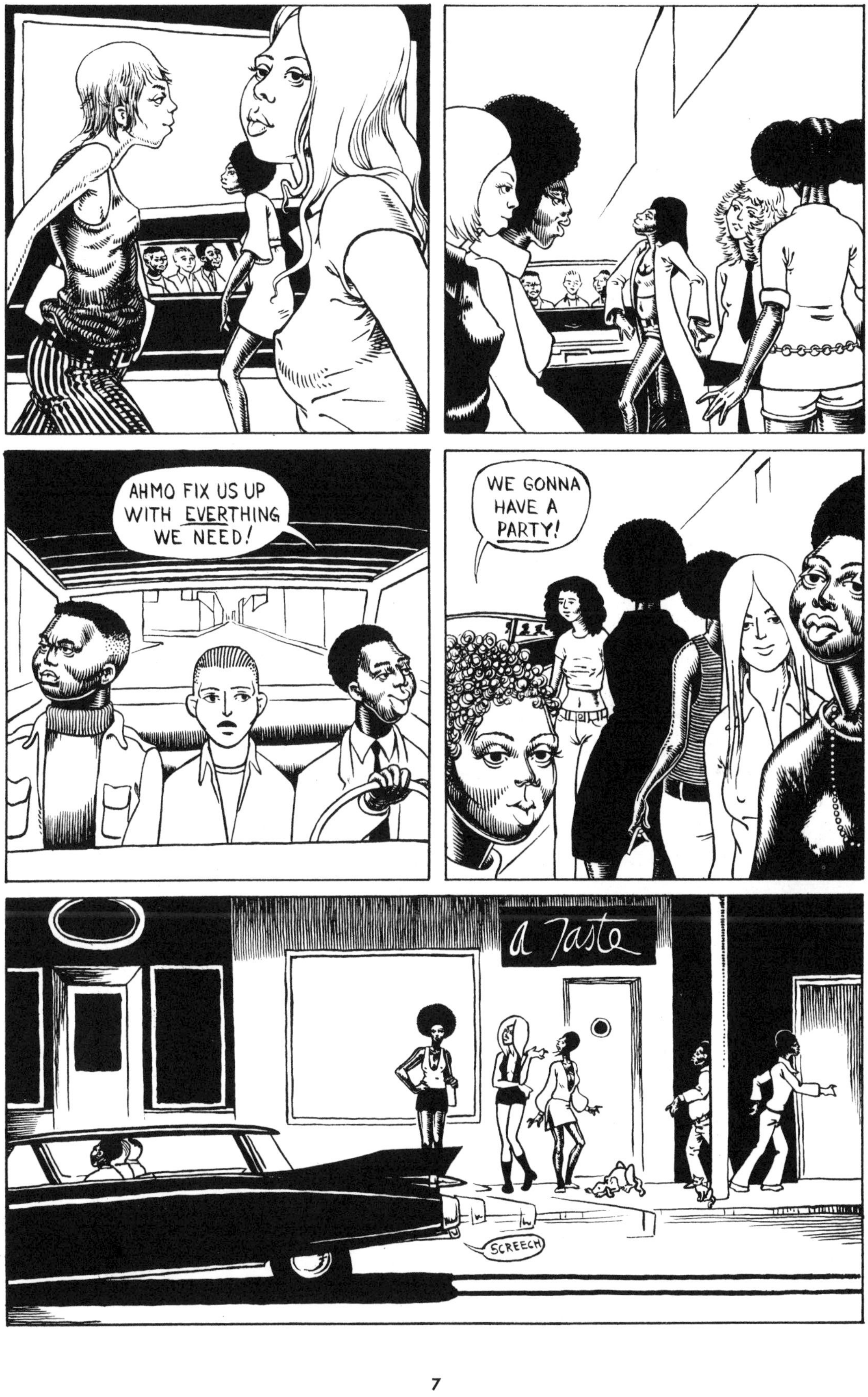
AHMO FIX US UP WITH EVERTHING WE NEED!
WE GONNA HAVE A PARTY!
a Taste
SCREECH

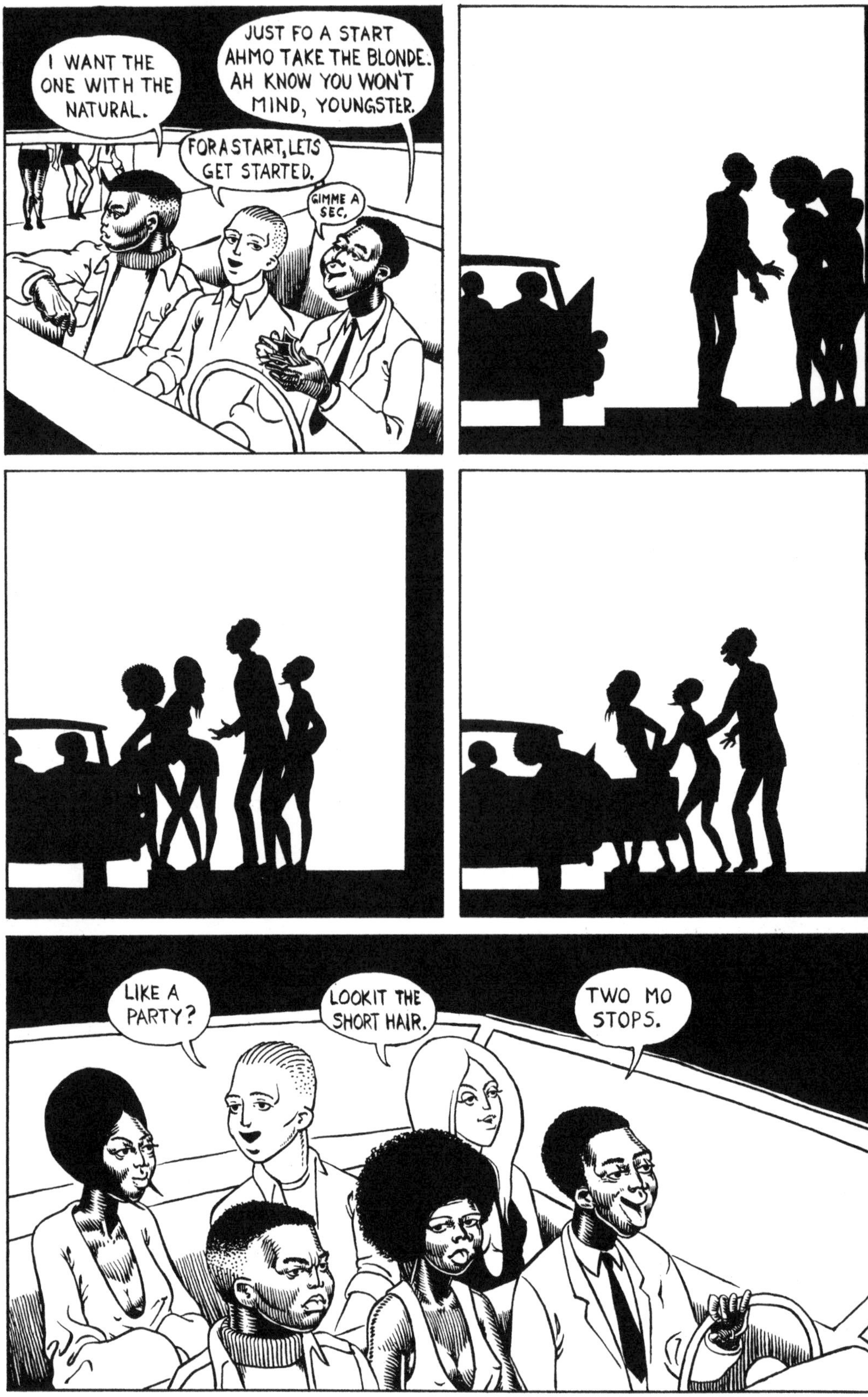
I WANT THE ONE WITH THE NATURAL.
JUST FO A START AHMO TAKE THE BLONDE. AH KNOW YOU WON'T MIND, YOUNGSTER.
FOR A START, LETS GET STARTED.
GIMME A SEC,
LIKE A PARTY?
LOOKIT THE SHORT HAIR.
TWO MO STOPS.

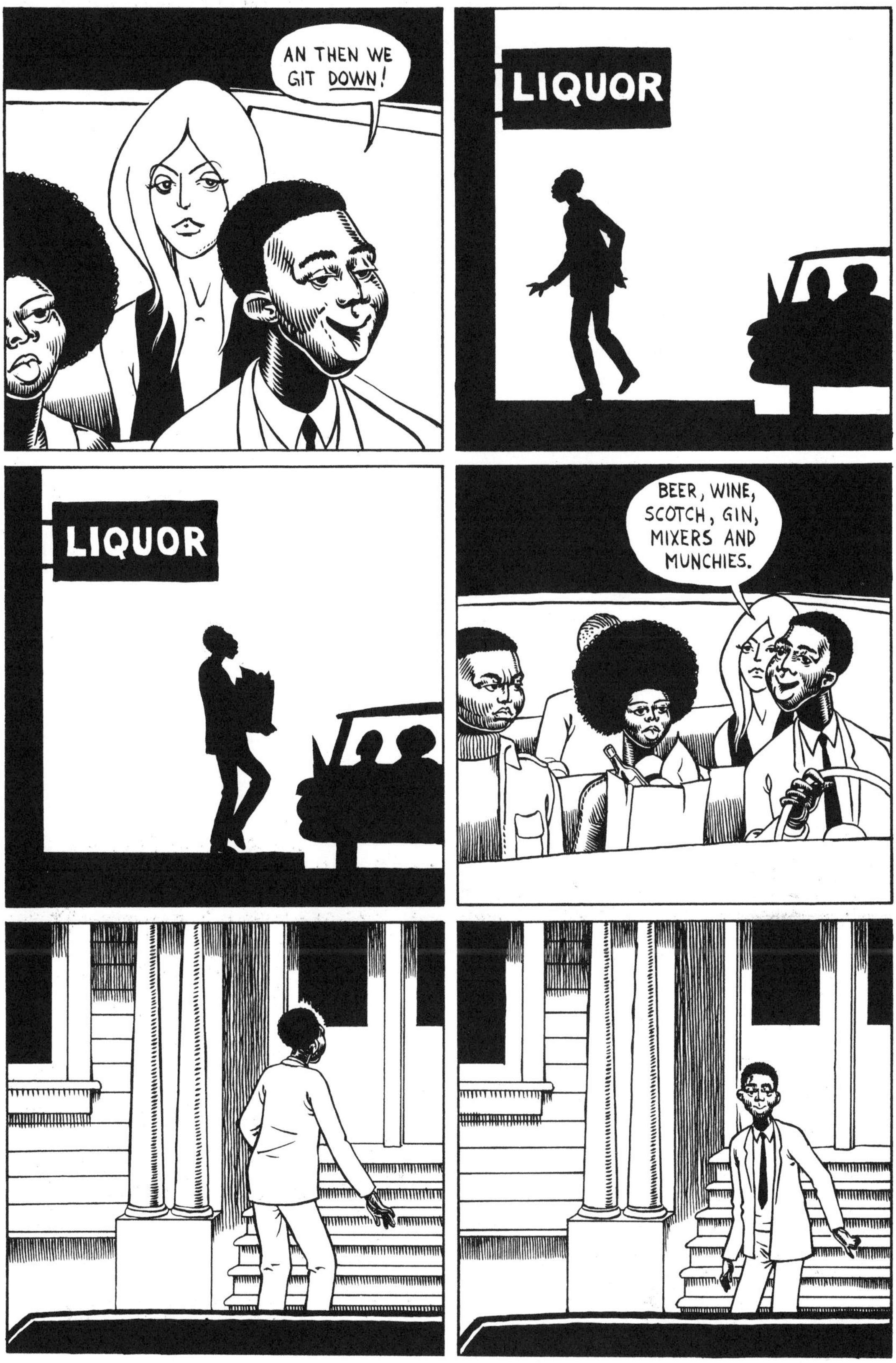
AN THEN WE GIT DOWN!
LIQUOR
LIQUOR
BEER, WINE, SCOTCH, GIN, MIXERS AND MUNCHIES.

ACID, HASH, COKE, REDS, SPEED, SMACK. WHATEVAH IS YO DESIAH.
I'LL TAKE SOME ACID.
AN NOW, MAH CHILLUN, LET US TO THE PLEASURE DOME.
WE SEE YOU FELLAS LATER.
EVAH MADE IT WITH BLACK MEAT B'FO, SUGAH?
NO. EVER BEEN FUCKED BY A DUDE WHO'S LOADED ON ACID AND AIN'T HAD NO PUSSY FOR 3½ YEARS?
NO.

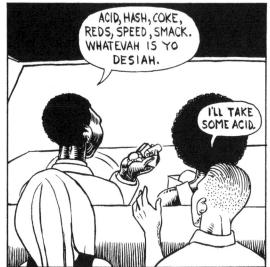

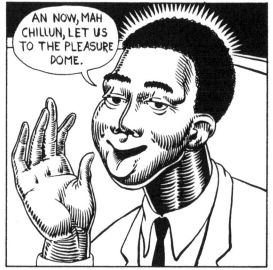

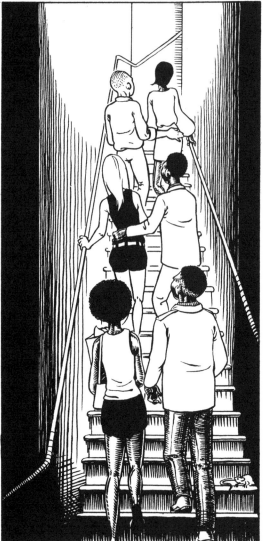

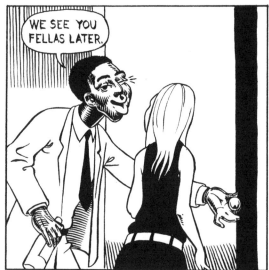

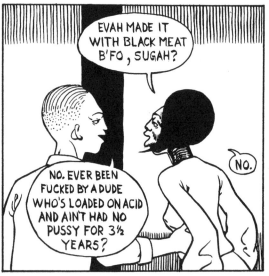

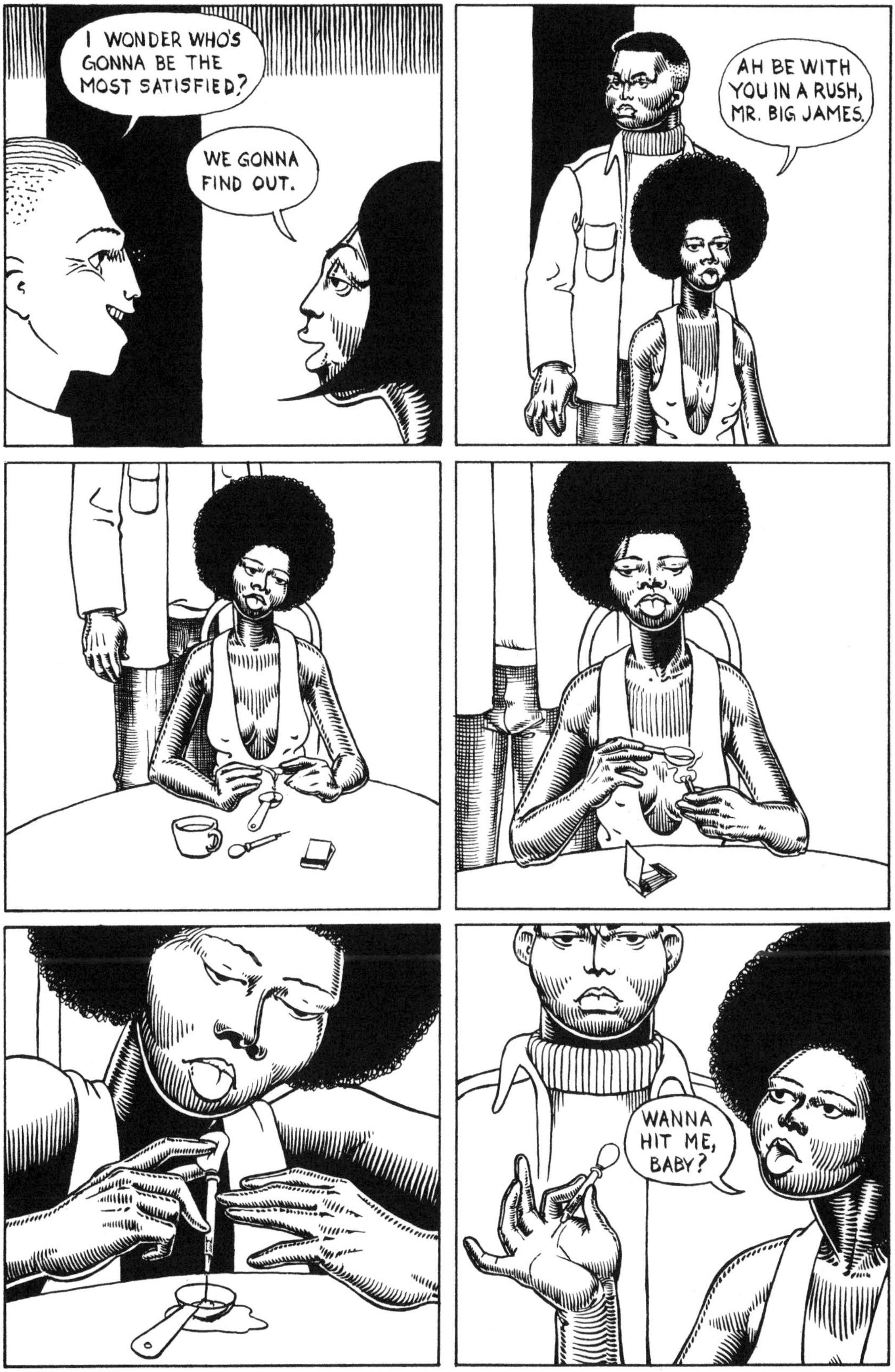
I WONDER WHO'S GONNA BE THE MOST SATISFIED?
WE GONNA FIND OUT.
AH BE WITH YOU IN A RUSH, MR. BIG JAMES.
WANNA HIT ME, BABY?

DON'T WORRY ABOUT IT, LOVER. I'LL DO IT.

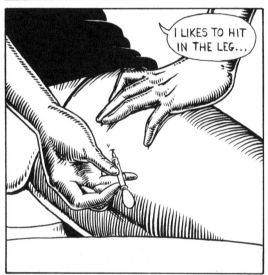
I LIKES TO HIT IN THE LEG...

...SO MY ARMS BE PRETTY FOR YOU, BABY.

BABY?

PRICK.

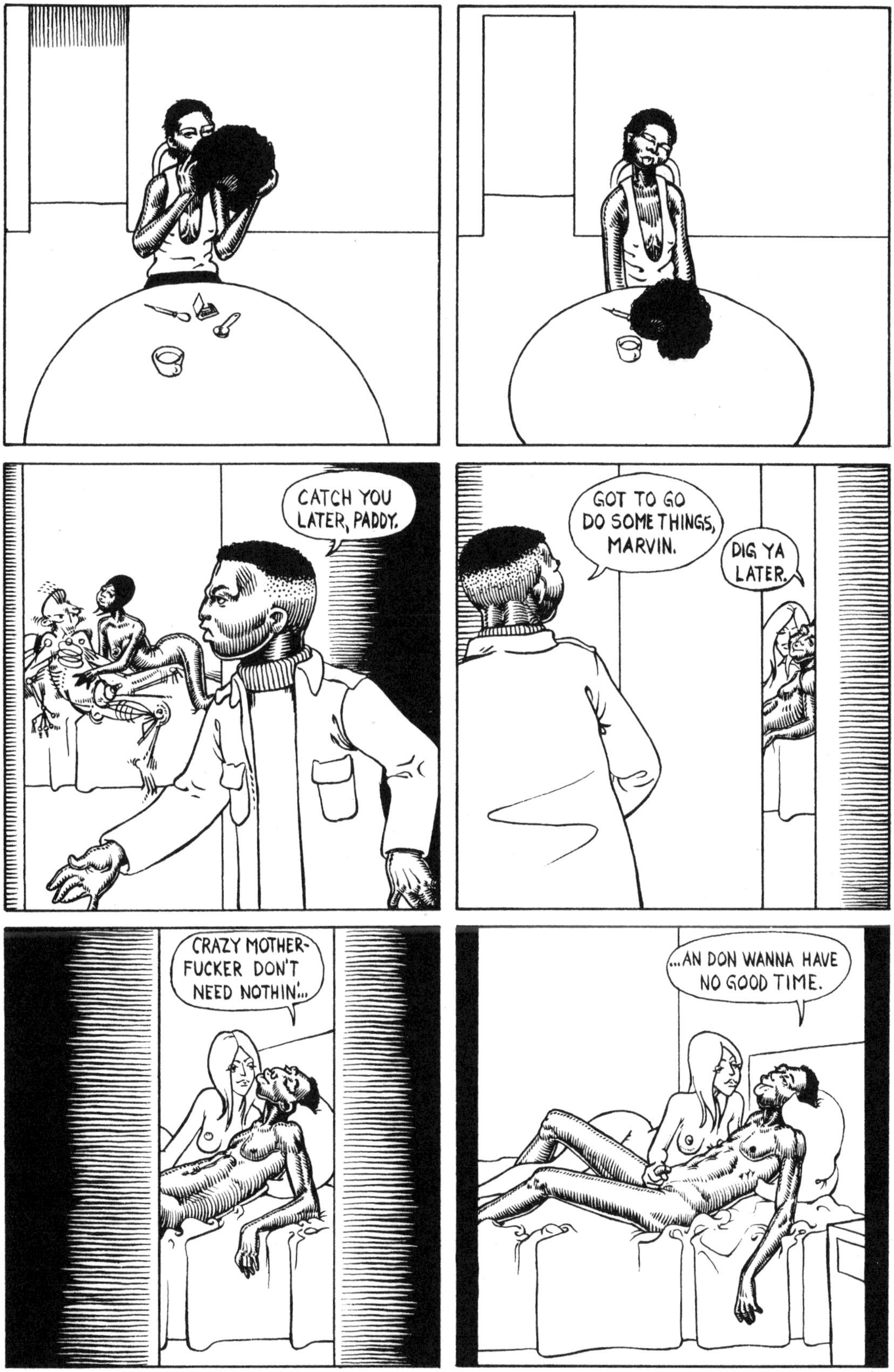
CATCH YOU LATER, PADDY.
GOT TO GO DO SOME THINGS, MARVIN.
DIG YA LATER.
CRAZY MOTHER-FUCKER DON'T NEED NOTHIN'...
...AN DON WANNA HAVE NO GOOD TIME.

WANT S'MORE HEAD, BABY?
YEAH, BOTH WAYS.
OOOUUUH
WHAT WHAT?
COME AGAIN?

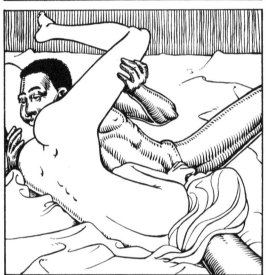

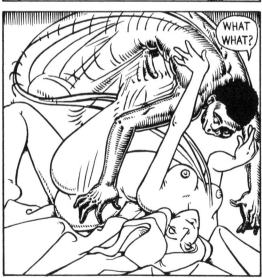

OOOUUUH.
THAT'S WHAT AH THOUGHT YOU SAID.
THE GATES ARE SWING-ING OPEN.
AH SHALL BE RELEASED.
AAOOOH, BABY.
FREE AT LAST.

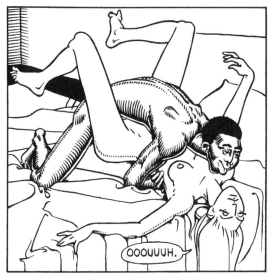

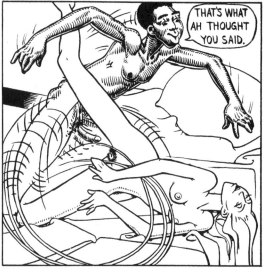

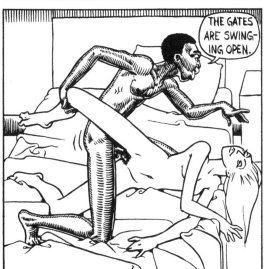

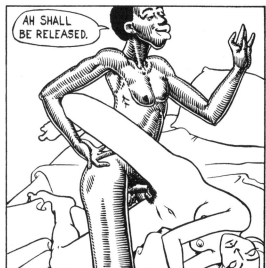

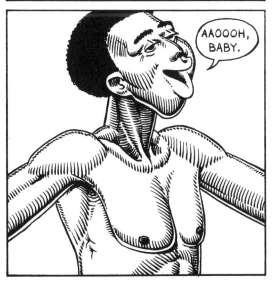

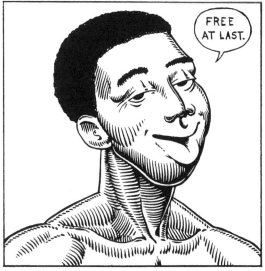

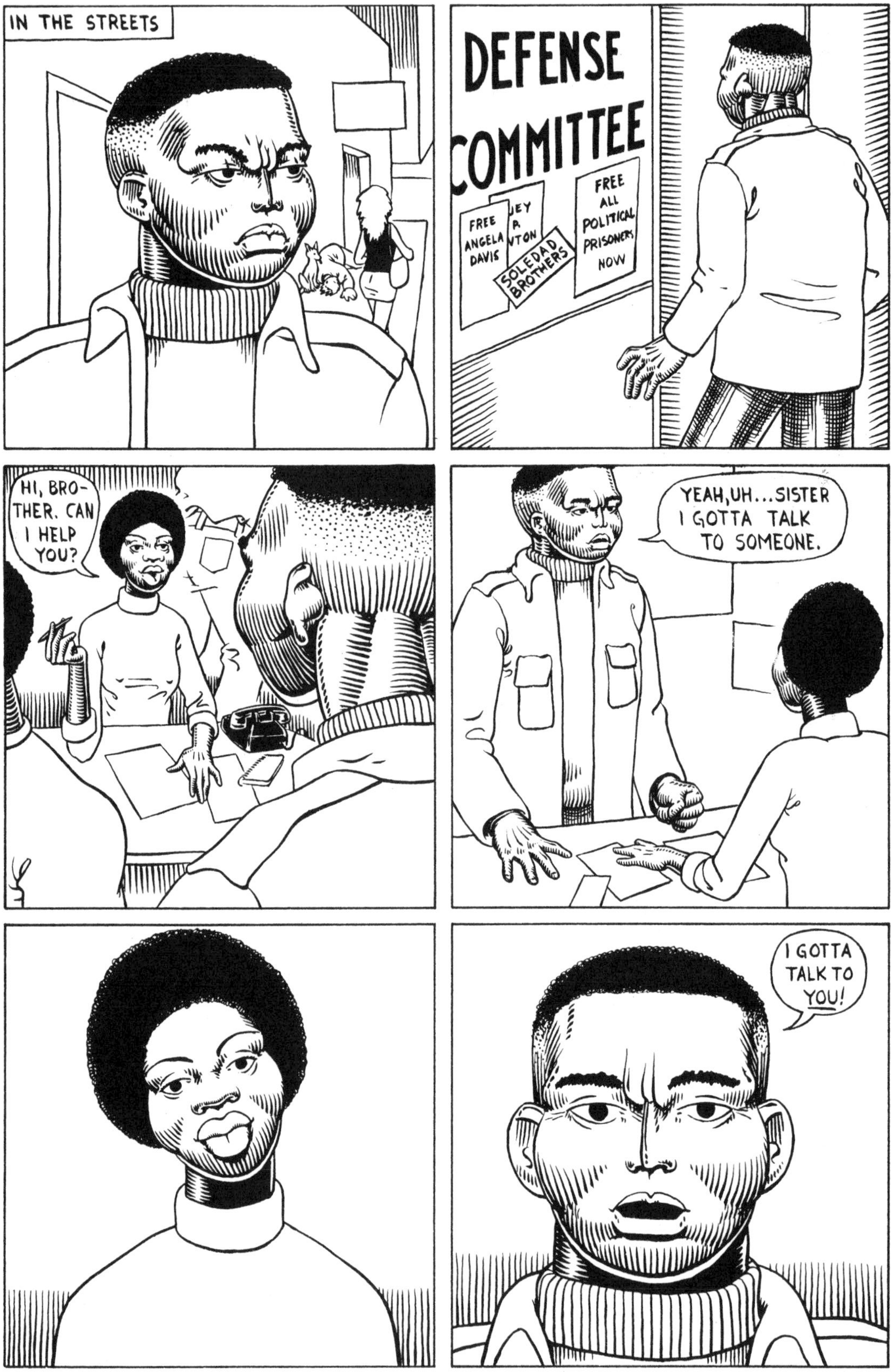
IN THE STREETS
DEFENSE COMMITTEE
FREE ANGELA DAVIS
SOLEDAD BROTHERS
FREE ALL POLITICAL PRISONERS NOW
HI, BROTHER. CAN I HELP YOU?
YEAH, UH... SISTER I GOTTA TALK TO SOMEONE.
I GOTTA TALK TO YOU!

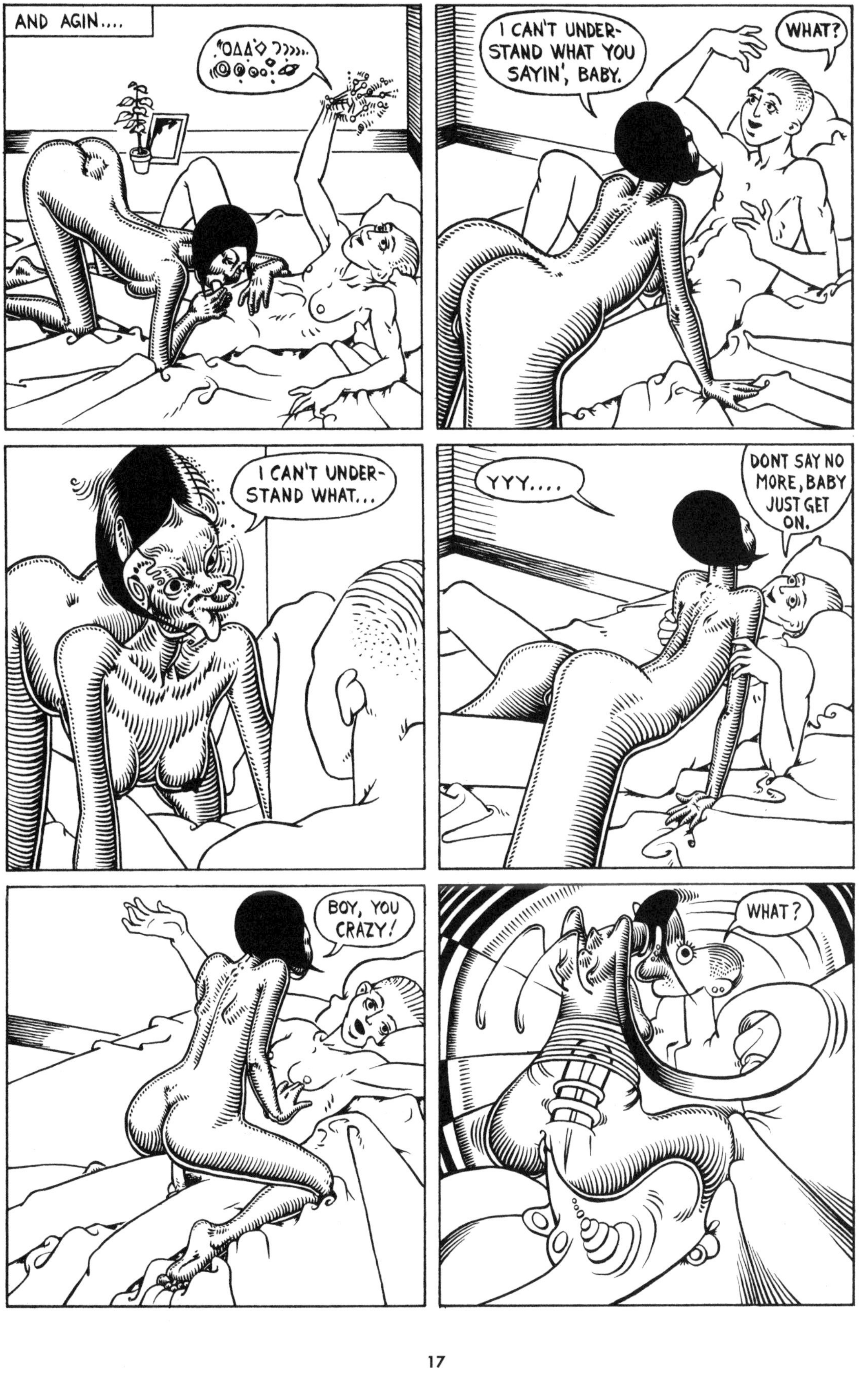
AND AGIN....
I CAN'T UNDER-STAND WHAT YOU SAYIN', BABY.
WHAT?
I CAN'T UNDER-STAND WHAT...
YYY....
DONT SAY NO MORE, BABY JUST GET ON.
BOY, YOU CRAZY!
WHAT?

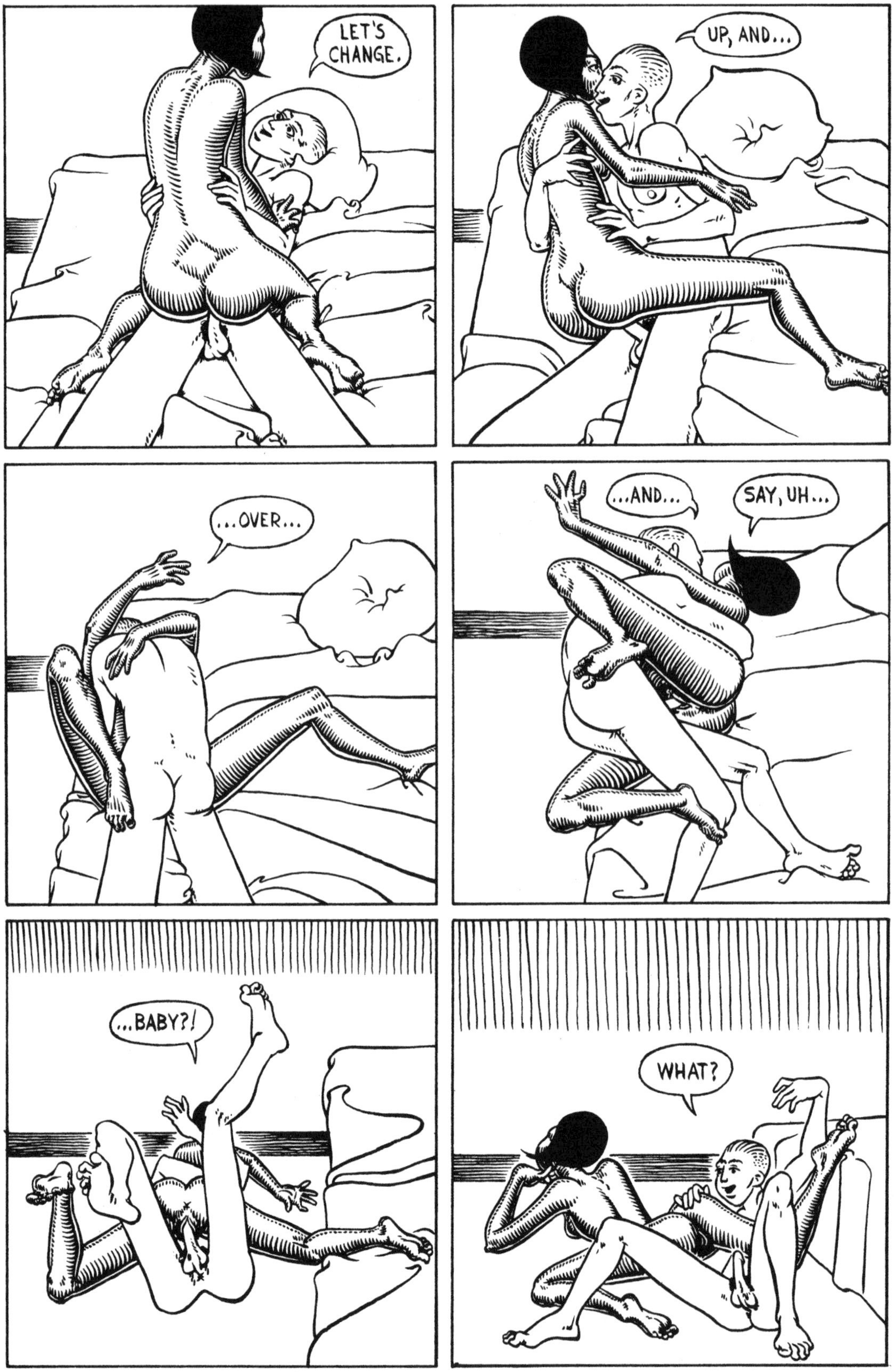
LET'S CHANGE.
UP, AND...
...OVER...
...AND...
SAY, UH...
...BABY?!
WHAT?

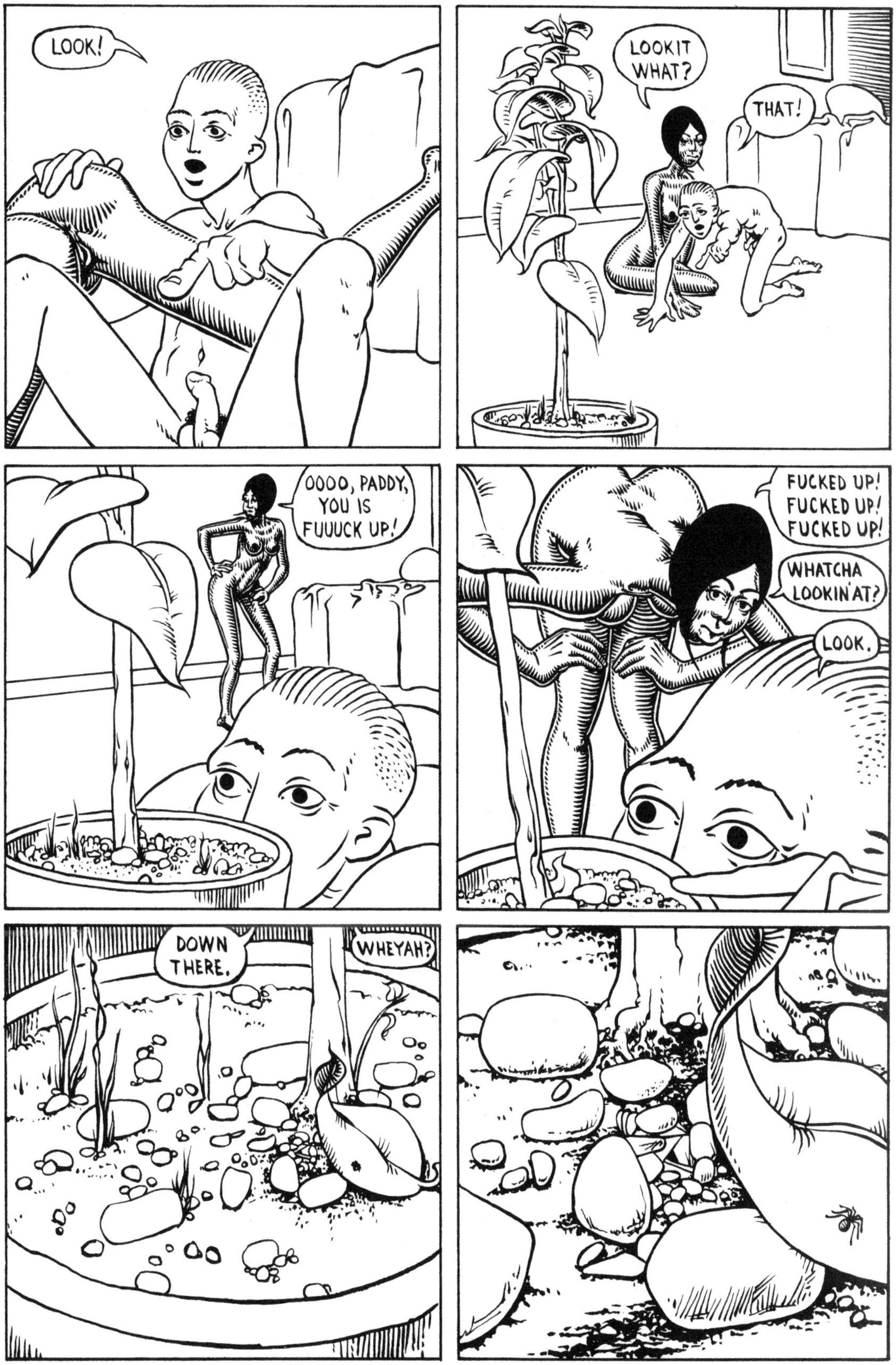
LOOK!
LOOKIT WHAT?
THAT!
OOOO, PADDY, YOU IS FUUUCK UP!
FUCKED UP! FUCKED UP! FUCKED UP!
WHATCHA LOOKIN'AT?
LOOK.
DOWN THERE.
WHEYAH?

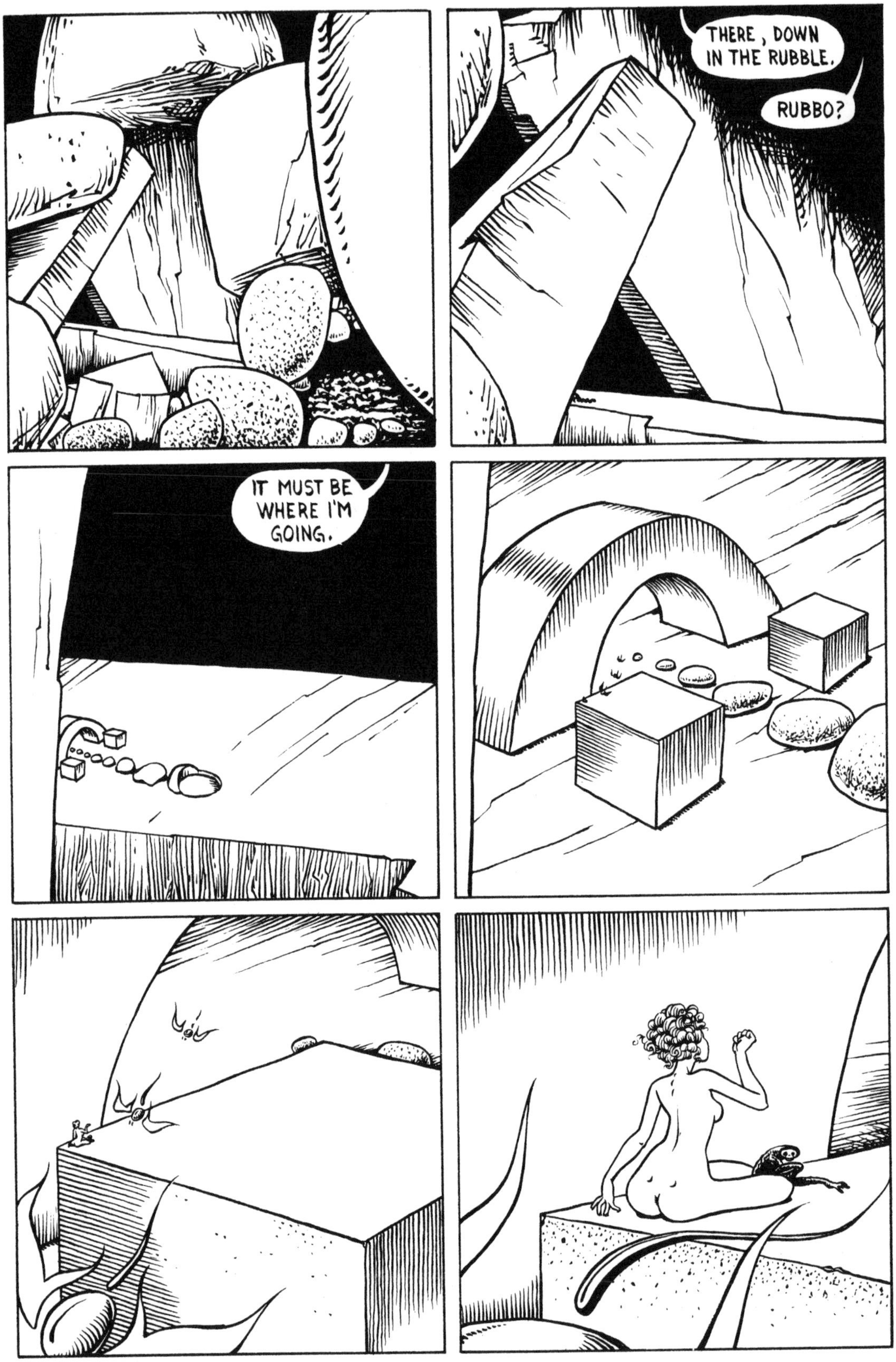
THERE, DOWN IN THE RUBBLE.
RUBBO?
IT MUST BE WHERE I'M GOING.

A CUNT IN THE HAND?

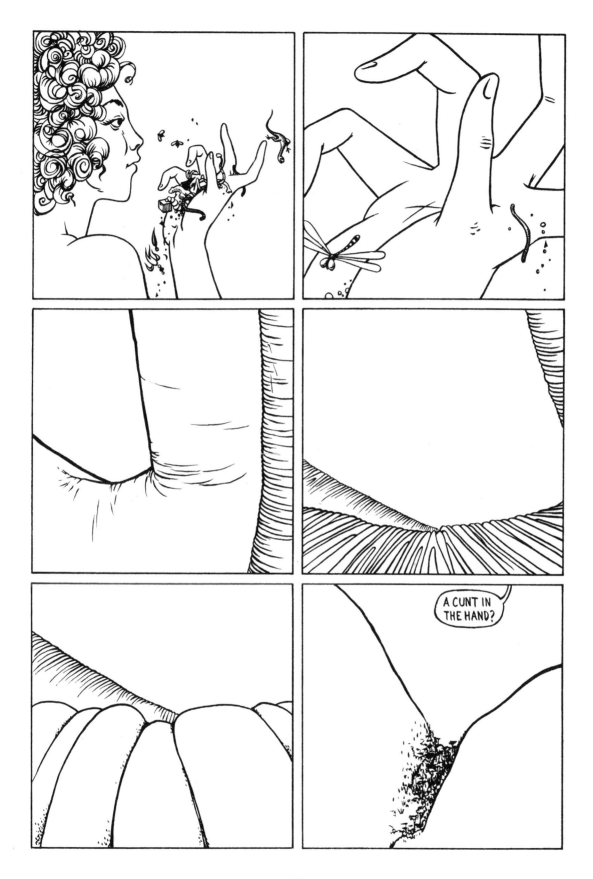

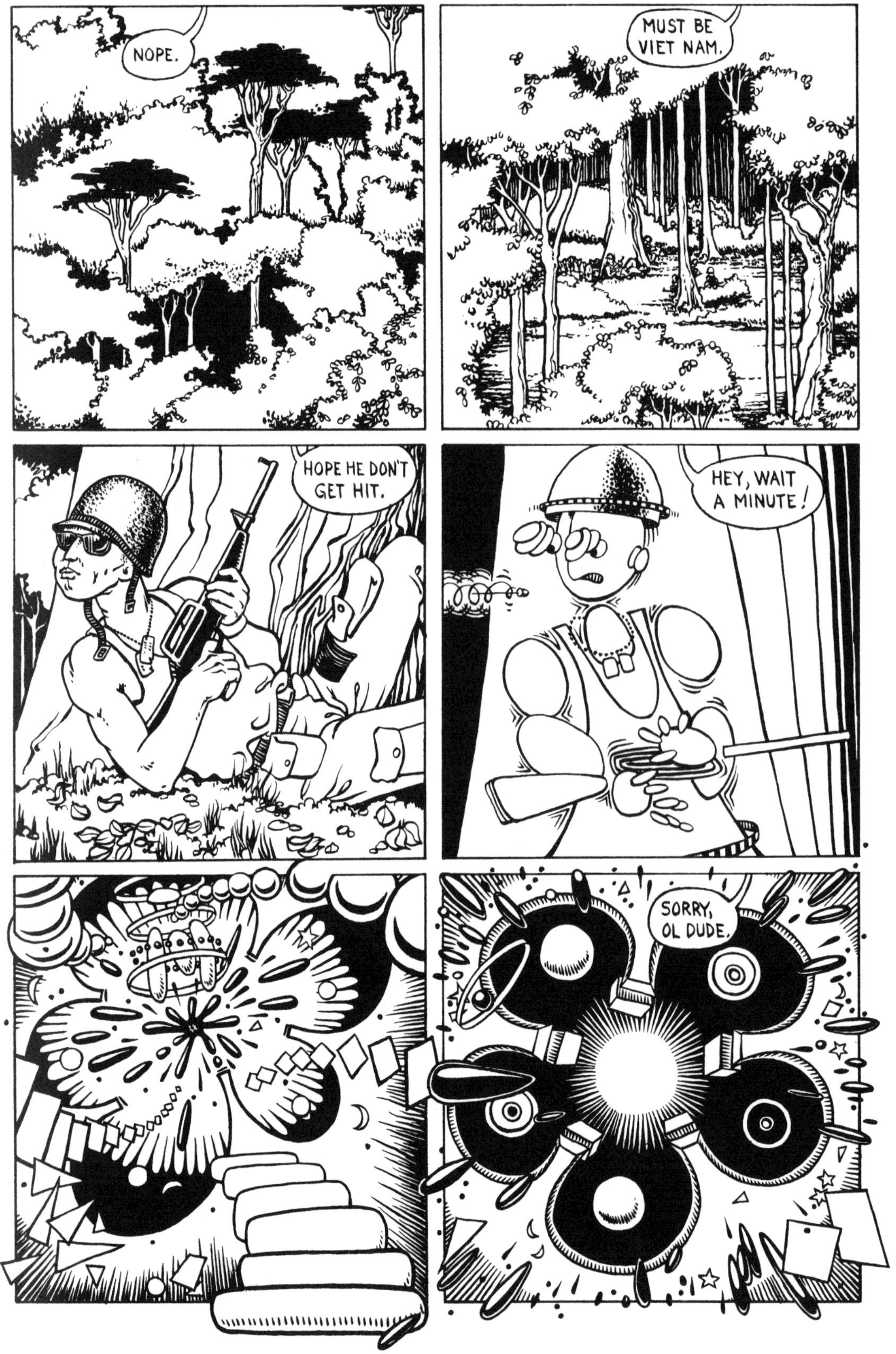
NOPE.
MUST BE VIET NAM.
HOPE HE DON'T GET HIT.
HEY, WAIT A MINUTE!
SORRY, OL DUDE.

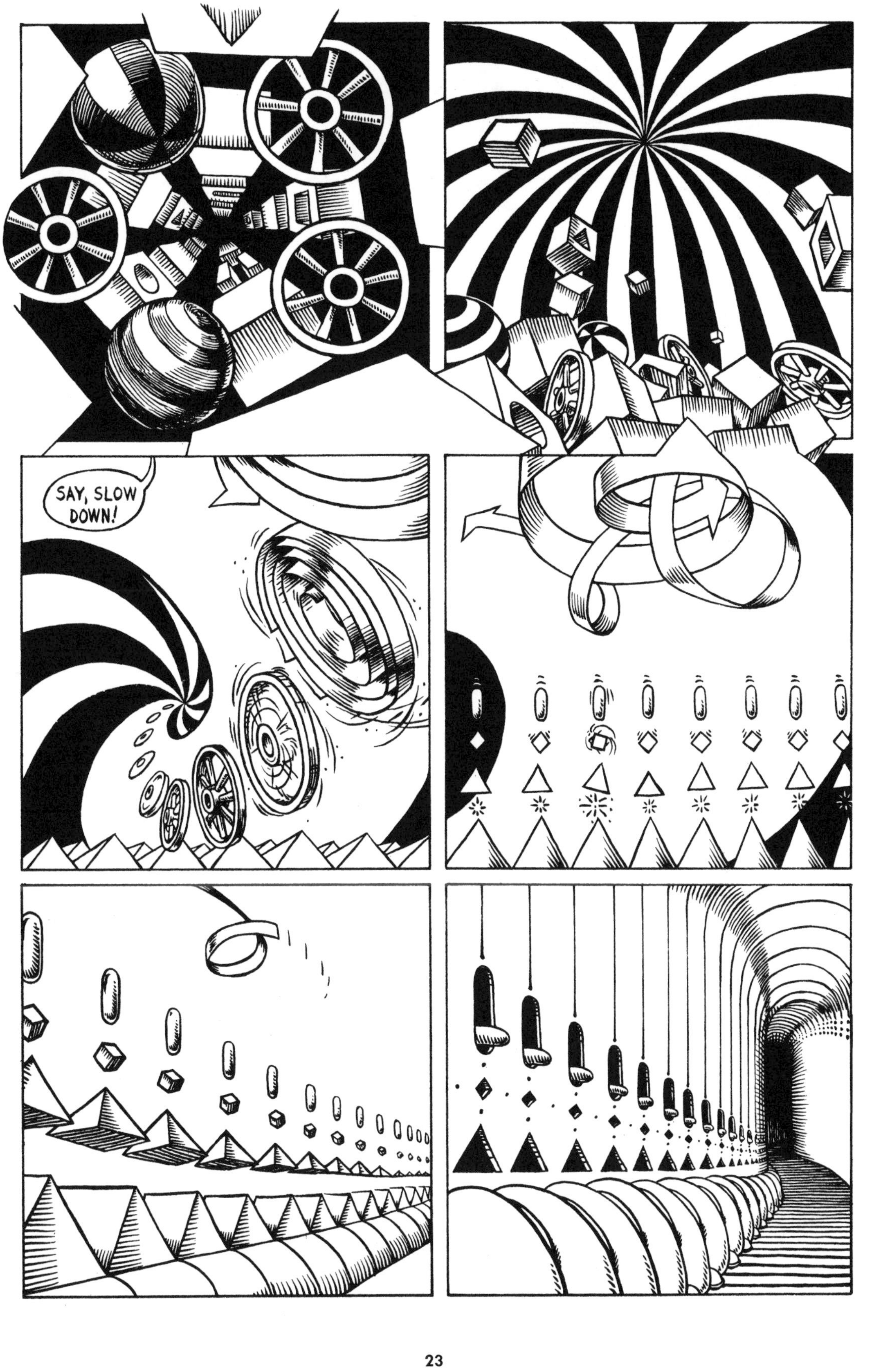
SAY, SLOW DOWN!

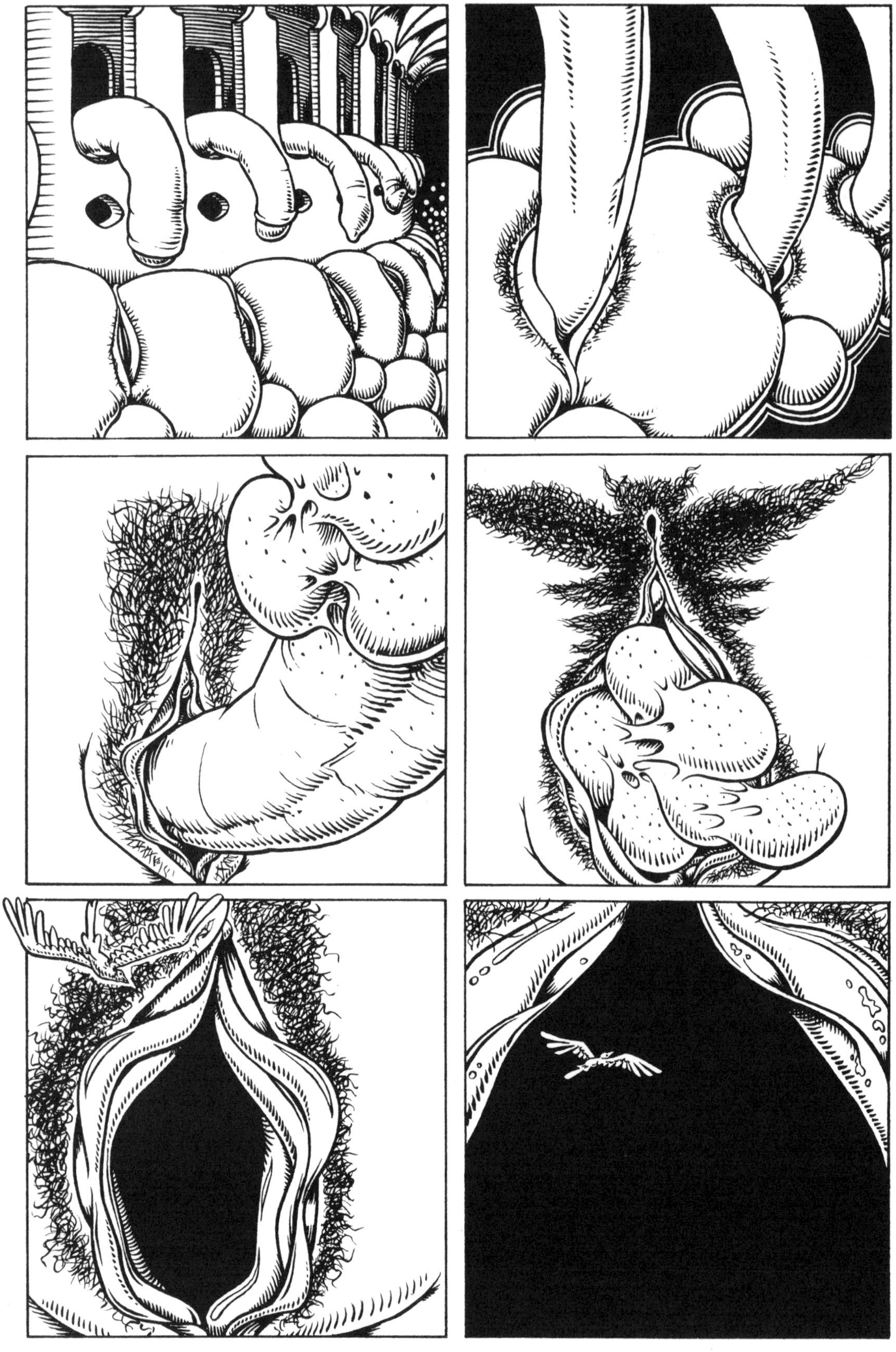

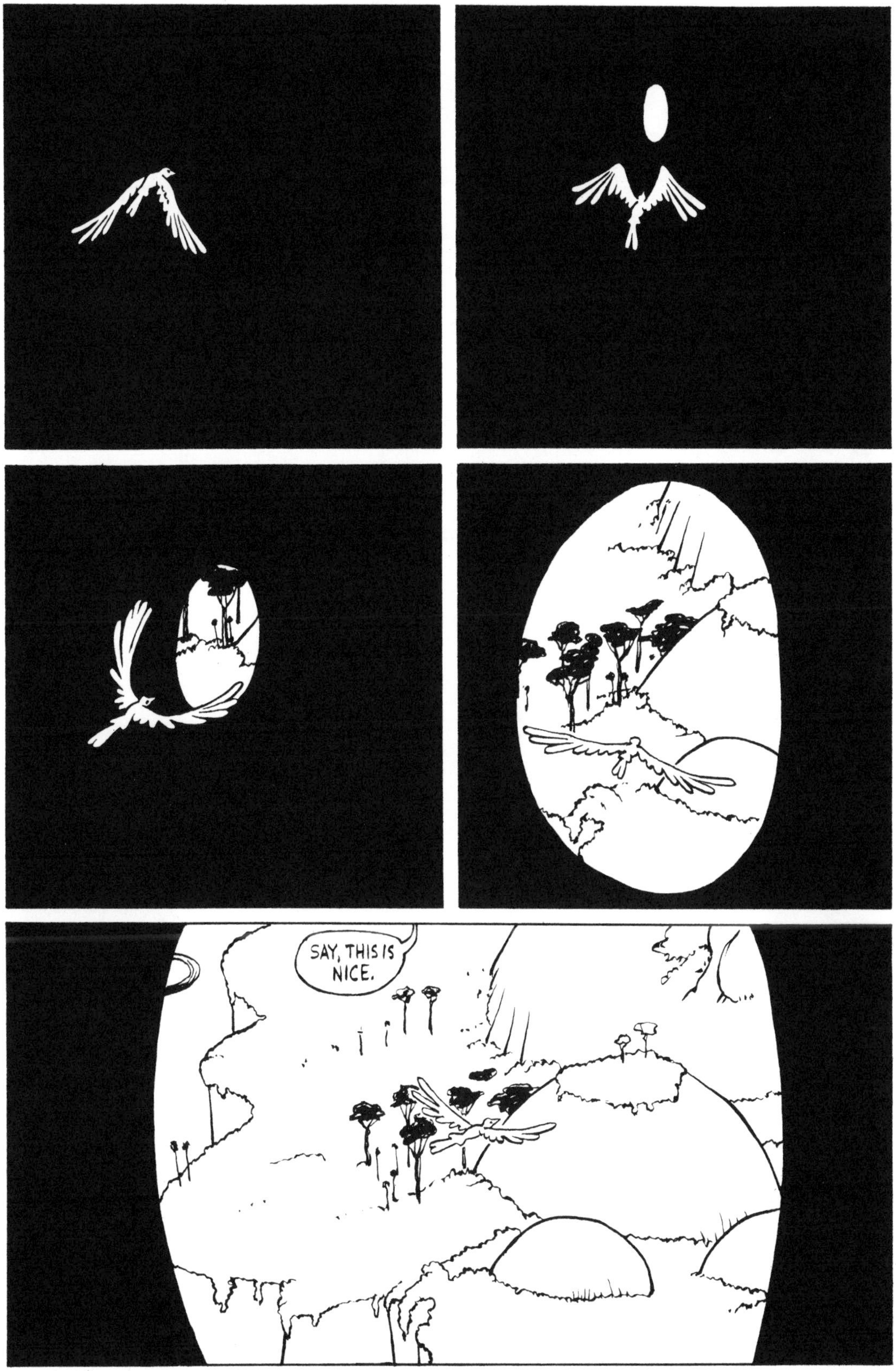
SAY, THIS IS NICE.

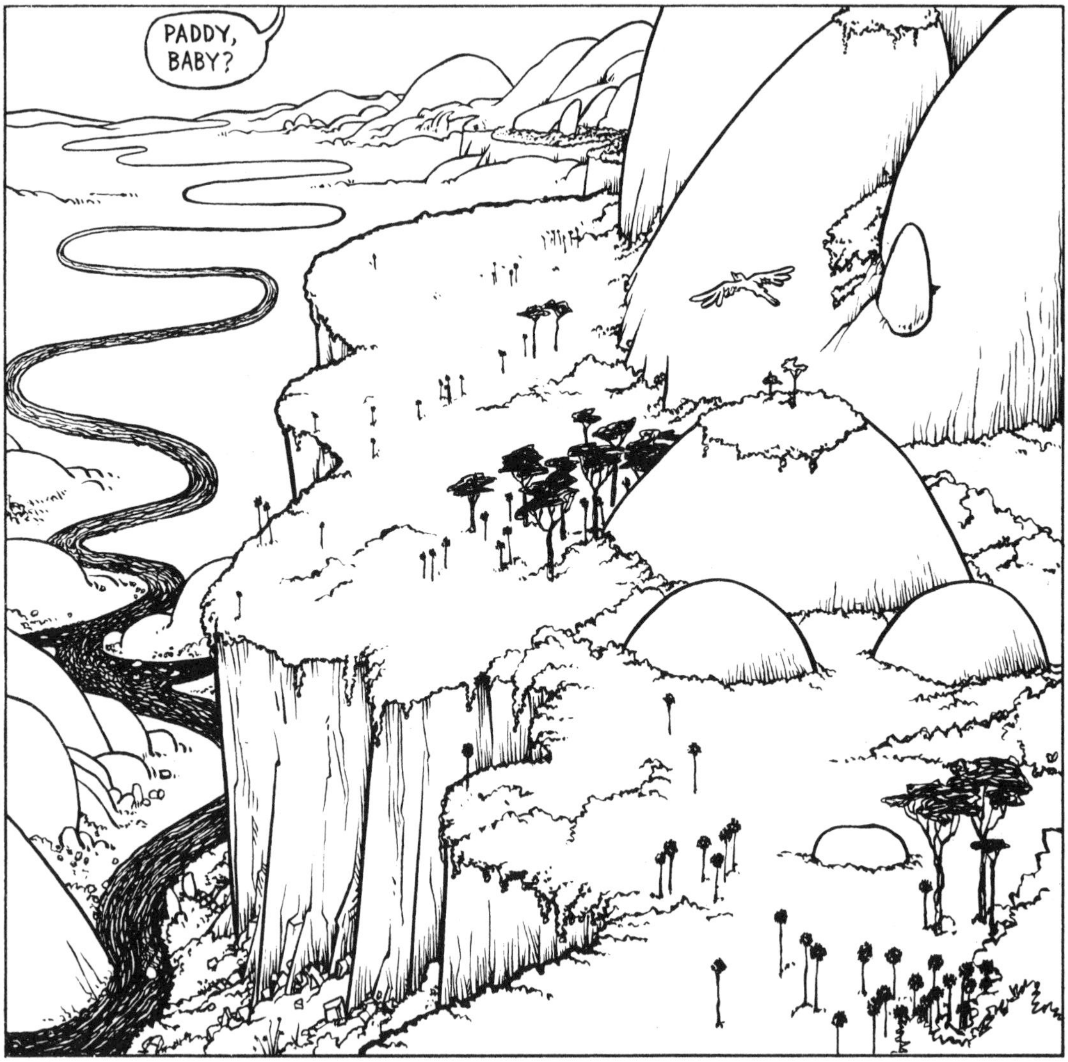
PADDY, BABY?

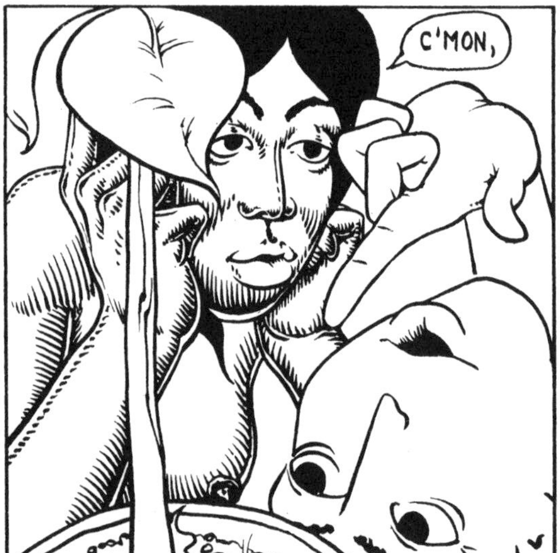
C'MON,

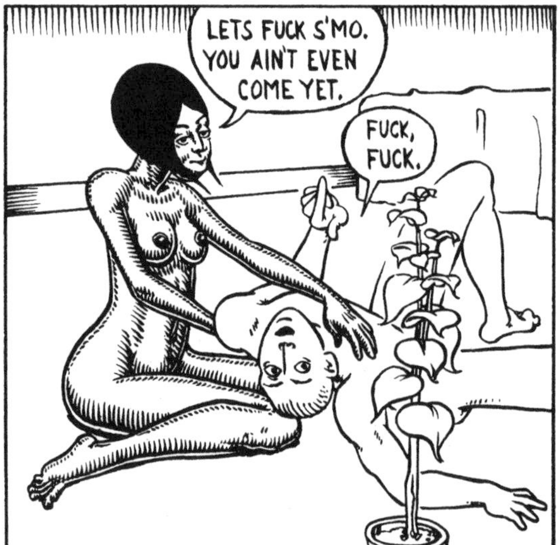
LETS FUCK S'MO. YOU AIN'T EVEN COME YET.
FUCK, FUCK.

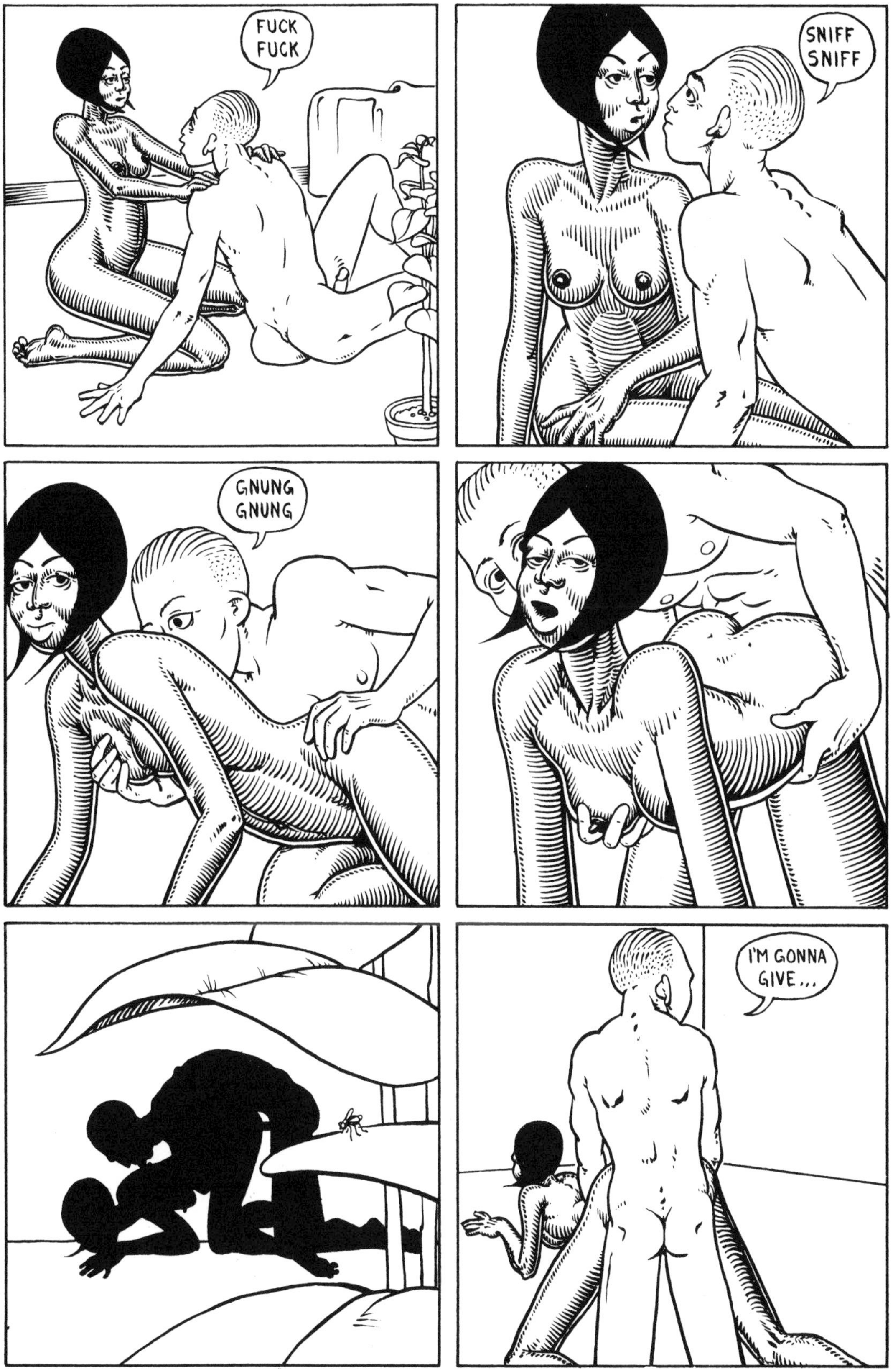
FUCK FUCK
SNIFF SNIFF
GNUNG GNUNG
I'M GONNA GIVE...

...A COUPLE GALLONS TO YA, BABE.
HEY
IS YOU SATISFIED, OR IS YOU GOIN' OFF INTO YO THING AGIN?
WHAT?
OH, HI!
OH, FUCK.
FUCK FUCK

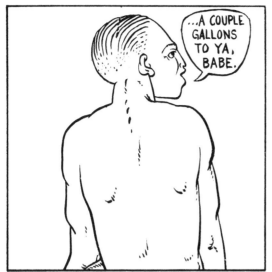

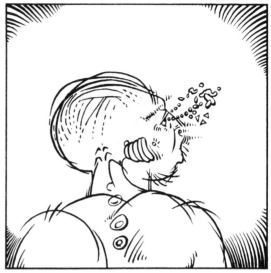

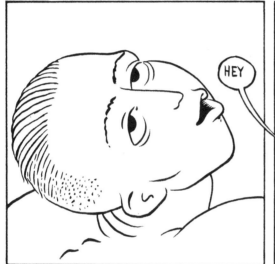

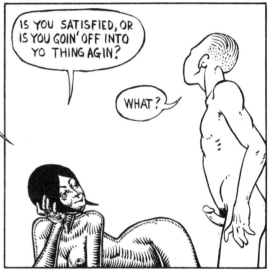

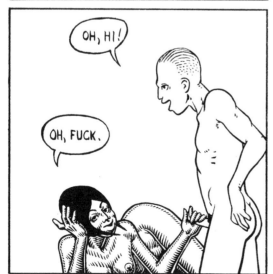

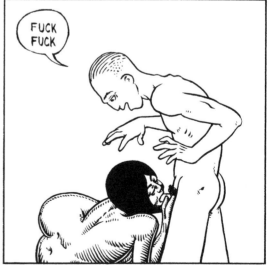

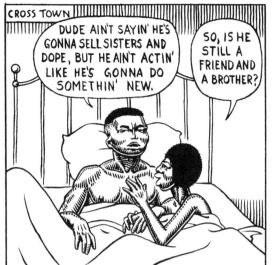

CROSS TOWN

DUDE AIN'T SAYIN' HE'S GONNA SELL SISTERS AND DOPE, BUT HE AIN'T ACTIN' LIKE HE'S GONNA DO SOMETHIN' NEW.

SO, IS HE STILL A FRIEND AND A BROTHER?

SO FAR.

BABY, I DIG HOW TIGHT YOU HAD TO BE WITH YOUR BROTHERS IN THE JOINT,...

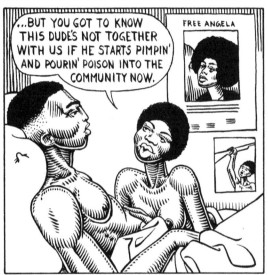

...BUT YOU GOT TO KNOW THIS DUDE'S NOT TOGETHER WITH US IF HE STARTS PIMPIN' AND POURIN' POISON INTO THE COMMUNITY NOW.

FREE ANGELA

I KNOW YOU DON'T WANT TO TURN ON YOUR BROTHER, JAMES, BUT DON'T TURN ON YOUR PEOPLE EITHER.

YOU SAY OUR STRUGGLE IS YOUR CAUSE, YOU SAY THE CAT IS A FRIEND,

THEN EDUCATE HIM. MAKE HIM UNDERSTAND HOW HE'S DES- TROYING US WITH THE SHIT HE'S DOING. TALK TRUTH TO HIM, BABY, DON'T KEEP ON BEING SI- LENT.

WELL, MAYBE I WON'T BE TAKIN' UP WITH HIM.

IF YOU DON'T WANT TO TRY TO CHANGE HIM, AT LEAST DON'T GIVE HIM THE ENCOURAGEMENT HE GETS FROM SEEING YOU DON'T GIVE A FUCK WHAT HE'S DOING TO HIS PEOPLE. CUT HIM LOOSE!

29

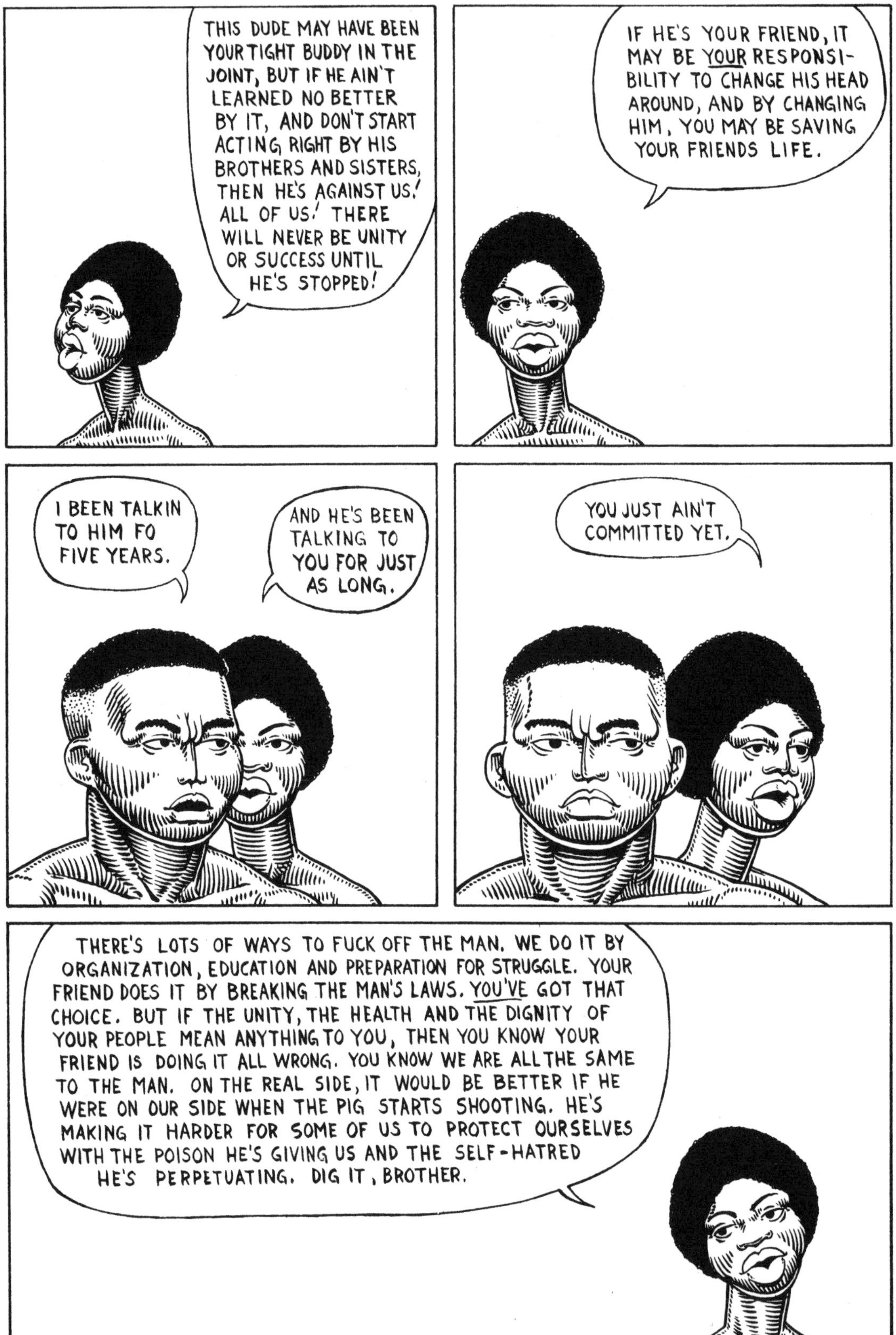
THIS DUDE MAY HAVE BEEN YOUR TIGHT BUDDY IN THE JOINT, BUT IF HE AIN'T LEARNED NO BETTER BY IT, AND DON'T START ACTING RIGHT BY HIS BROTHERS AND SISTERS, THEN HE'S AGAINST US! ALL OF US! THERE WILL NEVER BE UNITY OR SUCCESS UNTIL HE'S STOPPED!
IF HE'S YOUR FRIEND, IT MAY BE YOUR RESPONSIBILITY TO CHANGE HIS HEAD AROUND, AND BY CHANGING HIM, YOU MAY BE SAVING YOUR FRIENDS LIFE.
I BEEN TALKIN TO HIM FO FIVE YEARS.
AND HE'S BEEN TALKING TO YOU FOR JUST AS LONG.
YOU JUST AIN'T COMMITTED YET.
THERE'S LOTS OF WAYS TO FUCK OFF THE MAN. WE DO IT BY ORGANIZATION, EDUCATION AND PREPARATION FOR STRUGGLE. YOUR FRIEND DOES IT BY BREAKING THE MAN'S LAWS. YOU'VE GOT THAT CHOICE. BUT IF THE UNITY, THE HEALTH AND THE DIGNITY OF YOUR PEOPLE MEAN ANYTHING TO YOU, THEN YOU KNOW YOUR FRIEND IS DOING IT ALL WRONG. YOU KNOW WE ARE ALL THE SAME TO THE MAN. ON THE REAL SIDE, IT WOULD BE BETTER IF HE WERE ON OUR SIDE WHEN THE PIG STARTS SHOOTING. HE'S MAKING IT HARDER FOR SOME OF US TO PROTECT OURSELVES WITH THE POISON HE'S GIVING US AND THE SELF-HATRED HE'S PERPETUATING. DIG IT, BROTHER.

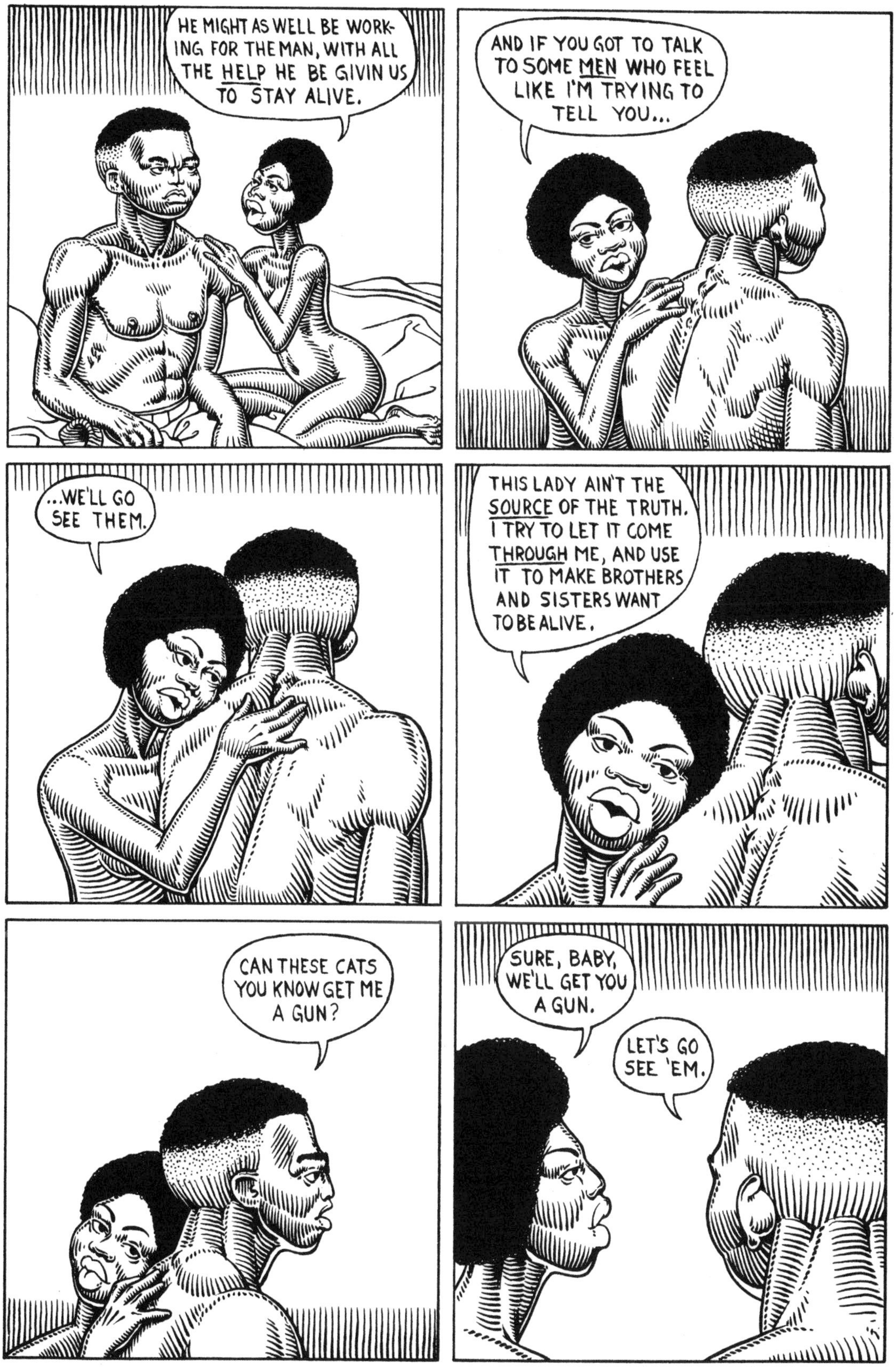
HE MIGHT AS WELL BE WORKING FOR THE MAN, WITH ALL THE HELP HE BE GIVIN US TO STAY ALIVE.
AND IF YOU GOT TO TALK TO SOME MEN WHO FEEL LIKE I'M TRYING TO TELL YOU...
...WE'LL GO SEE THEM.
THIS LADY AIN'T THE SOURCE OF THE TRUTH. I TRY TO LET IT COME THROUGH ME, AND USE IT TO MAKE BROTHERS AND SISTERS WANT TO BE ALIVE.
CAN THESE CATS YOU KNOW GET ME A GUN?
SURE, BABY, WE'LL GET YOU A GUN.
LET'S GO SEE 'EM.

BACK AT DE DOME AGIN.
SAY, LITTLE GIRL LONELY WHAT'S GOIN' ON?
IS YOU GIVIN' AWAY ANY MO SHIT, DADDY?
BE WELCOME, MA CHILD, AND WE SHALL CELEBRATE FREEDOM.
DO IT HERE, BABY.
AND COOK UP ENOUGH FO THIS ONE...
...AND DON'T FO-GIT, THEYS LOTS MO WHEY THAT COME FROM.

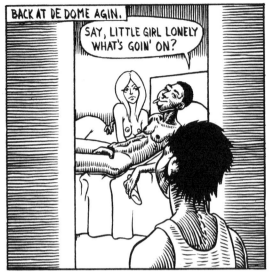

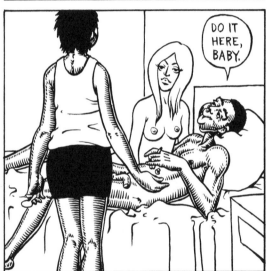

HOW KIN YOU HAVE IT SO TOGETHER AFTER ONE DAY ON THE STREETS?

PRAYER, BABY.

GOOD SHIT.

GOD GAVE ME WOMEN AND DOPE TO SELL, AND A BANK ACCOUNT TO KEEP MA BREAD WHILE I WAS LOCKED UP.

AN WHAT YOU GONNA DO NOW THAT YOU OUT?

PRAY FO MONEY, BABY, LOTS OF MONEY.

IS YOU GETTIN YO WOMEN TOGETHER AGIN?

WELL, I'LL TELL YOU, ANY TIME YO MAN CAN'T KEEP YOU HIGH OR IN NEW CLOTHES,

...YOU COME AROUND AND ASK ME AGIN.

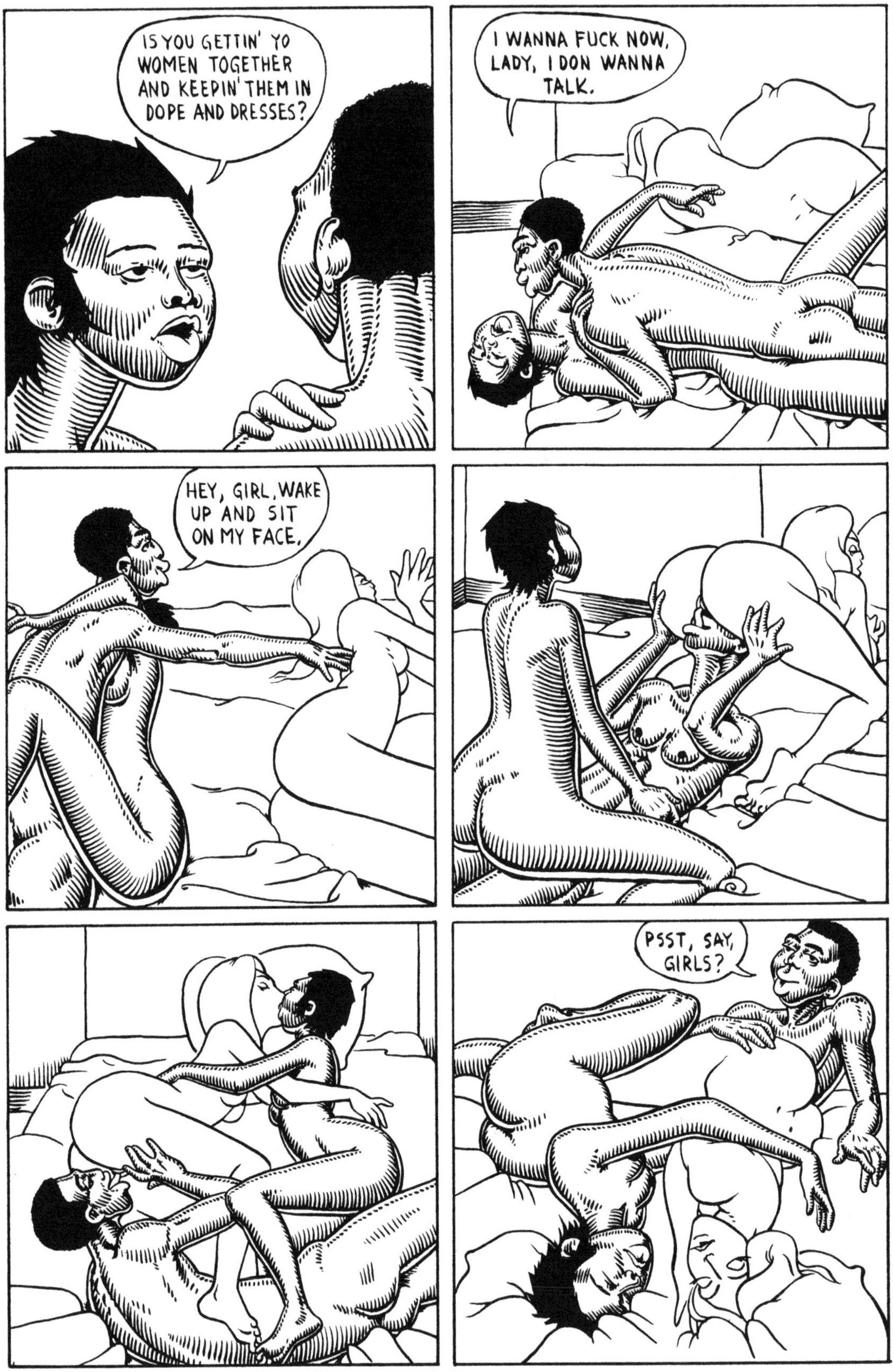
IS YOU GETTIN' YO WOMEN TOGETHER AND KEEPIN' THEM IN DOPE AND DRESSES?
I WANNA FUCK NOW, LADY, I DON WANNA TALK.
HEY, GIRL, WAKE UP AND SIT ON MY FACE.
PSST, SAY, GIRLS?

FUCKIN' HYPES.
SAY, MAN, CAN YOU SLOW THIS DUDE DOWN?
I'LL BRING YOU UP I'LL BRING YOU DOWN I'LL BRING YOU RIGHT AROUND TO WHERE YOU WANT TO BE.
GOT A JOINT?
WELCOME TO DE SLUMBER PARTY
OL ACID FREAK AINT HAD ENOUGH YET.
I AINT EITHER, BABY.

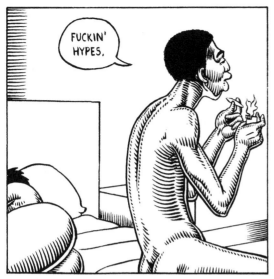

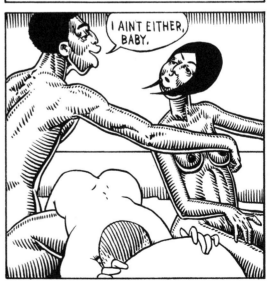

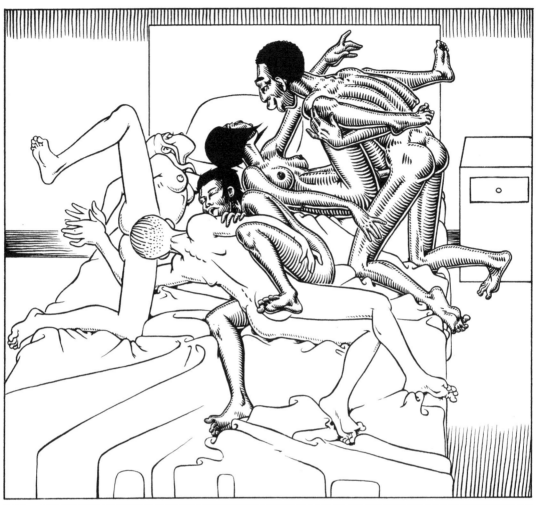

SAY, M'MAN, HOWYA DOIN'?

SOLID, HOMEBOY.

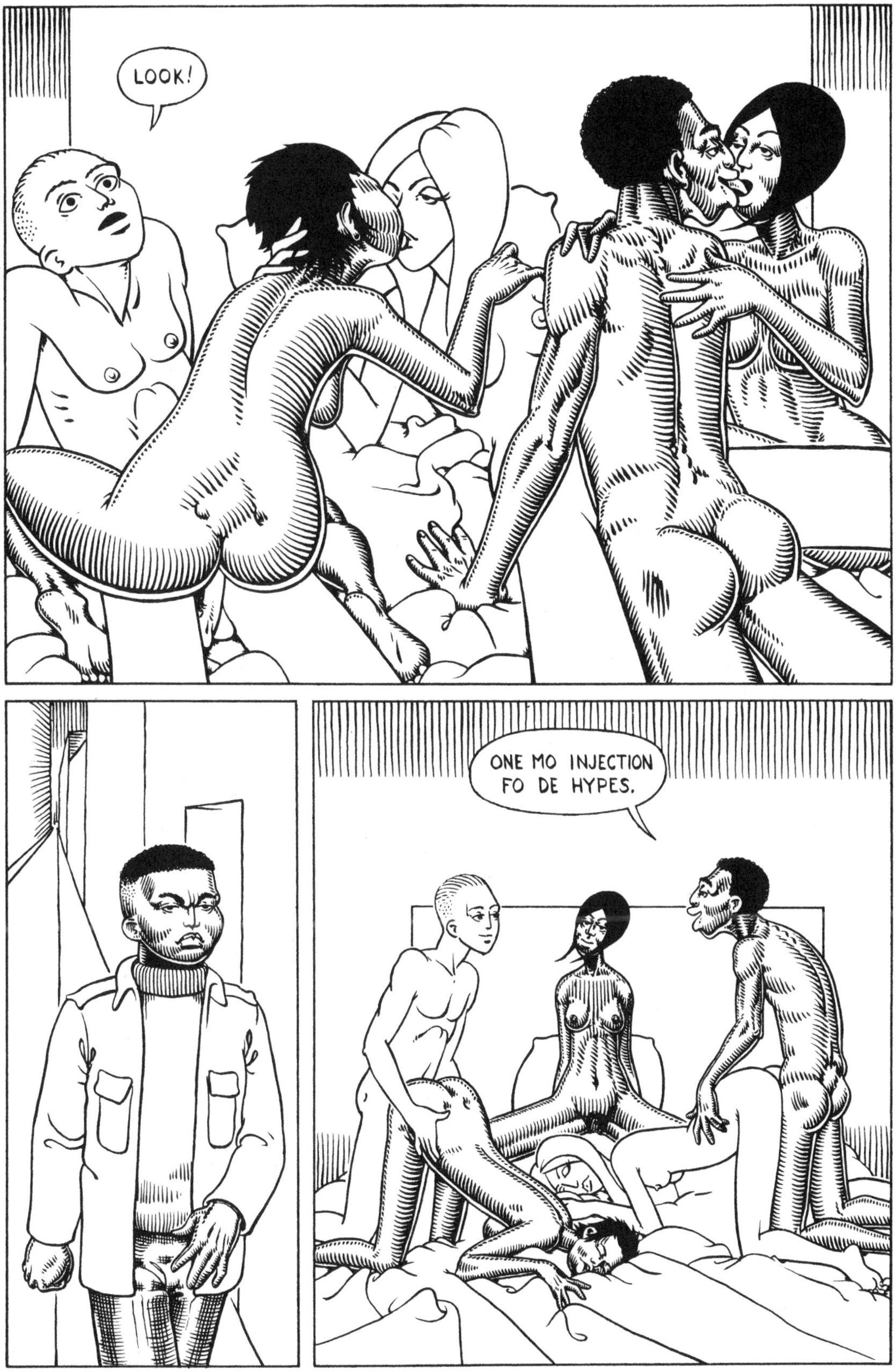
LOOK!
ONE MO INJECTION FO DE HYPES.

OOOOOO...

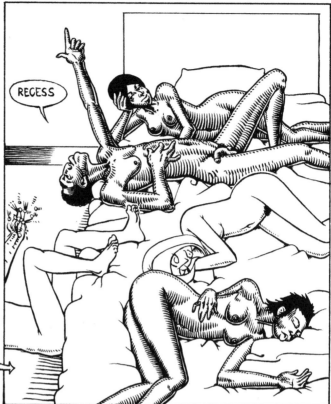

RECESS

...WEEEEE!

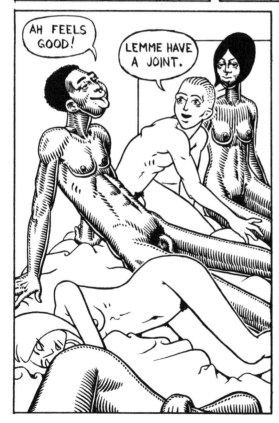

AH FEELS GOOD!

LEMME HAVE A JOINT.

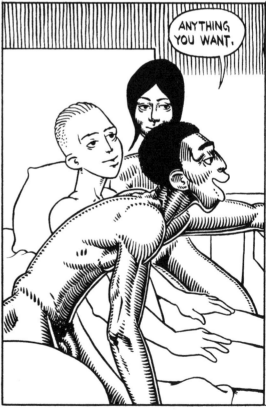

ANYTHING YOU WANT.

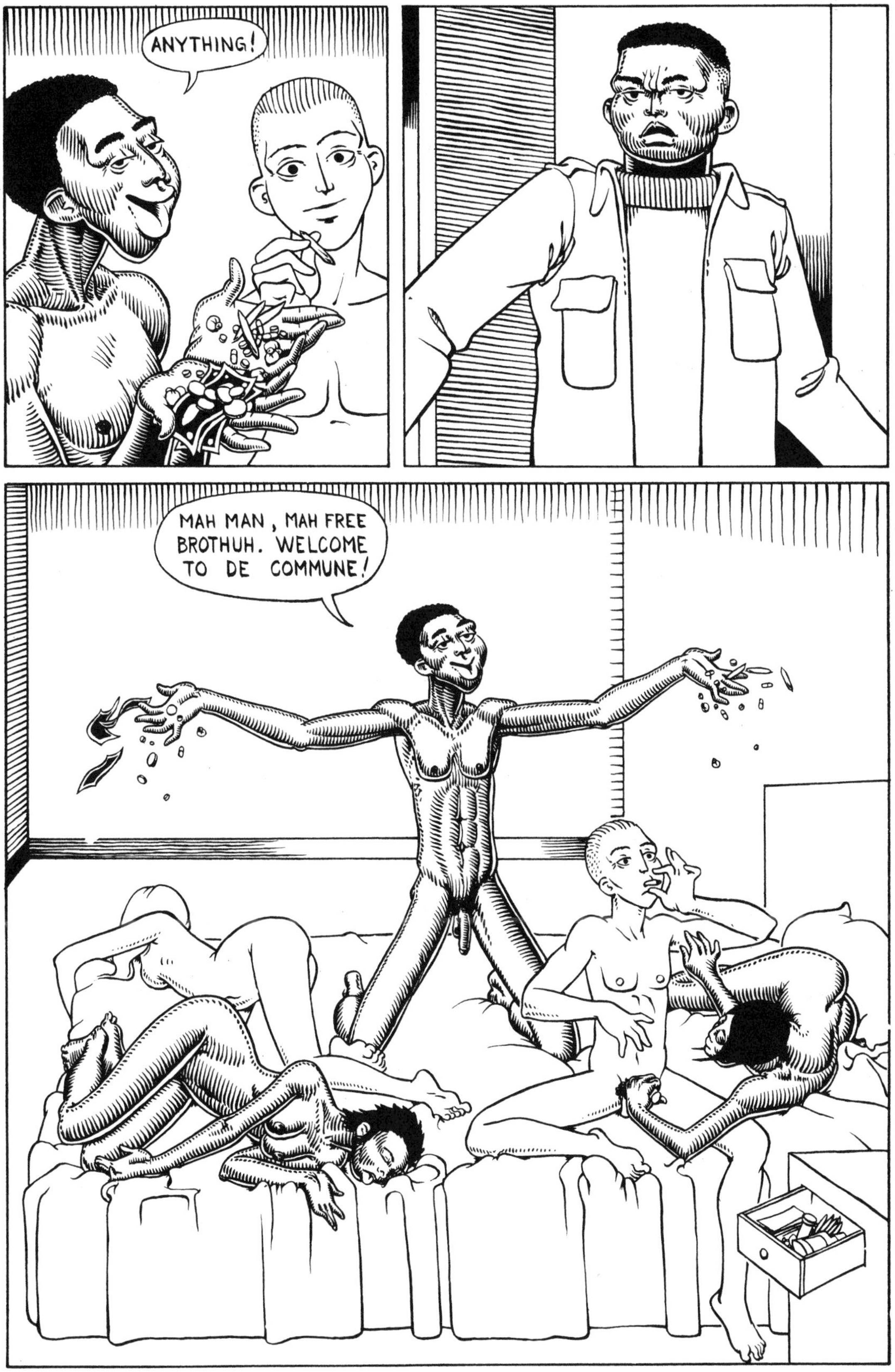
ANYTHING!
MAH MAN, MAH FREE BROTHUH. WELCOME TO DE COMMUNE!

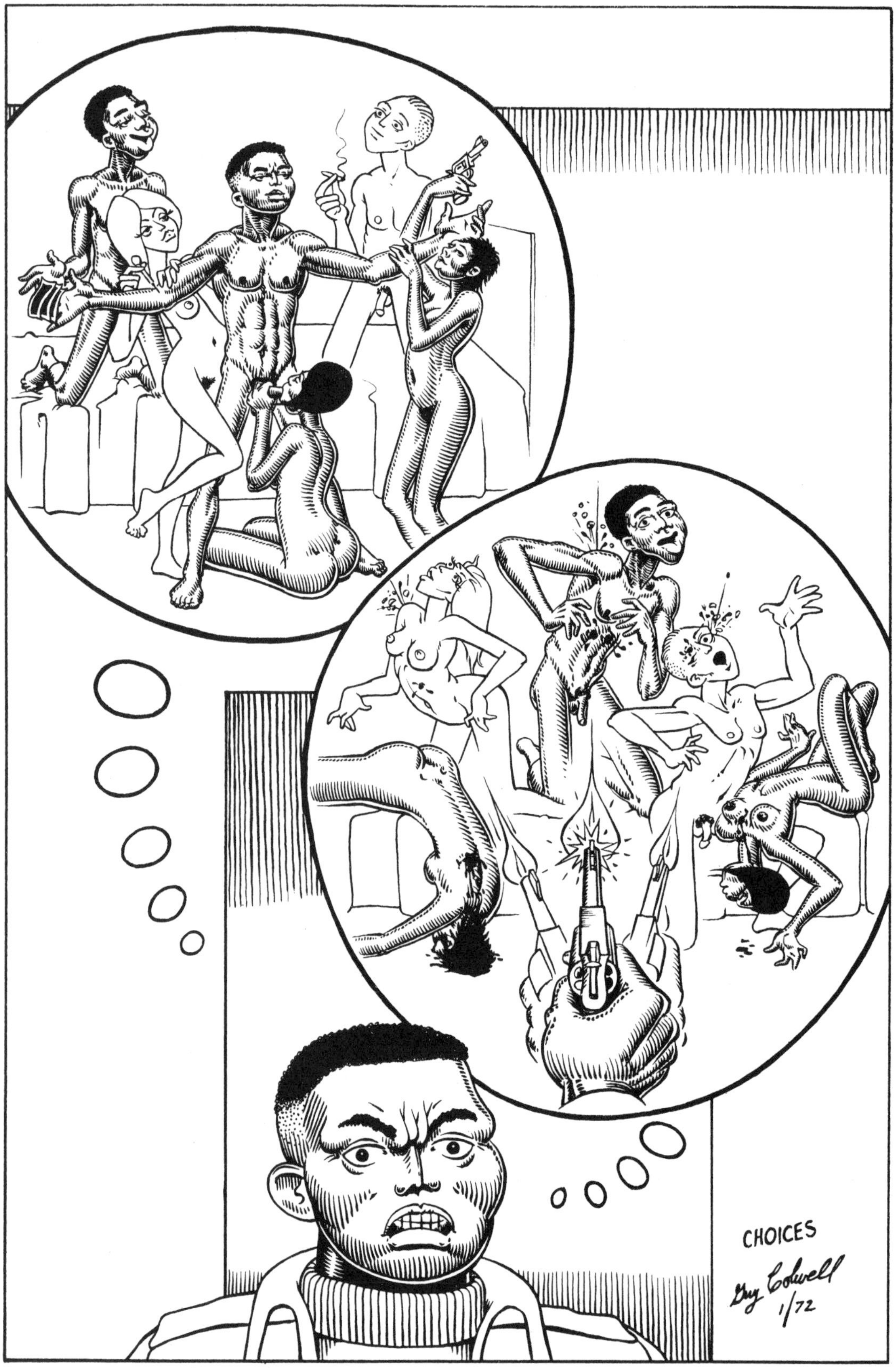
CHOICES
Guy Colwell
1/72

INNER CITY ROMANCE #2
(1972)
by Patrick Rosenkranz

"*Inner City Romance* #2 was begun at the Good Times Commune. It wove in the communal aspect to the story, followed the political thread that came out of the first book in the character of James, and let the junky heroin addiction stuff trail off. The big issue when I started doing comics and joined the commune was Peace, primarily the anti–Vietnam War struggles and the concern about nuclear holocaust. My participation was primarily to join in many demonstrations — mostly peaceful but some that included police on horseback charging into the crowds and beating demonstrators, tear gas, rage, and chaos. I was most active during the war years as part of the Good Times Commune. We not only went to the demonstrations, but I was becoming a journalist and political cartoonist, and we would support many other resistance groups with coverage and promotion. When the White Panther Party in San Francisco began having a lot of conflict with the police, I became a close observer, writing articles about their work and police problems — and when some of them got into a shootout with some cops and were arrested, I covered their trial as a courtroom quick sketch artist."

Colwell began his second comic book as three- and four-panel serialized strips for the *San Francisco Good Times* comics pages in 1972.

"I always called *Radical Rock* a rock opera. I'm not sure how or why I chose to do it in verse, but after I had done one strip of it for the *Good Times* "Comics Trips" page, there it was, a little rhyming verse poem. So I just went with this. An excited fan I met somewhere, probably at a show opening, told me he liked it so much he recited the entire 'libretto' to a live audience at some sort of poetry slam."

It would never be made into a Broadway hit or a movie like *Hair*, though, which was tailored for entertainment, not revolution.

"*Inner City Romance* #2 was probably the most political of all my books in the way it called for vigorous revolutionary action against police oppression and, as suggested in the 'Planet Earth' song sequence, change on an international scale was needed."

Radical Rock, oil on canvas, 1972. This painting became the wraparound front/back cover of *Inner City Romance* #2. Colwell had attended an outdoor rock concert that was disrupted by undercover police making drug arrests, and he witnessed the audience rise up and fight back.

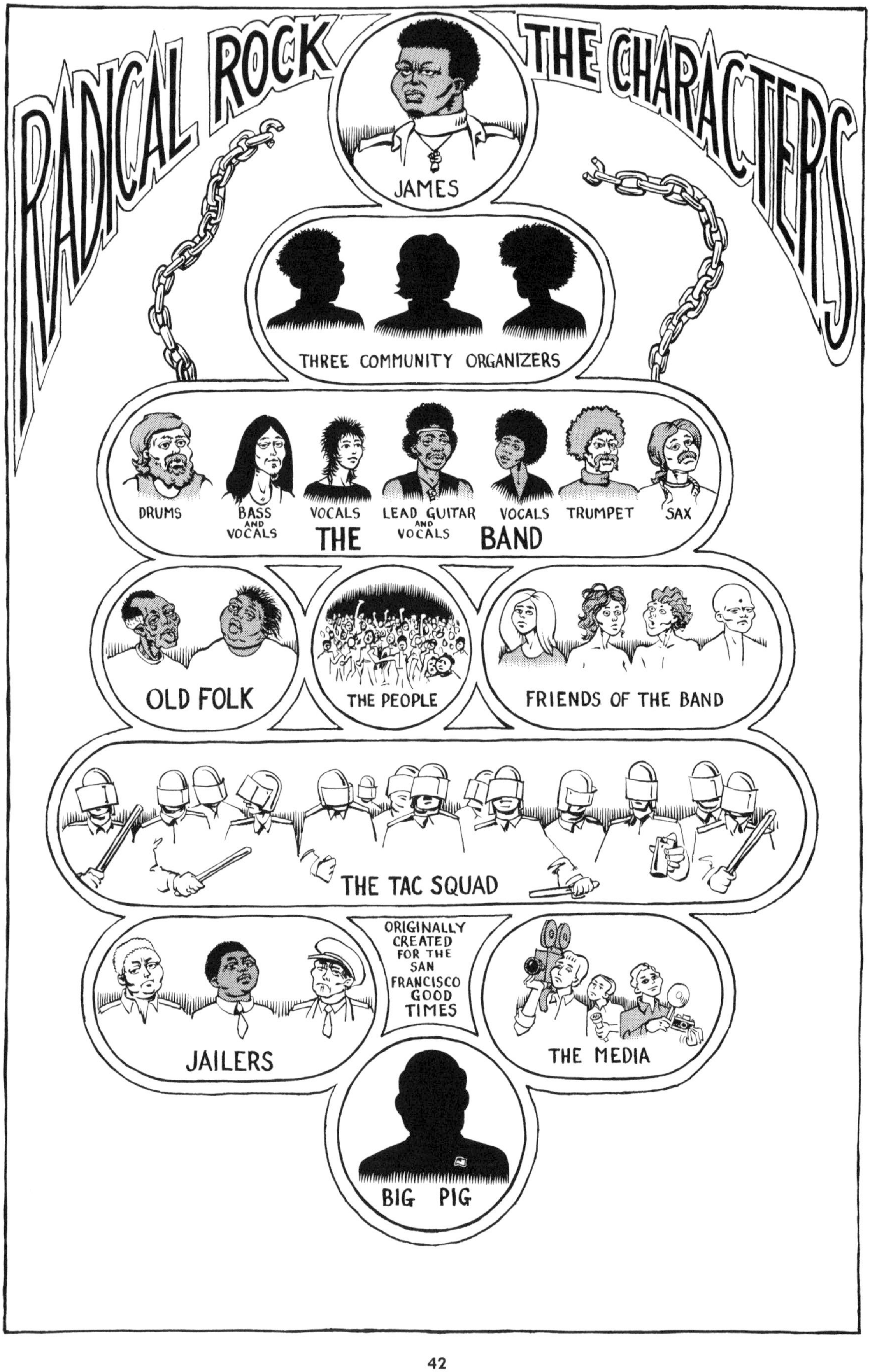
RADICAL ROCK
THE CHARACTERS
JAMES
THREE COMMUNITY ORGANIZERS
DRUMS
BASS AND VOCALS
VOCALS
LEAD GUITAR AND VOCALS
VOCALS
TRUMPET
SAX
THE BAND
OLD FOLK
THE PEOPLE
FRIENDS OF THE BAND
THE TAC SQUAD
JAILERS
ORIGINALLY CREATED FOR THE SAN FRANCISCO GOOD TIMES
THE MEDIA
BIG PIG

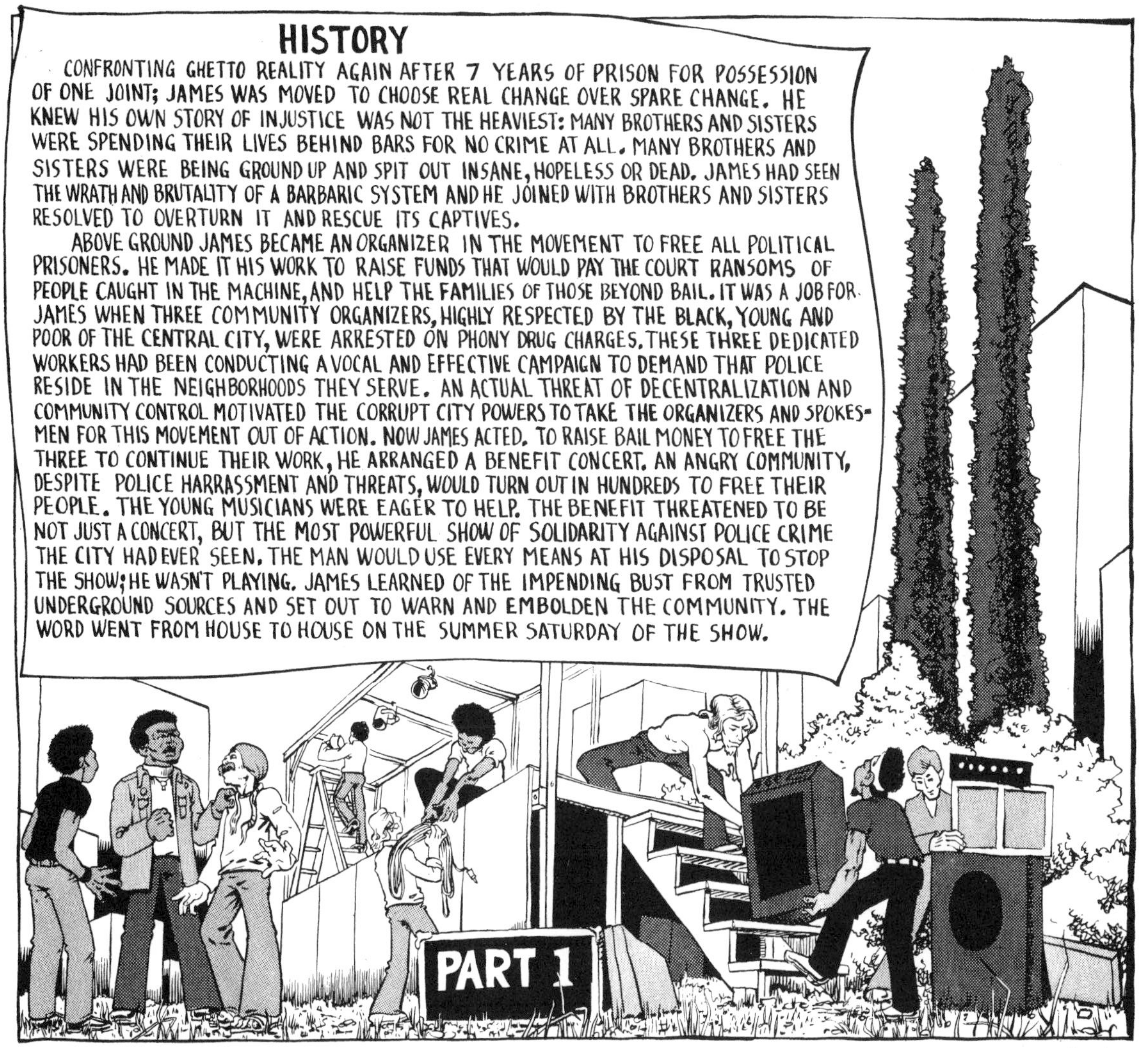
HISTORY
CONFRONTING GHETTO REALITY AGAIN AFTER 7 YEARS OF PRISON FOR POSSESSION OF ONE JOINT; JAMES WAS MOVED TO CHOOSE REAL CHANGE OVER SPARE CHANGE. HE KNEW HIS OWN STORY OF INJUSTICE WAS NOT THE HEAVIEST: MANY BROTHERS AND SISTERS WERE SPENDING THEIR LIVES BEHIND BARS FOR NO CRIME AT ALL. MANY BROTHERS AND SISTERS WERE BEING GROUND UP AND SPIT OUT INSANE, HOPELESS OR DEAD. JAMES HAD SEEN THE WRATH AND BRUTALITY OF A BARBARIC SYSTEM AND HE JOINED WITH BROTHERS AND SISTERS RESOLVED TO OVERTURN IT AND RESCUE ITS CAPTIVES.
ABOVE GROUND JAMES BECAME AN ORGANIZER IN THE MOVEMENT TO FREE ALL POLITICAL PRISONERS. HE MADE IT HIS WORK TO RAISE FUNDS THAT WOULD PAY THE COURT RANSOMS OF PEOPLE CAUGHT IN THE MACHINE, AND HELP THE FAMILIES OF THOSE BEYOND BAIL. IT WAS A JOB FOR JAMES WHEN THREE COMMUNITY ORGANIZERS, HIGHLY RESPECTED BY THE BLACK, YOUNG AND POOR OF THE CENTRAL CITY, WERE ARRESTED ON PHONY DRUG CHARGES. THESE THREE DEDICATED WORKERS HAD BEEN CONDUCTING A VOCAL AND EFFECTIVE CAMPAIGN TO DEMAND THAT POLICE RESIDE IN THE NEIGHBORHOODS THEY SERVE. AN ACTUAL THREAT OF DECENTRALIZATION AND COMMUNITY CONTROL MOTIVATED THE CORRUPT CITY POWERS TO TAKE THE ORGANIZERS AND SPOKESMEN FOR THIS MOVEMENT OUT OF ACTION. NOW JAMES ACTED. TO RAISE BAIL MONEY TO FREE THE THREE TO CONTINUE THEIR WORK, HE ARRANGED A BENEFIT CONCERT. AN ANGRY COMMUNITY, DESPITE POLICE HARRASSMENT AND THREATS, WOULD TURN OUT IN HUNDREDS TO FREE THEIR PEOPLE. THE YOUNG MUSICIANS WERE EAGER TO HELP. THE BENEFIT THREATENED TO BE NOT JUST A CONCERT, BUT THE MOST POWERFUL SHOW OF SOLIDARITY AGAINST POLICE CRIME THE CITY HAD EVER SEEN. THE MAN WOULD USE EVERY MEANS AT HIS DISPOSAL TO STOP THE SHOW; HE WASN'T PLAYING. JAMES LEARNED OF THE IMPENDING BUST FROM TRUSTED UNDERGROUND SOURCES AND SET OUT TO WARN AND EMBOLDEN THE COMMUNITY. THE WORD WENT FROM HOUSE TO HOUSE ON THE SUMMER SATURDAY OF THE SHOW.
PART 1

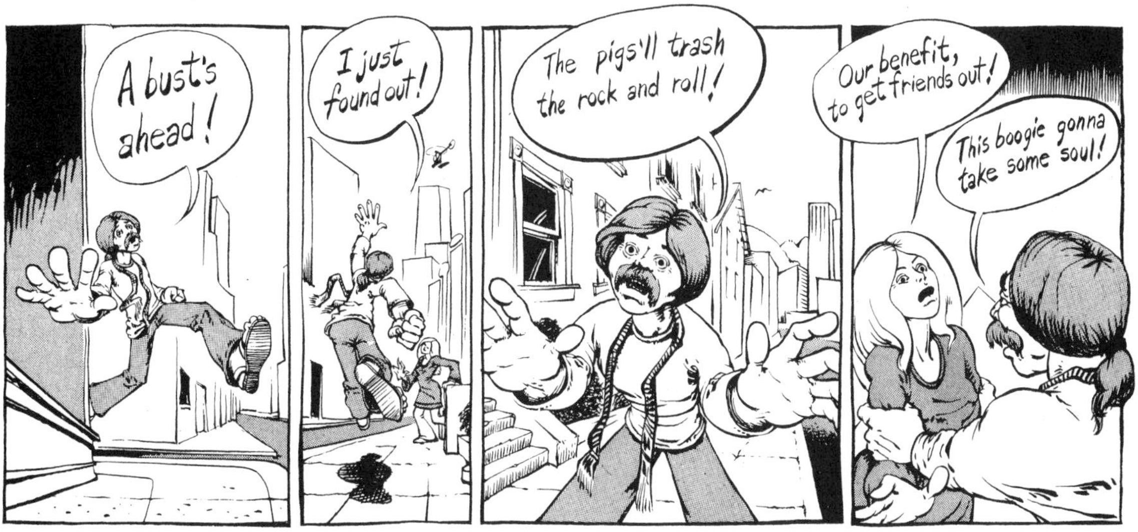
A bust's ahead!
I just found out!
The pigs'll trash the rock and roll!
Our benefit, to get friends out!
This boogie gonna take some soul!

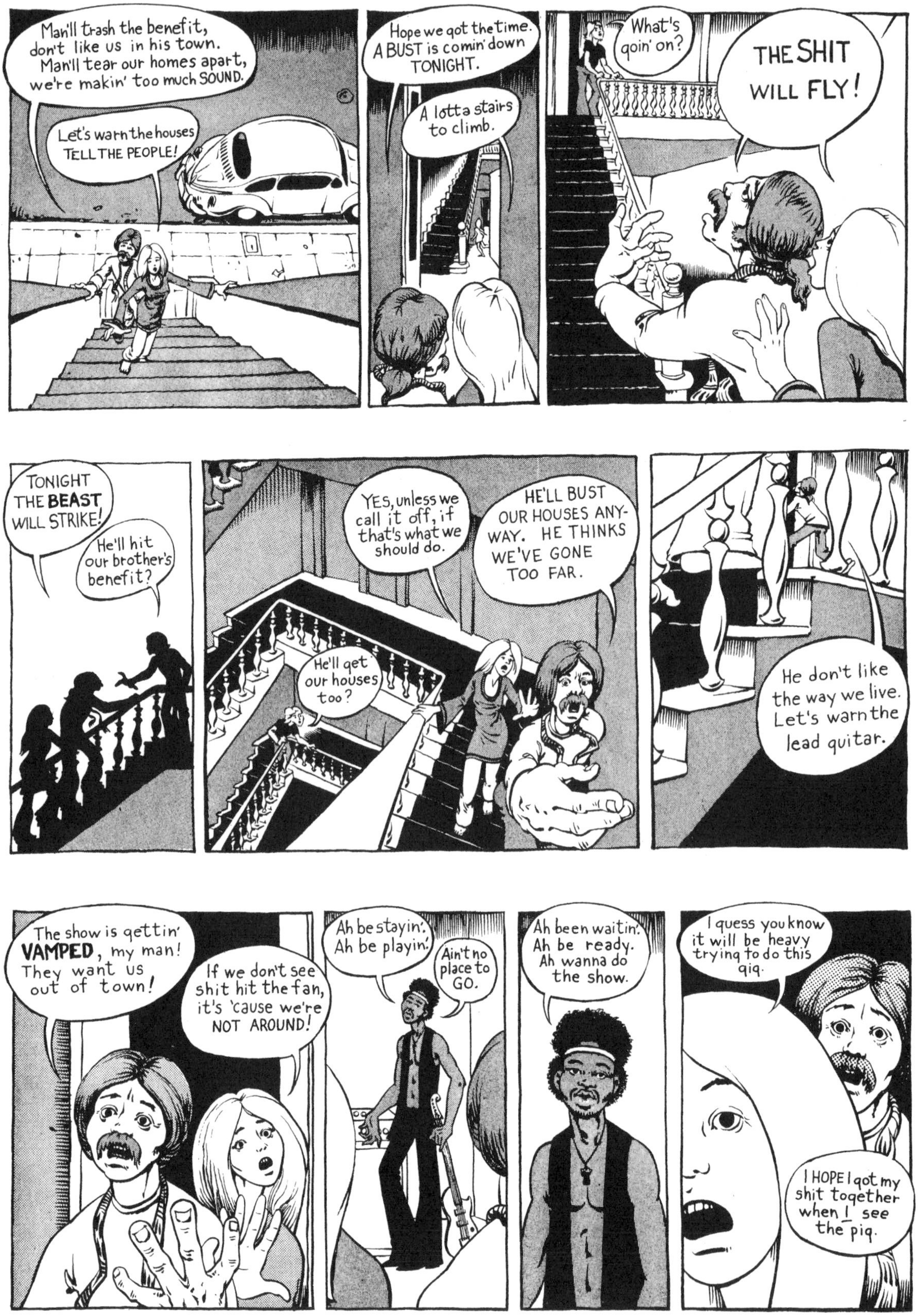
Man'll trash the benefit, don't like us in his town. Man'll tear our homes apart, we're makin' too much SOUND.
Let's warn the houses TELL THE PEOPLE!
Hope we got the time. A BUST is comin' down TONIGHT.
A lotta stairs to climb.
What's goin' on?
THE SHIT WILL FLY!
TONIGHT THE BEAST WILL STRIKE!
He'll hit our brother's benefit?
YES, unless we call it off, if that's what we should do.
HE'LL BUST OUR HOUSES ANYWAY. HE THINKS WE'VE GONE TOO FAR.
He'll get our houses too?
He don't like the way we live. Let's warn the lead guitar.
The show is gettin' VAMPED, my man! They want us out of town!
If we don't see shit hit the fan, it's 'cause we're NOT AROUND!
Ah be stayin'. Ah be playin'.
Ain't no place to GO.
Ah been waitin'. Ah be ready. Ah wanna do the show.
I guess you know it will be heavy trying to do this gig.
I HOPE I got my shit together when I see the gig.

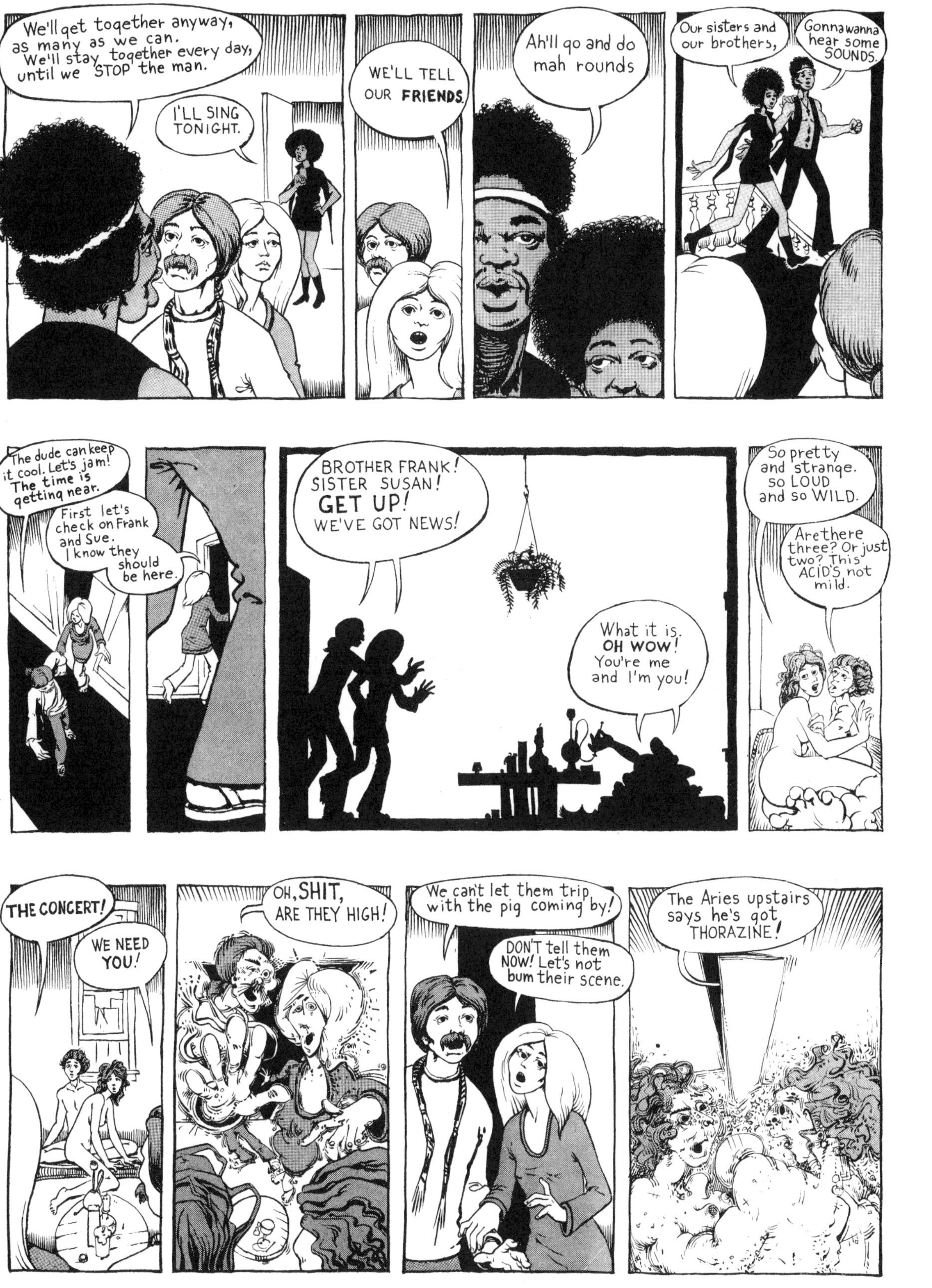

We'll get together anyway, as many as we can. We'll stay together every day, until we STOP the man.
I'LL SING TONIGHT.
WE'LL TELL OUR FRIENDS.
Ah'll go and do mah rounds
Our sisters and our brothers,
Gonnawanna hear some SOUNDS.
The dude can keep it cool. Let's jam! The time is getting near.
First let's check on Frank and Sue. I know they should be here.
BROTHER FRANK! SISTER SUSAN! GET UP! WE'VE GOT NEWS!
What it is. OH WOW! You're me and I'm you!
So pretty and strange. so LOUD and so WILD.
Are there three? Or just two? This ACID'S not mild.
THE CONCERT!
WE NEED YOU!
OH, SHIT, ARE THEY HIGH!
We can't let them trip with the pig coming by!
DON'T tell them NOW! Let's not bum their scene.
The Aries upstairs says he's got THORAZINE!

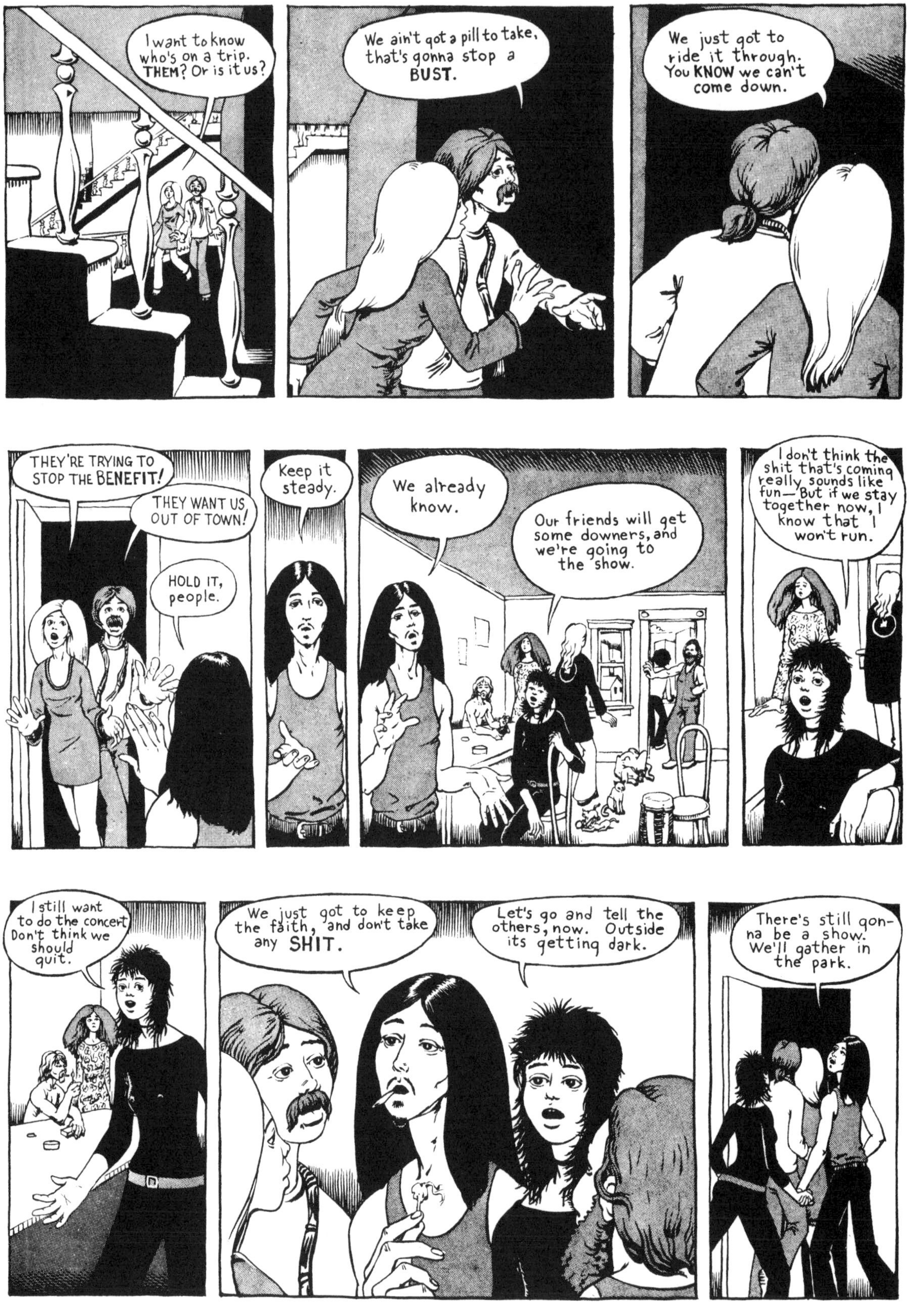
I want to know who's on a trip. THEM? Or is it us?
We ain't got a pill to take, that's gonna stop a BUST.
We just got to ride it through. You KNOW we can't come down.
THEY'RE TRYING TO STOP THE BENEFIT!
THEY WANT US OUT OF TOWN!
HOLD IT, people.
Keep it steady.
We already know.
Our friends will get some downers, and we're going to the show.
I don't think the shit that's coming really sounds like fun— But if we stay together now, I know that I won't run.
I still want to do the concert Don't think we should quit.
We just got to keep the faith, and don't take any SHIT.
Let's go and tell the others, now. Outside its getting dark.
There's still gonna be a show. We'll gather in the park.

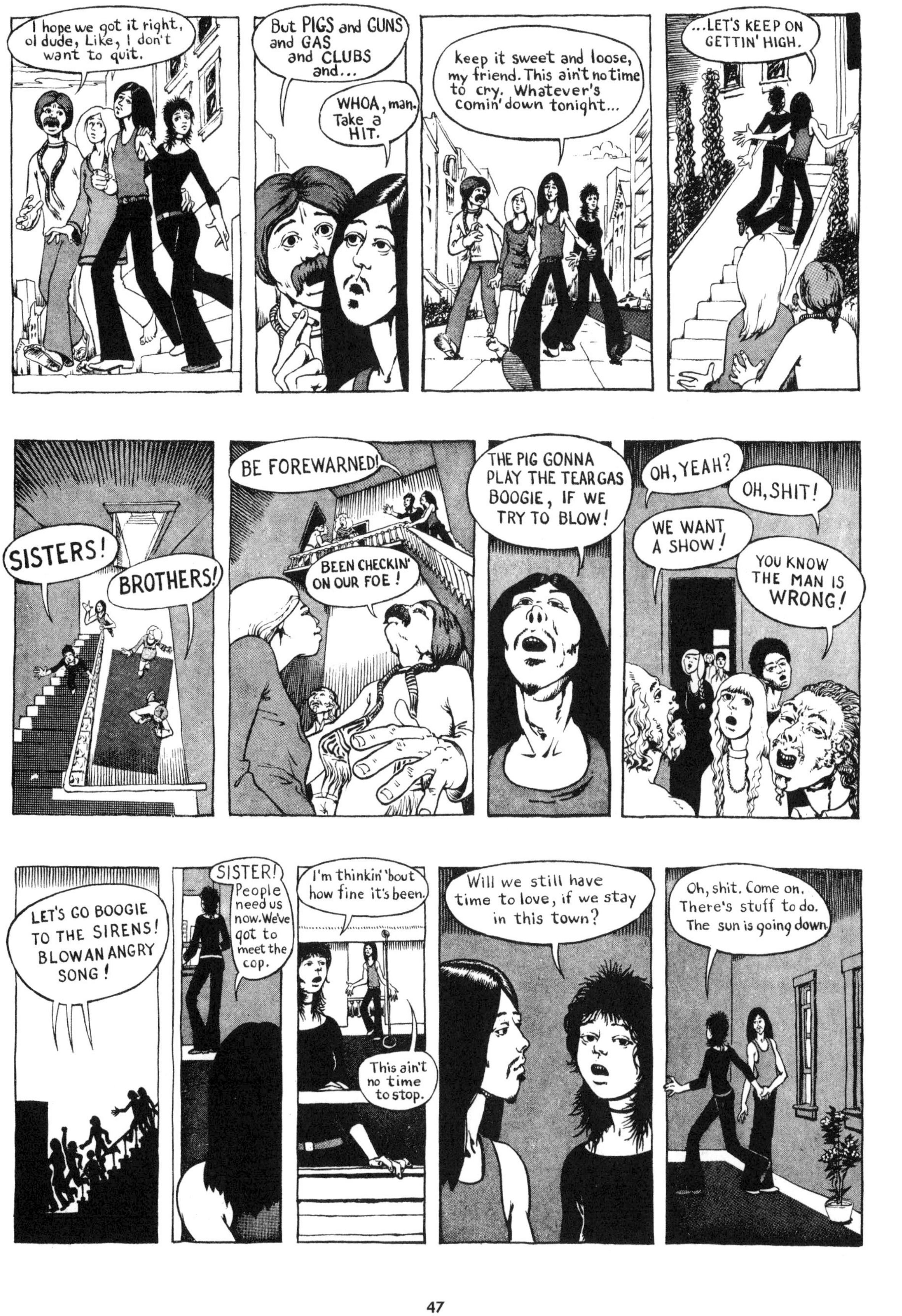
I hope we got it right, ol dude, Like, I don't want to quit.
But PIGS and GUNS and GAS and CLUBS and...
WHOA, man. Take a HIT.
keep it sweet and loose, my friend. This ain't no time to cry. Whatever's comin' down tonight...
...LET'S KEEP ON GETTIN' HIGH.
SISTERS!
BROTHERS!
BE FOREWARNED!
BEEN CHECKIN' ON OUR FOE!
THE PIG GONNA PLAY THE TEARGAS BOOGIE, IF WE TRY TO BLOW!
OH, YEAH?
OH, SHIT!
WE WANT A SHOW!
YOU KNOW THE MAN IS WRONG!
LET'S GO BOOGIE TO THE SIRENS! BLOWAN ANGRY SONG!
SISTER! People need us now. We've got to meet the cop.
I'm thinkin' 'bout how fine it's been.
This ain't no time to stop.
Will we still have time to love, if we stay in this town?
Oh, shit. Come on. There's stuff to do. The sun is going down.

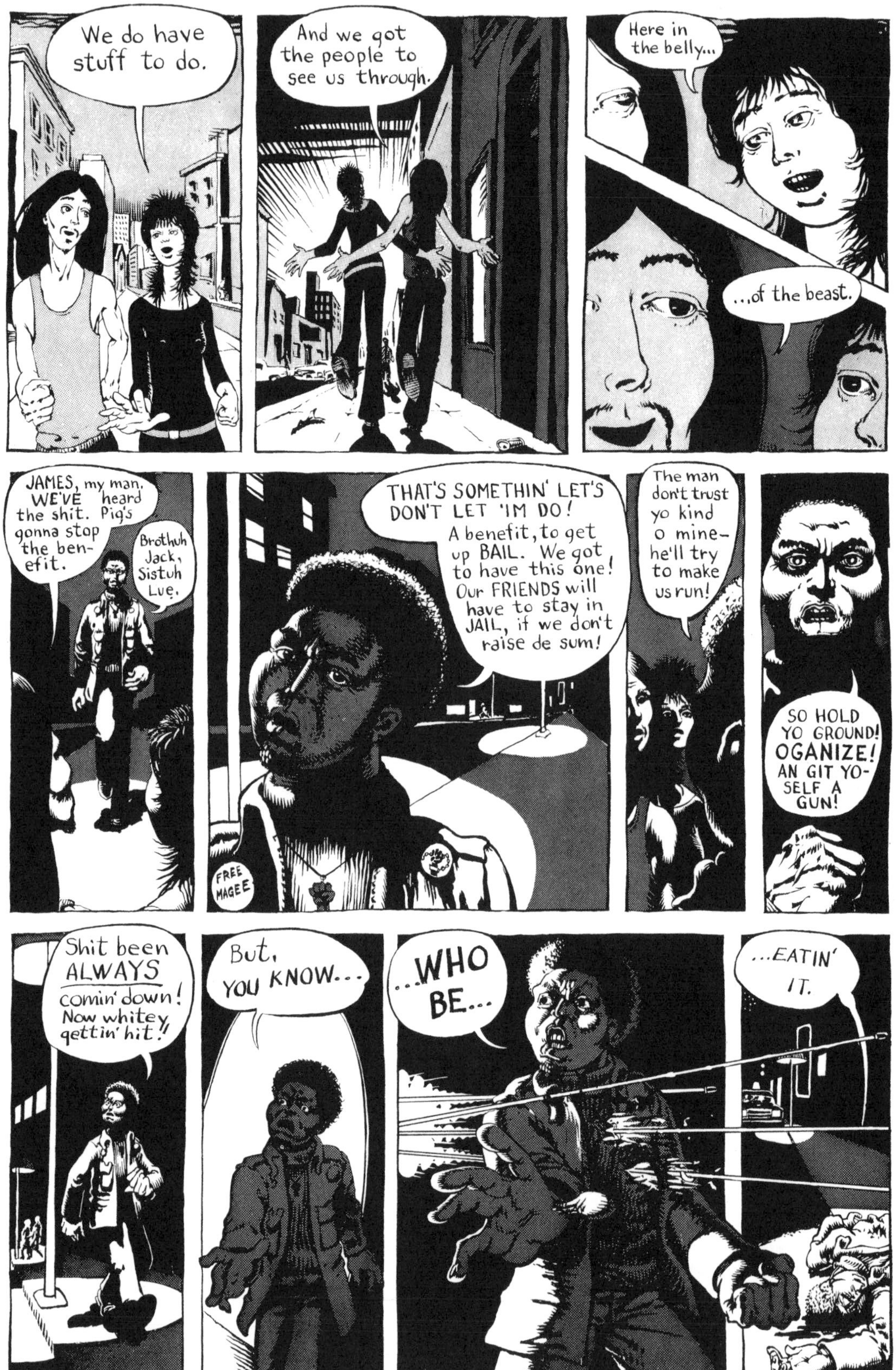

We do have stuff to do.
And we got the people to see us through.
Here in the belly...
...of the beast.
JAMES, my man. WE'VE heard the shit. Pig's gonna stop the benefit.
Brothuh Jack, Sistuh Lue.
THAT'S SOMETHIN' LET'S DON'T LET 'IM DO!
A benefit, to get up BAIL. We got to have this one! Our FRIENDS will have to stay in JAIL, if we don't raise de sum!
FREE MAGEE
The man don't trust yo kind o mine- he'll try to make us run!
SO HOLD YO GROUND! OGANIZE! AN GIT YO-SELF A GUN!
Shit been ALWAYS comin' down! Now whitey gettin' hit!
But, YOU KNOW...
...WHO BE...
...EATIN' IT.

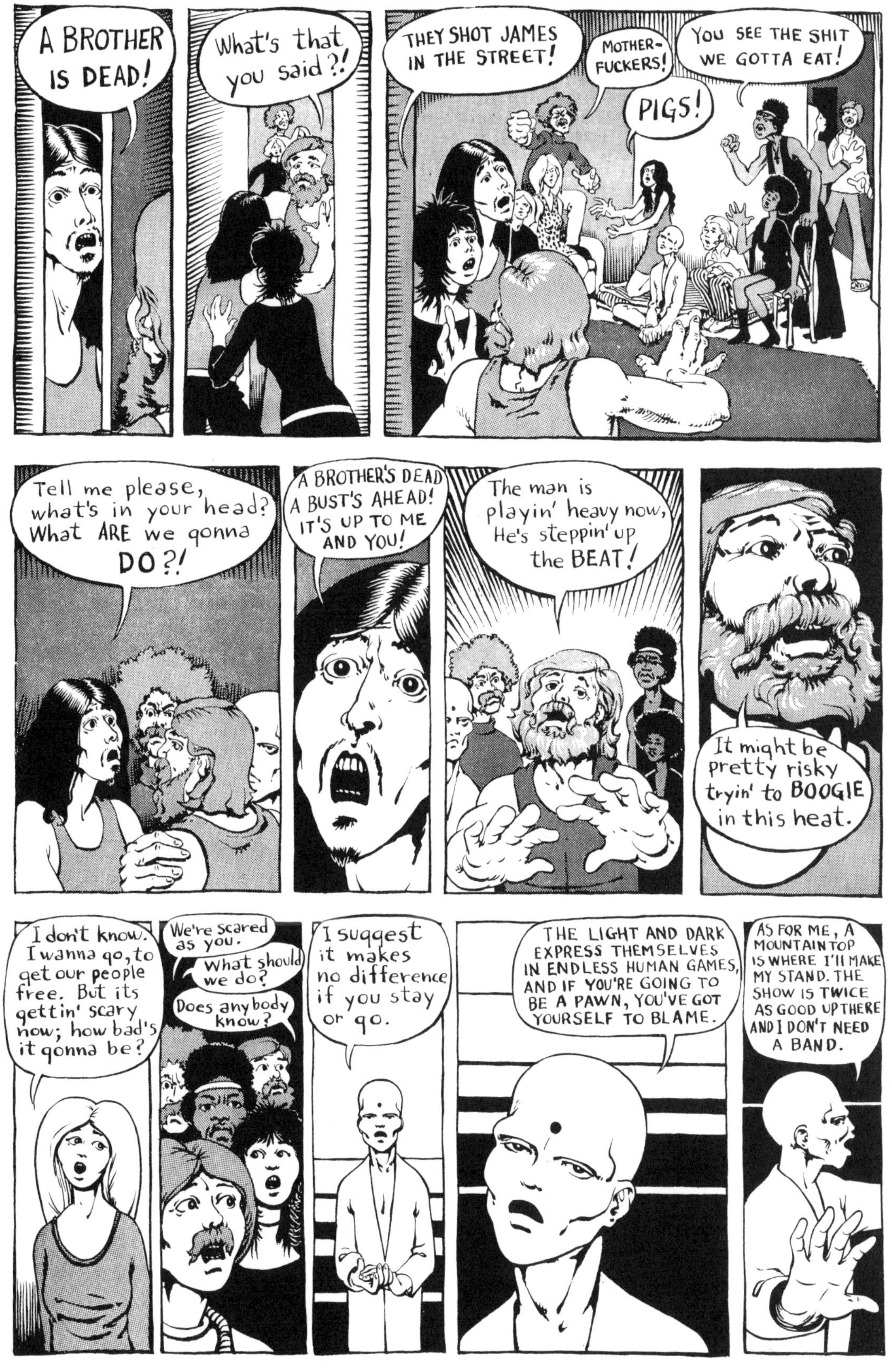
A BROTHER IS DEAD!
What's that you said?!
THEY SHOT JAMES IN THE STREET!
MOTHER-FUCKERS!
PIGS!
YOU SEE THE SHIT WE GOTTA EAT!
Tell me please, what's in your head? What ARE we gonna DO?!
A BROTHER'S DEAD A BUST'S AHEAD! IT'S UP TO ME AND YOU!
The man is playin' heavy now, He's steppin' up the BEAT!
It might be pretty risky tryin' to BOOGIE in this heat.
I don't know. I wanna go, to get our people free. But its gettin' scary now; how bad's it gonna be?
We're scared as you.
What should we do?
Does anybody know?
I suggest it makes no difference if you stay or go.
THE LIGHT AND DARK EXPRESS THEMSELVES IN ENDLESS HUMAN GAMES, AND IF YOU'RE GOING TO BE A PAWN, YOU'VE GOT YOURSELF TO BLAME.
AS FOR ME, A MOUNTAIN TOP IS WHERE I'LL MAKE MY STAND. THE SHOW IS TWICE AS GOOD UP THERE AND I DON'T NEED A BAND.

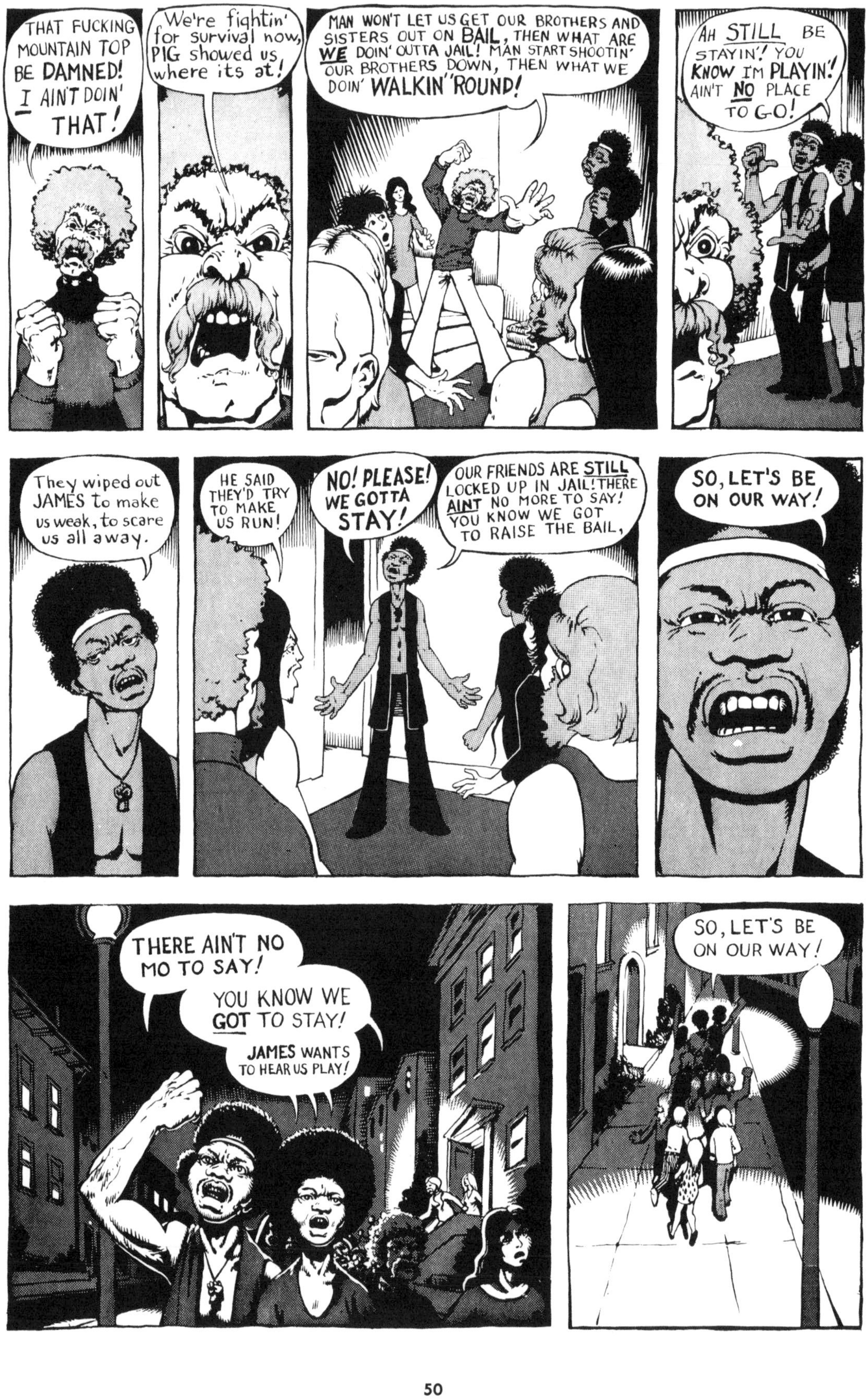
THAT FUCKING MOUNTAIN TOP BE DAMNED! I AIN'T DOIN' THAT!
We're fightin' for survival now, PIG showed us where its at!
MAN WON'T LET US GET OUR BROTHERS AND SISTERS OUT ON BAIL, THEN WHAT ARE WE DOIN' OUTTA JAIL! MAN START SHOOTIN' OUR BROTHERS DOWN, THEN WHAT WE DOIN' WALKIN' 'ROUND!
AH STILL BE STAYIN'! YOU KNOW I'M PLAYIN'! AIN'T NO PLACE TO GO!
They wiped out JAMES to make us weak, to scare us all away.
HE SAID THEY'D TRY TO MAKE US RUN!
NO! PLEASE! WE GOTTA STAY!
OUR FRIENDS ARE STILL LOCKED UP IN JAIL! THERE AINT NO MORE TO SAY! YOU KNOW WE GOT TO RAISE THE BAIL,
SO, LET'S BE ON OUR WAY!
THERE AIN'T NO MO TO SAY!
YOU KNOW WE GOT TO STAY!
JAMES WANTS TO HEAR US PLAY!
SO, LET'S BE ON OUR WAY!

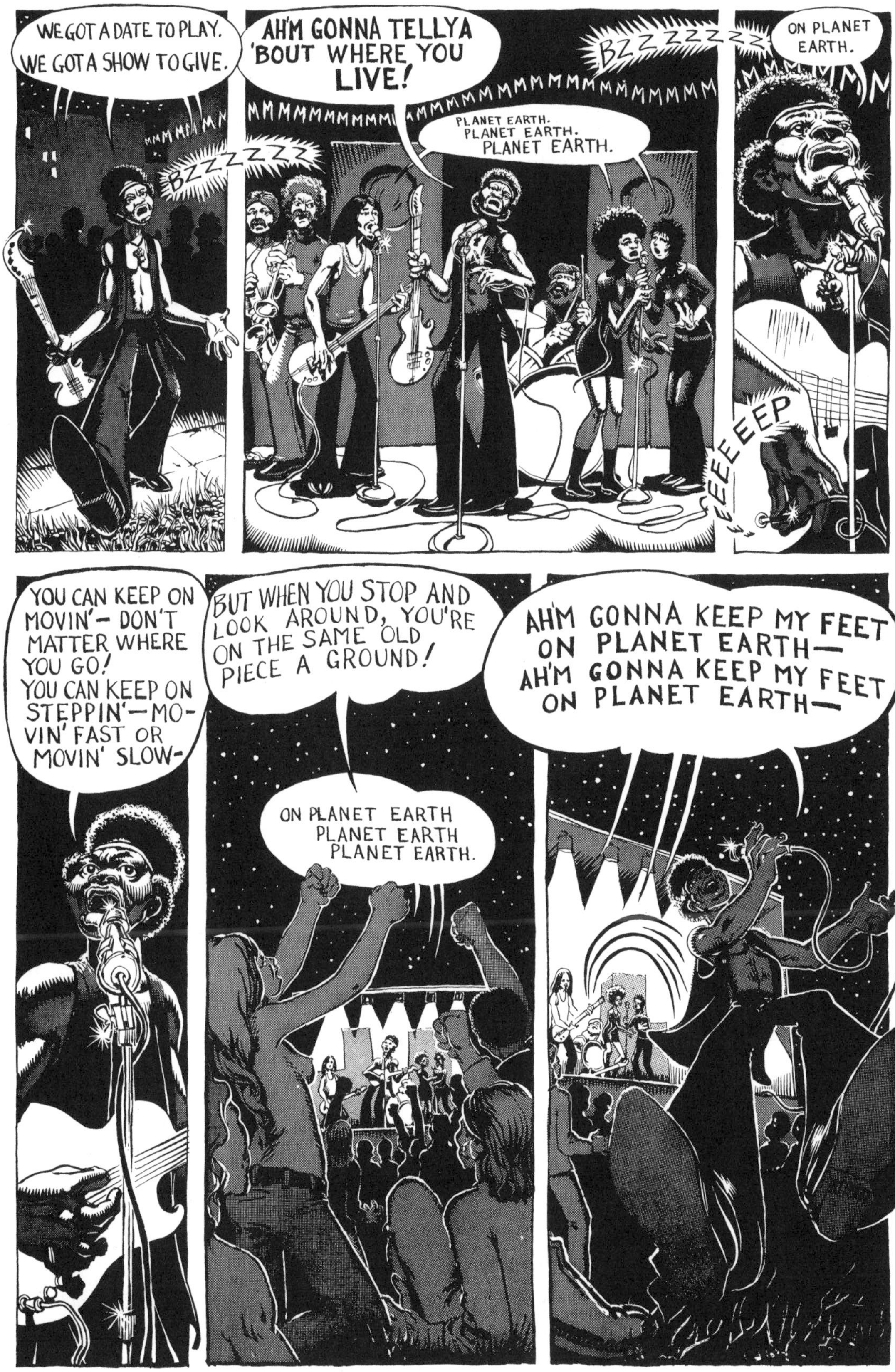
WE GOT A DATE TO PLAY.
WE GOT A SHOW TO GIVE.
BZZZZZZZ
AH'M GONNA TELLYA 'BOUT WHERE YOU LIVE!
PLANET EARTH. PLANET EARTH. PLANET EARTH.
BZZZZZZZ
ON PLANET EARTH.
EEEEEEP
YOU CAN KEEP ON MOVIN'— DON'T MATTER WHERE YOU GO! YOU CAN KEEP ON STEPPIN'—MOVIN' FAST OR MOVIN' SLOW-
BUT WHEN YOU STOP AND LOOK AROUND, YOU'RE ON THE SAME OLD PIECE A GROUND!
ON PLANET EARTH PLANET EARTH PLANET EARTH.
AH'M GONNA KEEP MY FEET ON PLANET EARTH— AH'M GONNA KEEP MY FEET ON PLANET EARTH—

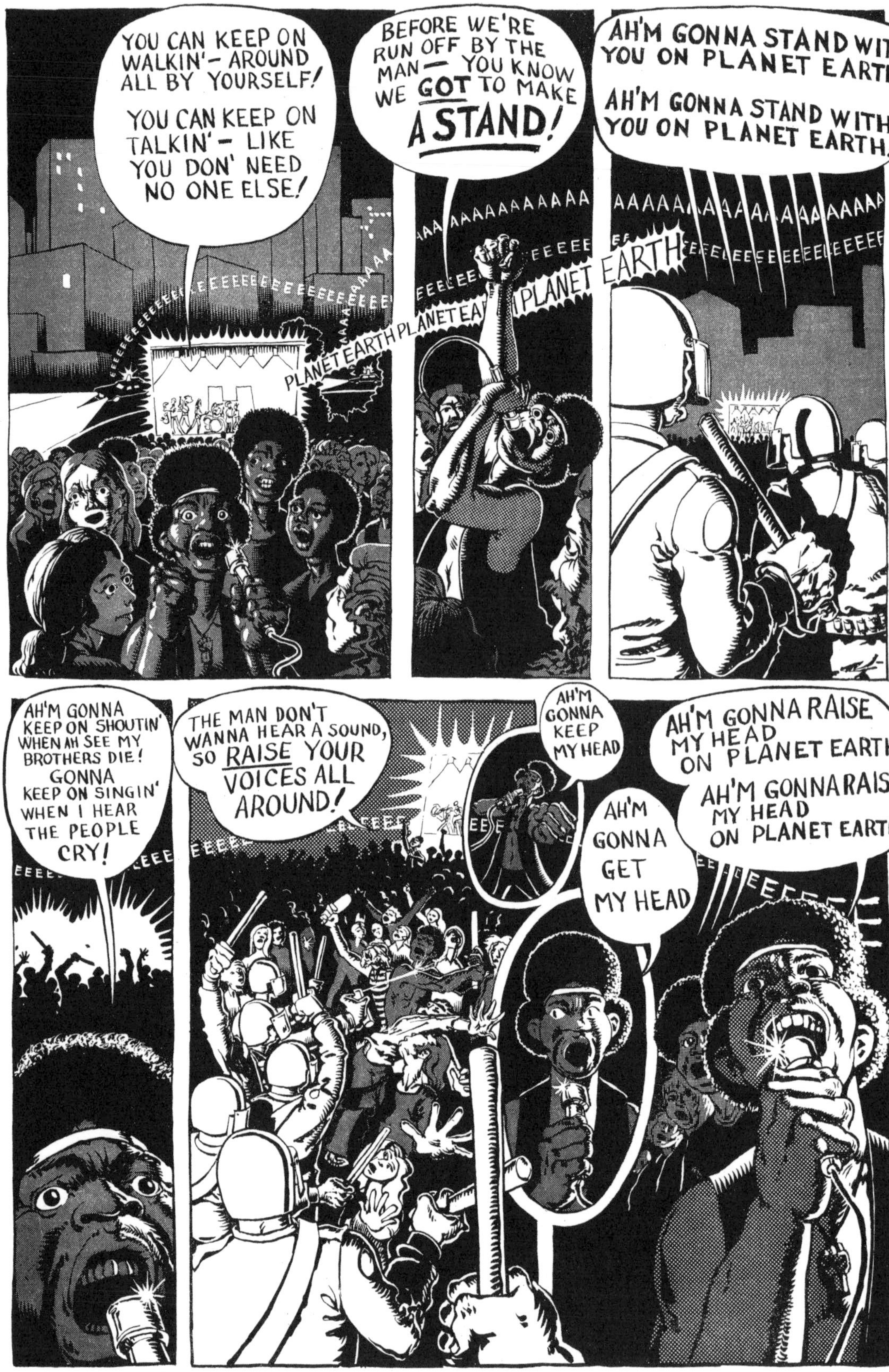

YOU CAN KEEP ON WALKIN'- AROUND ALL BY YOURSELF!
YOU CAN KEEP ON TALKIN' - LIKE YOU DON' NEED NO ONE ELSE!
PLANET EARTH PLANET EARTH PLANET EARTH
BEFORE WE'RE RUN OFF BY THE MAN— YOU KNOW WE GOT TO MAKE A STAND!
AH'M GONNA STAND WITH YOU ON PLANET EARTH!
AH'M GONNA STAND WITH YOU ON PLANET EARTH!
AH'M GONNA KEEP ON SHOUTIN' WHEN AH SEE MY BROTHERS DIE!
GONNA KEEP ON SINGIN' WHEN I HEAR THE PEOPLE CRY!
THE MAN DON'T WANNA HEAR A SOUND, SO RAISE YOUR VOICES ALL AROUND!
AH'M GONNA KEEP MY HEAD
AH'M GONNA GET MY HEAD
AH'M GONNA RAISE MY HEAD ON PLANET EARTH
AH'M GONNA RAISE MY HEAD ON PLANET EARTH

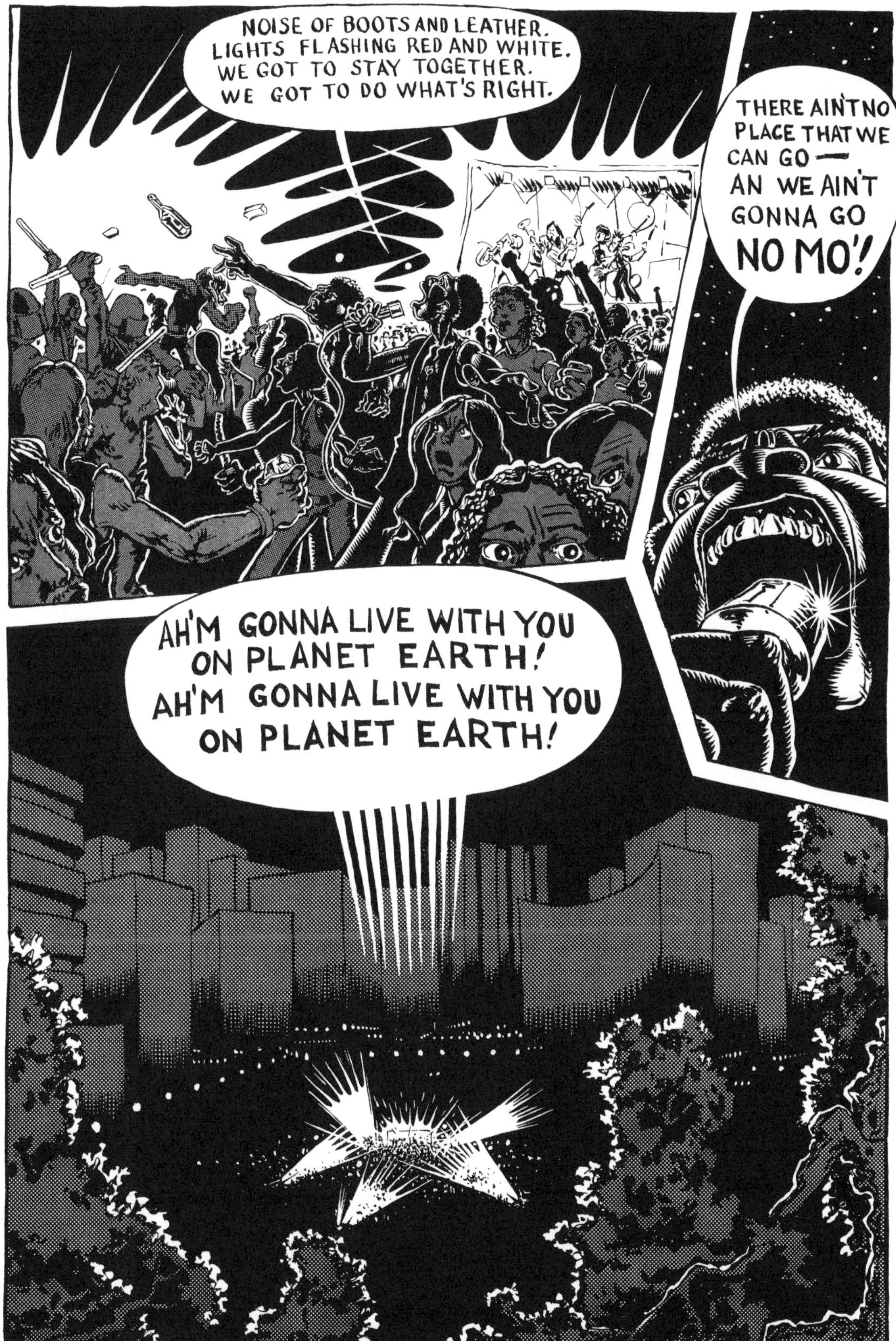
NOISE OF BOOTS AND LEATHER. LIGHTS FLASHING RED AND WHITE. WE GOT TO STAY TOGETHER. WE GOT TO DO WHAT'S RIGHT.
THERE AIN'T NO PLACE THAT WE CAN GO— AN WE AIN'T GONNA GO NO MO'!
AH'M GONNA LIVE WITH YOU ON PLANET EARTH! AH'M GONNA LIVE WITH YOU ON PLANET EARTH!

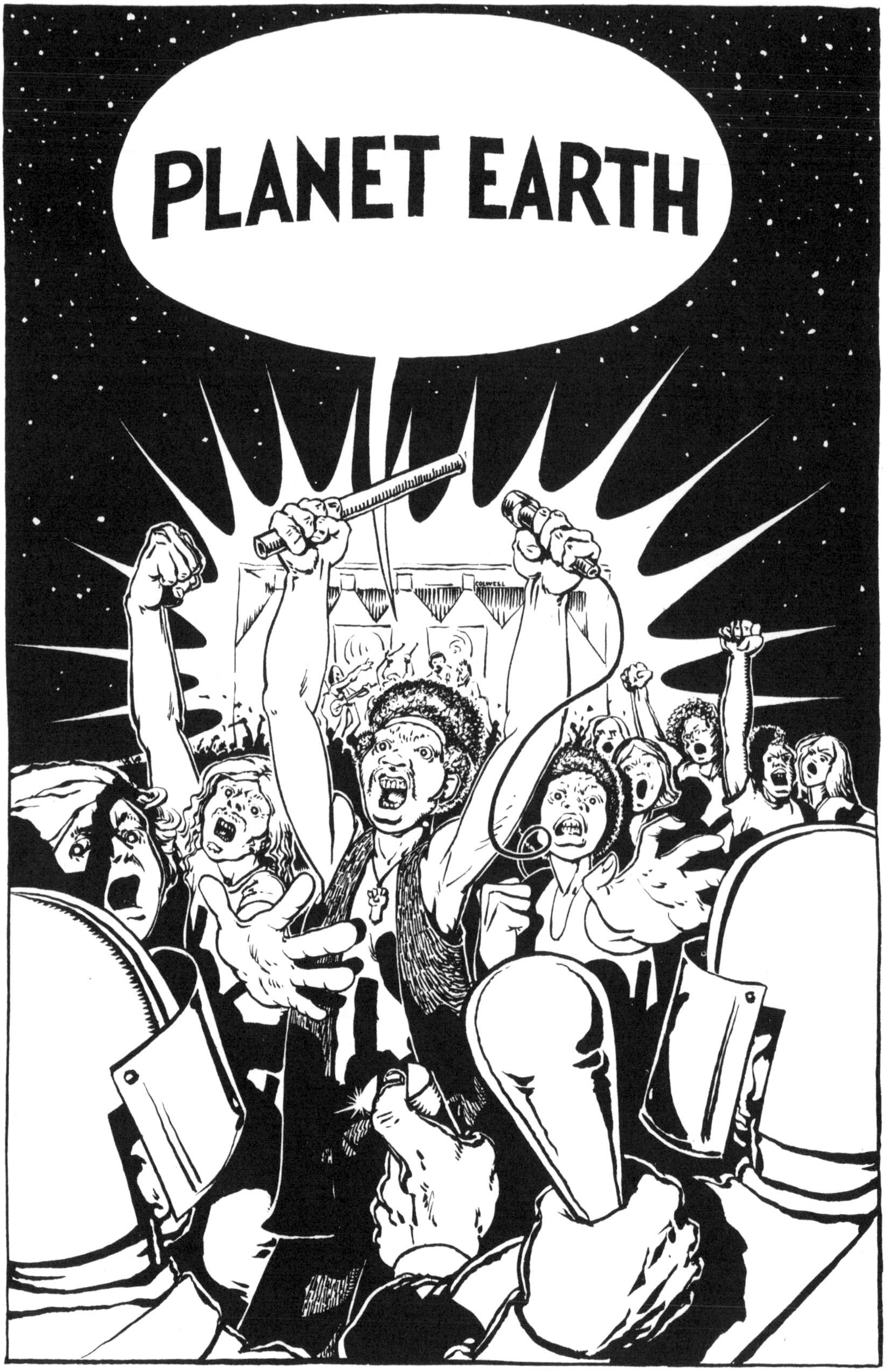
PLANET EARTH

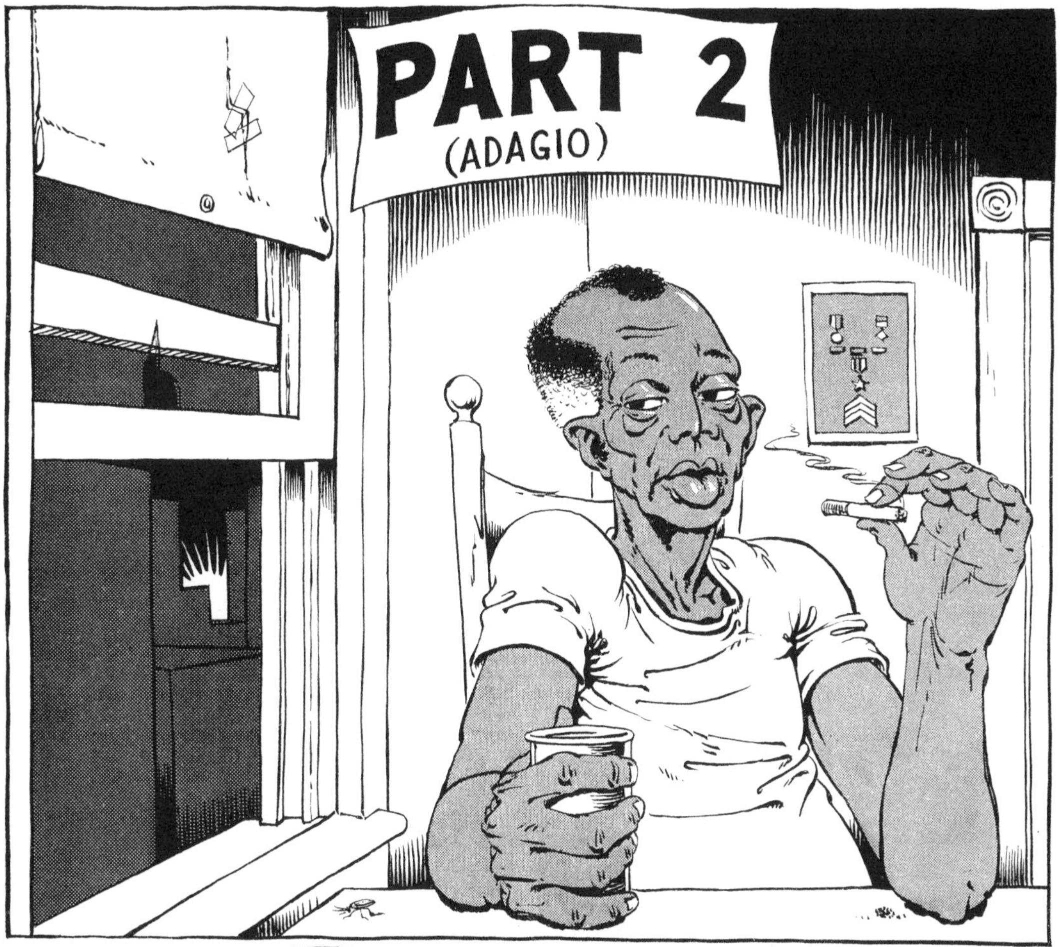
PART 2
(ADAGIO)

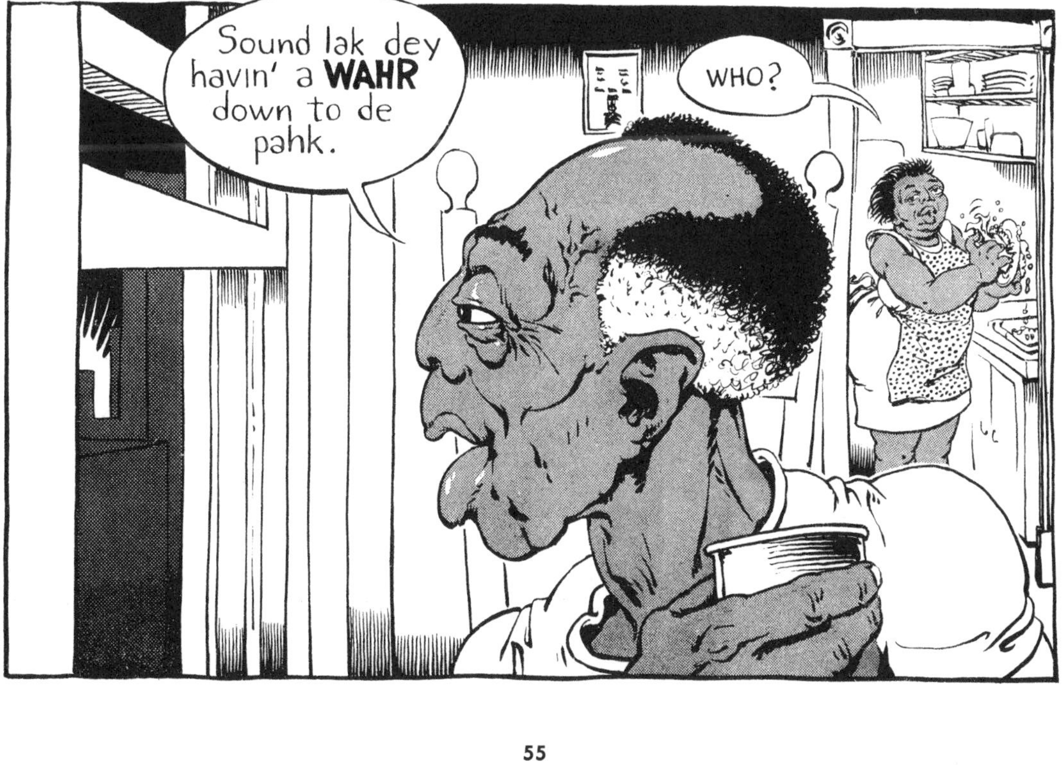
Sound lak dey havin' a WAHR down to de pahk.
WHO?

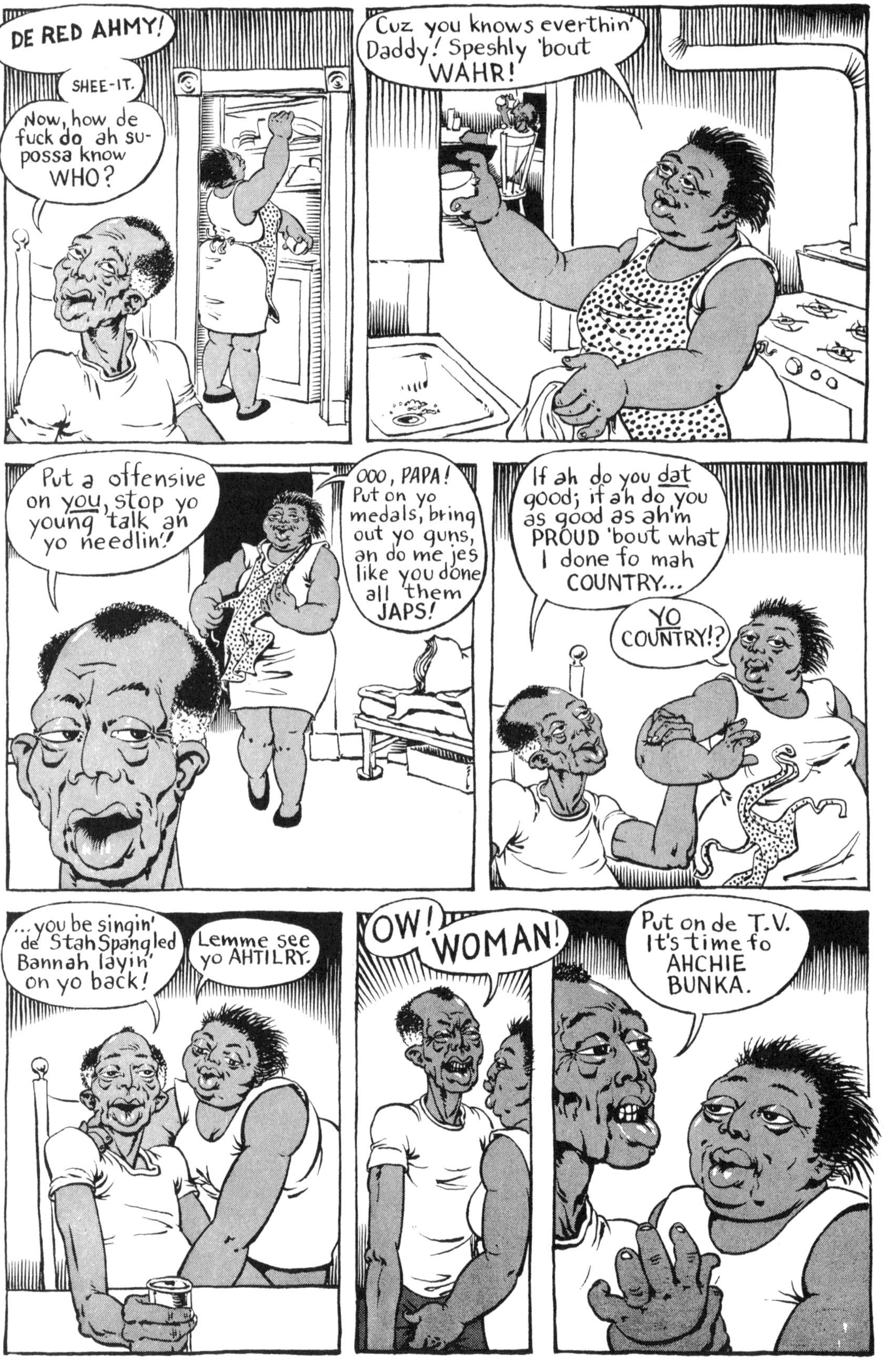
DE RED AHMY!
SHEE-IT.
Now, how de fuck do ah supossa know WHO?
Cuz you knows everthin' Daddy! Speshly 'bout WAHR!
Put a offensive on you, stop yo young talk an yo needlin'!
OOO, PAPA! Put on yo medals, bring out yo guns, an do me jes like you done all them JAPS!
If ah do you dat good; if ah do you as good as ah'm PROUD 'bout what I done fo mah COUNTRY...
YO COUNTRY!?
...you be singin' de Stah Spangled Bannah layin' on yo back!
Lemme see yo AHTILRY.
OW!
WOMAN!
Put on de T.V. It's time fo AHCHIE BUNKA.

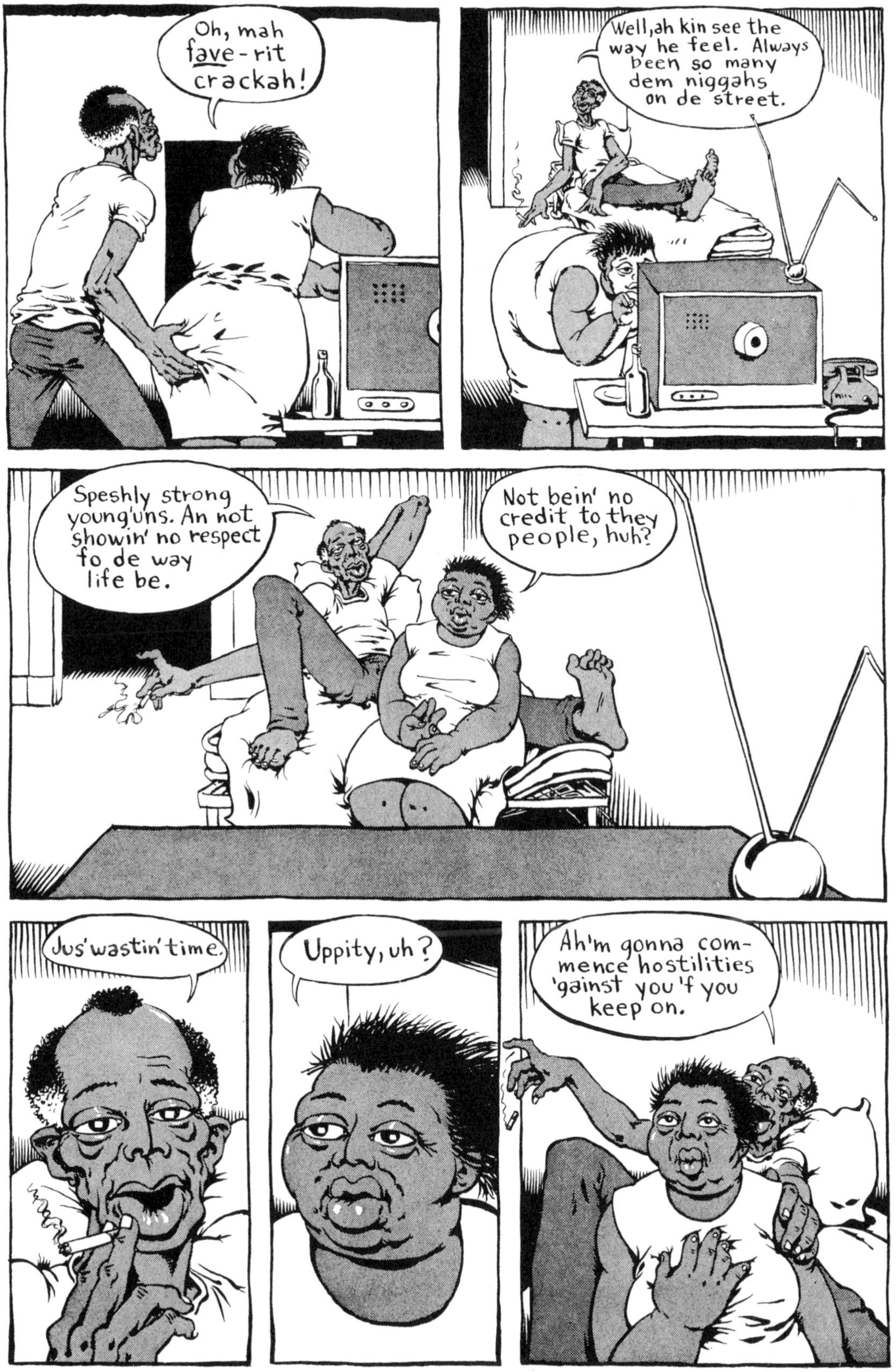
Oh, mah fave-rit crackah!
Well, ah kin see the way he feel. Always been so many dem niggahs on de street.
Speshly strong young'uns. An not showin' no respect fo de way life be.
Not bein' no credit to they people, huh?
Jus' wastin' time.
Uppity, uh?
Ah'm gonna commence hostilities 'gainst you'f you keep on.

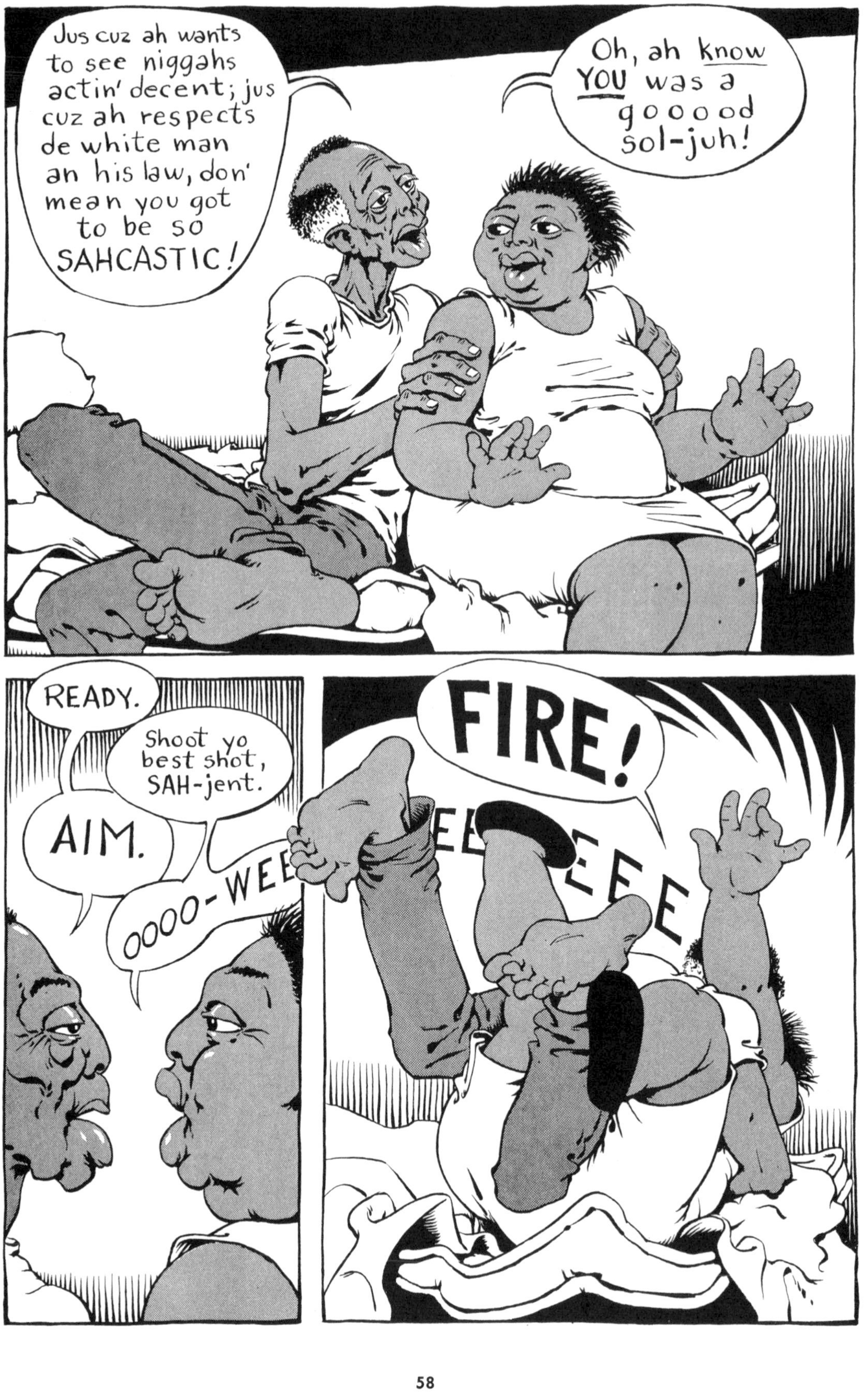

Jus cuz ah wants to see niggahs actin' decent; jus cuz ah respects de white man an his law, don' mean you got to be so SAHCASTIC!
Oh, ah know YOU was a goooood sol-juh!
READY.
Shoot yo best shot, SAH-jent.
AIM.
OOOO-WEE
FIRE!

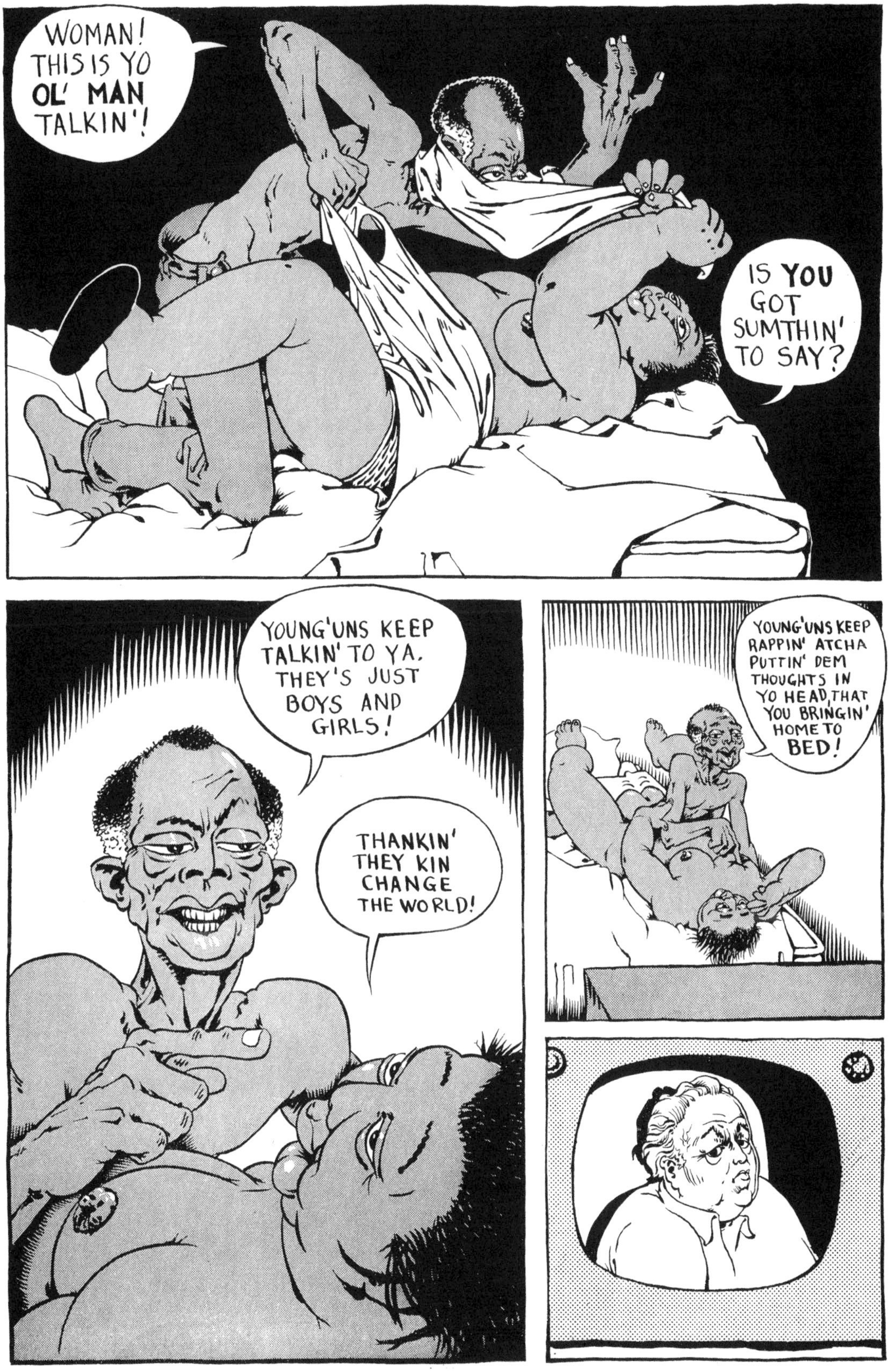
WOMAN! THIS IS YO OL' MAN TALKIN'!
IS YOU GOT SUMTHIN' TO SAY?
YOUNG'UNS KEEP TALKIN' TO YA. THEY'S JUST BOYS AND GIRLS!
THANKIN' THEY KIN CHANGE THE WORLD!
YOUNG'UNS KEEP RAPPIN' ATCHA PUTTIN' DEM THOUGHTS IN YO HEAD, THAT YOU BRINGIN' HOME TO BED!

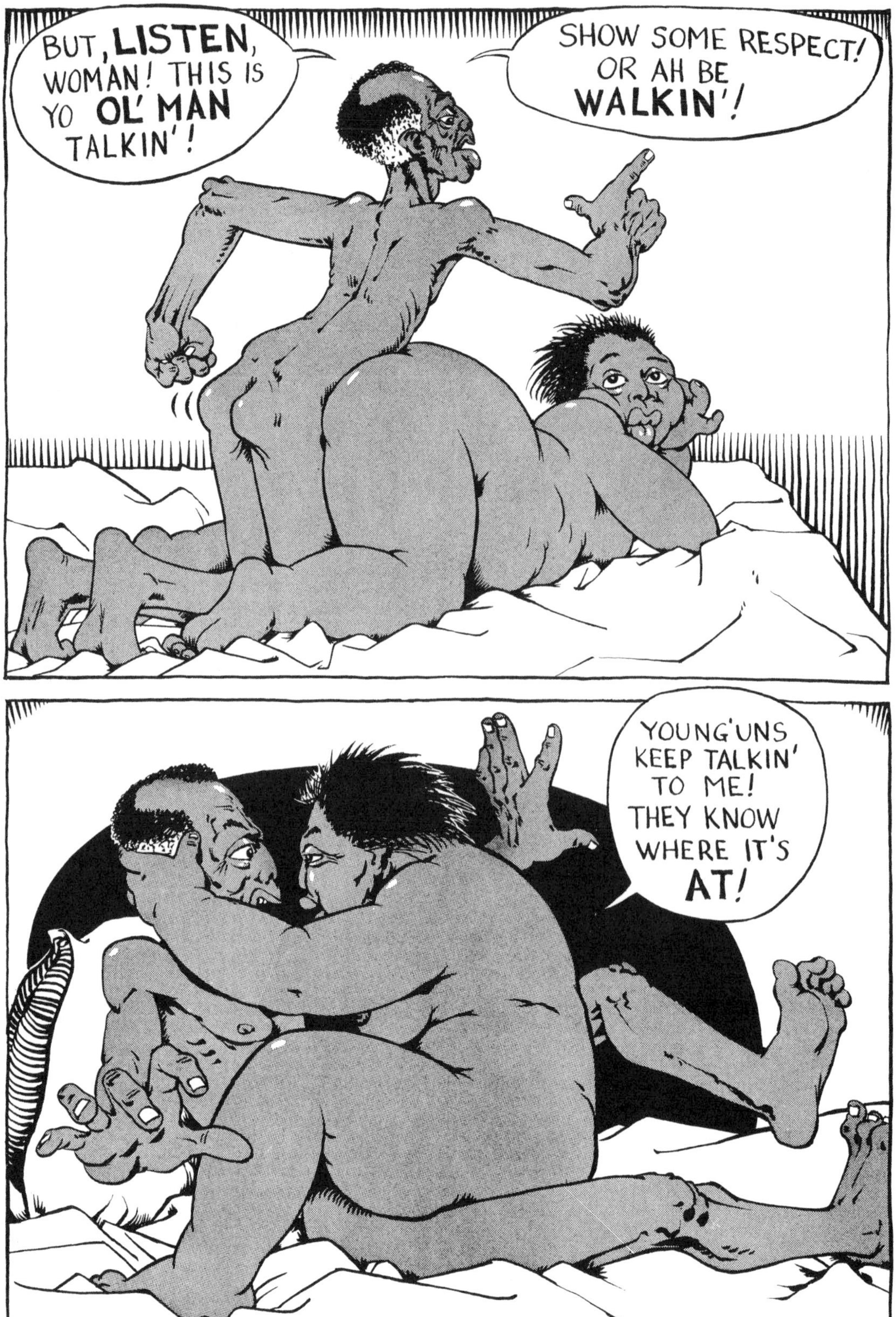
BUT, LISTEN, WOMAN! THIS IS YO OL' MAN TALKIN'!
SHOW SOME RESPECT! OR AH BE WALKIN'!
YOUNG'UNS KEEP TALKIN' TO ME! THEY KNOW WHERE IT'S AT!

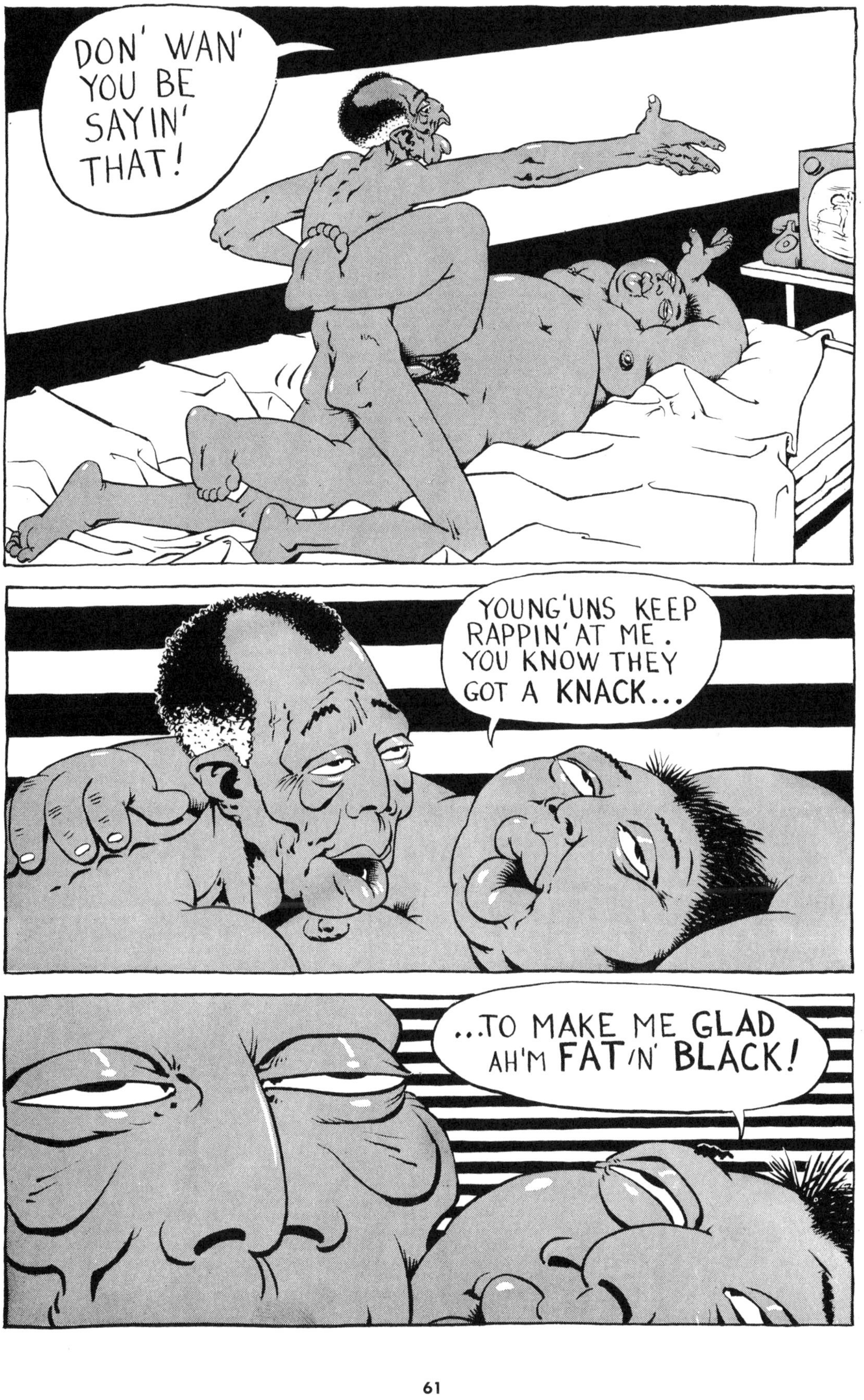
DON' WAN' YOU BE SAYIN' THAT!
YOUNG'UNS KEEP RAPPIN' AT ME. YOU KNOW THEY GOT A KNACK...
...TO MAKE ME GLAD AH'M FAT 'N' BLACK!

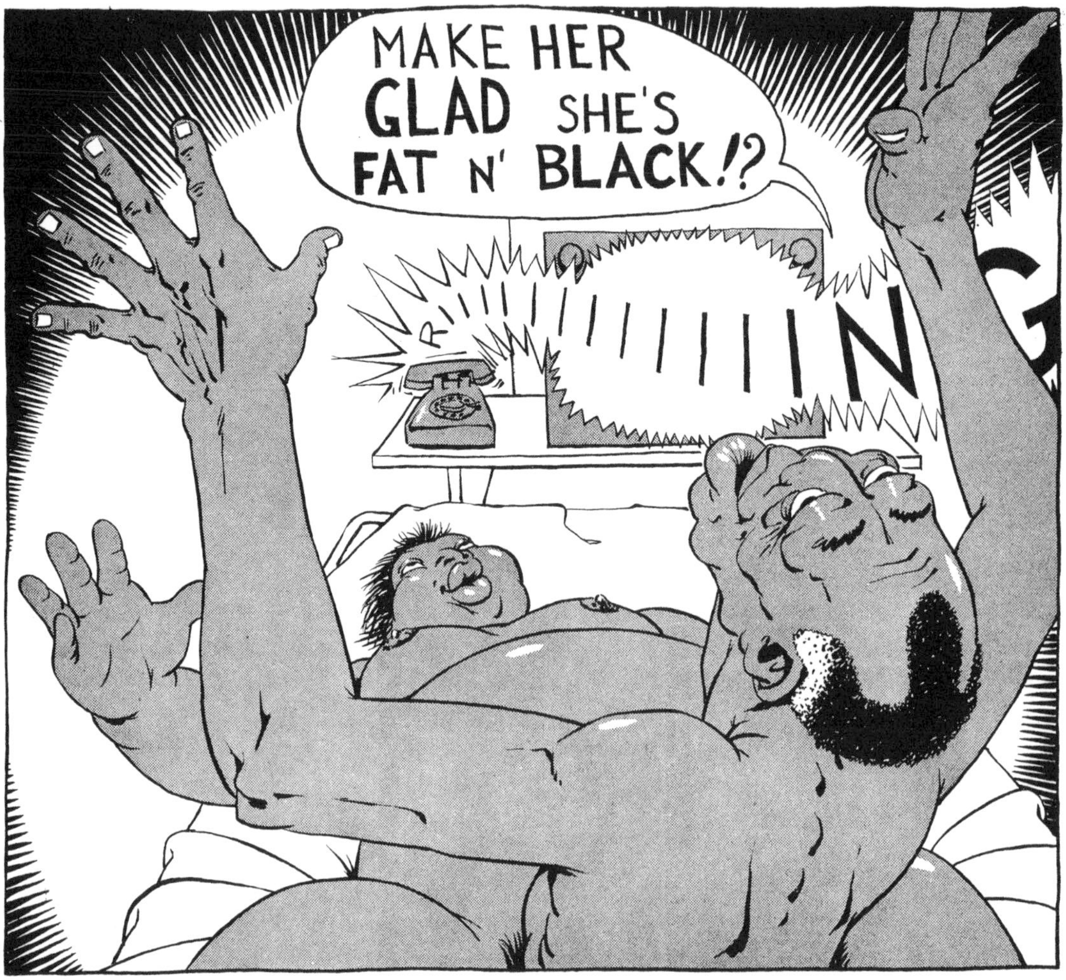
MAKE HER GLAD SHE'S FAT N' BLACK!?
RIIIIIIIIIIIING

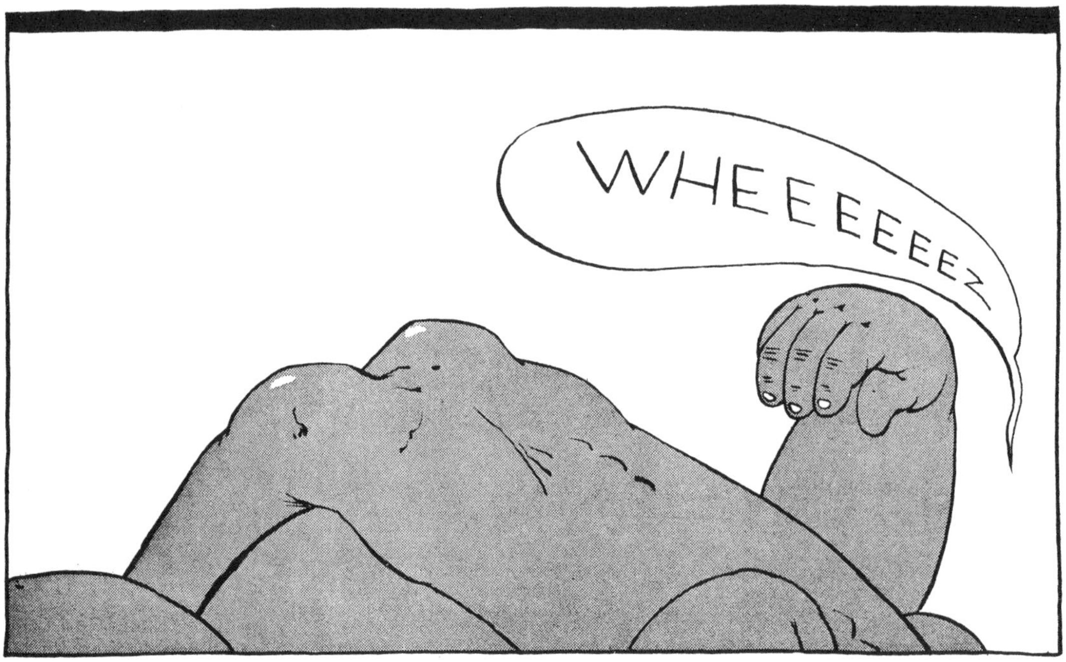
WHEEEEEEZ

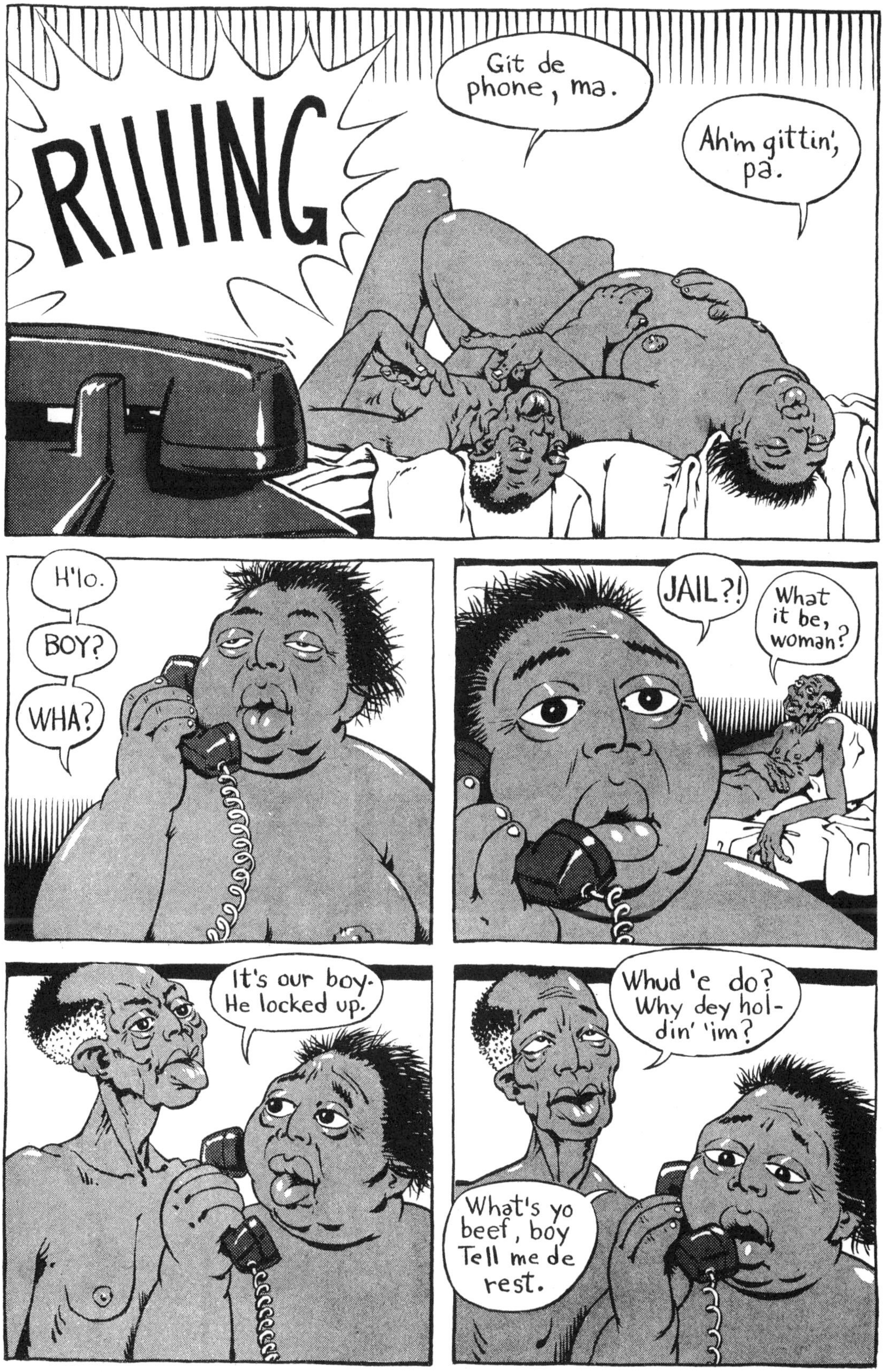
RIIIING
Git de phone, ma.
Ah'm gittin', pa.
H'lo.
BOY?
WHA?
JAIL?!
What it be, woman?
It's our boy. He locked up.
Whud 'e do? Why dey hol-din' 'im?
What's yo beef, boy Tell me de rest.

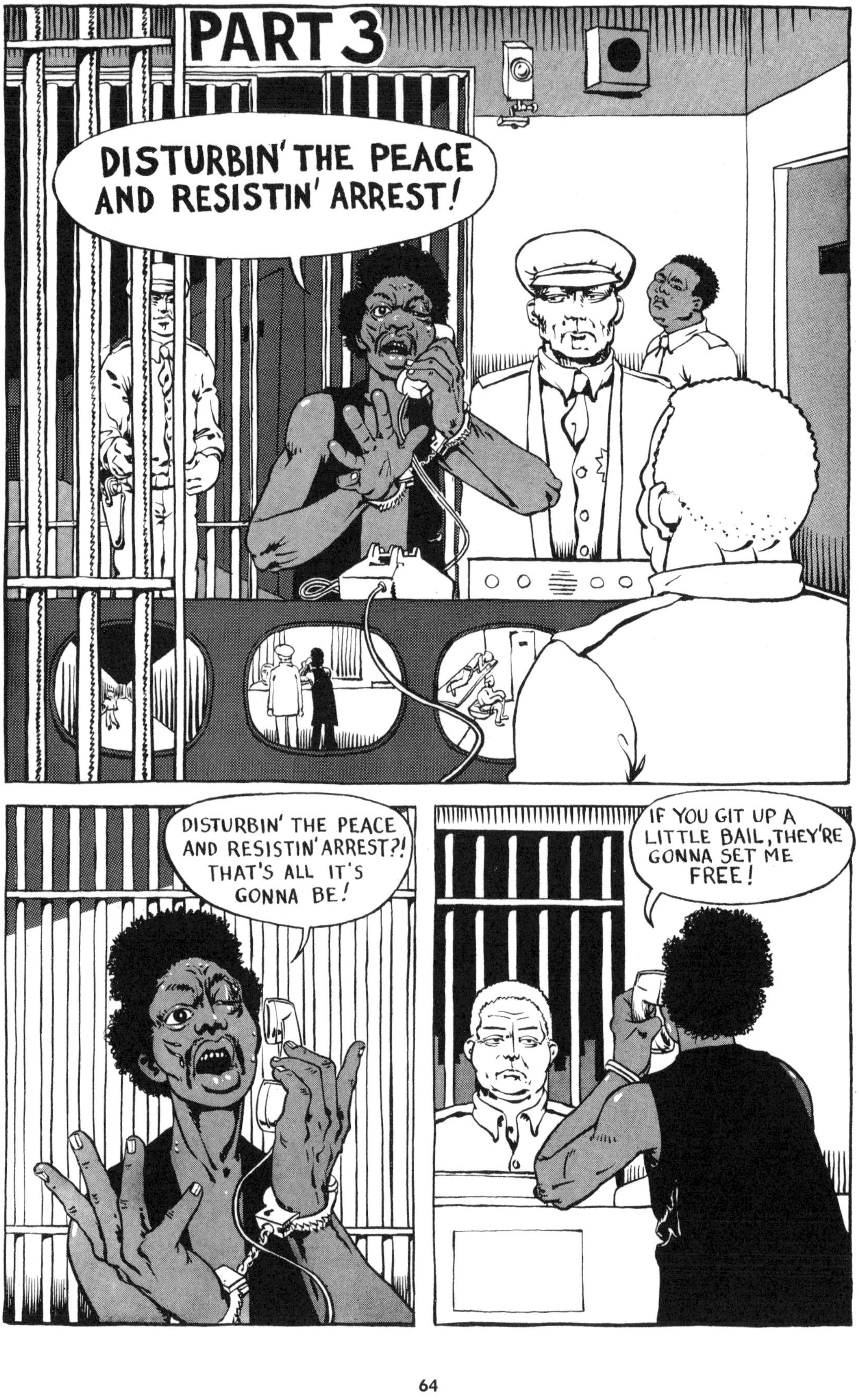
PART 3
DISTURBIN' THE PEACE AND RESISTIN' ARREST!
DISTURBIN' THE PEACE AND RESISTIN' ARREST?! THAT'S ALL IT'S GONNA BE!
IF YOU GIT UP A LITTLE BAIL, THEY'RE GONNA SET ME FREE!

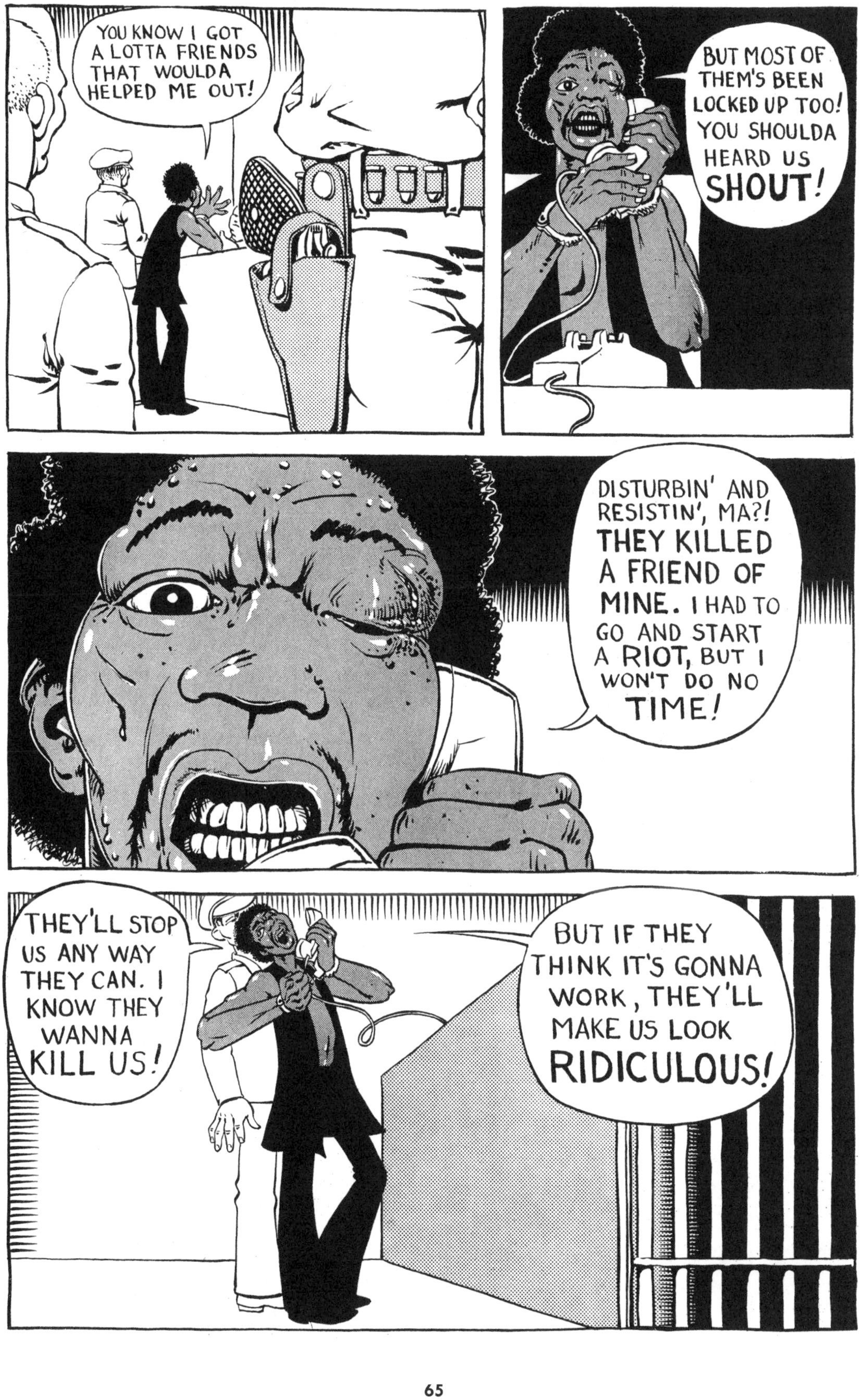
YOU KNOW I GOT A LOTTA FRIENDS THAT WOULDA HELPED ME OUT!
BUT MOST OF THEM'S BEEN LOCKED UP TOO! YOU SHOULDA HEARD US SHOUT!
DISTURBIN' AND RESISTIN', MA?! THEY KILLED A FRIEND OF MINE. I HAD TO GO AND START A RIOT, BUT I WON'T DO NO TIME!
THEY'LL STOP US ANY WAY THEY CAN. I KNOW THEY WANNA KILL US!
BUT IF THEY THINK IT'S GONNA WORK, THEY'LL MAKE US LOOK RIDICULOUS!

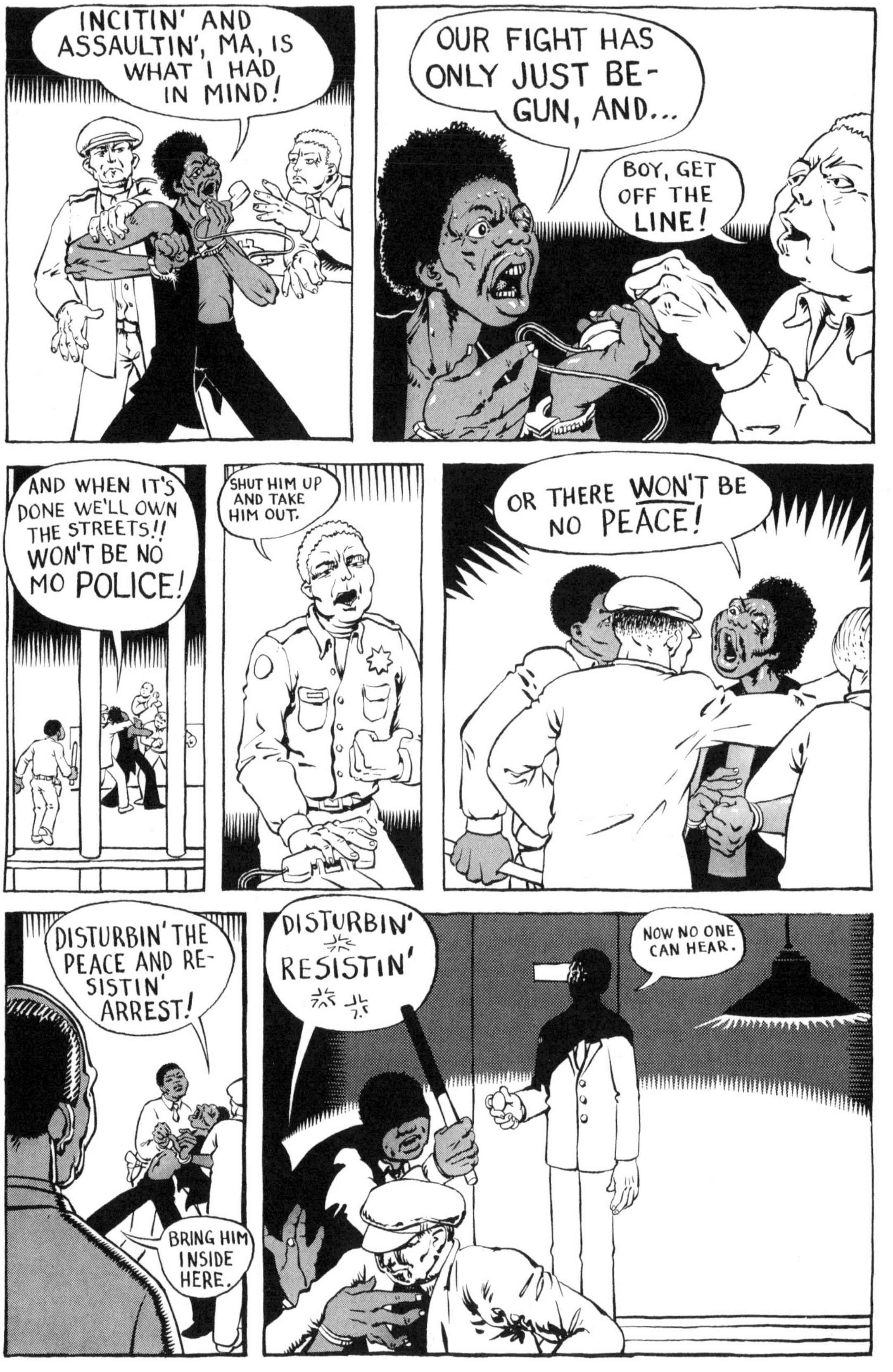
INCITIN' AND ASSAULTIN', MA, IS WHAT I HAD IN MIND!
OUR FIGHT HAS ONLY JUST BE-GUN, AND...
BOY, GET OFF THE LINE!
AND WHEN IT'S DONE WE'LL OWN THE STREETS!! WON'T BE NO MO POLICE!
SHUT HIM UP AND TAKE HIM OUT.
OR THERE WON'T BE NO PEACE!
DISTURBIN' THE PEACE AND RE-SISTIN' ARREST!
BRING HIM INSIDE HERE.
DISTURBIN' RESISTIN'
NOW NO ONE CAN HEAR.

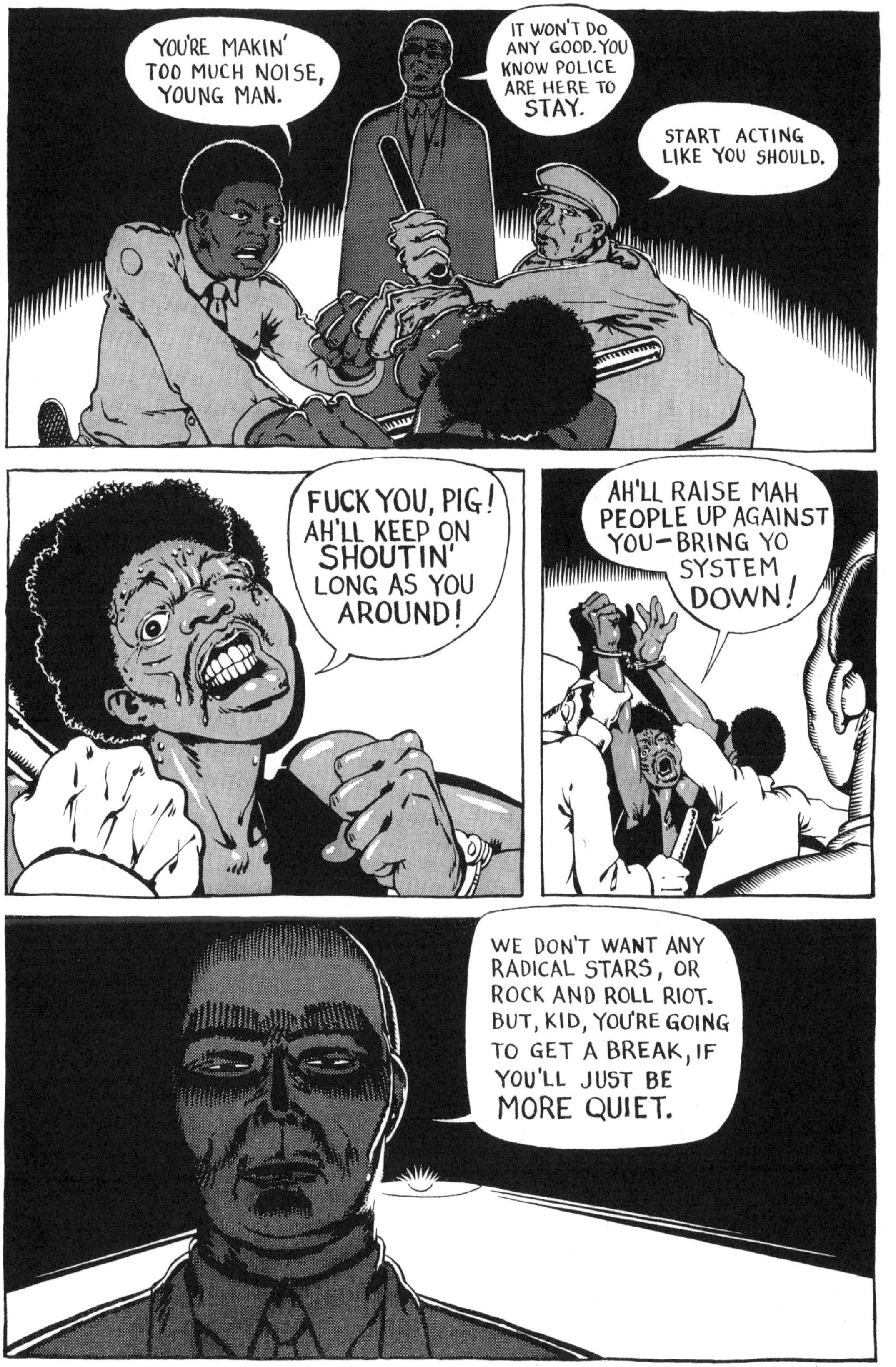
YOU'RE MAKIN' TOO MUCH NOISE, YOUNG MAN.
IT WON'T DO ANY GOOD. YOU KNOW POLICE ARE HERE TO STAY.
START ACTING LIKE YOU SHOULD.
FUCK YOU, PIG! AH'LL KEEP ON SHOUTIN' LONG AS YOU AROUND!
AH'LL RAISE MAH PEOPLE UP AGAINST YOU—BRING YO SYSTEM DOWN!
WE DON'T WANT ANY RADICAL STARS, OR ROCK AND ROLL RIOT. BUT, KID, YOU'RE GOING TO GET A BREAK, IF YOU'LL JUST BE MORE QUIET.

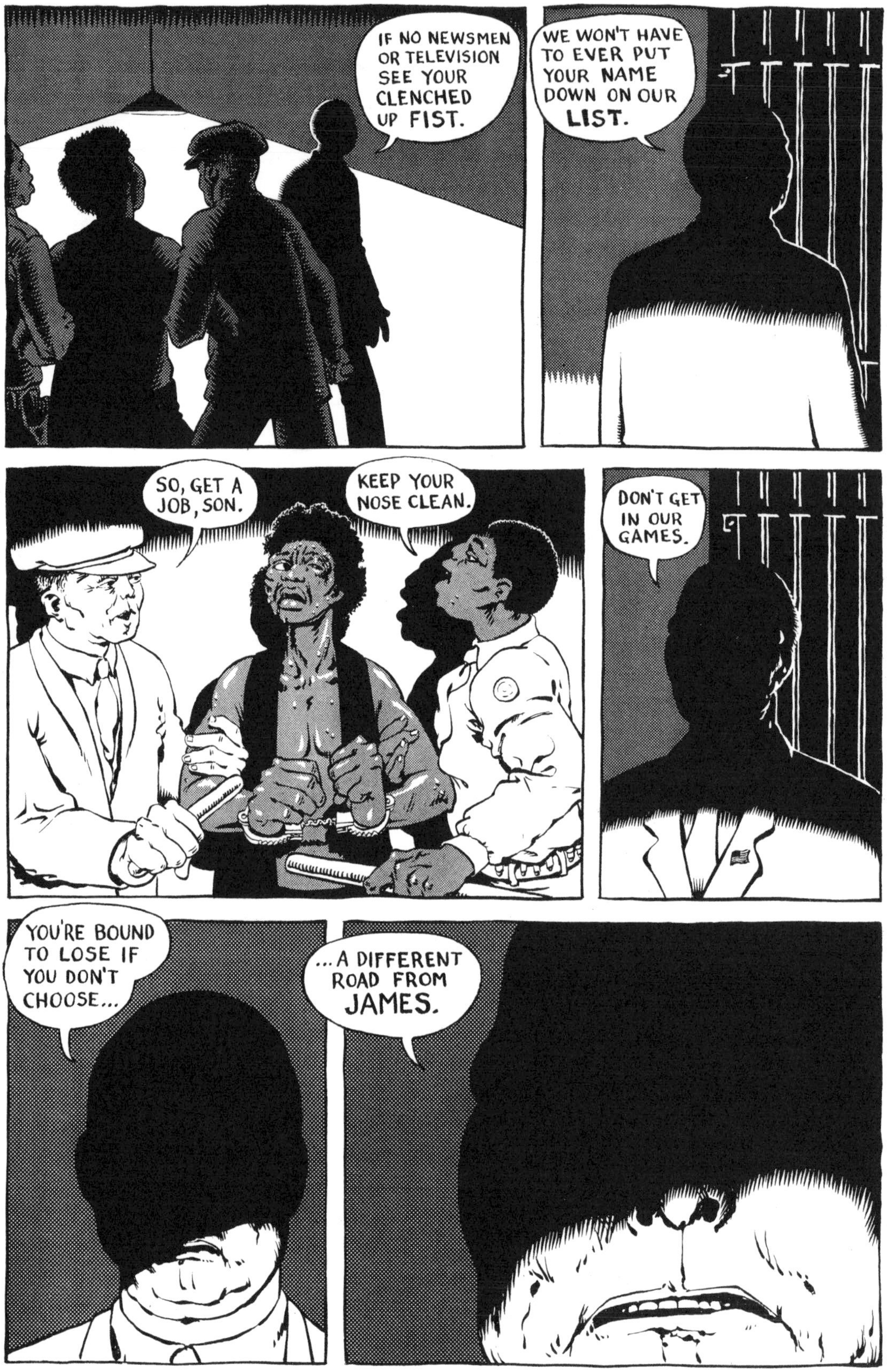
IF NO NEWSMEN OR TELEVISION SEE YOUR CLENCHED UP FIST.
WE WON'T HAVE TO EVER PUT YOUR NAME DOWN ON OUR LIST.
SO, GET A JOB, SON.
KEEP YOUR NOSE CLEAN.
DON'T GET IN OUR GAMES.
YOU'RE BOUND TO LOSE IF YOU DON'T CHOOSE...
...A DIFFERENT ROAD FROM JAMES.

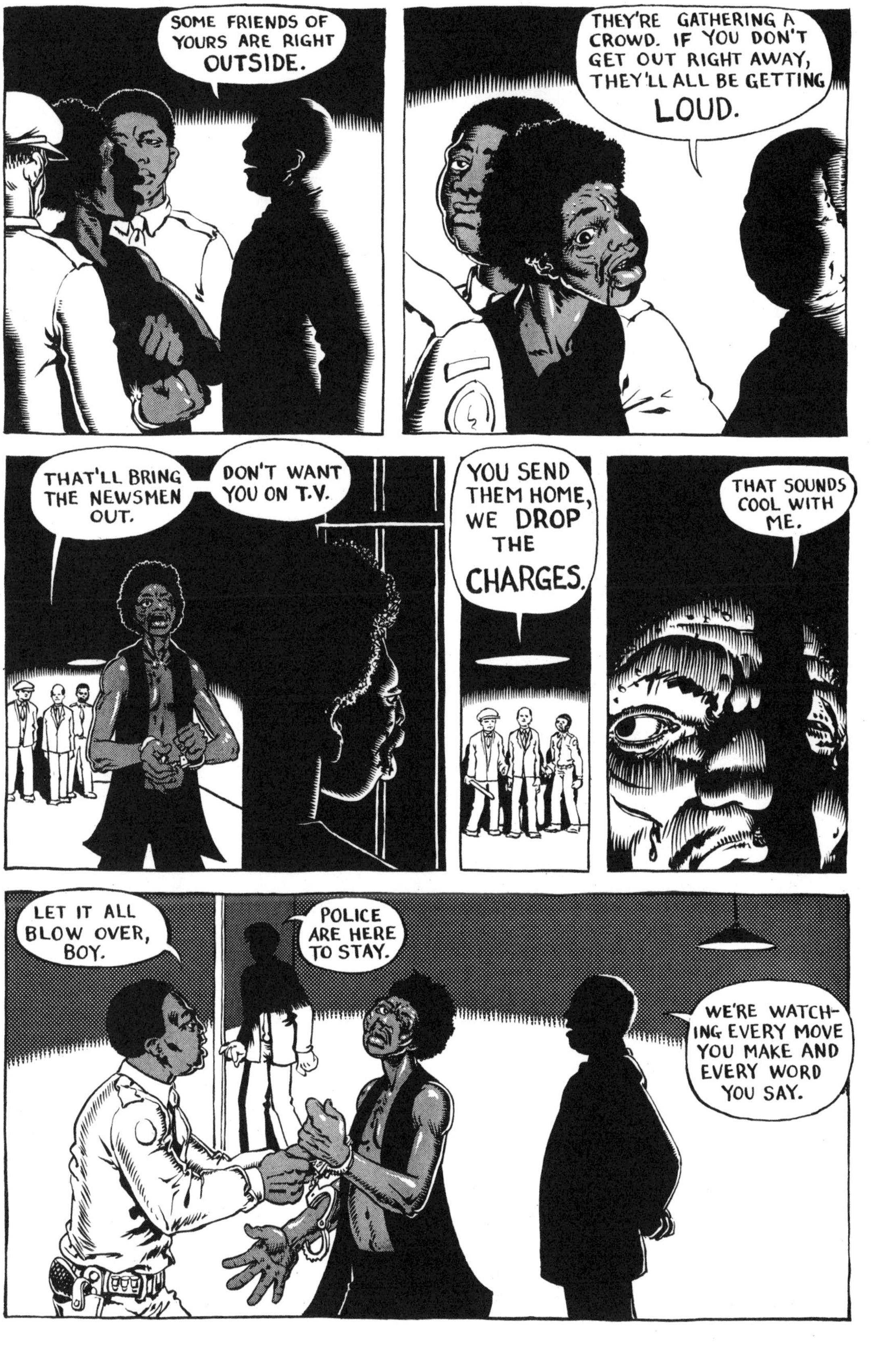
SOME FRIENDS OF YOURS ARE RIGHT OUTSIDE.
THEY'RE GATHERING A CROWD. IF YOU DON'T GET OUT RIGHT AWAY, THEY'LL ALL BE GETTING LOUD.
THAT'LL BRING THE NEWSMEN OUT.
DON'T WANT YOU ON T.V.
YOU SEND THEM HOME, WE DROP THE CHARGES.
THAT SOUNDS COOL WITH ME.
LET IT ALL BLOW OVER, BOY.
POLICE ARE HERE TO STAY.
WE'RE WATCHING EVERY MOVE YOU MAKE AND EVERY WORD YOU SAY.

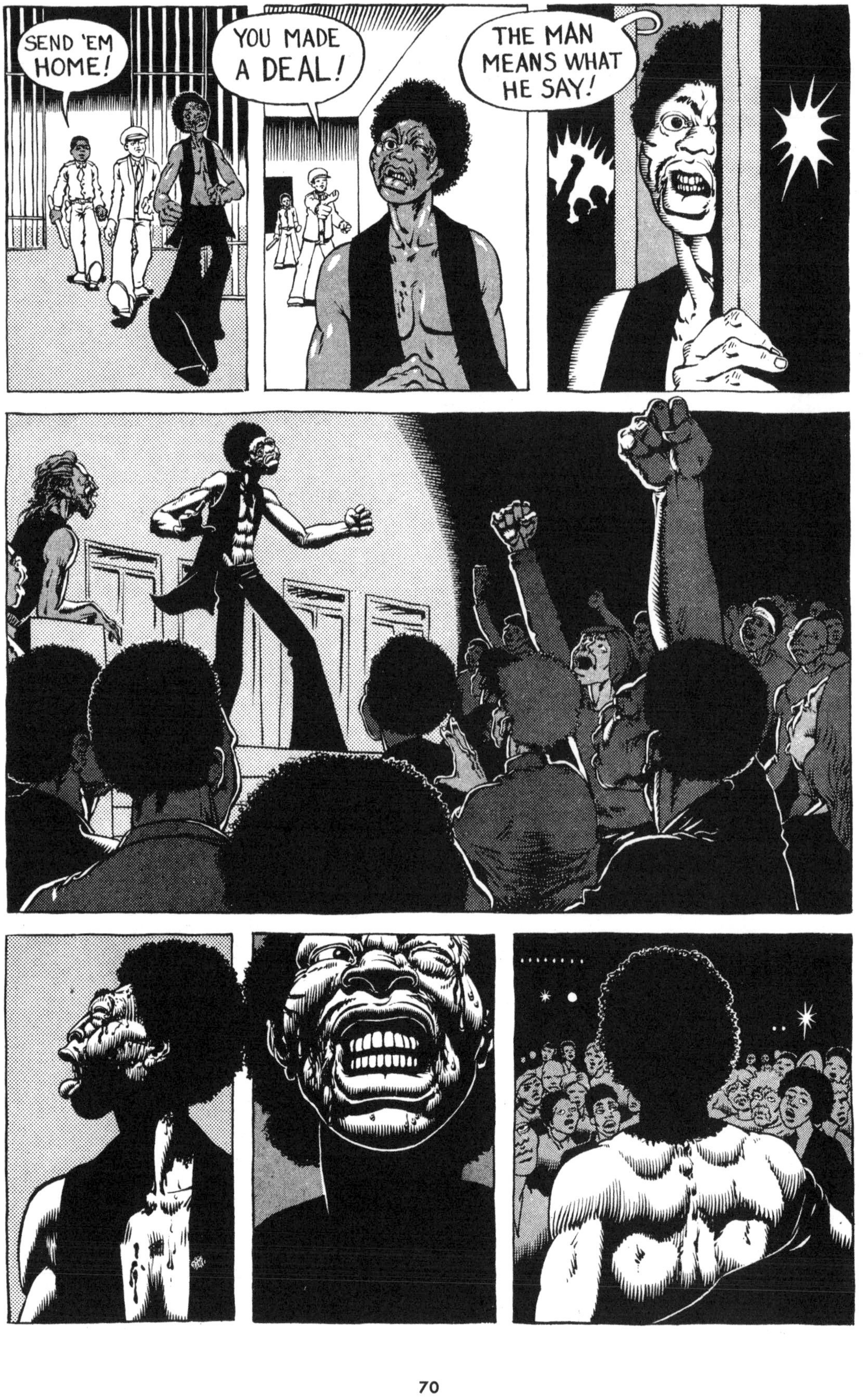
SEND 'EM HOME!
YOU MADE A DEAL!
THE MAN MEANS WHAT HE SAY!

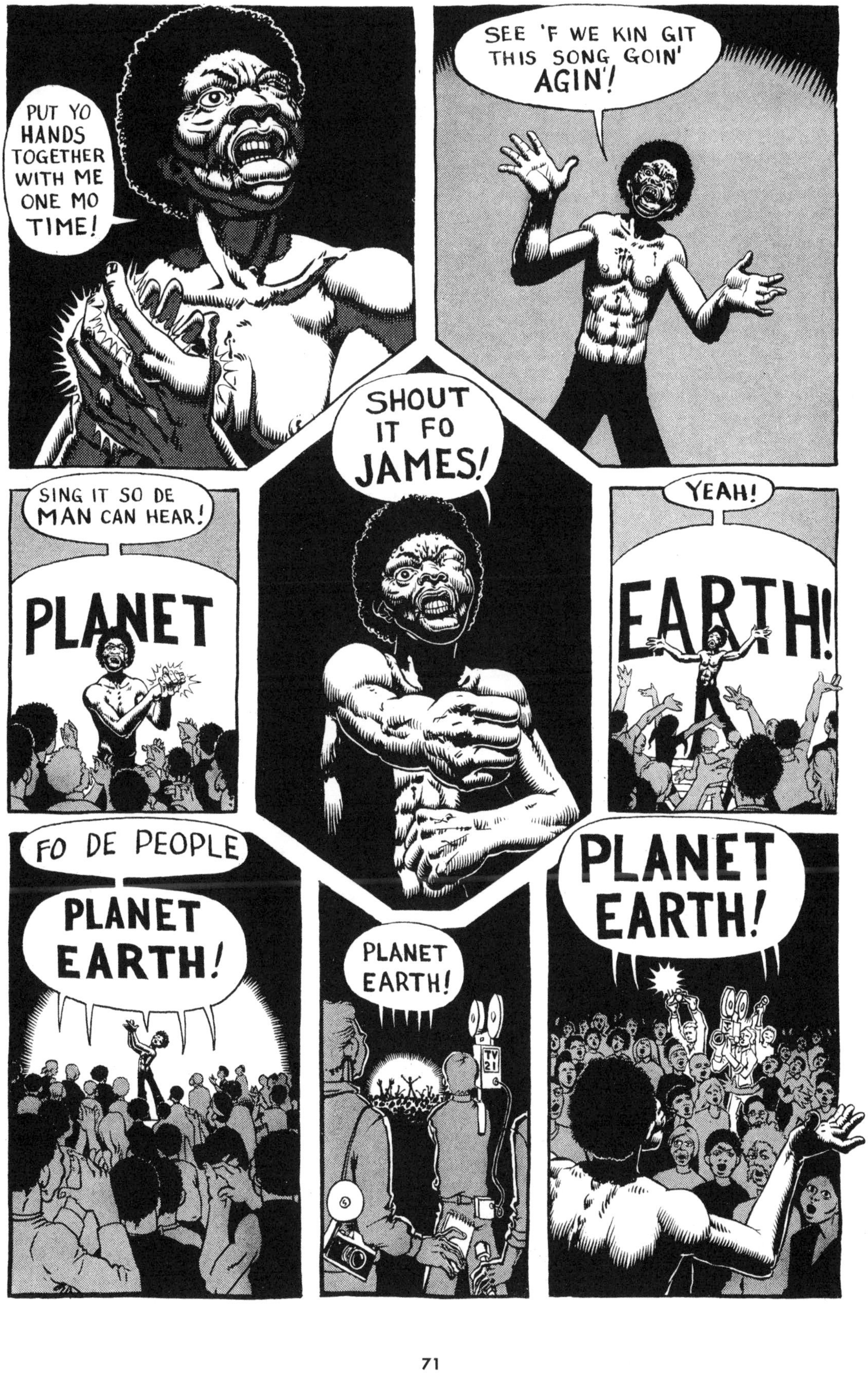
PUT YO HANDS TOGETHER WITH ME ONE MO TIME!
SEE 'F WE KIN GIT THIS SONG GOIN' AGIN'!
SHOUT IT FO JAMES!
SING IT SO DE MAN CAN HEAR!
PLANET
YEAH!
EARTH!
FO DE PEOPLE
PLANET EARTH!
PLANET EARTH!
PLANET EARTH!
TV 21

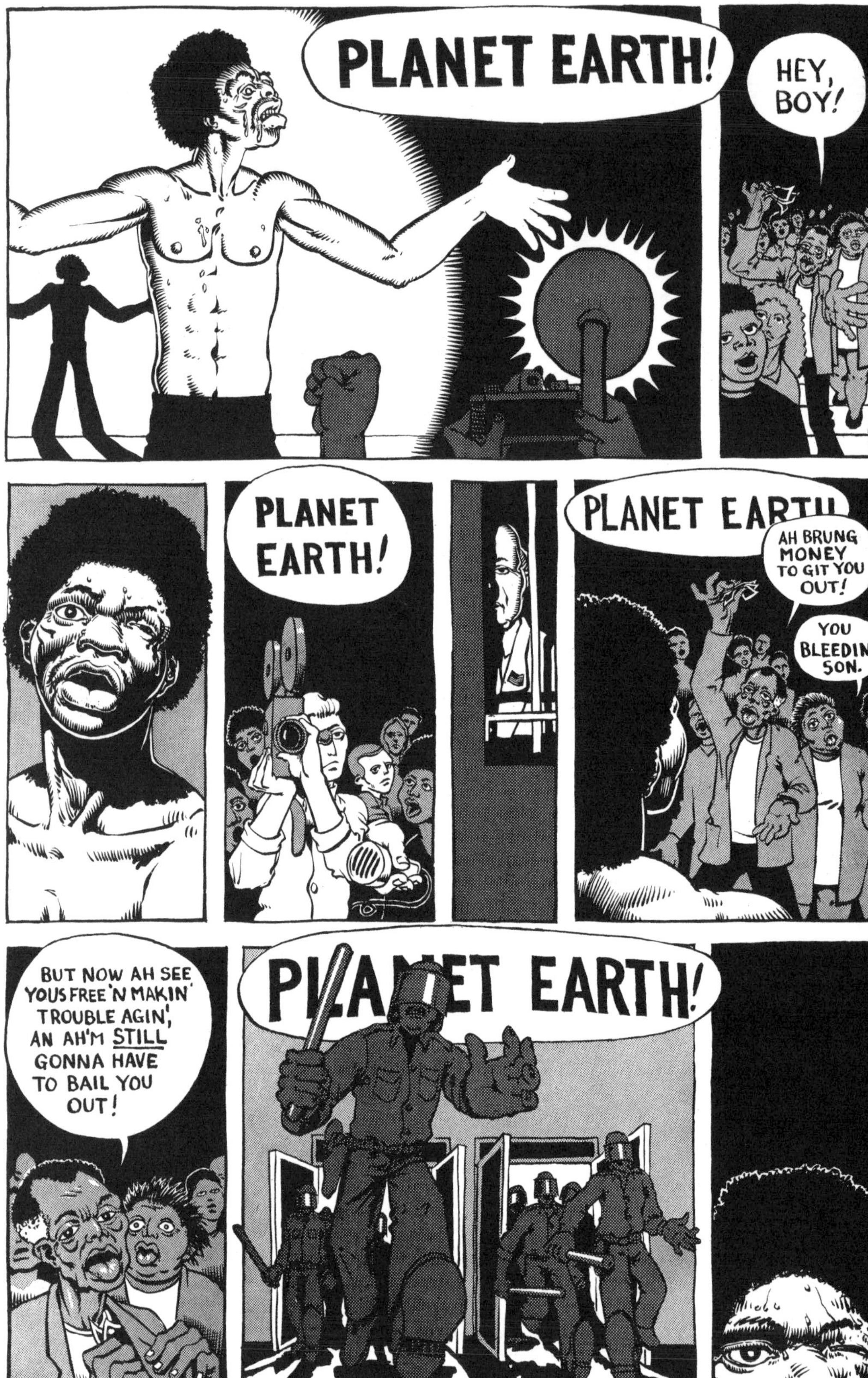
PLANET EARTH!
HEY, BOY!
PLANET EARTH!
PLANET EARTH
AH BRUNG MONEY TO GIT YOU OUT!
YOU BLEEDIN', SON.
BUT NOW AH SEE YOUS FREE 'N MAKIN' TROUBLE AGIN', AN AH'M STILL GONNA HAVE TO BAIL YOU OUT!
PLANET EARTH!

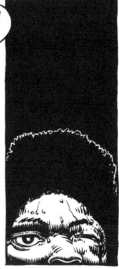

NO YOU AIN'T, PA.

WISH AH COULD STOP THE SHOW, PA, AN TALK TO YA NOW.

WISH AH COULD MAKE YA SEE IT DON'T MATTER YOU SPEND YO WHOLE LIFE BEIN' A GOOD SOLJUH FO DE MAN.

DIGGIN' HIM MOR'N YOU DIG YOSELF. KEEPIN' THE LAW THAT AIN'T YO LAW. WISH AH COULD MAKE YOU SEE YOU DON' MATTUH NO MO TO DE MAN THAN THEM NIGGUHS IN THE STREETS YOU ALWAYS TALKIN' ABOUT.

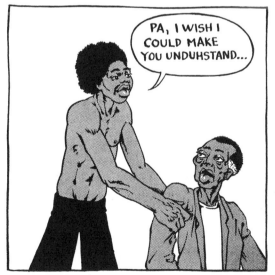

PA, I WISH I COULD MAKE YOU UNDUHSTAND...

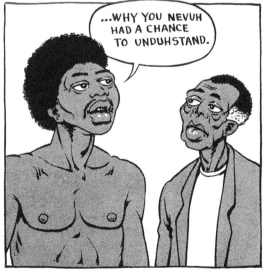

...WHY YOU NEVUH HAD A CHANCE TO UNDUHSTAND.

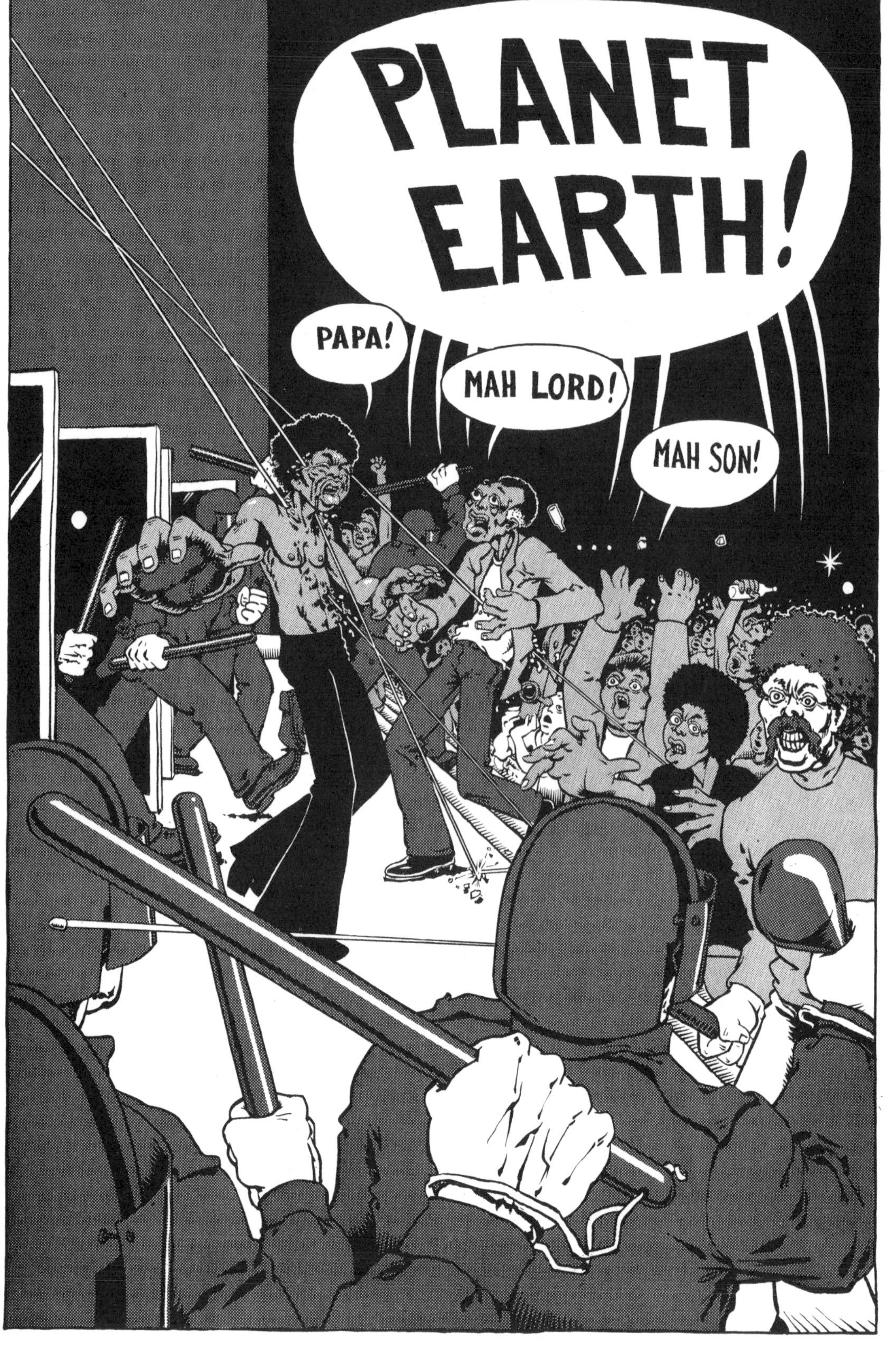
PLANET EARTH!
PAPA!
MAH LORD!
MAH SON!

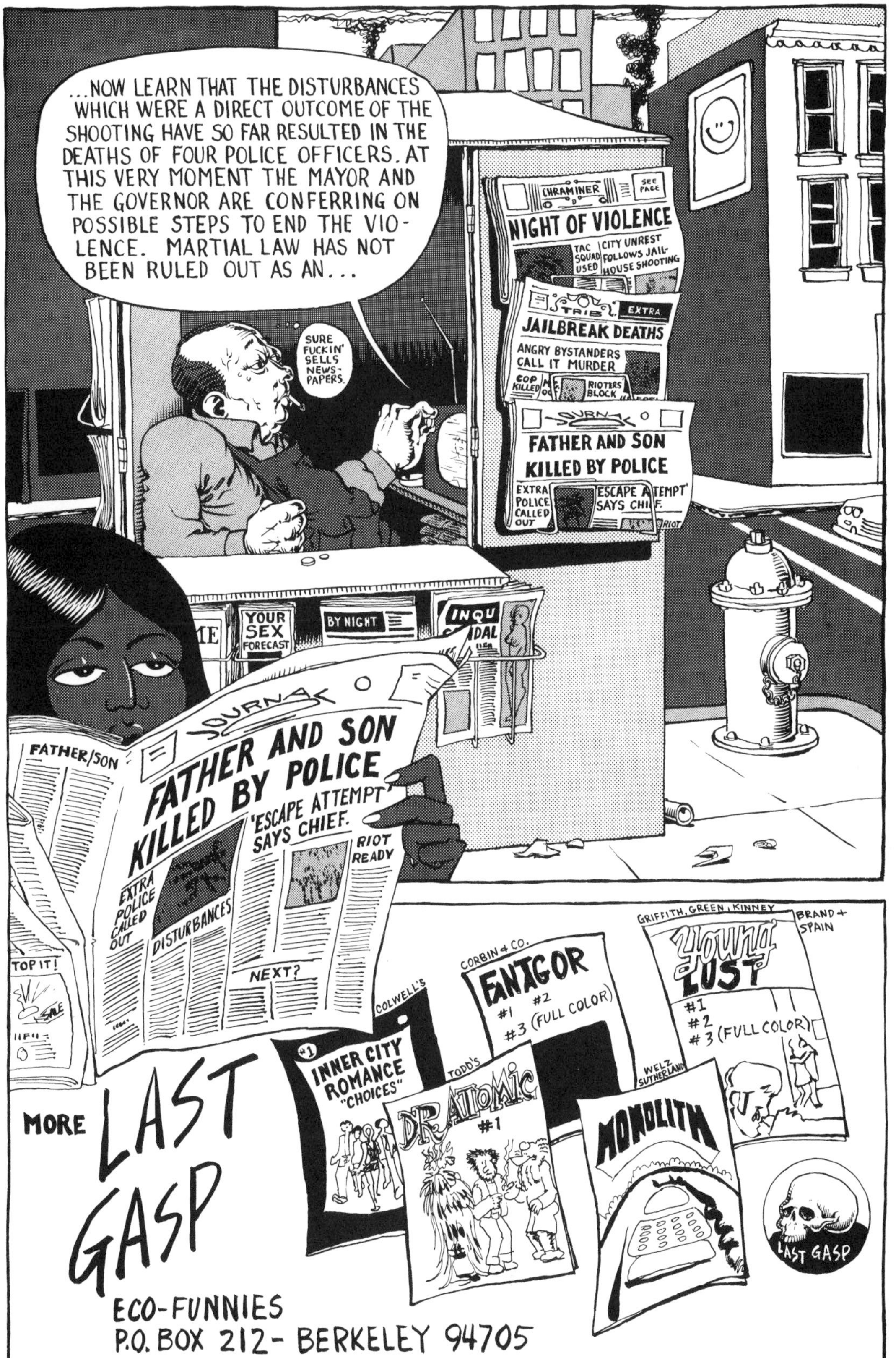
...NOW LEARN THAT THE DISTURBANCES WHICH WERE A DIRECT OUTCOME OF THE SHOOTING HAVE SO FAR RESULTED IN THE DEATHS OF FOUR POLICE OFFICERS. AT THIS VERY MOMENT THE MAYOR AND THE GOVERNOR ARE CONFERRING ON POSSIBLE STEPS TO END THE VIO-LENCE. MARTIAL LAW HAS NOT BEEN RULED OUT AS AN...
SURE FUCKIN' SELLS NEWS-PAPERS.
CHRAMINER
SEE PAGE
NIGHT OF VIOLENCE
TAC SQUAD USED
CITY UNREST FOLLOWS JAIL-HOUSE SHOOTING
TRIB
EXTRA
JAILBREAK DEATHS
ANGRY BYSTANDERS CALL IT MURDER
COP KILLED
RIOTERS BLOCK
JOURNAL
FATHER AND SON KILLED BY POLICE
EXTRA POLICE CALLED OUT
'ESCAPE ATTEMPT' SAYS CHIEF.
RIOT
YOUR SEX FORECAST
BY NIGHT
FATHER/SON
JOURNAL
FATHER AND SON KILLED BY POLICE
'ESCAPE ATTEMPT' SAYS CHIEF.
RIOT READY
EXTRA POLICE CALLED OUT
DISTURBANCES
NEXT?
TOP IT!
MORE LAST GASP
ECO-FUNNIES
P.O. BOX 212- BERKELEY 94705
COLWELL'S
#1 INNER CITY ROMANCE "CHOICES"
CORBIN + CO.
FANTAGOR
#1 #2 #3 (FULL COLOR)
TODD'S
DR. ATOMIC #1
GRIFFITH, GREEN, KINNEY
BRAND + SPAIN
YOUNG LUST
#1 #2 #3 (FULL COLOR)
WELZ SUTHERLAND
MONOLITH
LAST GASP

INNER CITY ROMANCE #3
(1977)
by Patrick Rosenkranz

"*Inner City Romance* #3 turned out to be perhaps the best comic I ever did in terms of artistic quality and psychological depth. Being very infused with love and happiness at that time, I lavished more dense and intricate detail on the pages of this book than any other. By doing a series of dreams dreamed by convicts, I could explore both social and personal issues in a way that was engaging visually yet thought-provoking politically and psychologically. Prison and its consequences take awhile to forget or process or incorporate into the consciousness, but the great power of all these events was beginning to recede, and my art was turning in new directions. This was a very useful book to me in that it helped me a lot to purge my own post-traumatic nightmares about prison and to just focus on the political action that was going on then. I had also by then published three of my oil paintings on the covers of my comics and began feeling it was almost worth doing comics just for the exposure it gave to my fine art."

Five years passed between *Inner City Romance* #2 and #3.

"I didn't have any set plan to do *Inner City Romance* regularly, but I would go back again and again to this title for all the comics I drew throughout the '70s. Between #2 and #3, the Vietnam War ended, I got married, I concentrated on painting and sort of settled down. I was making a little money doing exhibitions and selling paintings, and getting more money for reprints of my comics in Europe, so I finally decided to do another. I think maybe it was the Europeans' love of comics that stimulated me to do more."

Jail, oil on canvas, 1976. When Colwell painted this picture, the paranoia of prison was still hard to shake off, and it continued to be a theme in his work. This image appeared on the back cover of *Inner City Romance* #3, which explored the dreams of prison inmates.

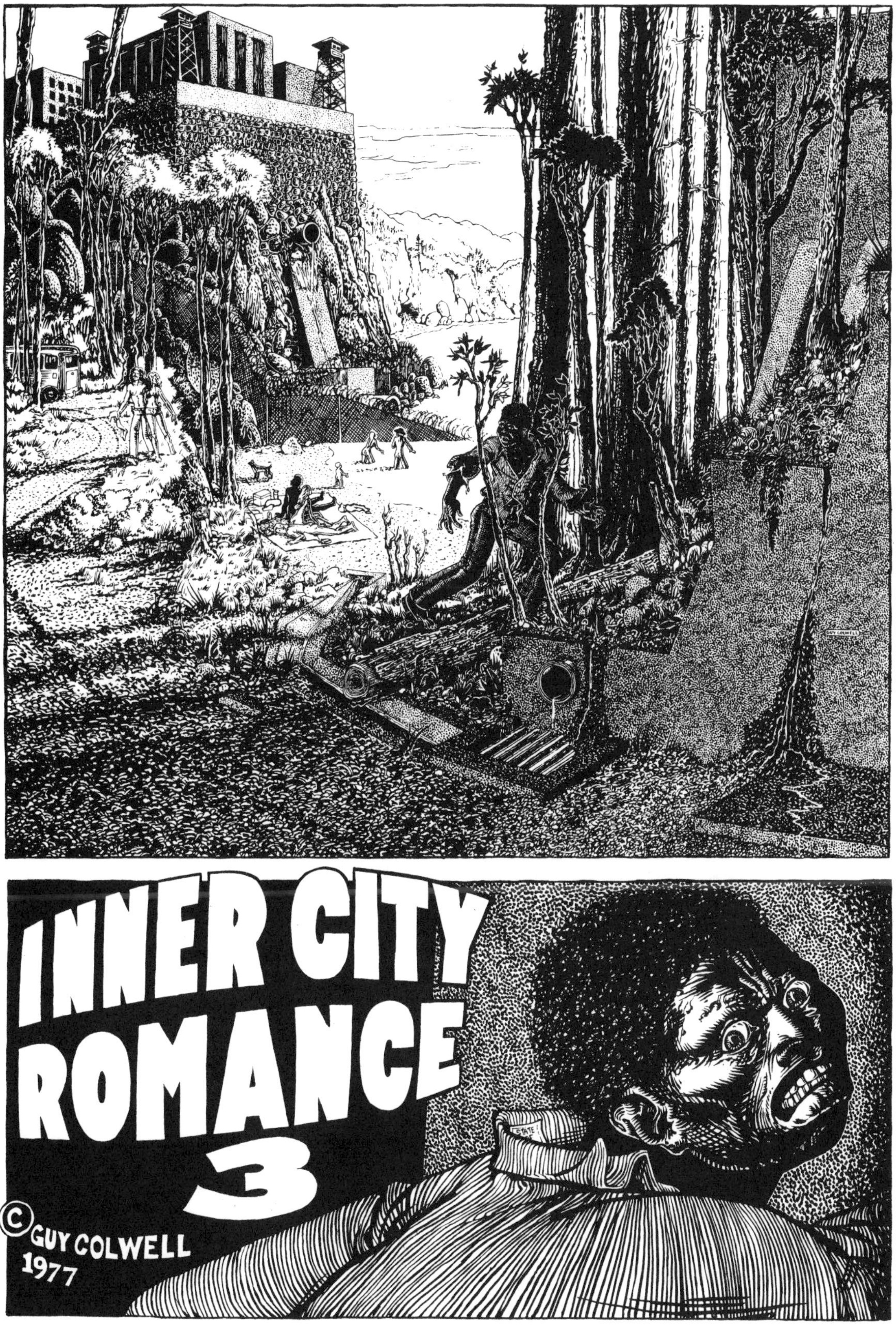
INNER CITY
ROMANCE
3
© GUY COLWELL
1977

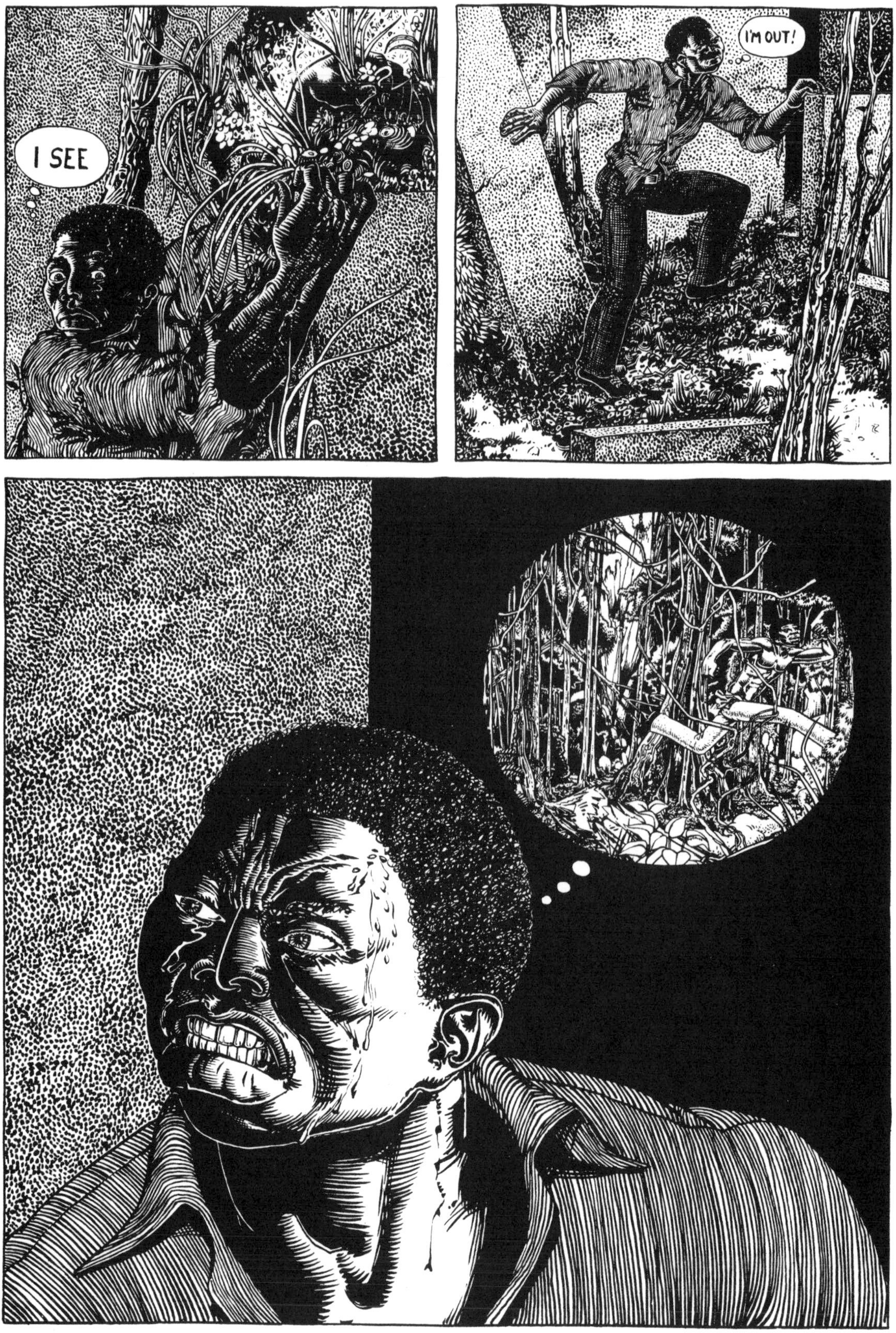
I SEE
I'M OUT!

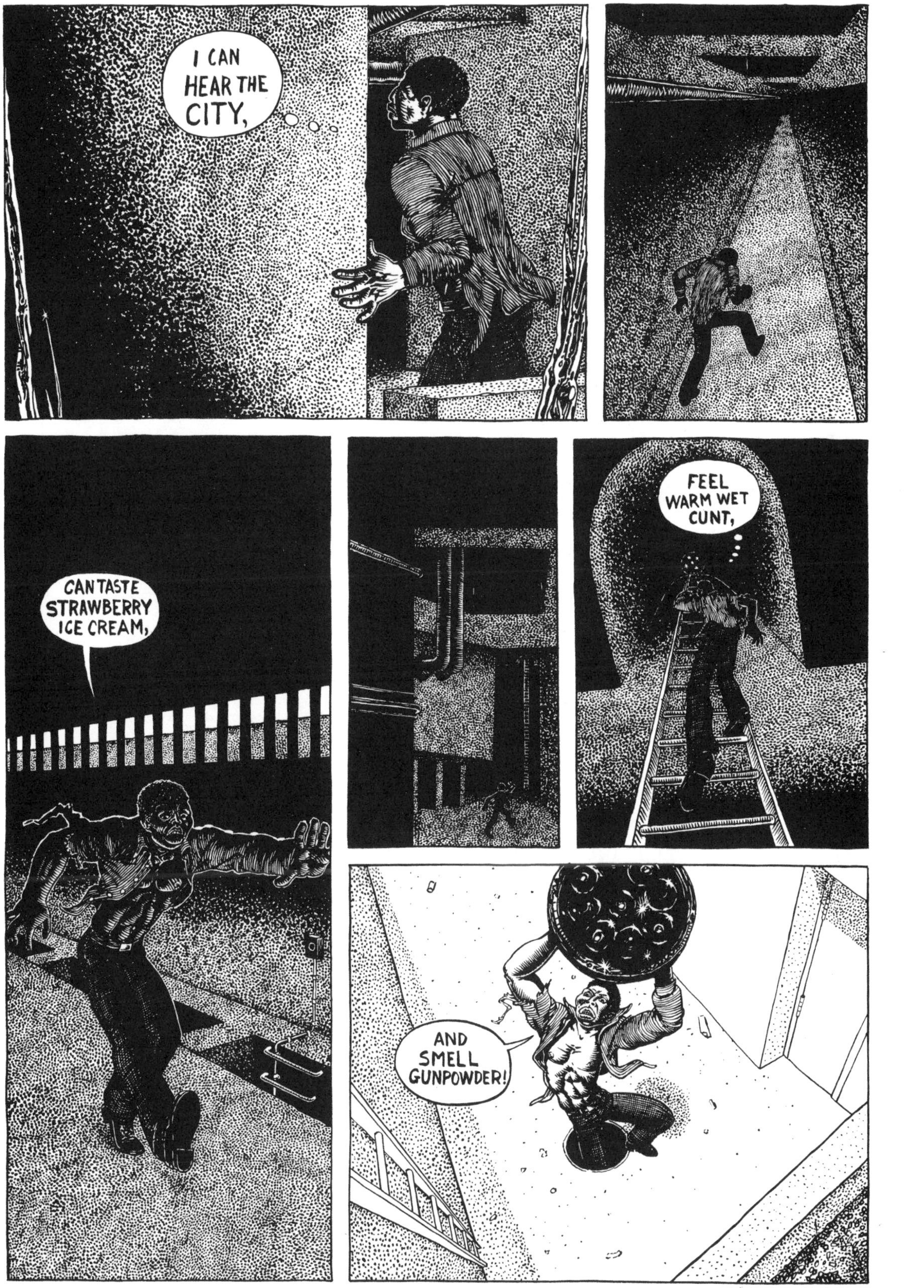
I CAN HEAR THE CITY,
CAN TASTE STRAWBERRY ICE CREAM,
FEEL WARM WET CUNT,
AND SMELL GUNPOWDER!

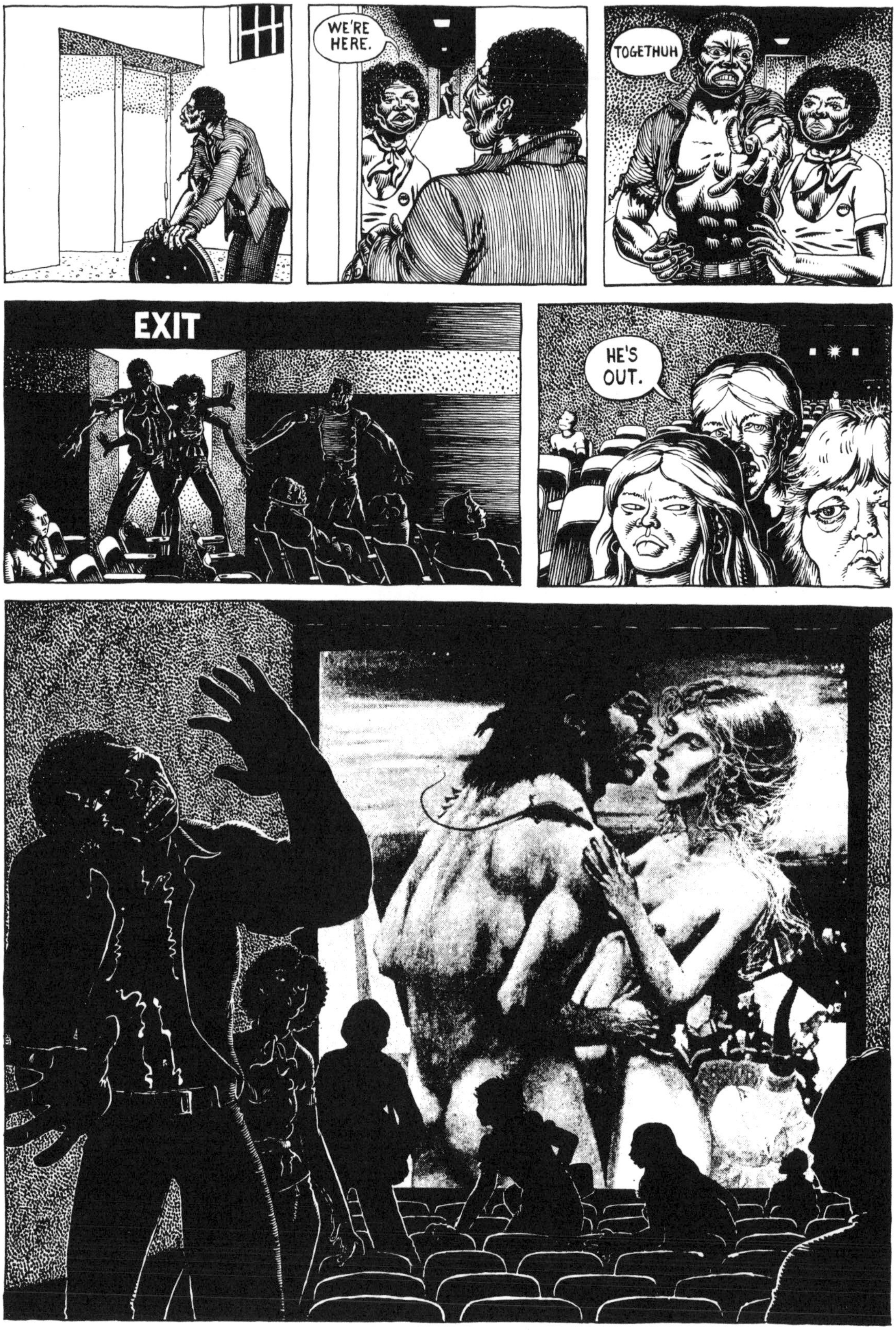
WE'RE HERE.
TOGETHUH
EXIT
HE'S OUT.

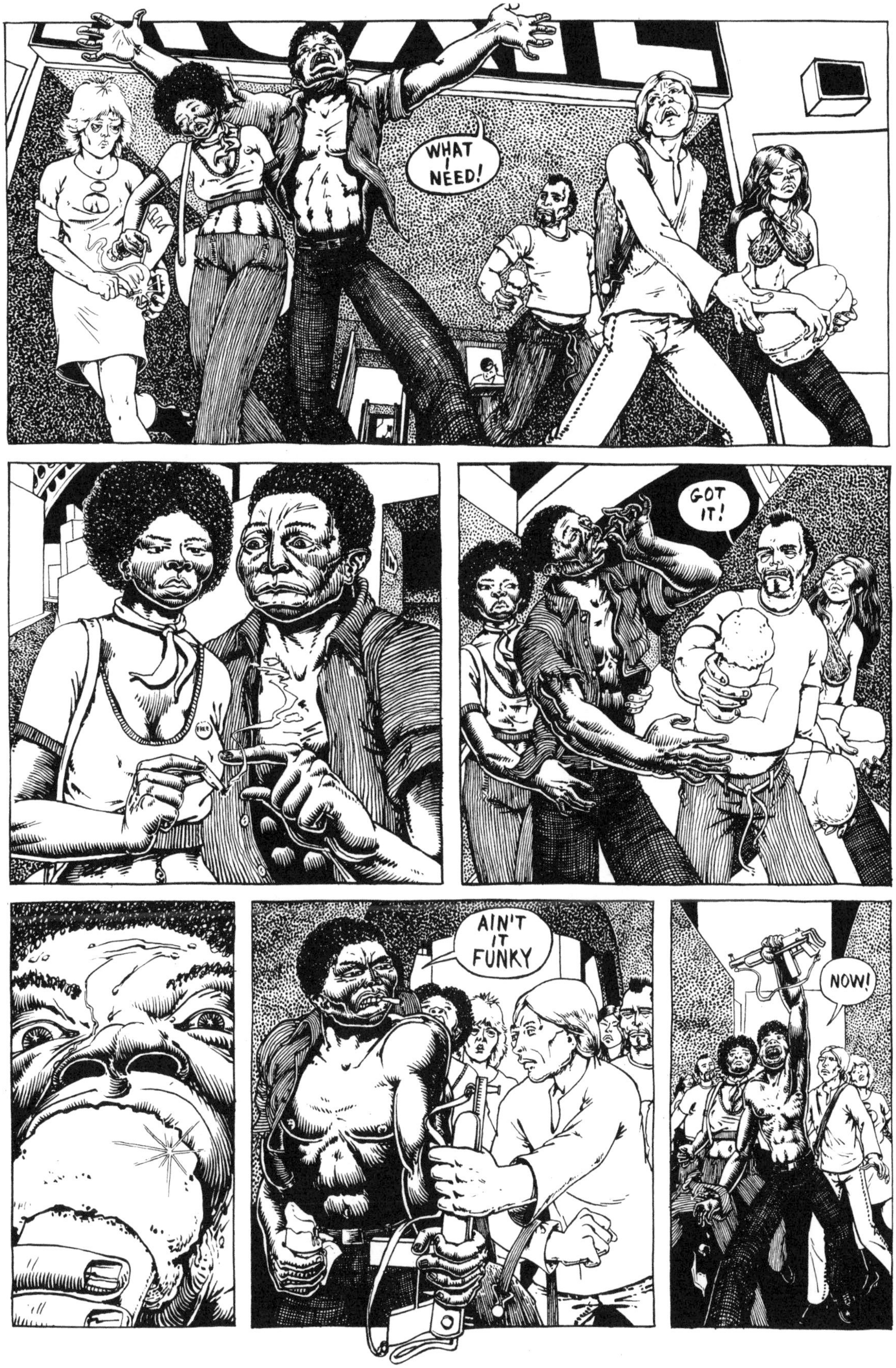
WHAT I NEED!
GOT IT!
AIN'T IT FUNKY
NOW!

OH, BABIES!
YEARS AND YEARS
WE'LL LOVE
AND DO THE WORK.
BUST OUR PEOPLE OUT!

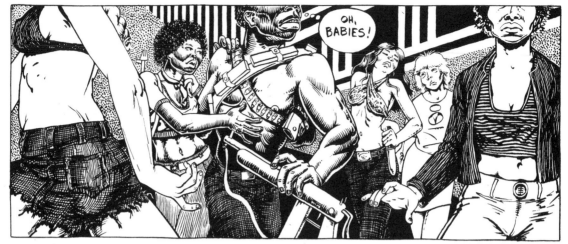

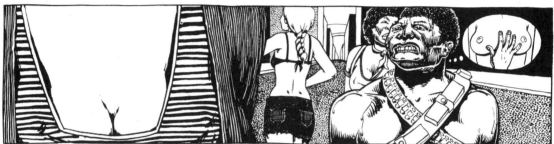

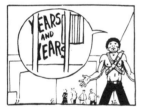

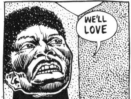

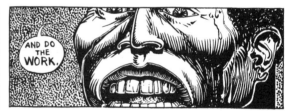

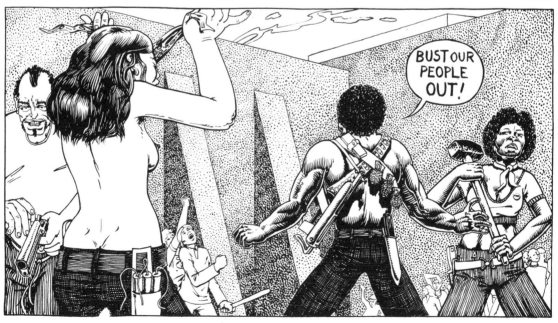

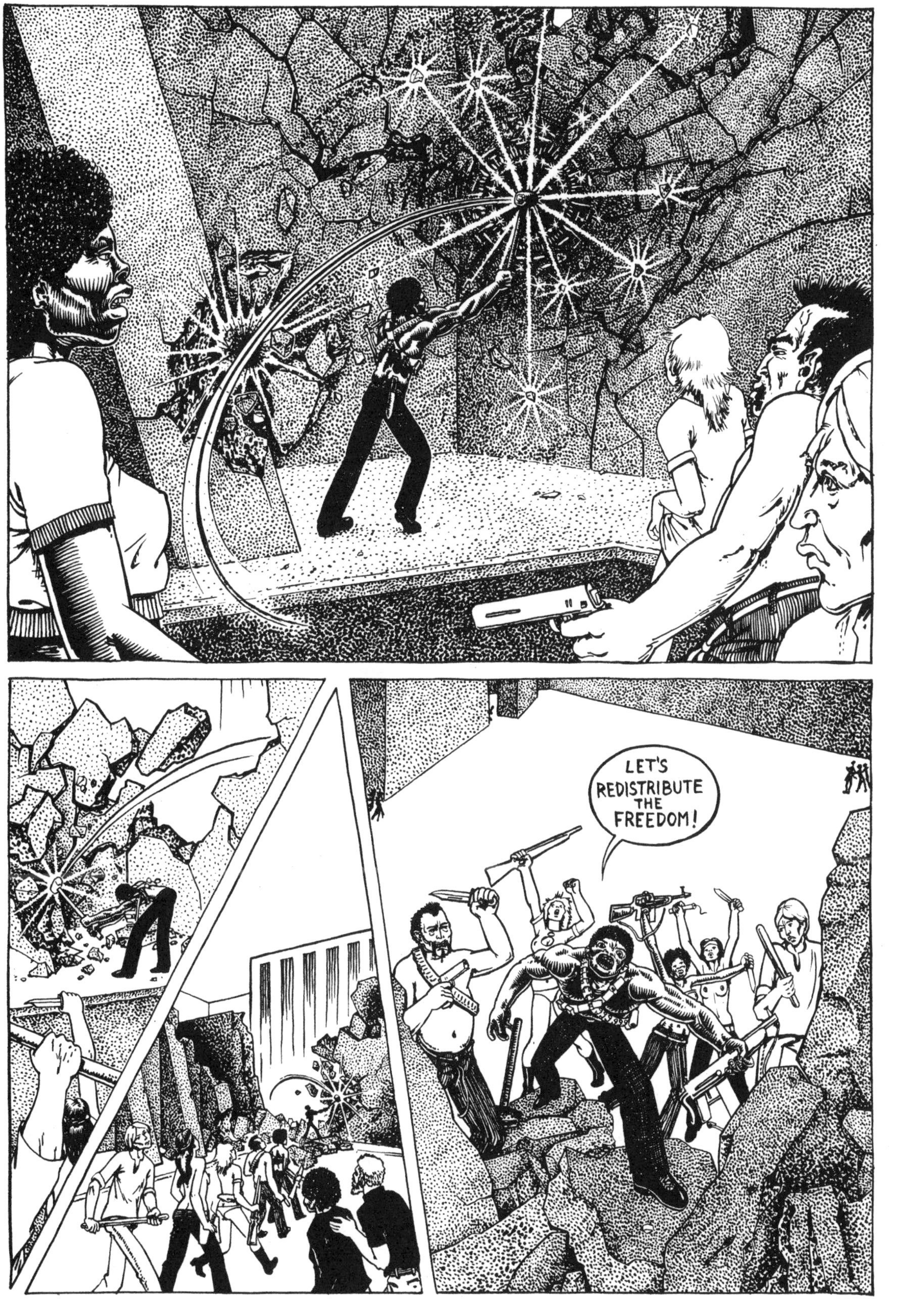
LET'S
REDISTRIBUTE
THE
FREEDOM!

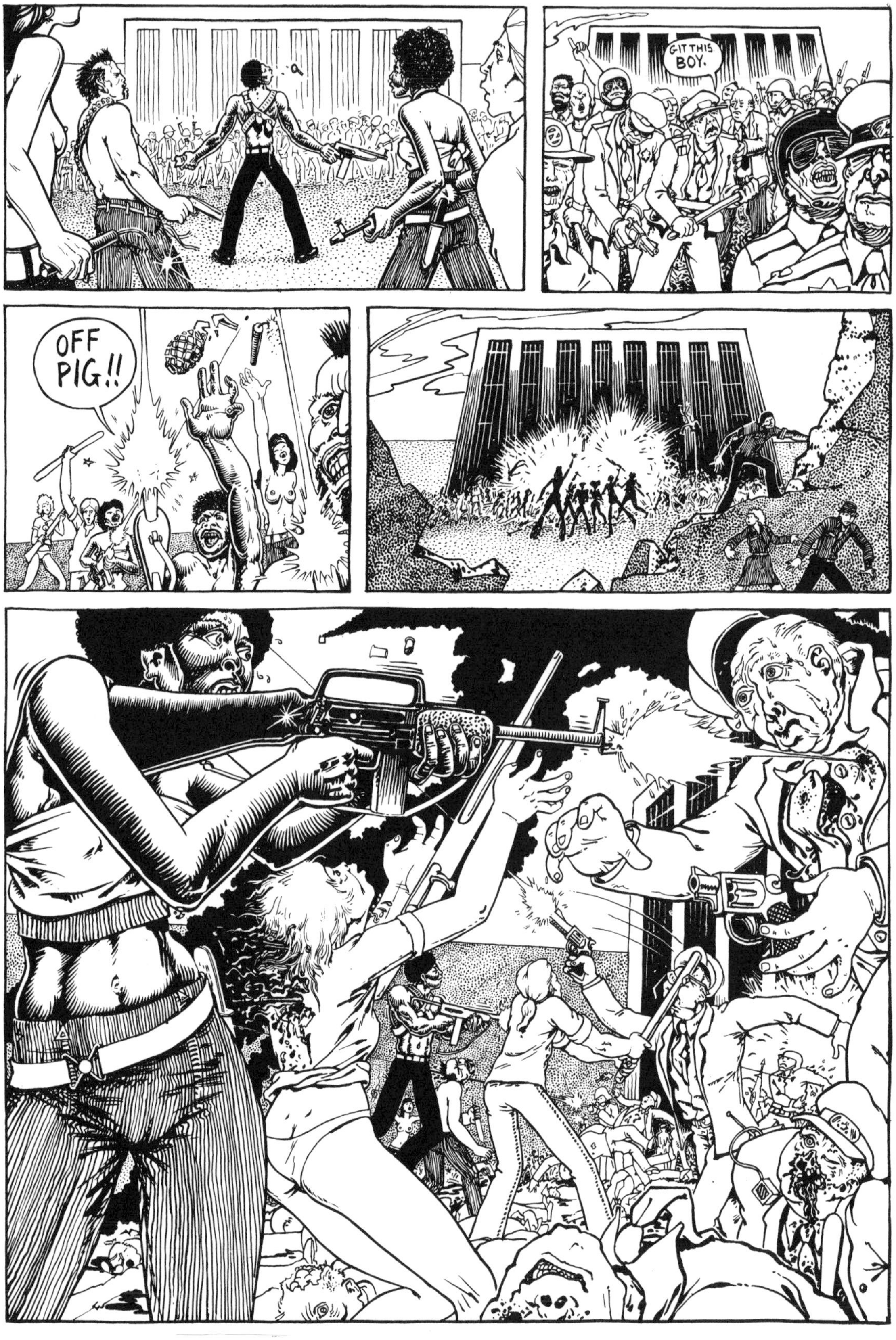
GIT THIS BOY.
OFF PIG!!

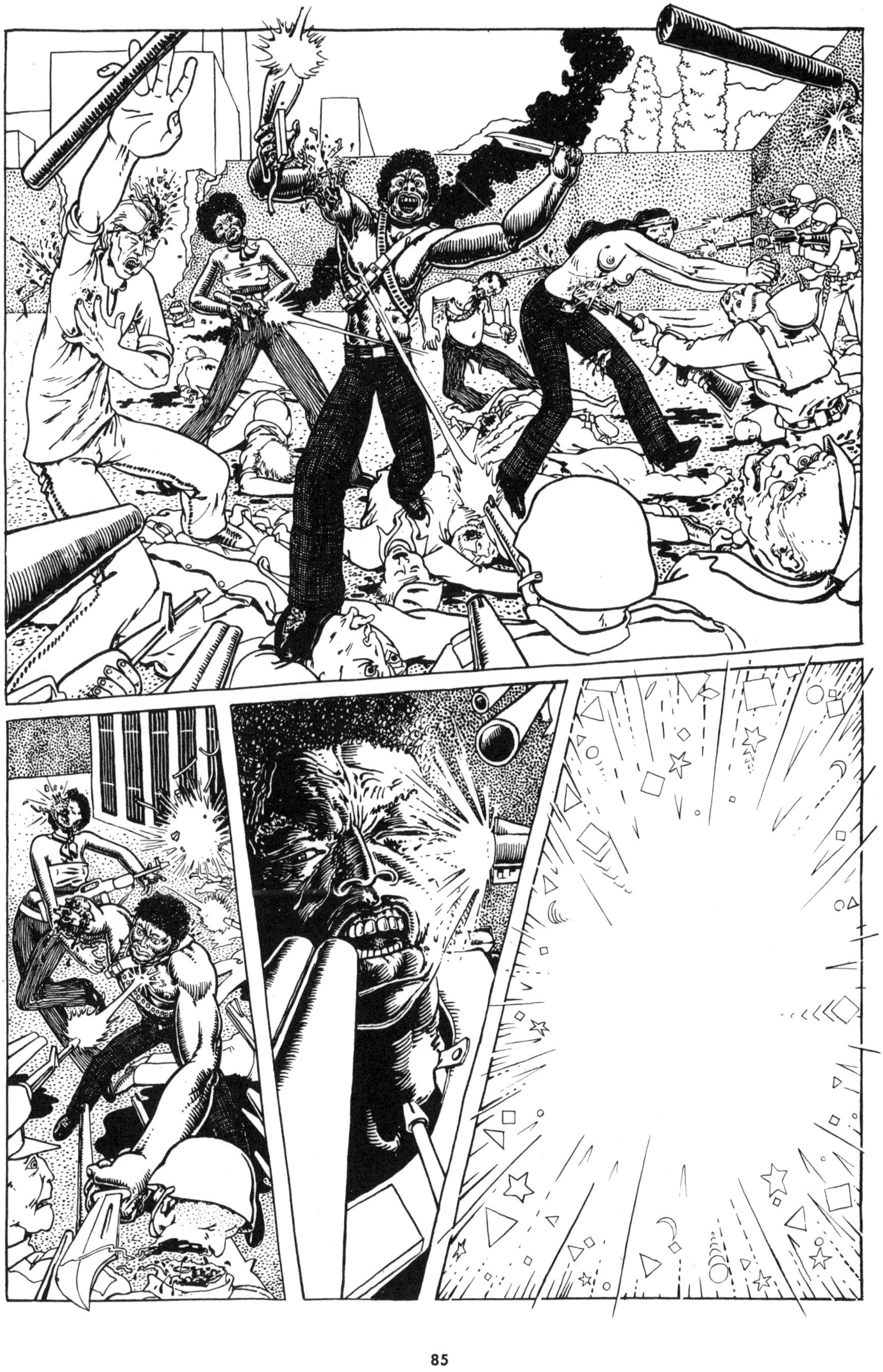

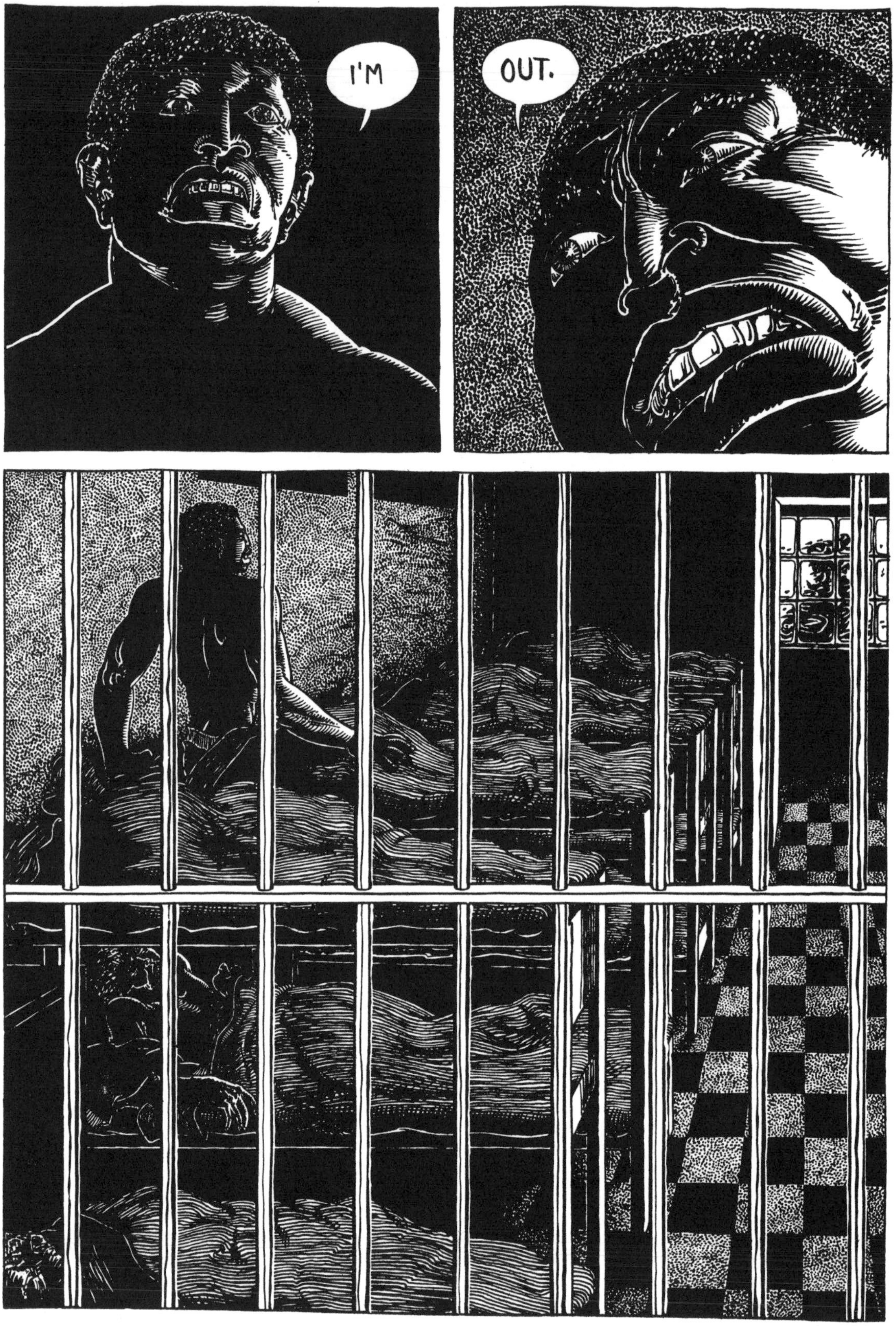
I'M
OUT.

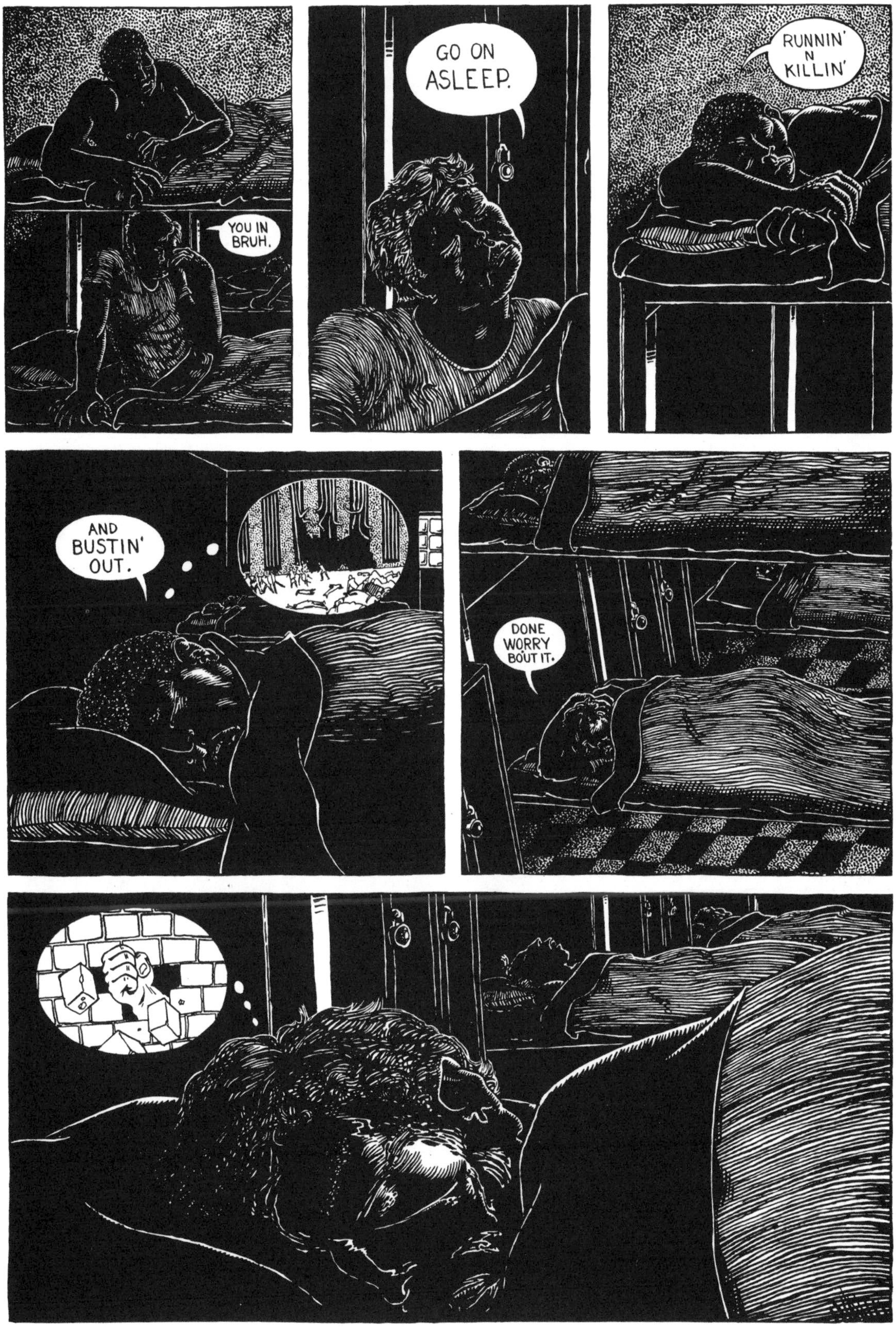
YOU IN BRUH.
GO ON ASLEEP.
RUNNIN' N KILLIN'
AND BUSTIN' OUT.
DONE WORRY BOUT IT.

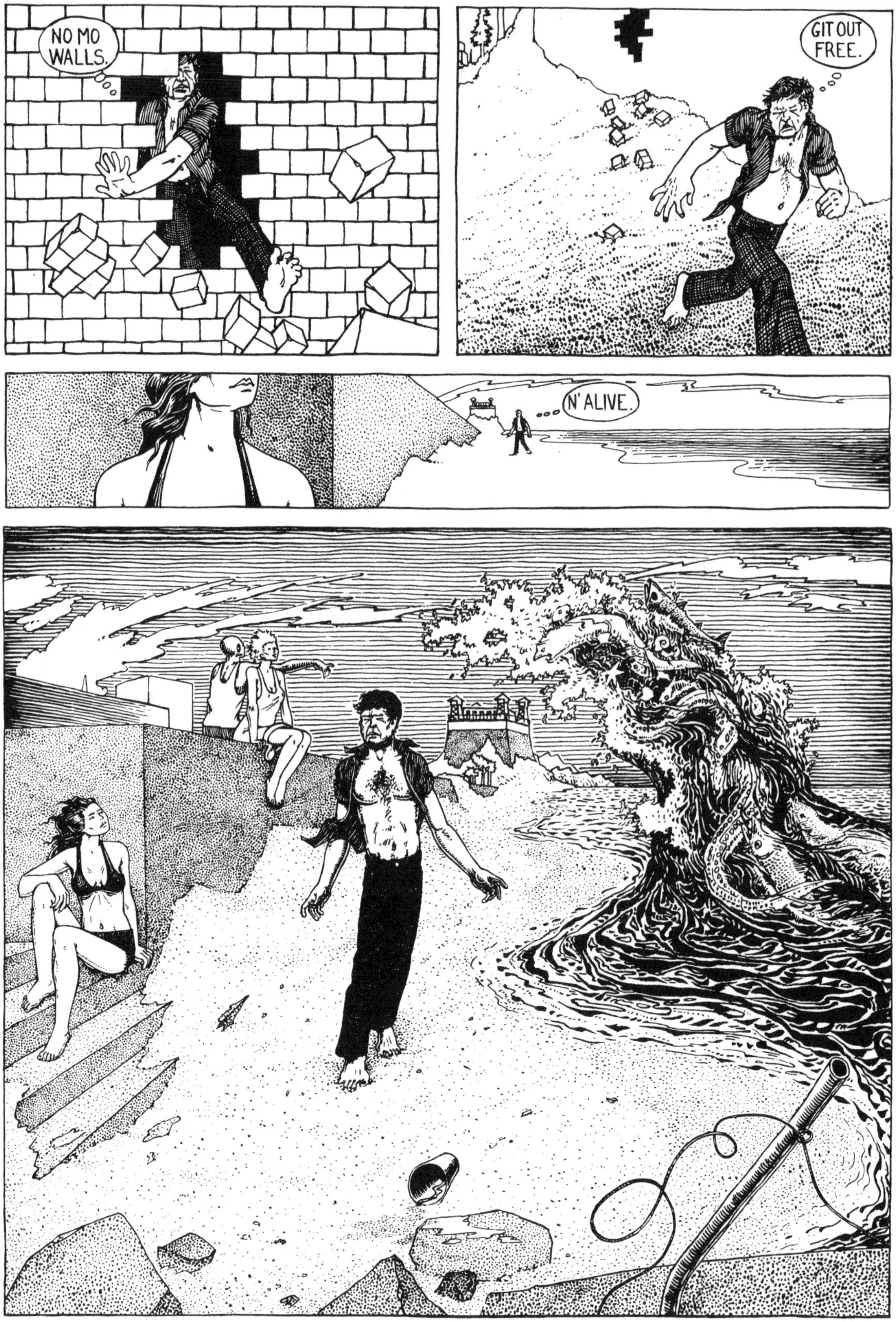
NO MO WALLS.
GIT OUT FREE.
N' ALIVE.

THIS WAY'S STILL DARK WITH WALLS.

YOU CAN GET THROUGH.

YOU GOT TO GO IN TO GET OUT.

I NEED SPACE.

I'LL TAKE YOU THERE.

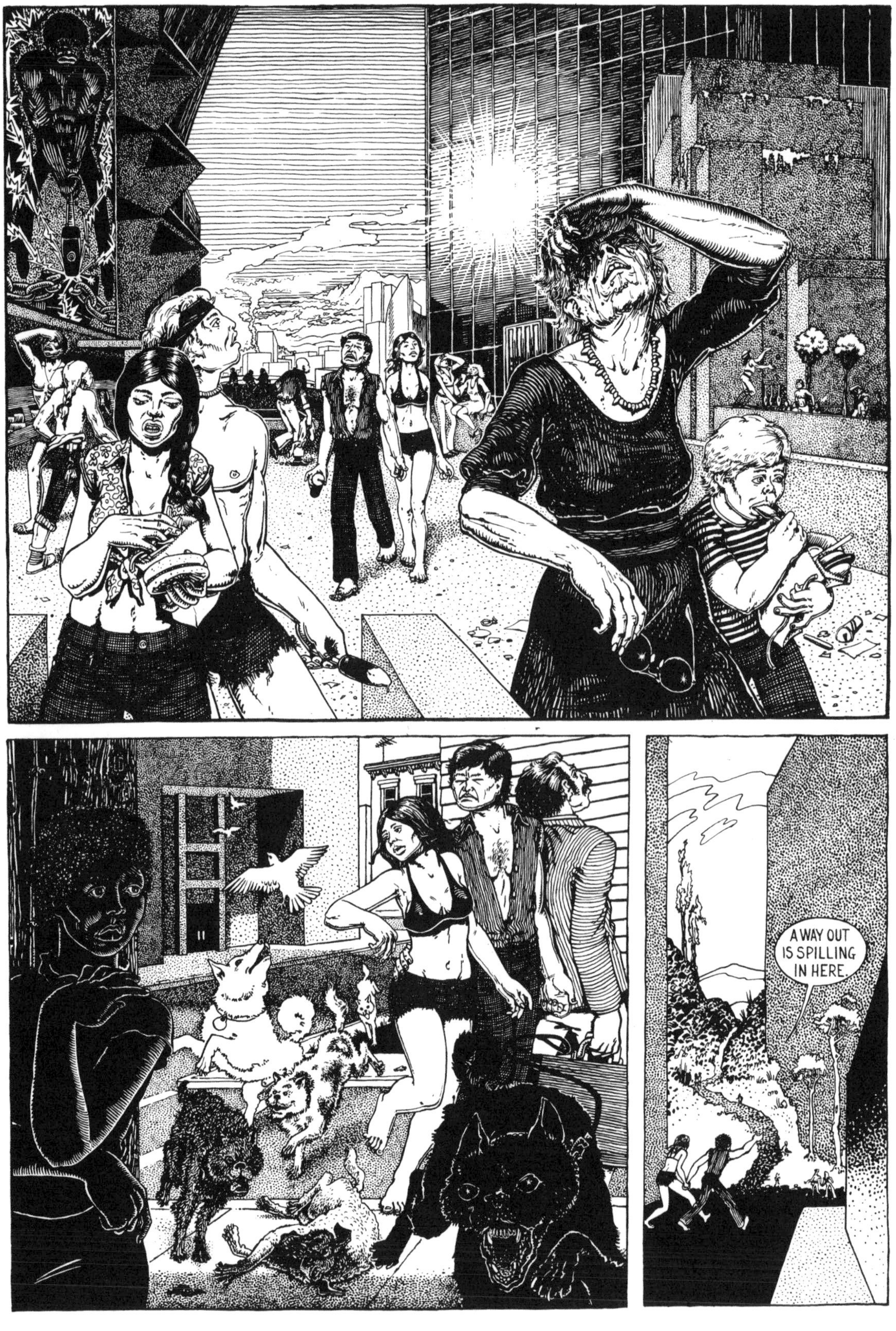
A WAY OUT IS SPILLING IN HERE.

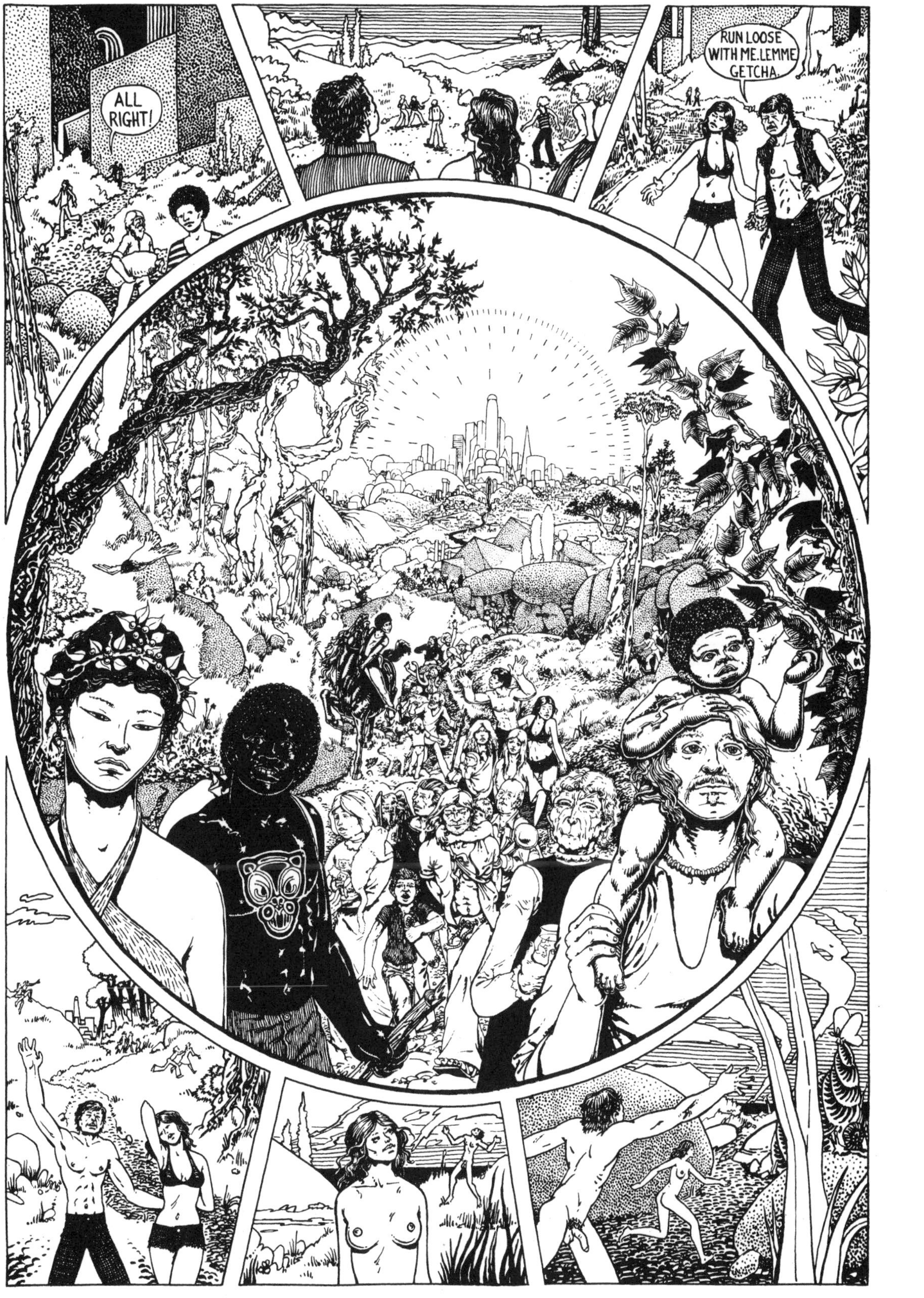
ALL RIGHT!
RUN LOOSE WITH ME. LEMME GETCHA.

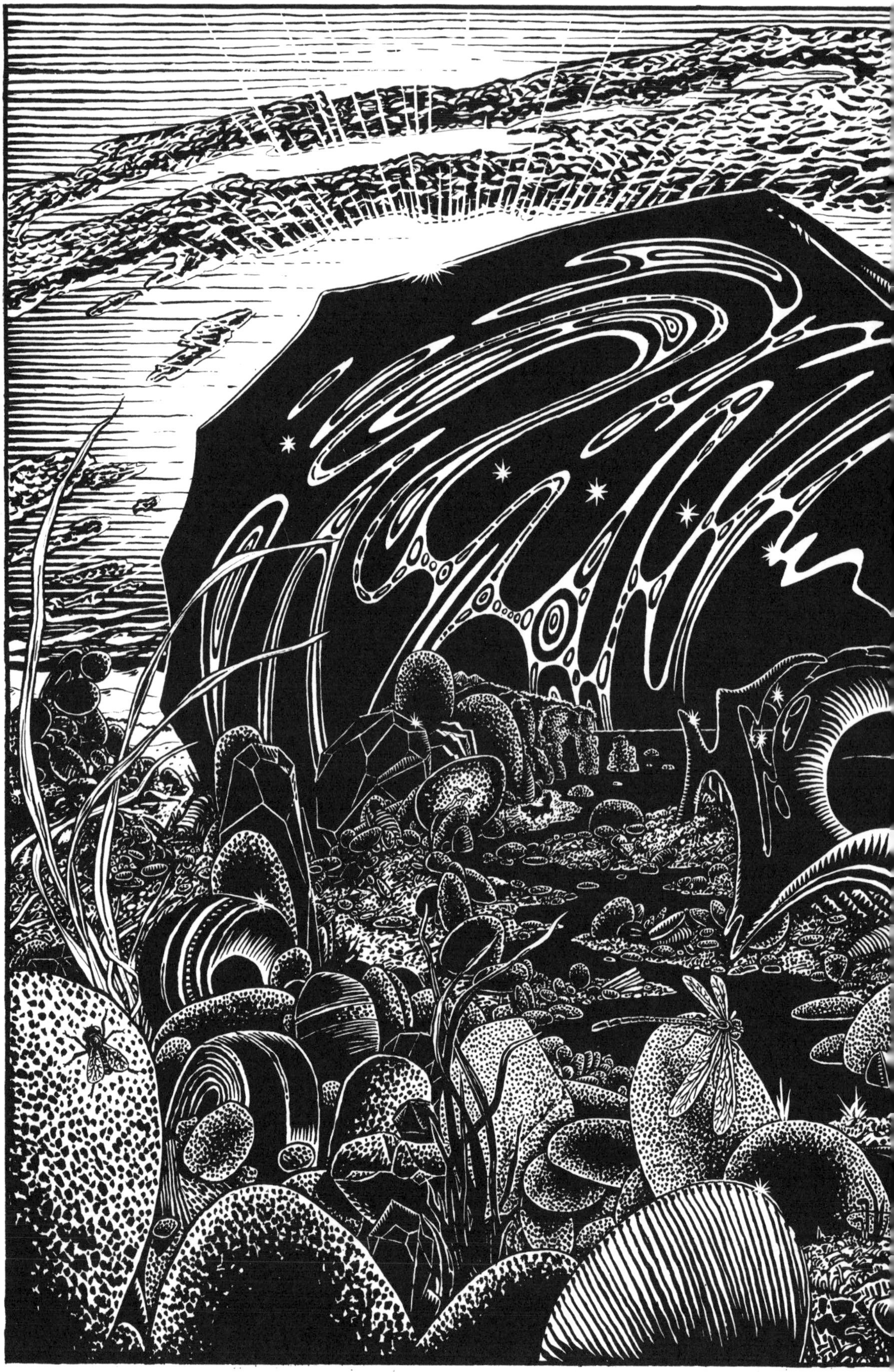

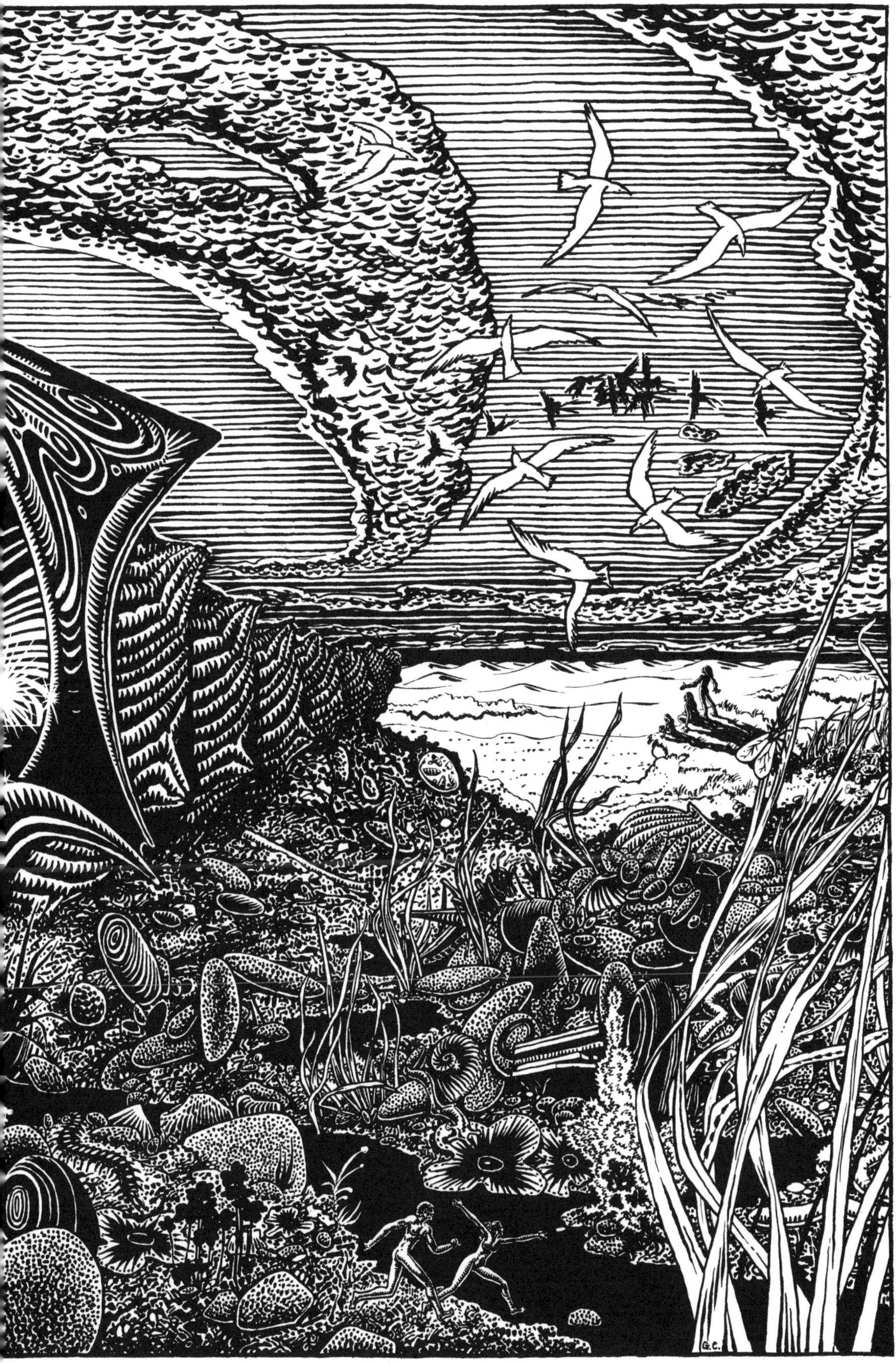

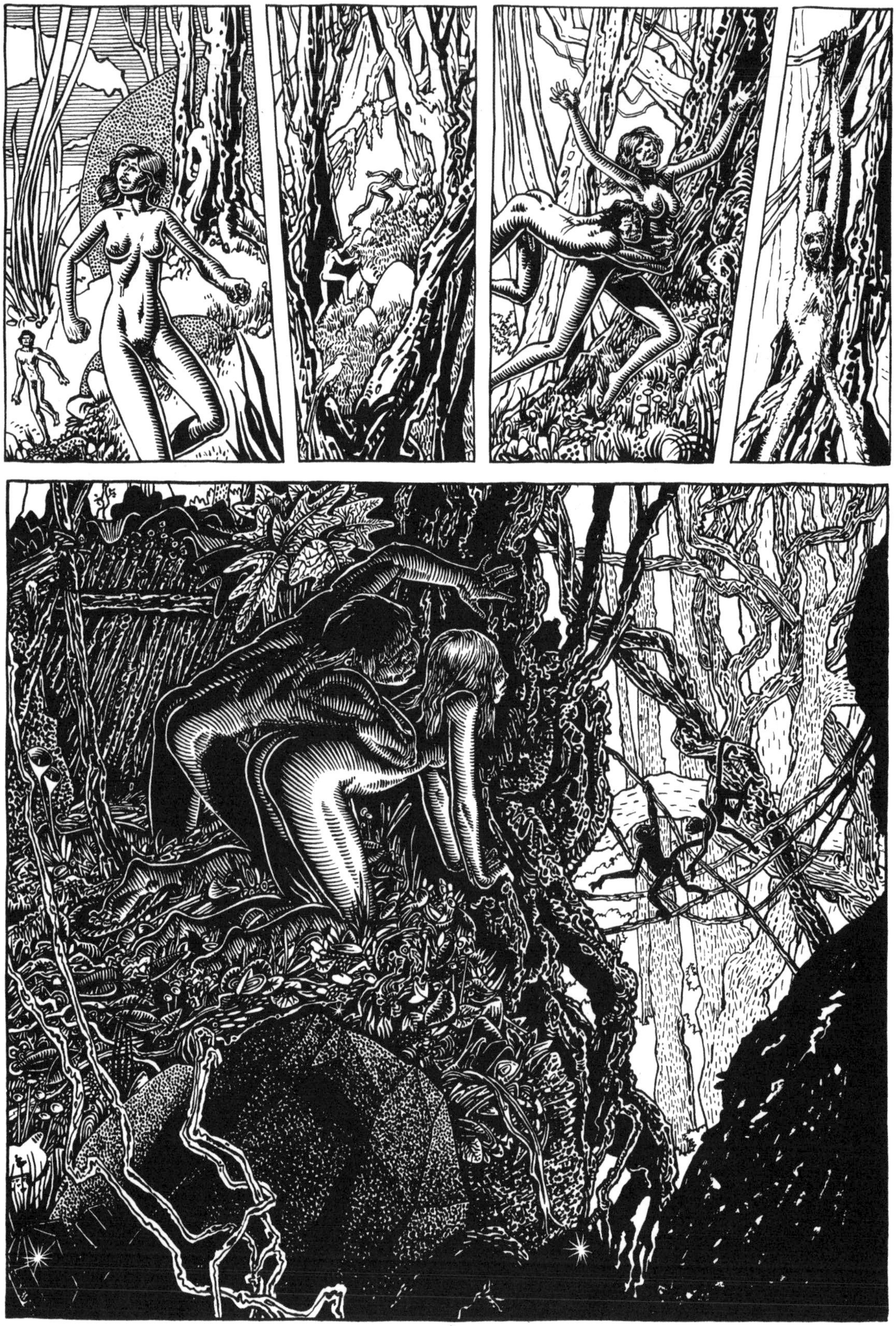

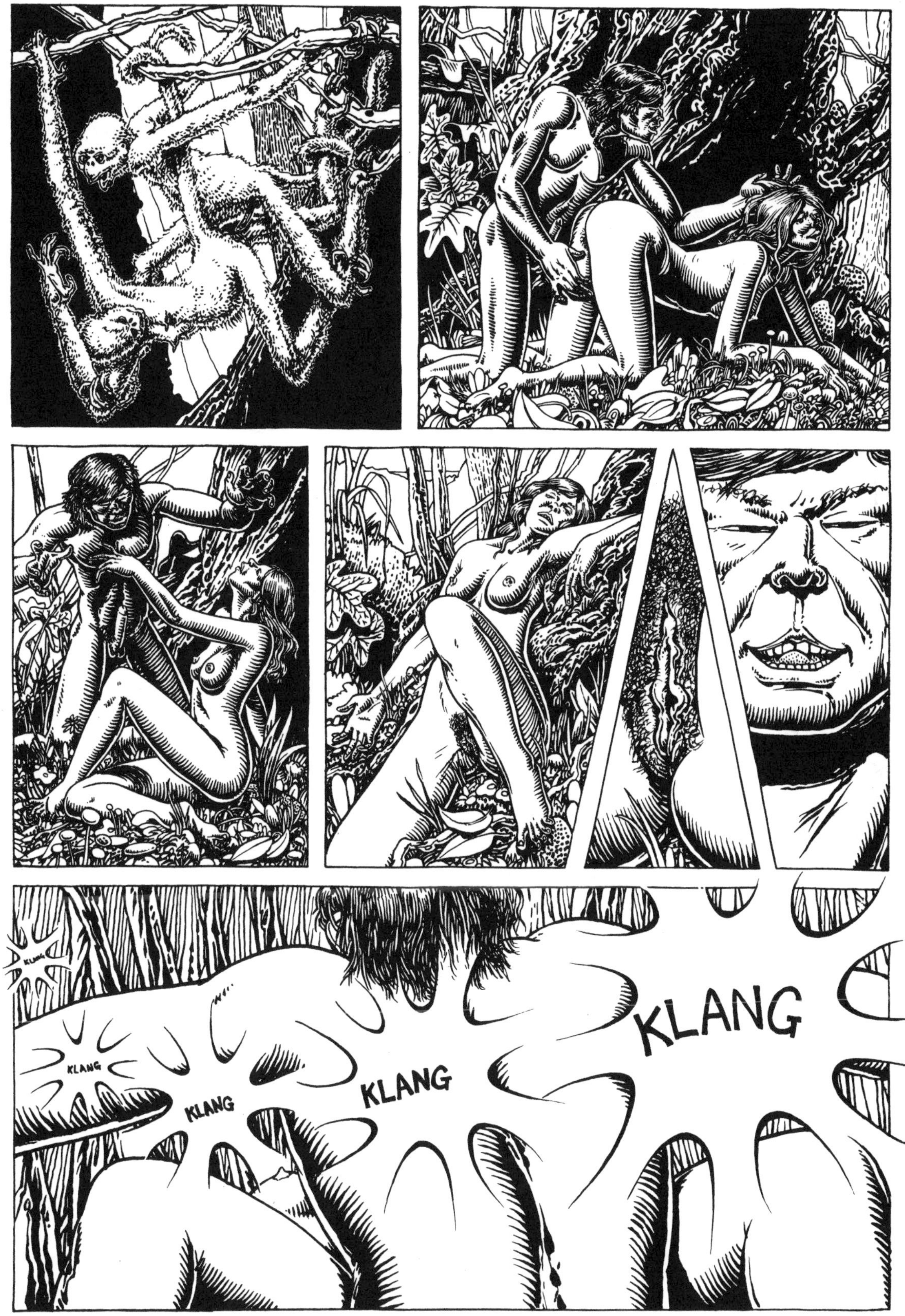
KLANG
KLANG
KLANG
KLANG
KLANG

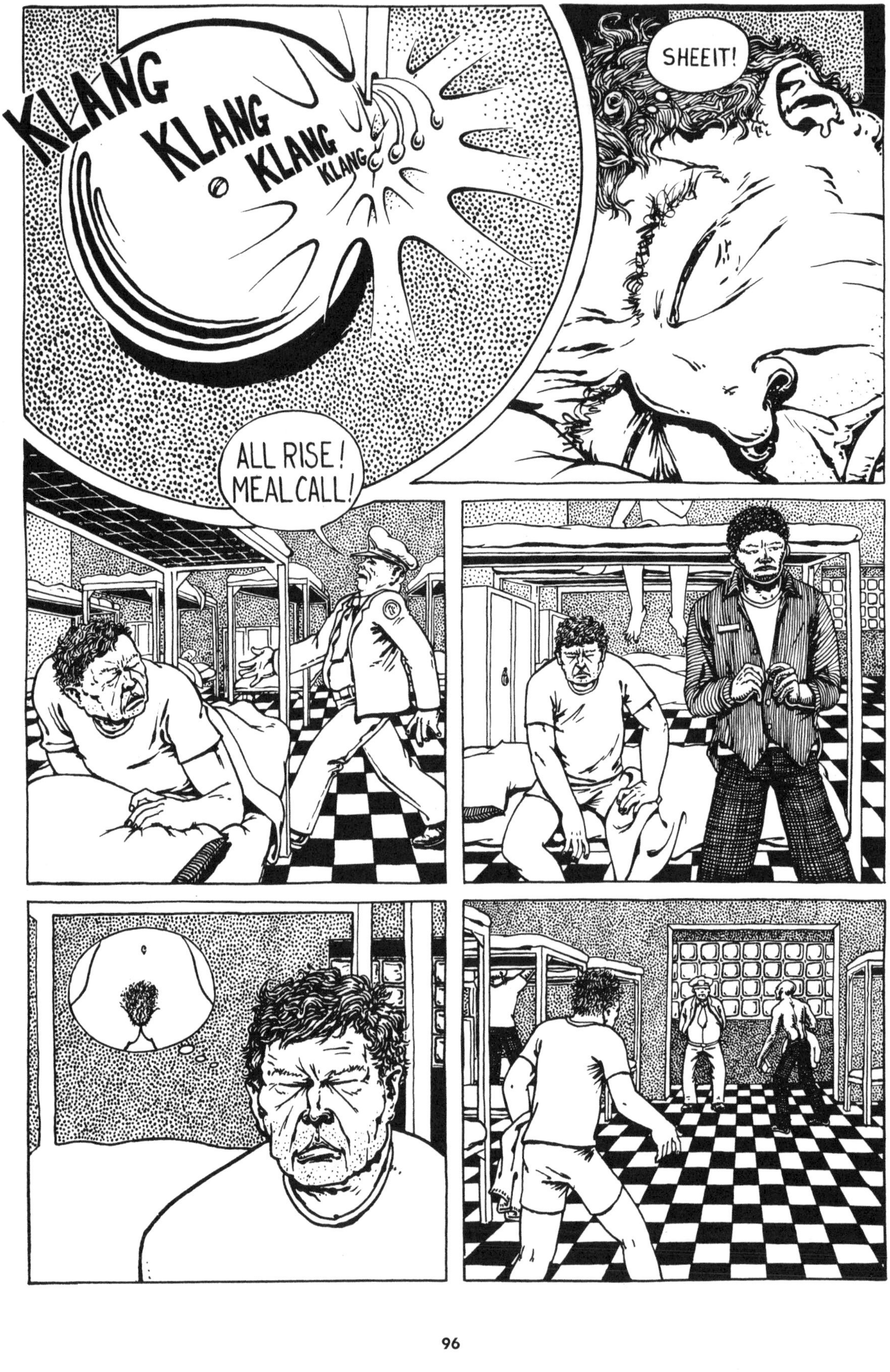
KLANG
KLANG
KLANG
KLANG
SHEEIT!
ALL RISE! MEAL CALL!

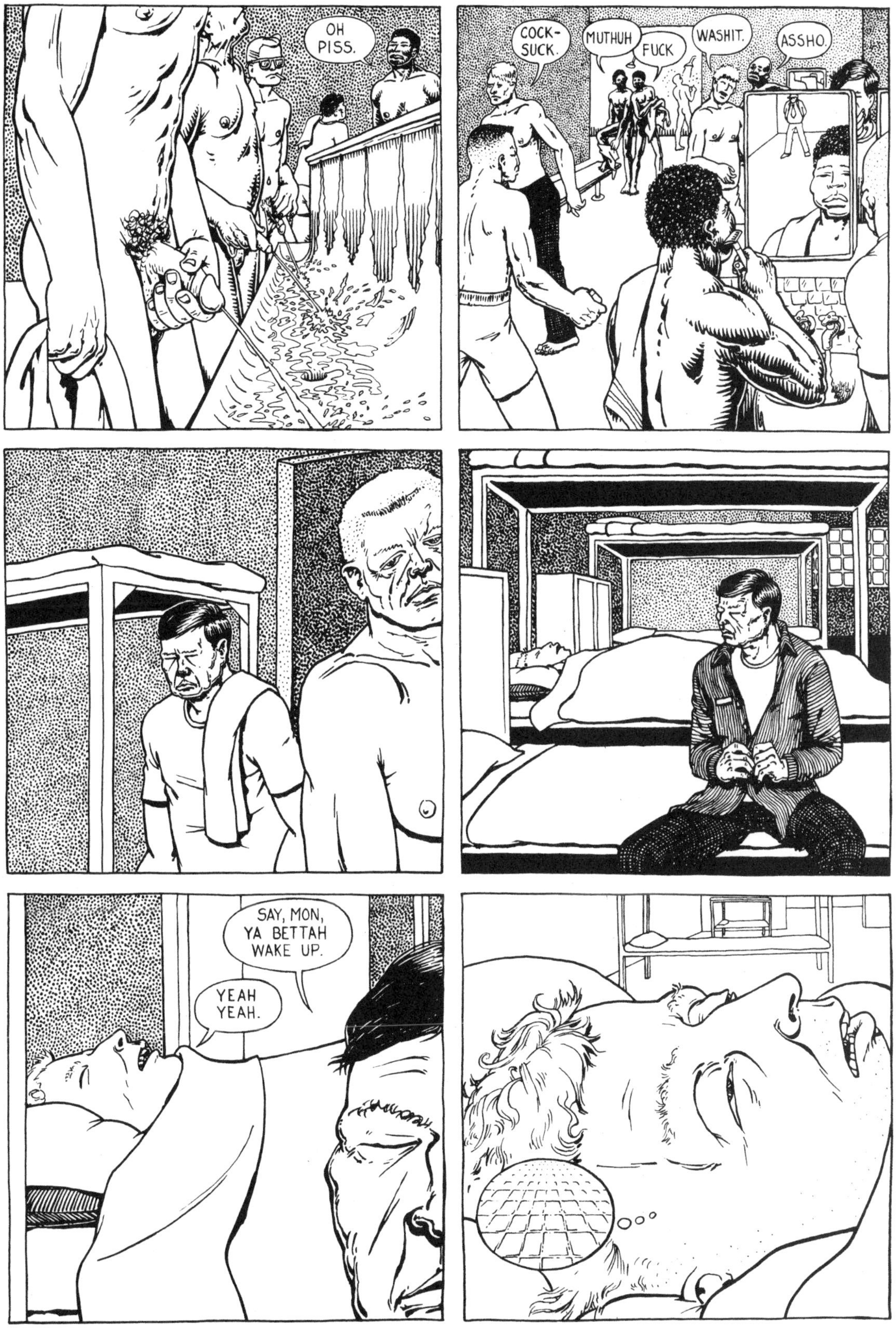
OH PISS.
COCK-SUCK.
MUTHUH
FUCK
WASHIT.
ASSHO.
SAY, MON, YA BETTAH WAKE UP.
YEAH YEAH.

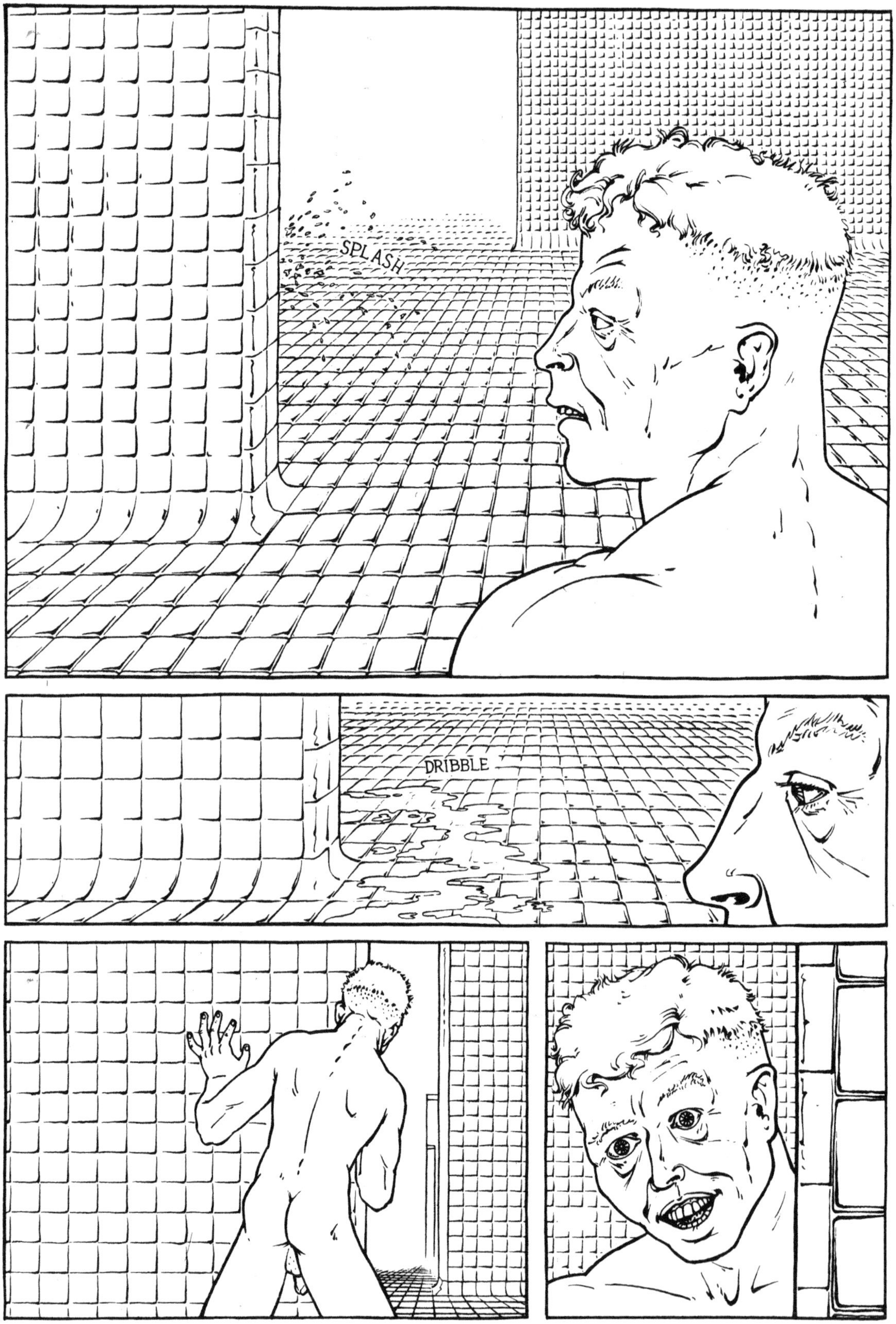
SPLASH
DRIBBLE

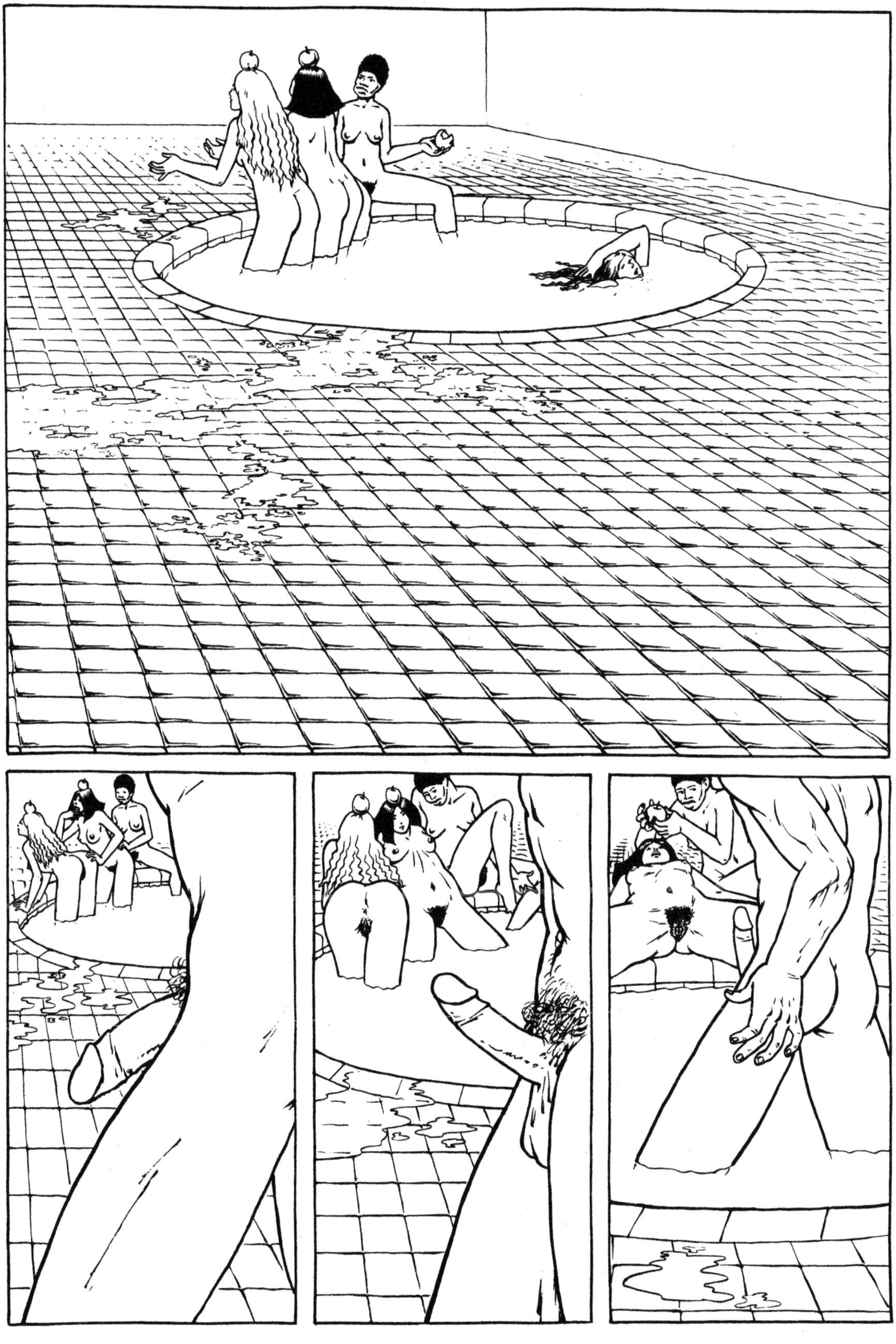

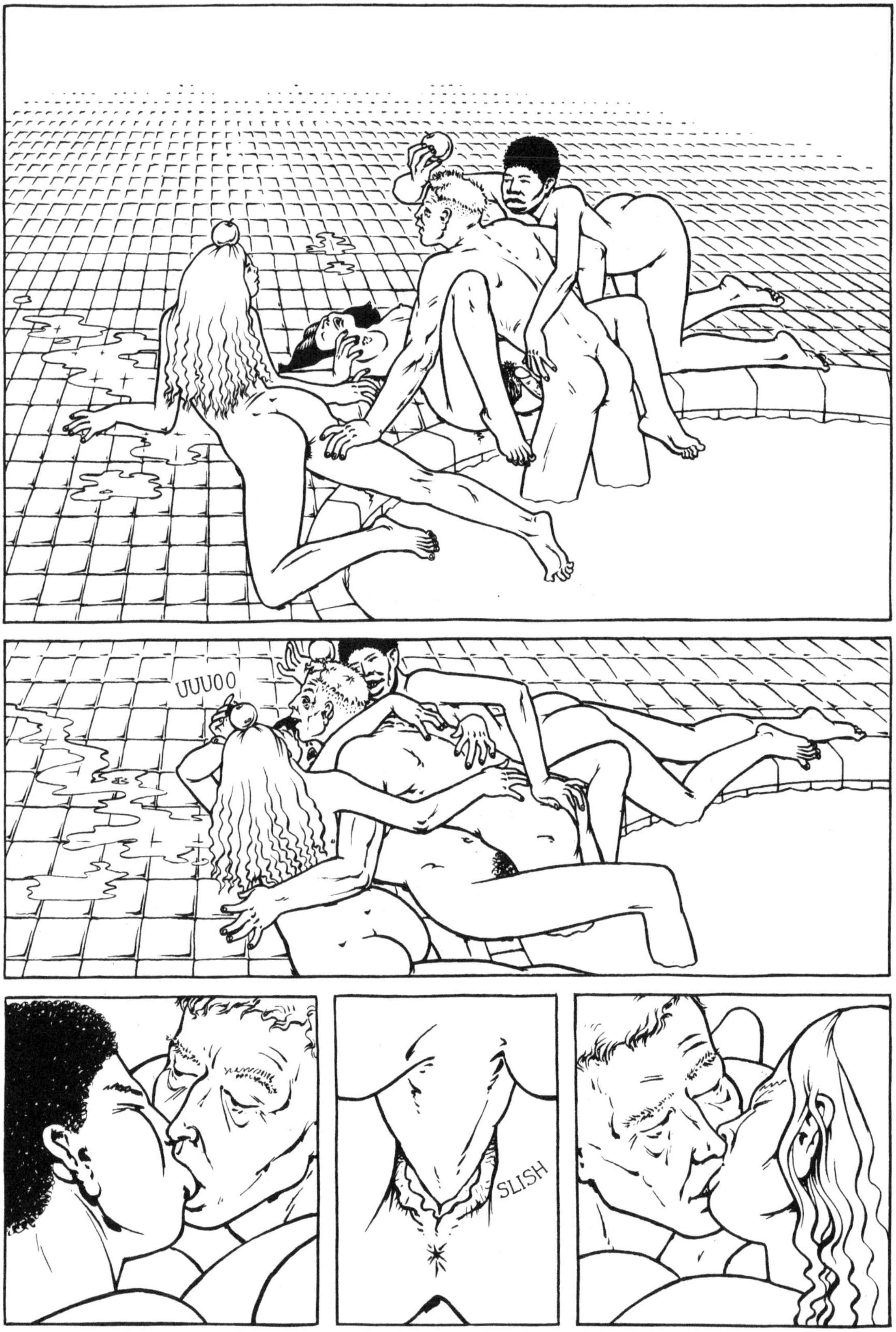
UUUOO
SLISH

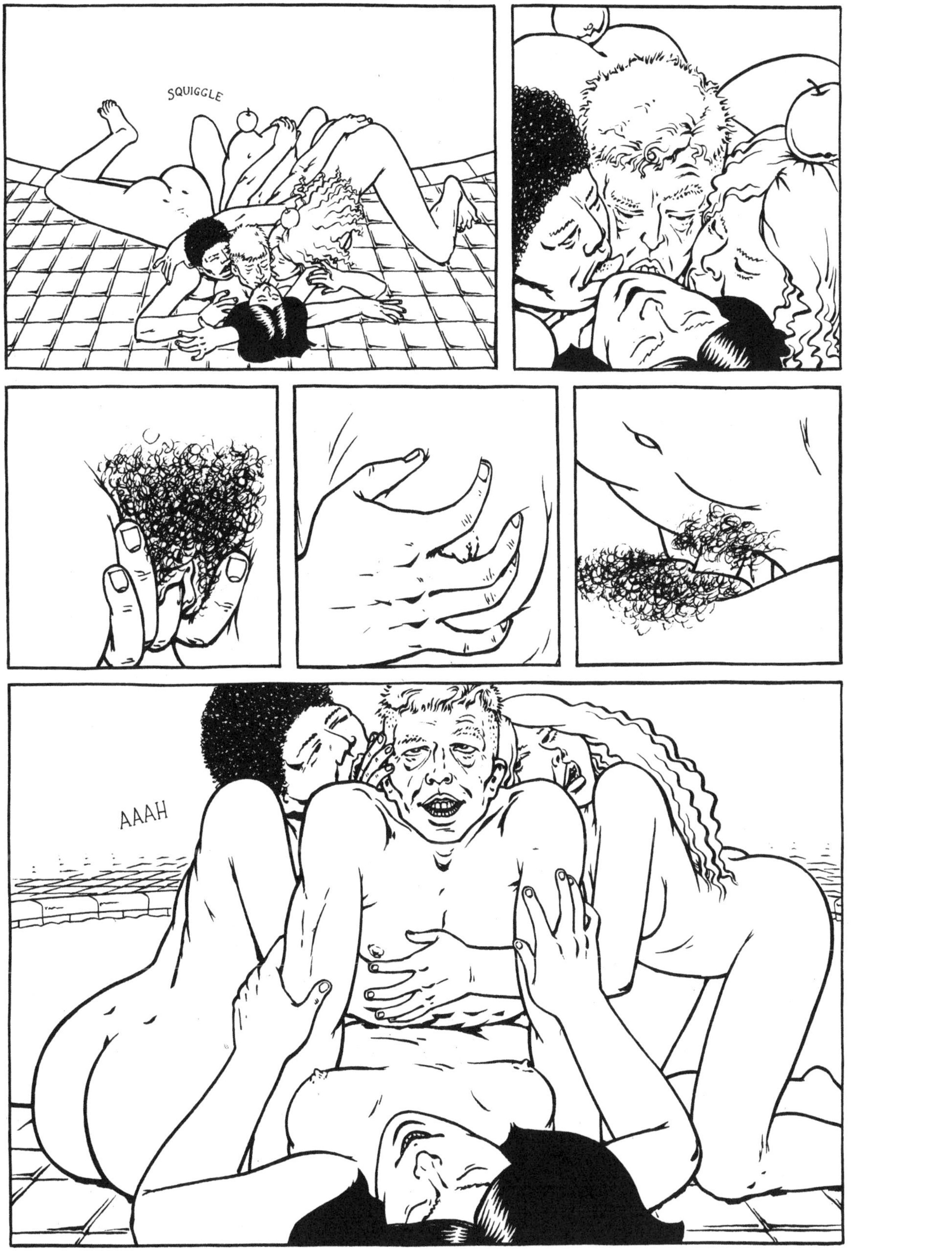
SQUIGGLE
AAAH

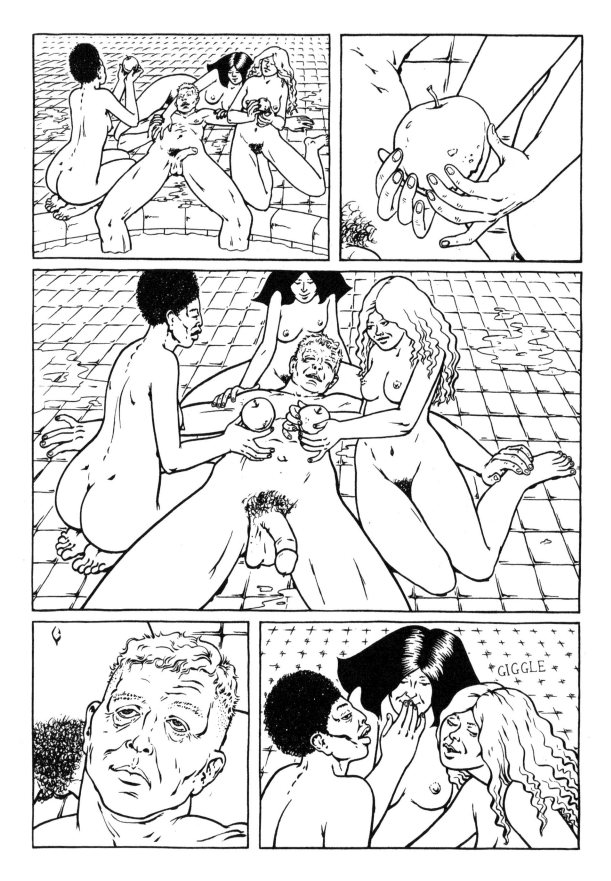

GIGGLE

HUH

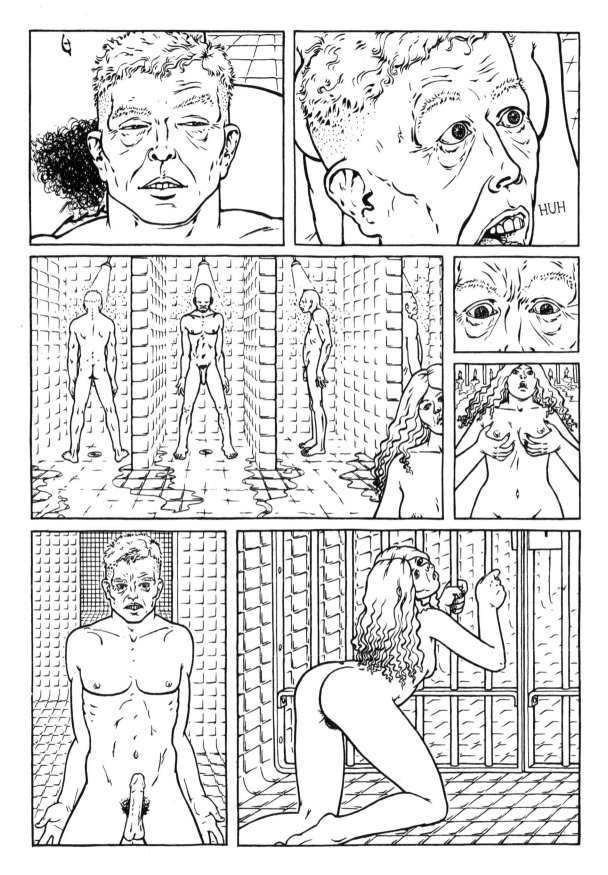

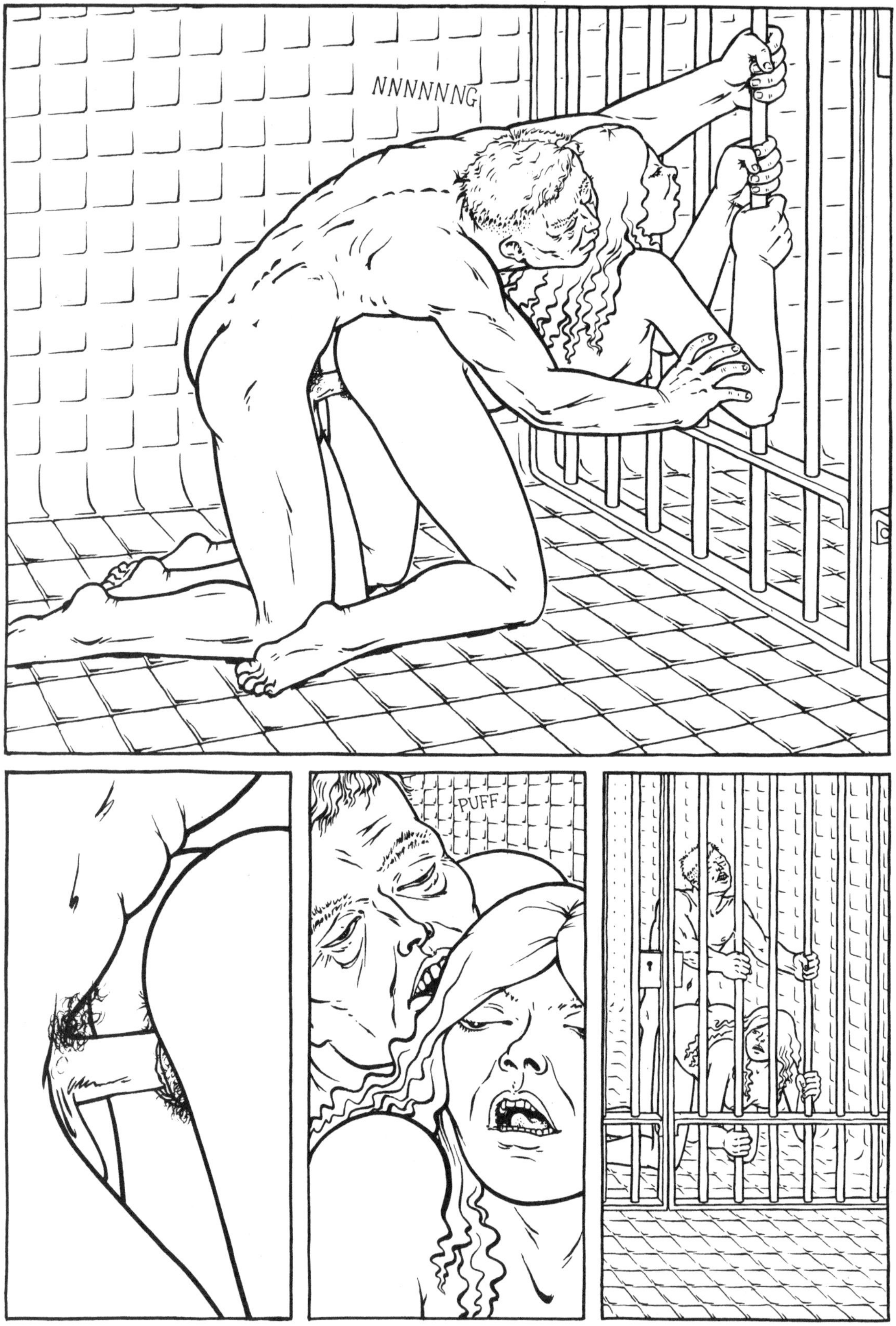
NNNNNNG
PUFF

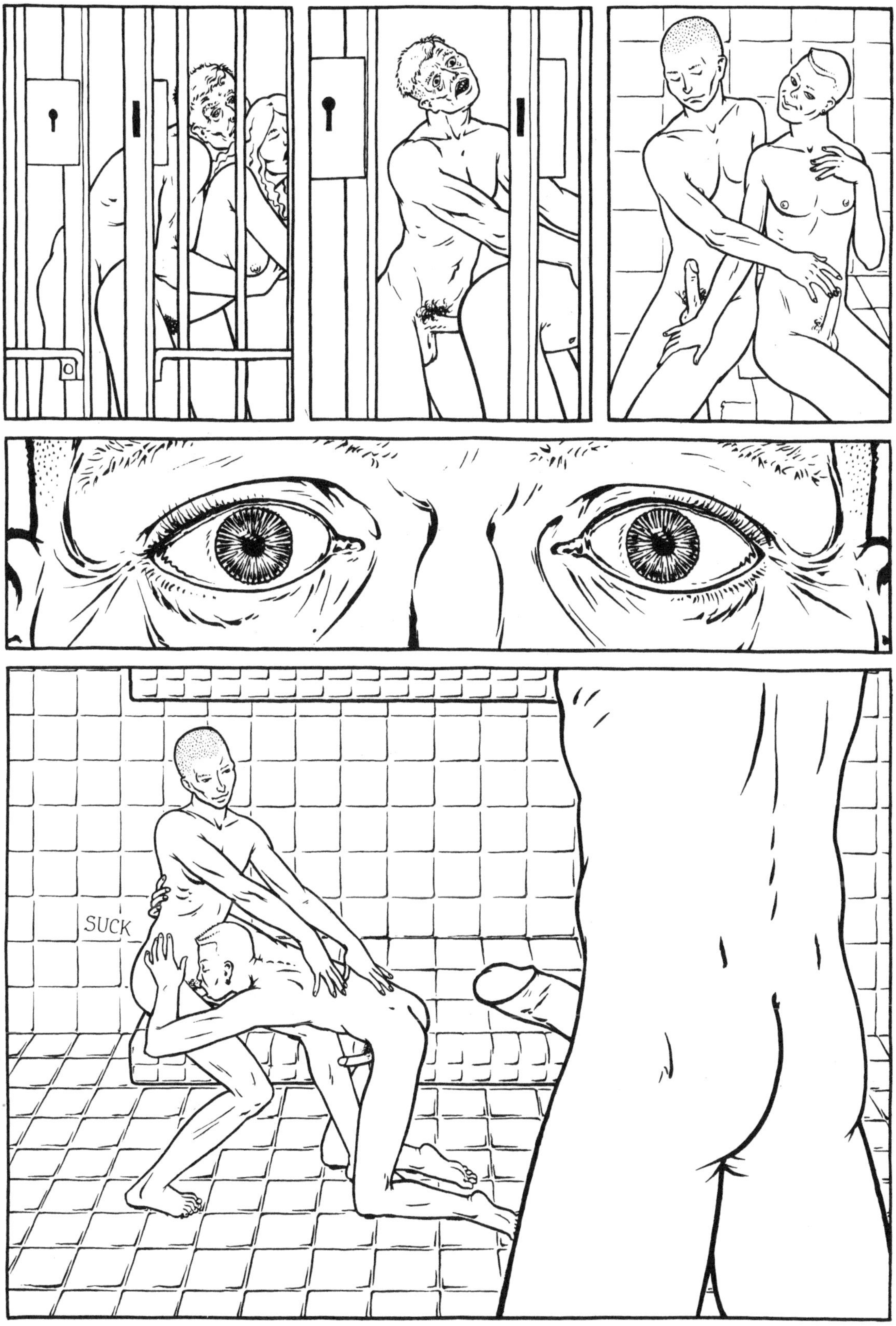
SUCK

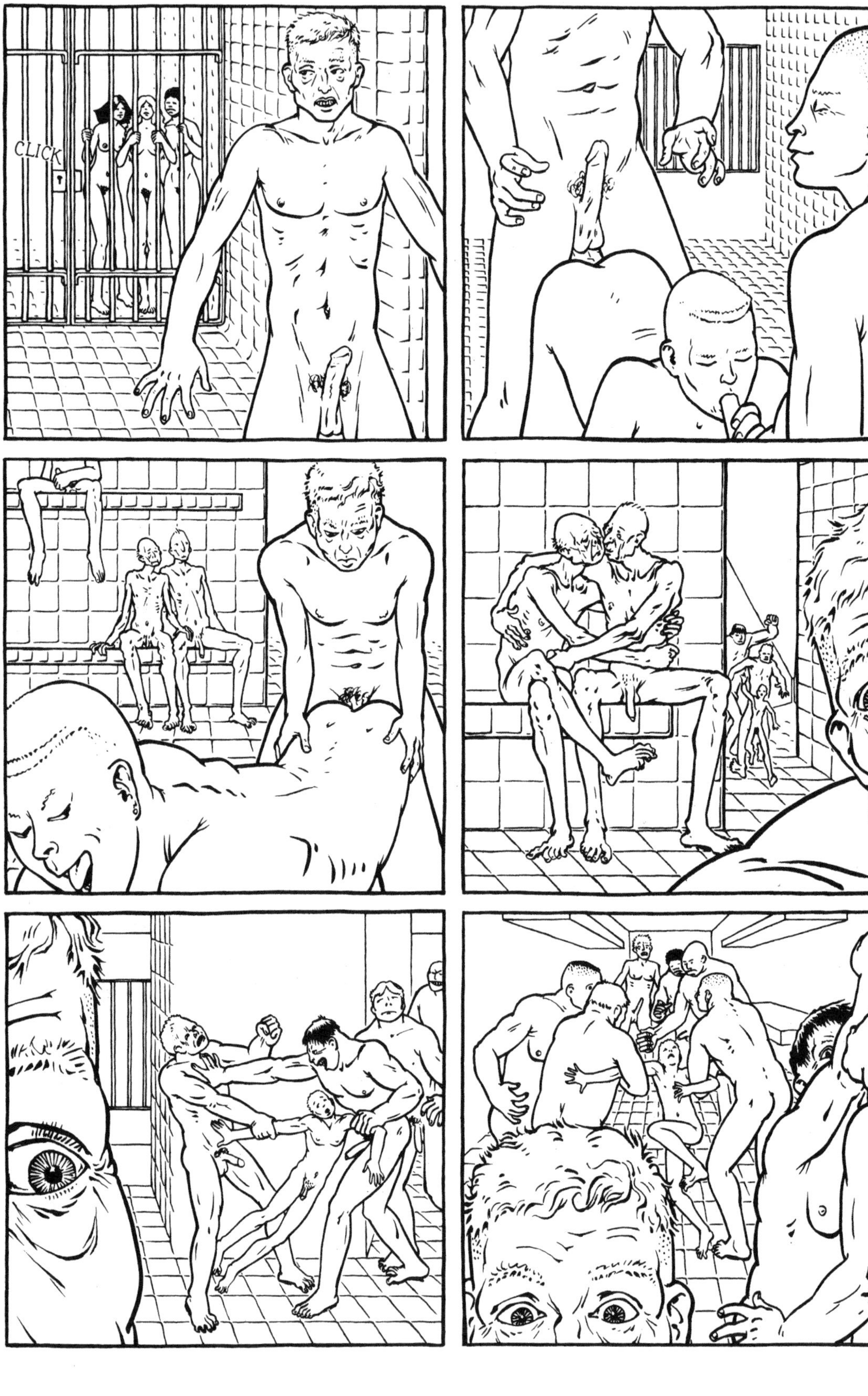
CLICK

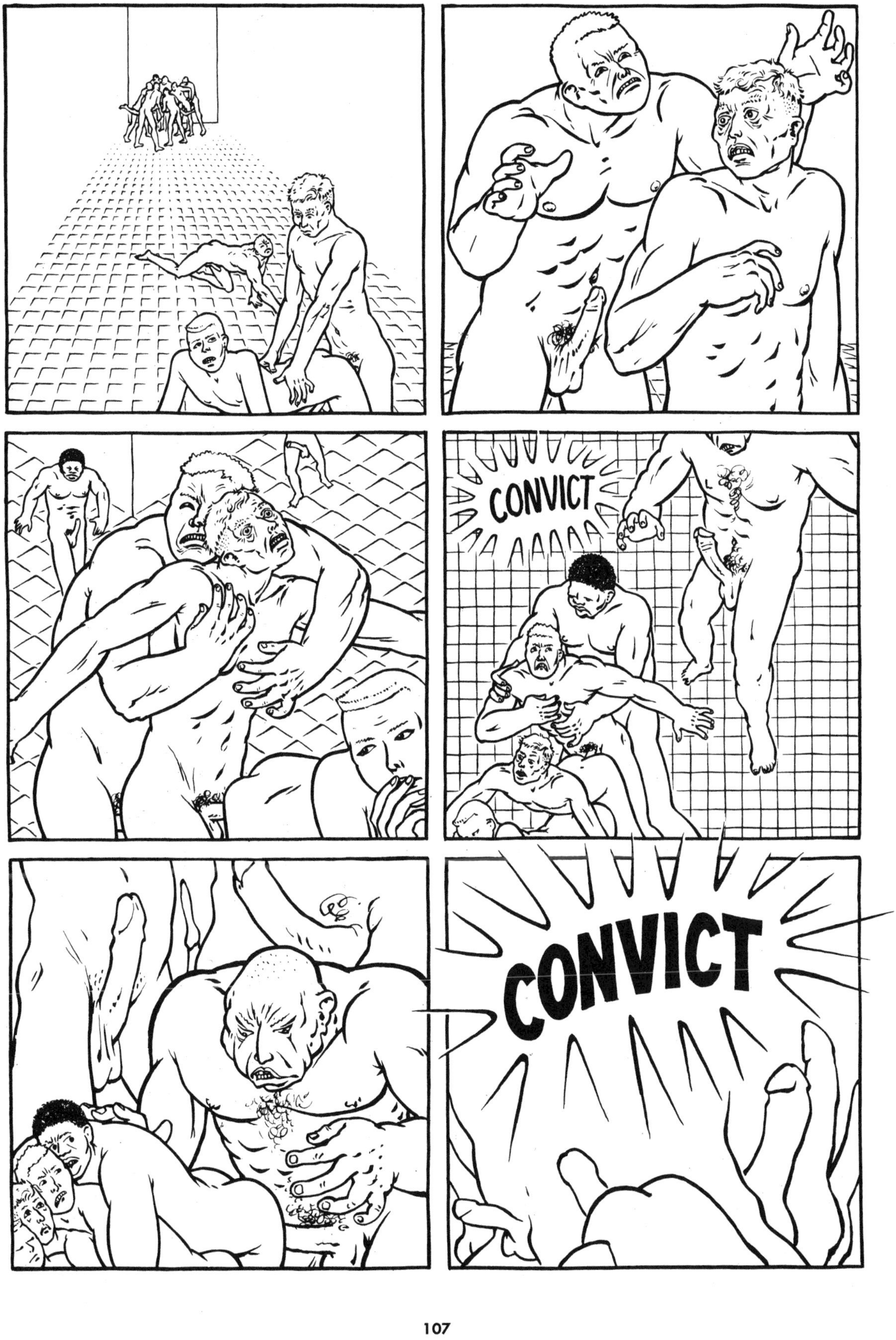
CONVICT
CONVICT

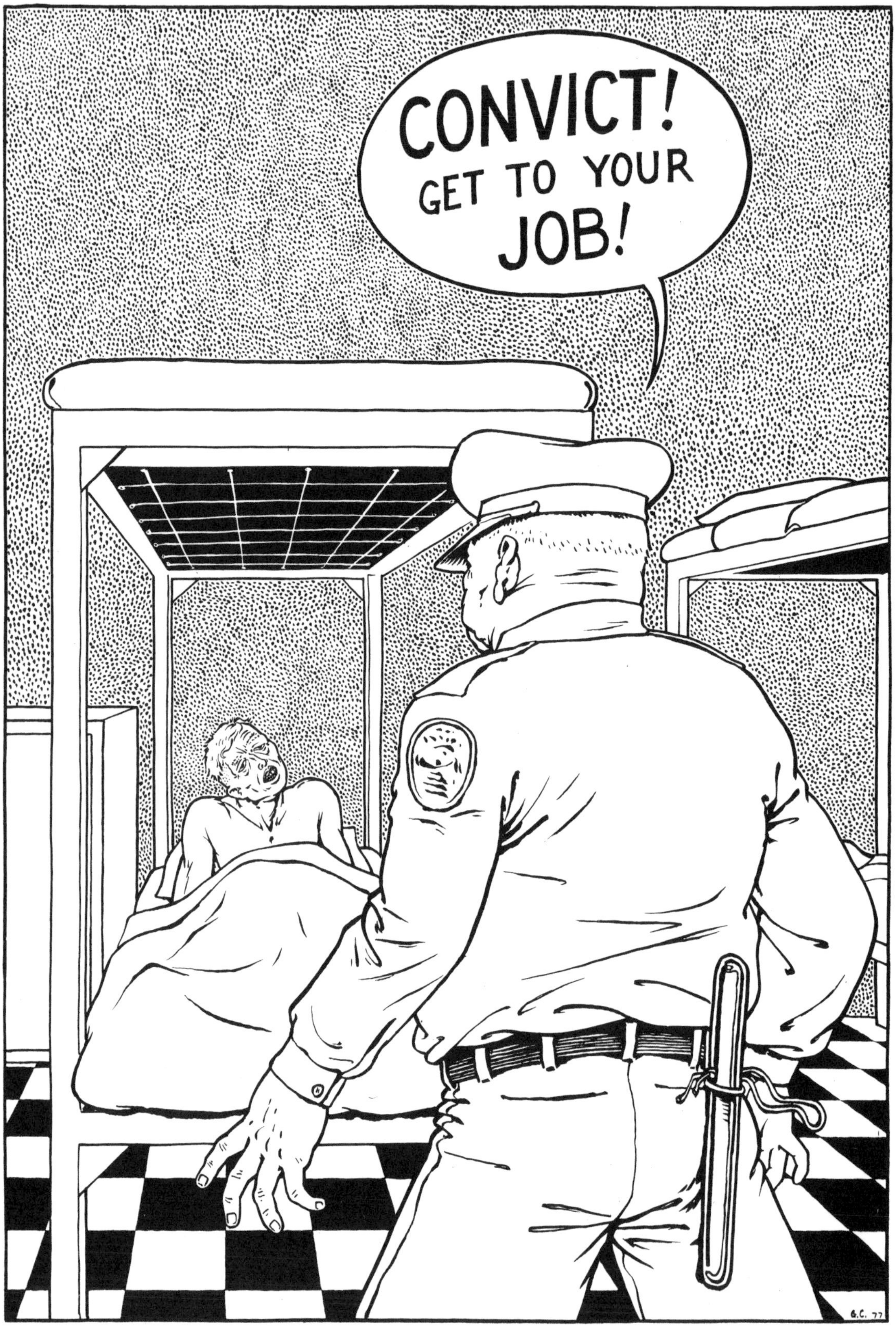
CONVICT! GET TO YOUR JOB!
G.C. 77

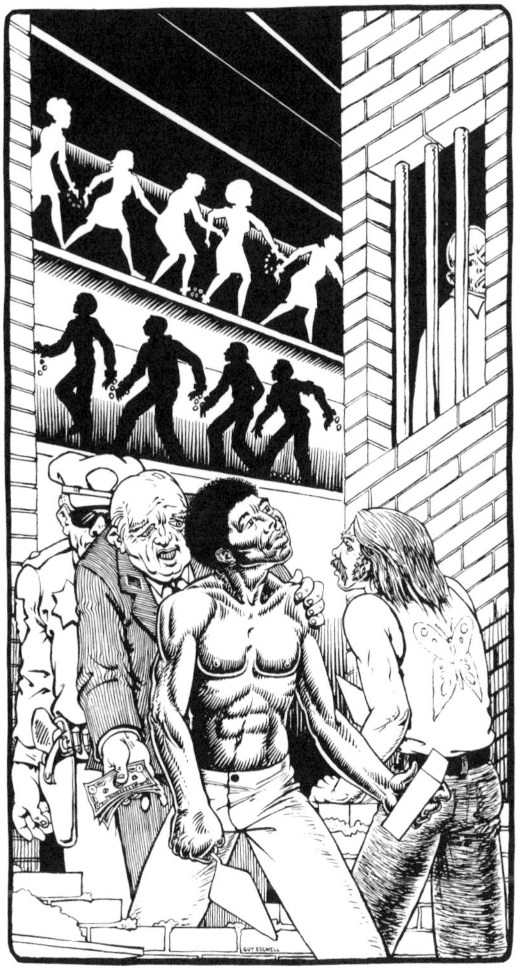
GUY COLWELL

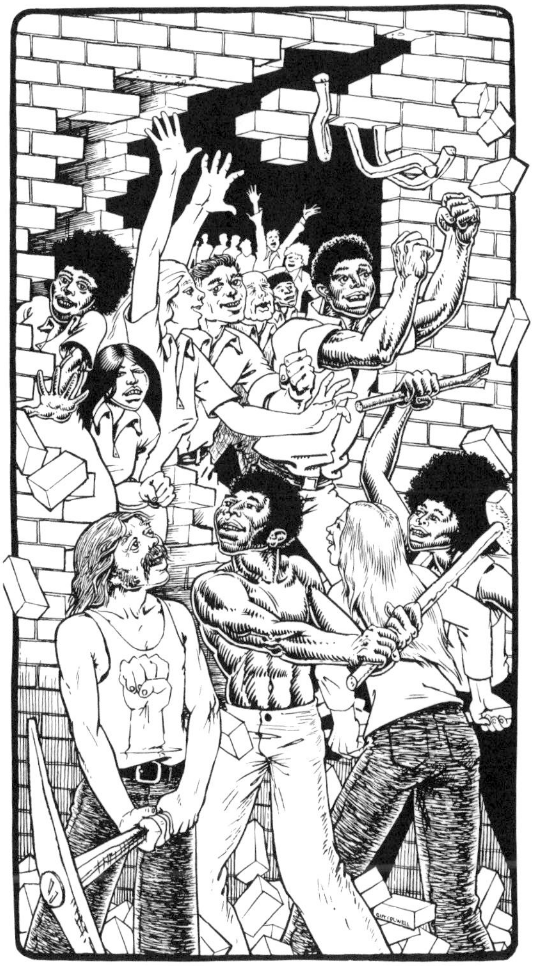
GUY COLWELL

LEFT: The original illustration from the inside front cover of *Inner City Romance* #3.
RIGHT: The original illustration from the inside back cover of that issue.

INNER CITY ROMANCE #4

(1977)

by Patrick Rosenkranz

"By *Inner City Romance* #4, I was focusing on other people's experiences of poverty and desperation, not on my own internal or social narrative. When I needed to raise some cash, as in the case of *Inner City Romance* #4, "Ramps," I sat down with a Rapidograph pen and went through the process of writing and drawing this story of life in a housing project in a period of only 30 days. This was the fastest I would ever do a comic book. The story was inspired by the struggle of very poor and elderly people living in the International Hotel in San Francisco. This old residence hotel in Chinatown became the focus of a major confrontation when landowners and the city teamed up to evict the tenants, who refused to leave and took over the management of the building themselves, holding out for more than a year until a large riot-equipped force finally removed them."

Colwell slows down time to portray the mindset of the skateboarder in the climax of this story, taking half a dozen pages to portray the character's last moments of life as he falls from the building ramp to the concrete below. This sequence has some visual and philosophical similarities to the 10-page sequence in *Inner City Romance* #1 that attempts to convey the subjective effects of LSD hallucinations.

"The brain is capable of some very stunning productions both by psychedelic ingestion and, I think, in the extremity of imminent death," said Colwell. "Think of the mental energy that gets put into an expression like 'my life flashed before my eyes' and the reports of vivid 'near death' experiences. Something is going on there. I'm atheistic about the possibility of life after death, but the episode of consciousness expansion that happens when we die will most probably be a remarkably brilliant and wondrous experience. The sequences in *Inner City Romance* #1 and #4 are an exploration of this potential. They are meant to be a serious contribution to the discussion of brain potential as a real biological fact, not just fantasy sequences."

Heat Wave, oil on canvas, 1976. This cover painting for *Inner City Romance* #4 explores the oppressive aspects of urban life. The sun's heat may be the apparent focus, but the real subject is the undercurrent of poverty, struggle, and alienation.

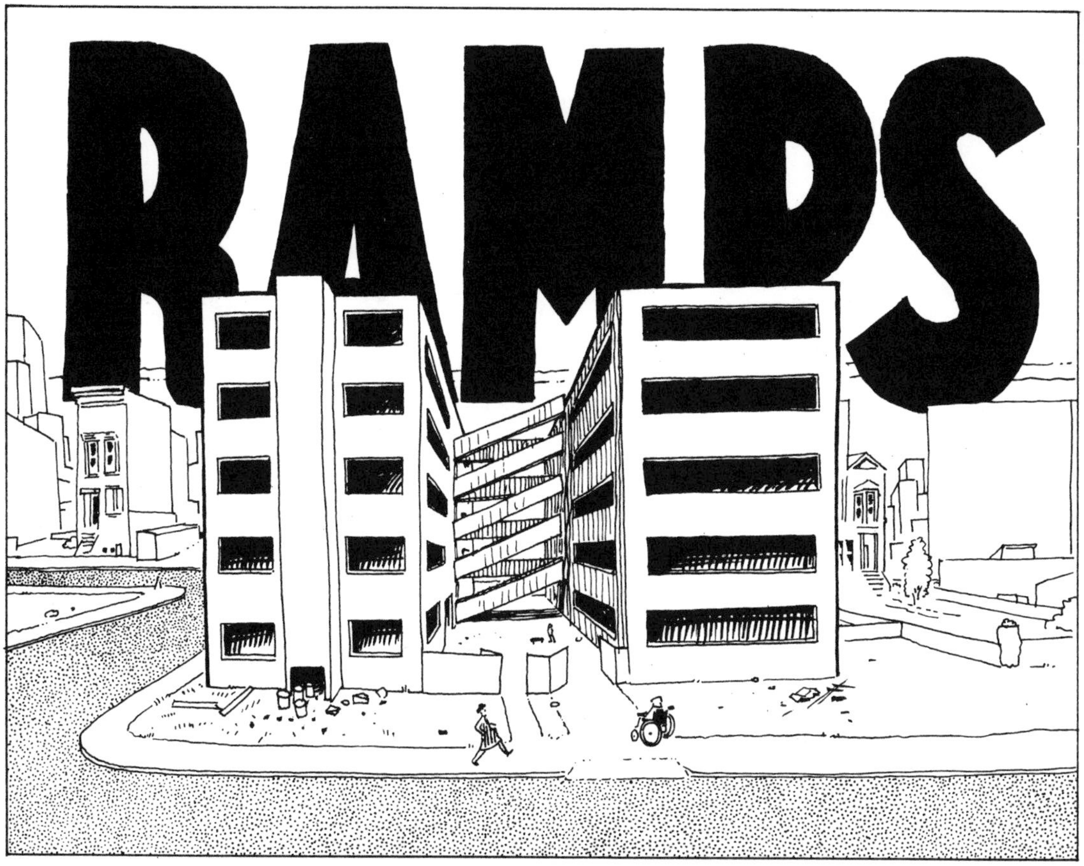
RAMPS

INNER CITY ROMANCE 4

©1977 GUY COLWELL

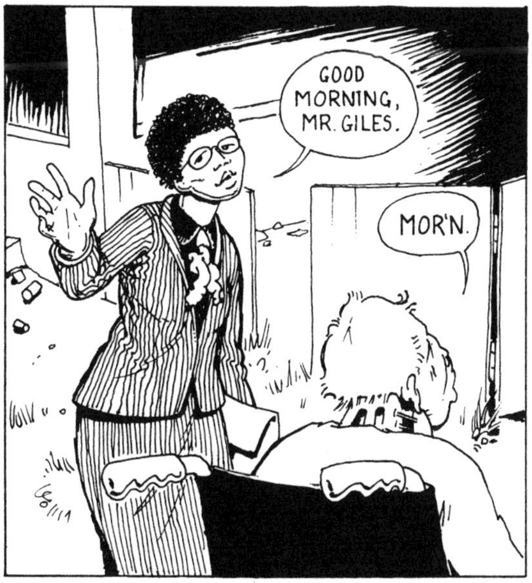
GOOD MORNING, MR. GILES.
MOR'N.

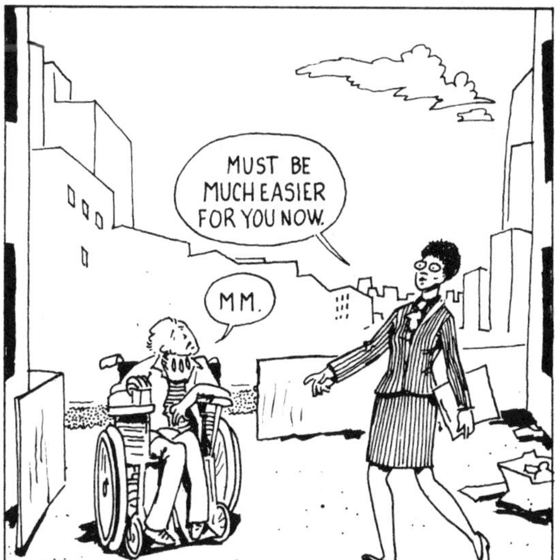
MUST BE MUCH EASIER FOR YOU NOW.
MM.

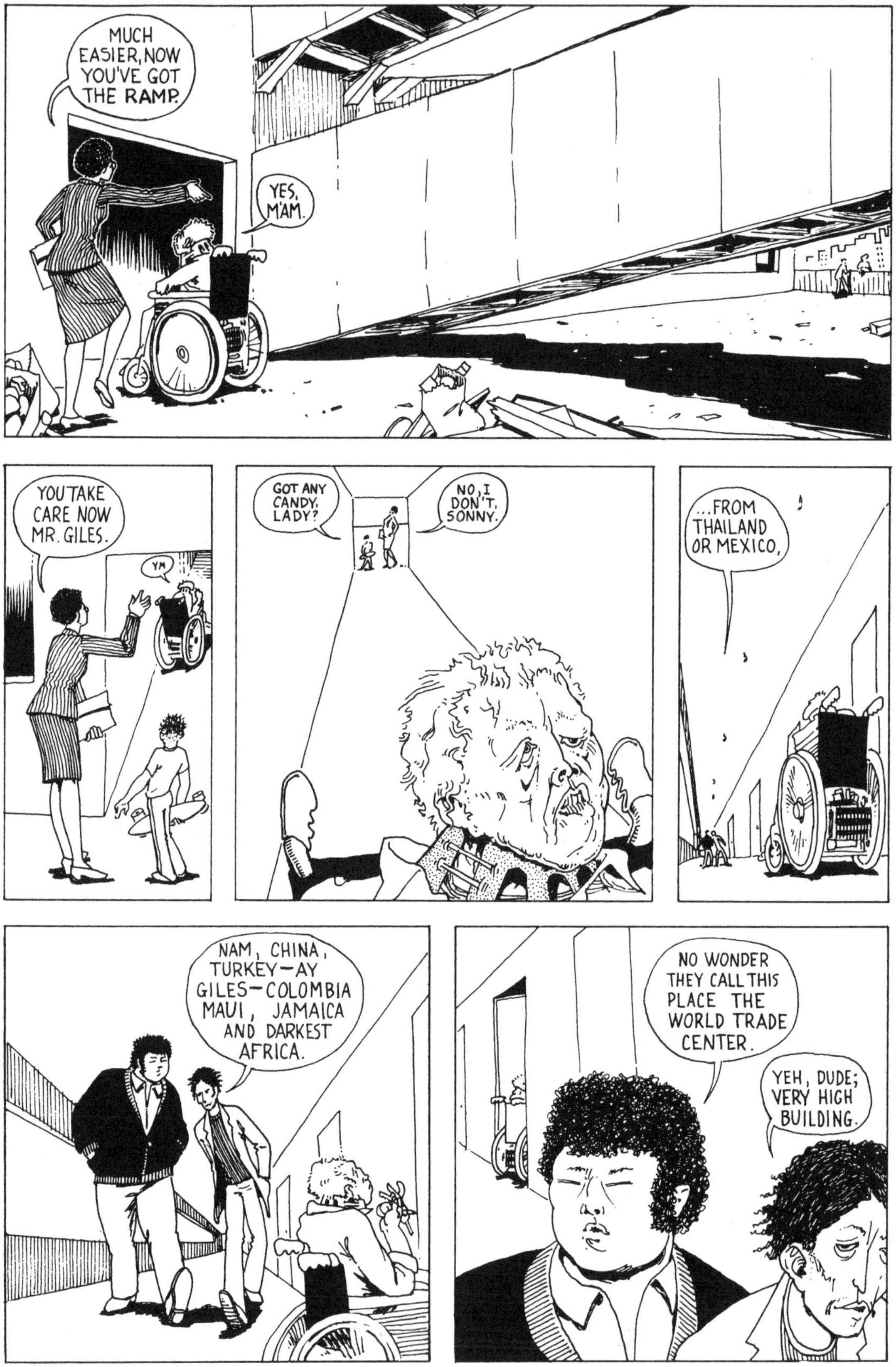
MUCH EASIER, NOW YOU'VE GOT THE RAMP.
YES, M'AM.
YOU TAKE CARE NOW MR. GILES.
YM
GOT ANY CANDY, LADY?
NO, I DON'T, SONNY.
...FROM THAILAND OR MEXICO,
NAM, CHINA, TURKEY—AY GILES—COLOMBIA MAUI, JAMAICA AND DARKEST AFRICA.
NO WONDER THEY CALL THIS PLACE THE WORLD TRADE CENTER.
YEH, DUDE; VERY HIGH BUILDING.

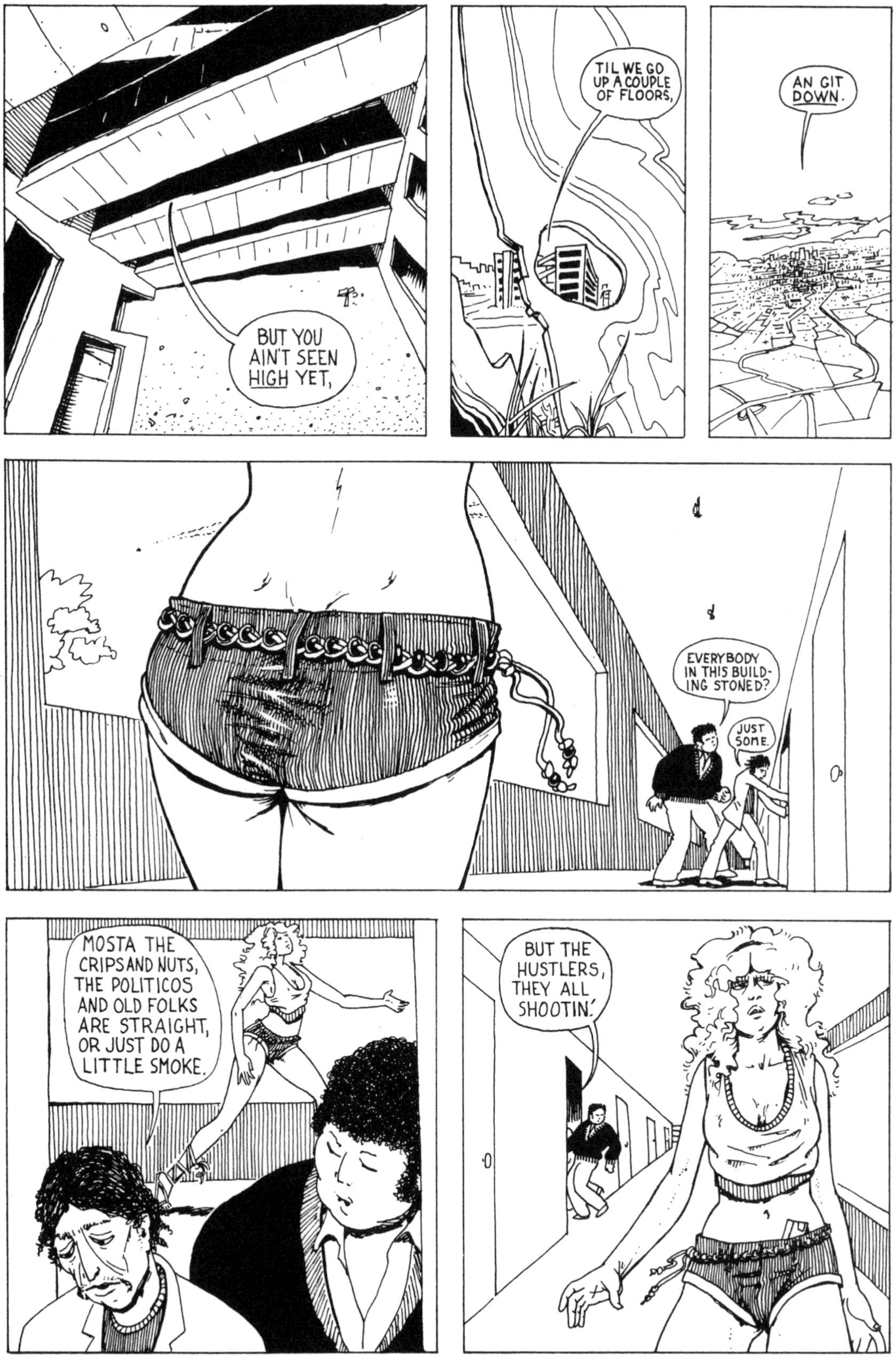
BUT YOU AIN'T SEEN HIGH YET,
TIL WE GO UP A COUPLE OF FLOORS,
AN GIT DOWN.
EVERYBODY IN THIS BUILDING STONED?
JUST SOME.
MOSTA THE CRIPSAND NUTS, THE POLITICOS AND OLD FOLKS ARE STRAIGHT, OR JUST DO A LITTLE SMOKE.
BUT THE HUSTLERS, THEY ALL SHOOTIN'.

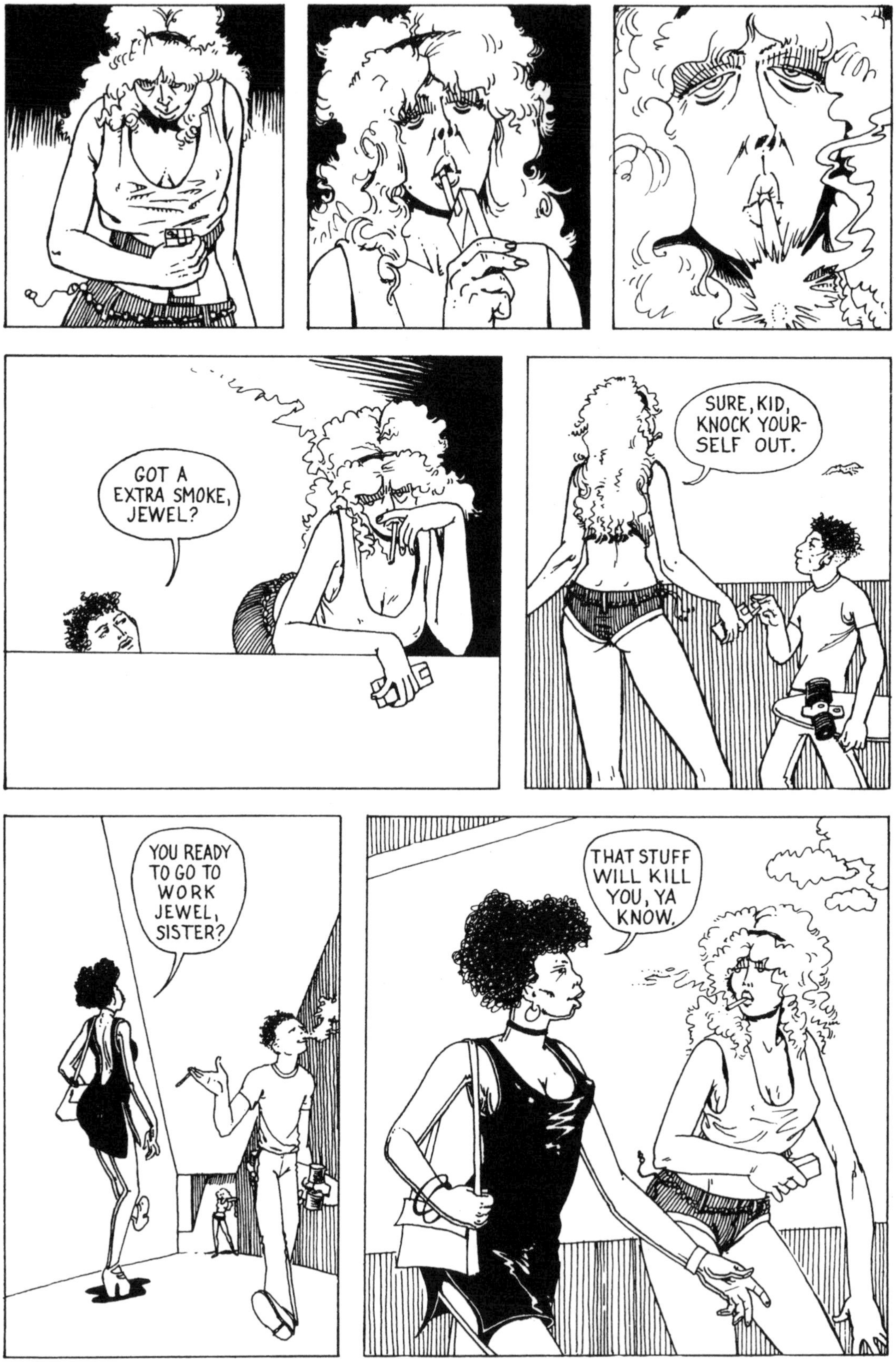
GOT A EXTRA SMOKE, JEWEL?
SURE, KID, KNOCK YOURSELF OUT.
YOU READY TO GO TO WORK JEWEL, SISTER?
THAT STUFF WILL KILL YOU, YA KNOW.

KNOK
KNOK
KNOK

MS. INGRUM.

NOTICE OF
INTENTION

WELL, GOOD MORNING MS. INGRUM. AREN'T WE LOOKING FINE TODAY. AND SUCH A NICE DAY TO GO OUT AND GET SOME EXERCISE AND DO SOME SHOPPING.

GOOD DAY DEAR, I DON'T FEEL SO GOOD. STILL HURTS FROM FALLING.

I'M GLAD WE HAVE THE RAMP NOW. IT WILL BE SO MUCH EASIER TO SHOP.

SO MUCH SAFER THAN THE STAIRS.

BUT THEY TOOK MY CHECK AGAIN, SO I WON'T BE SHOPPING FOR AWHILE I SUPPOSE.

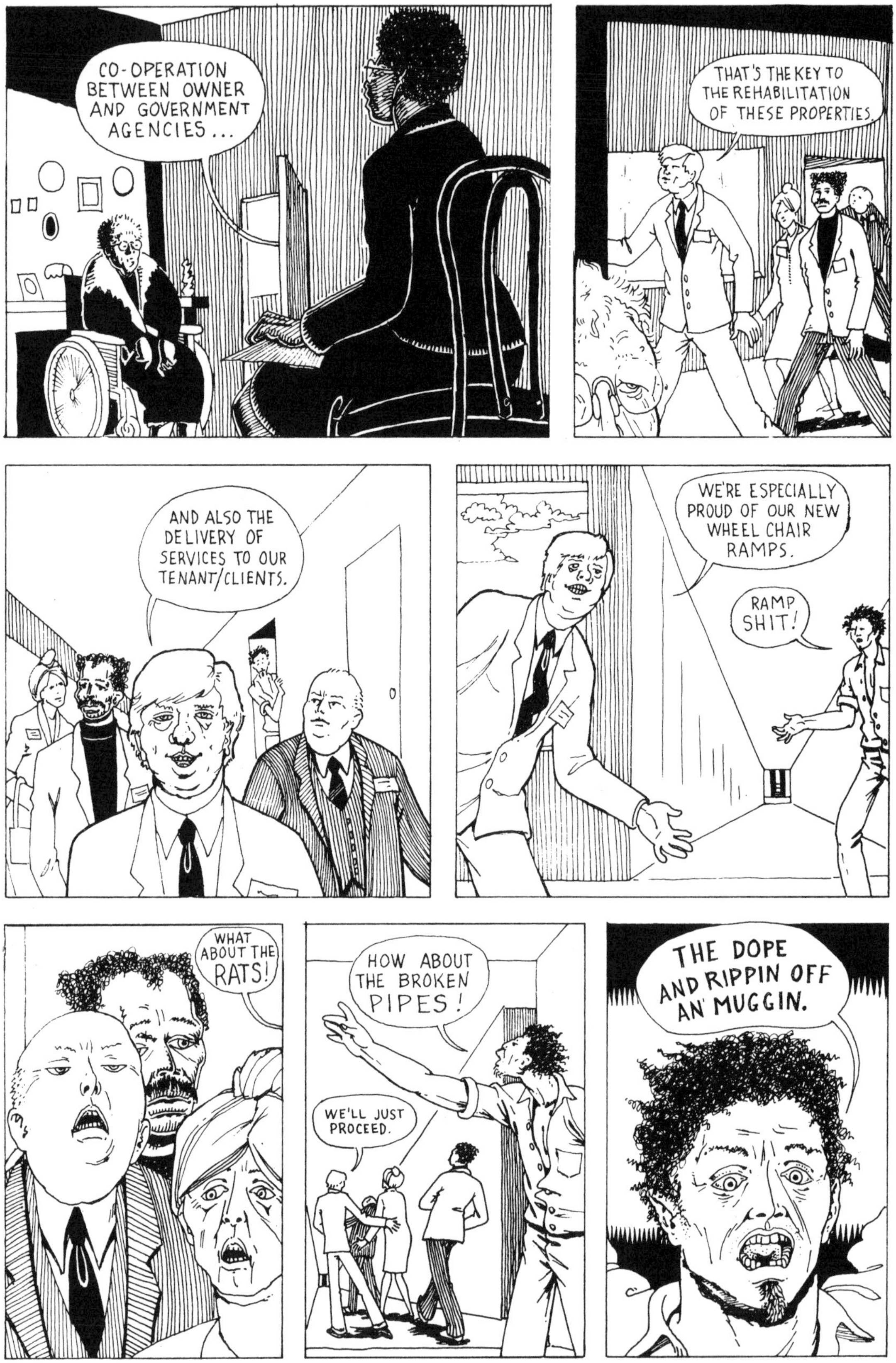

CO-OPERATION BETWEEN OWNER AND GOVERNMENT AGENCIES...
THAT'S THE KEY TO THE REHABILITATION OF THESE PROPERTIES.
AND ALSO THE DELIVERY OF SERVICES TO OUR TENANT/CLIENTS.
WE'RE ESPECIALLY PROUD OF OUR NEW WHEEL CHAIR RAMPS.
RAMP SHIT!
WHAT ABOUT THE RATS!
HOW ABOUT THE BROKEN PIPES!
WE'LL JUST PROCEED.
THE DOPE AND RIPPIN OFF AN' MUGGIN.

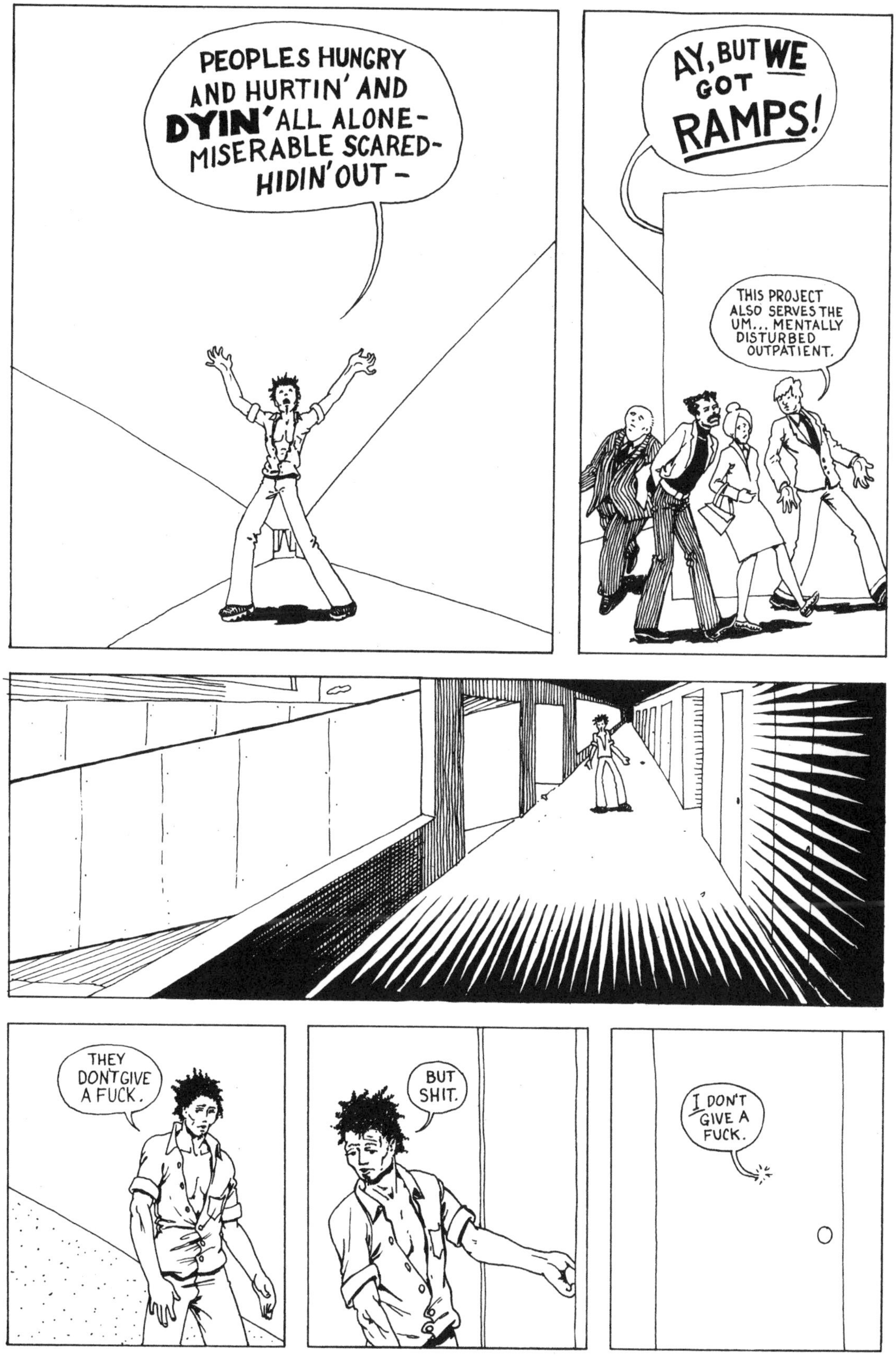
PEOPLES HUNGRY AND HURTIN' AND DYIN' ALL ALONE- MISERABLE SCARED- HIDIN' OUT -
AY, BUT WE GOT RAMPS!
THIS PROJECT ALSO SERVES THE UM... MENTALLY DISTURBED OUTPATIENT.
THEY DON'T GIVE A FUCK.
BUT SHIT.
I DON'T GIVE A FUCK.

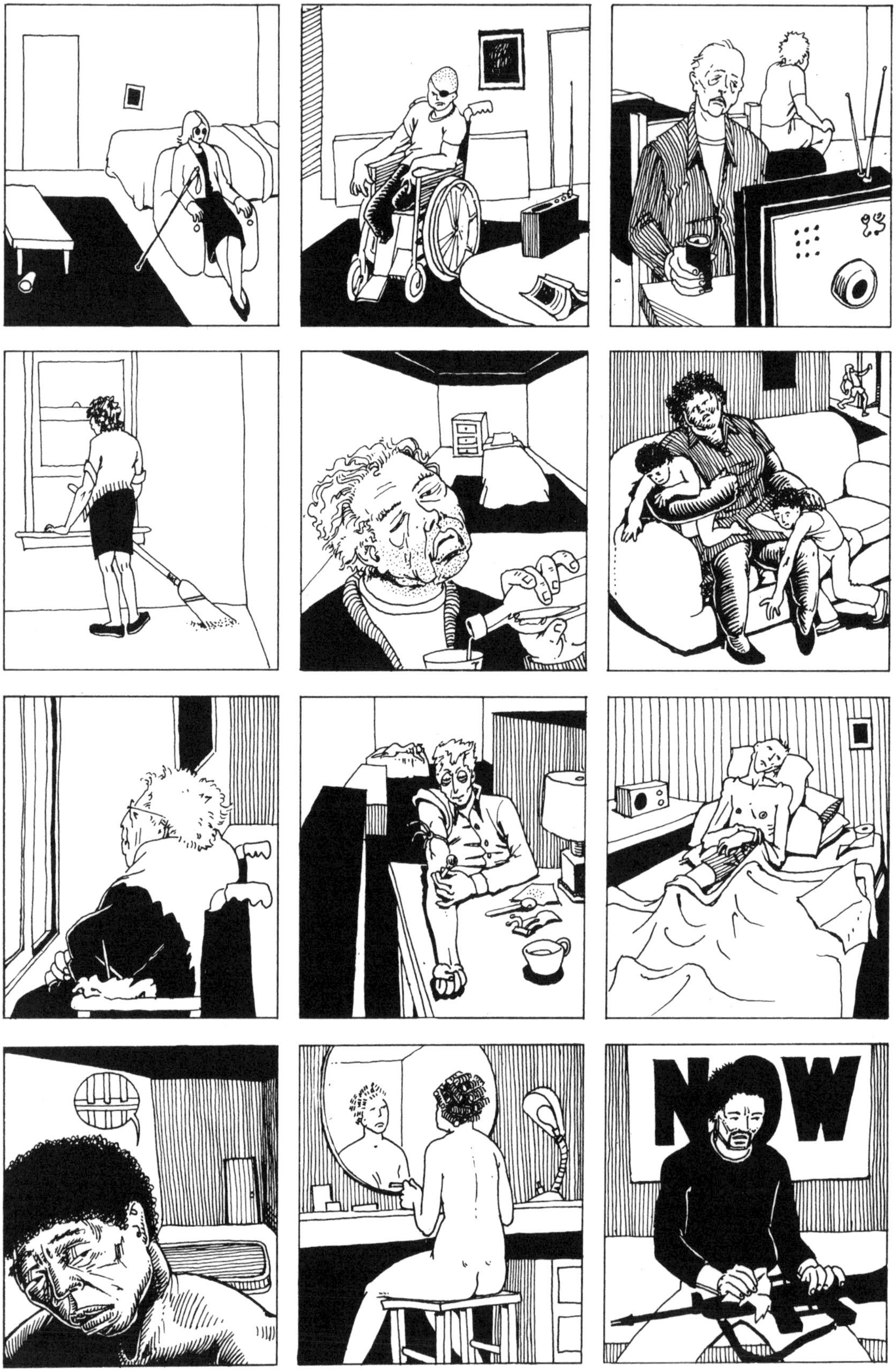
NOW

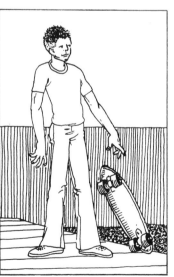

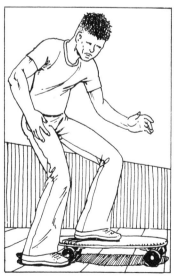

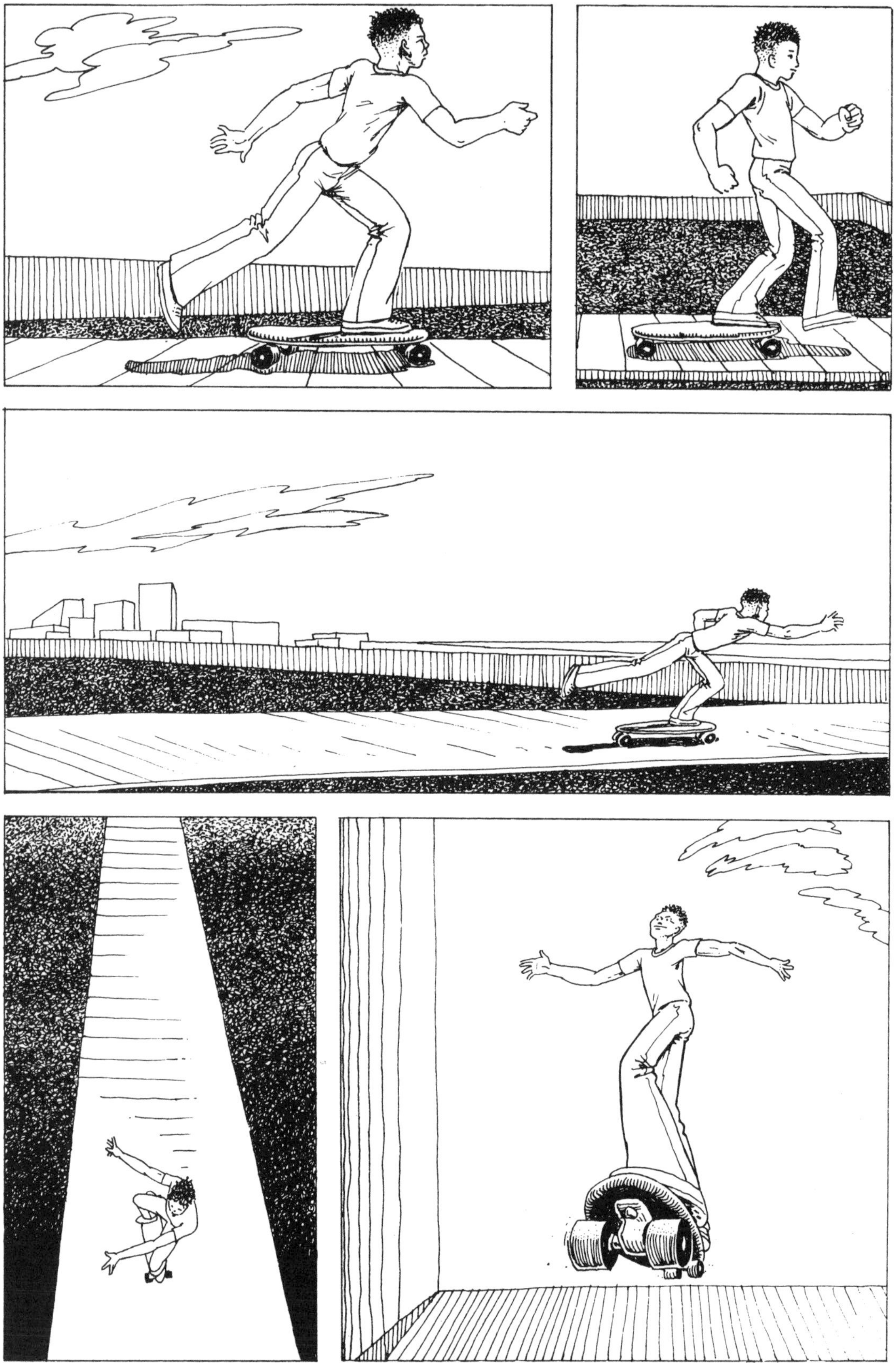

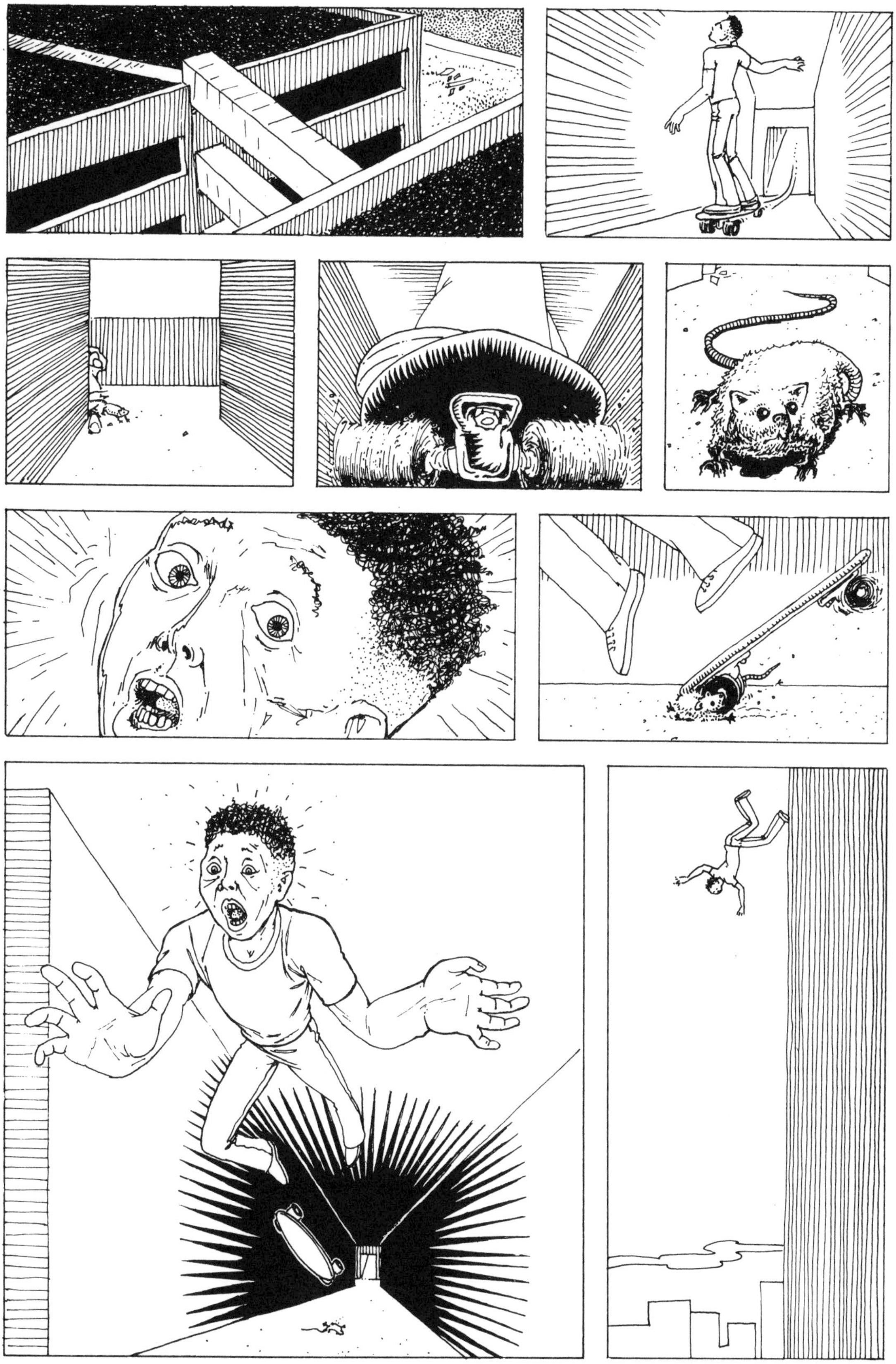

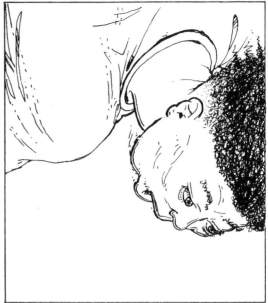
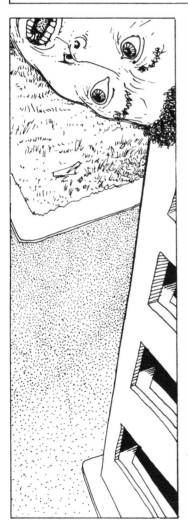
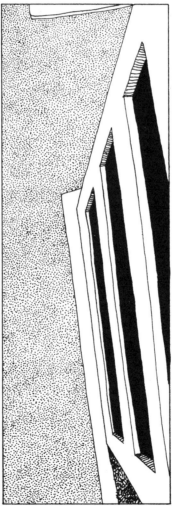
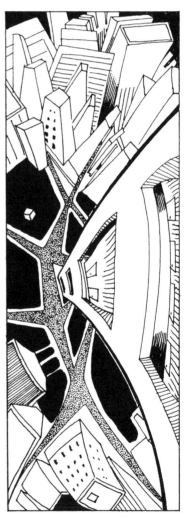

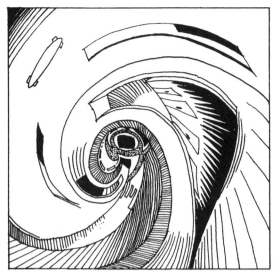
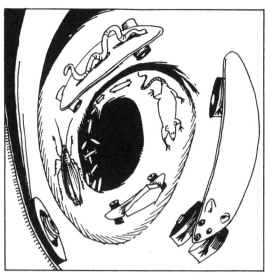
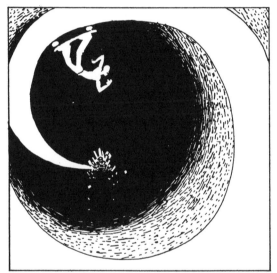

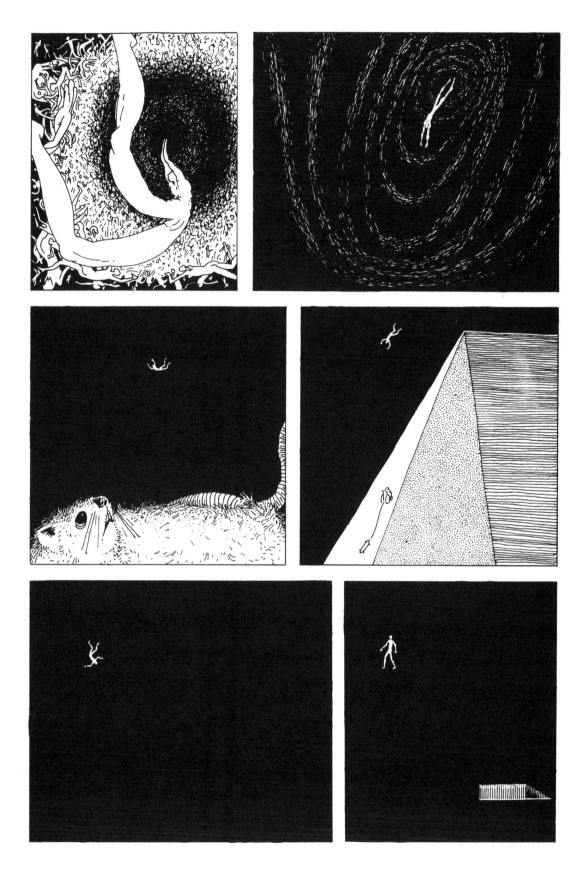

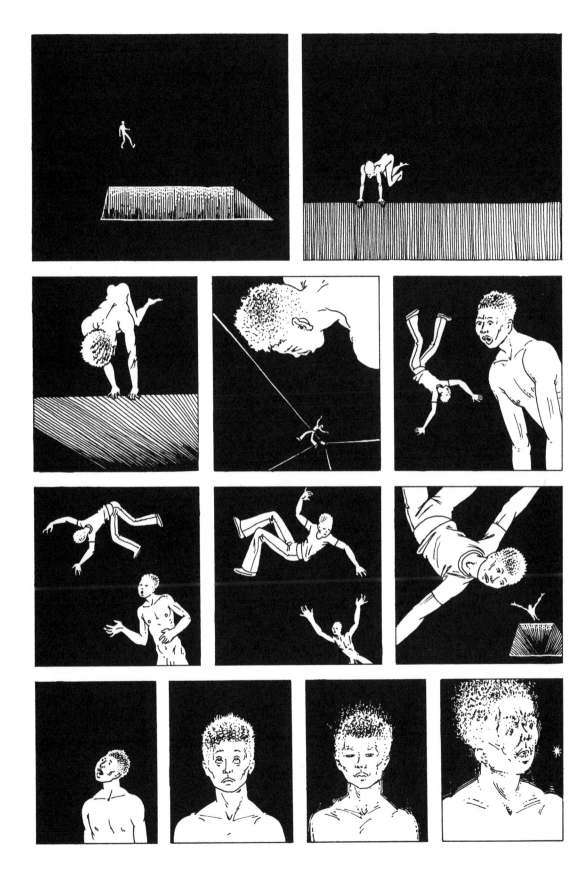

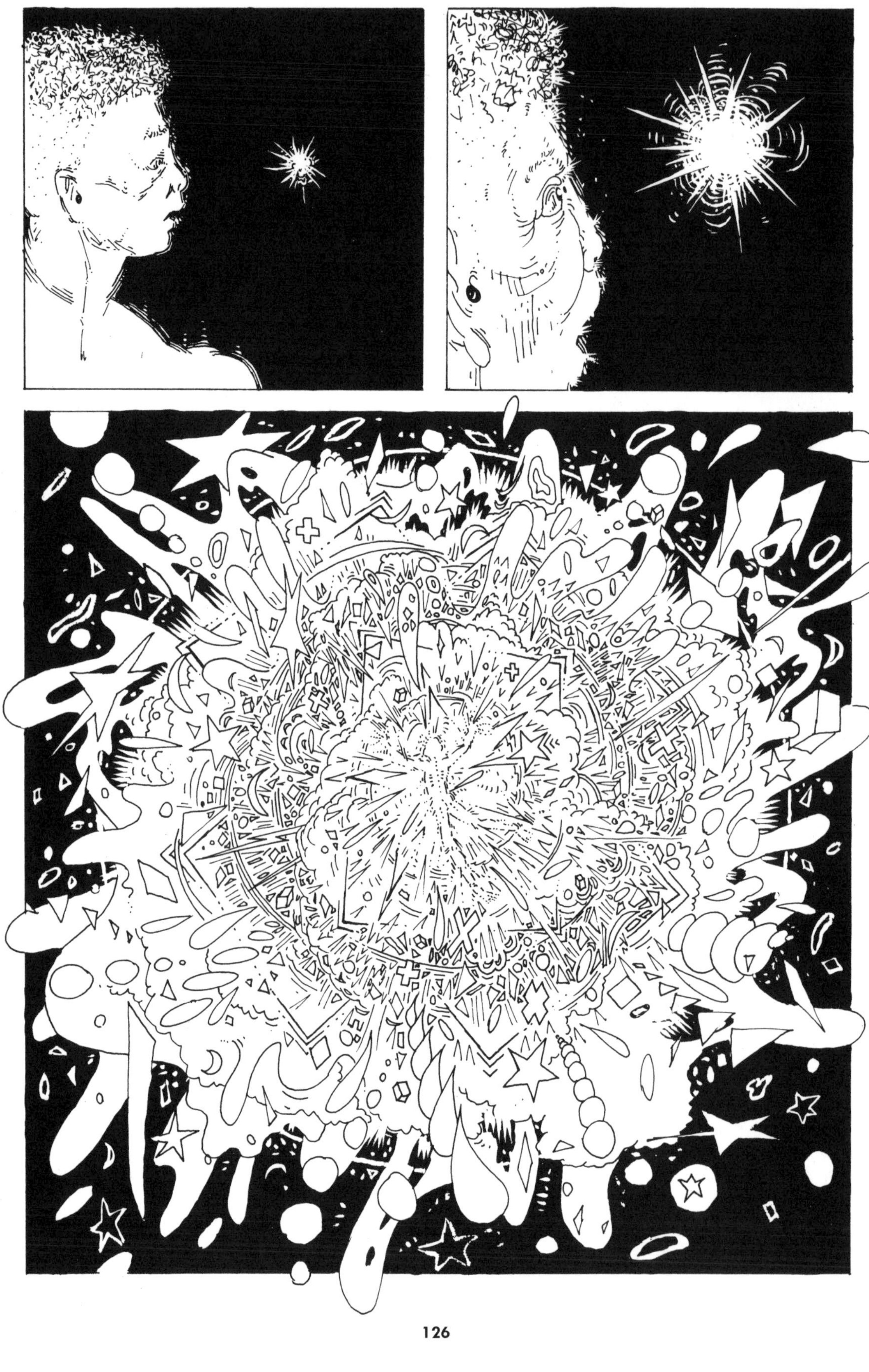

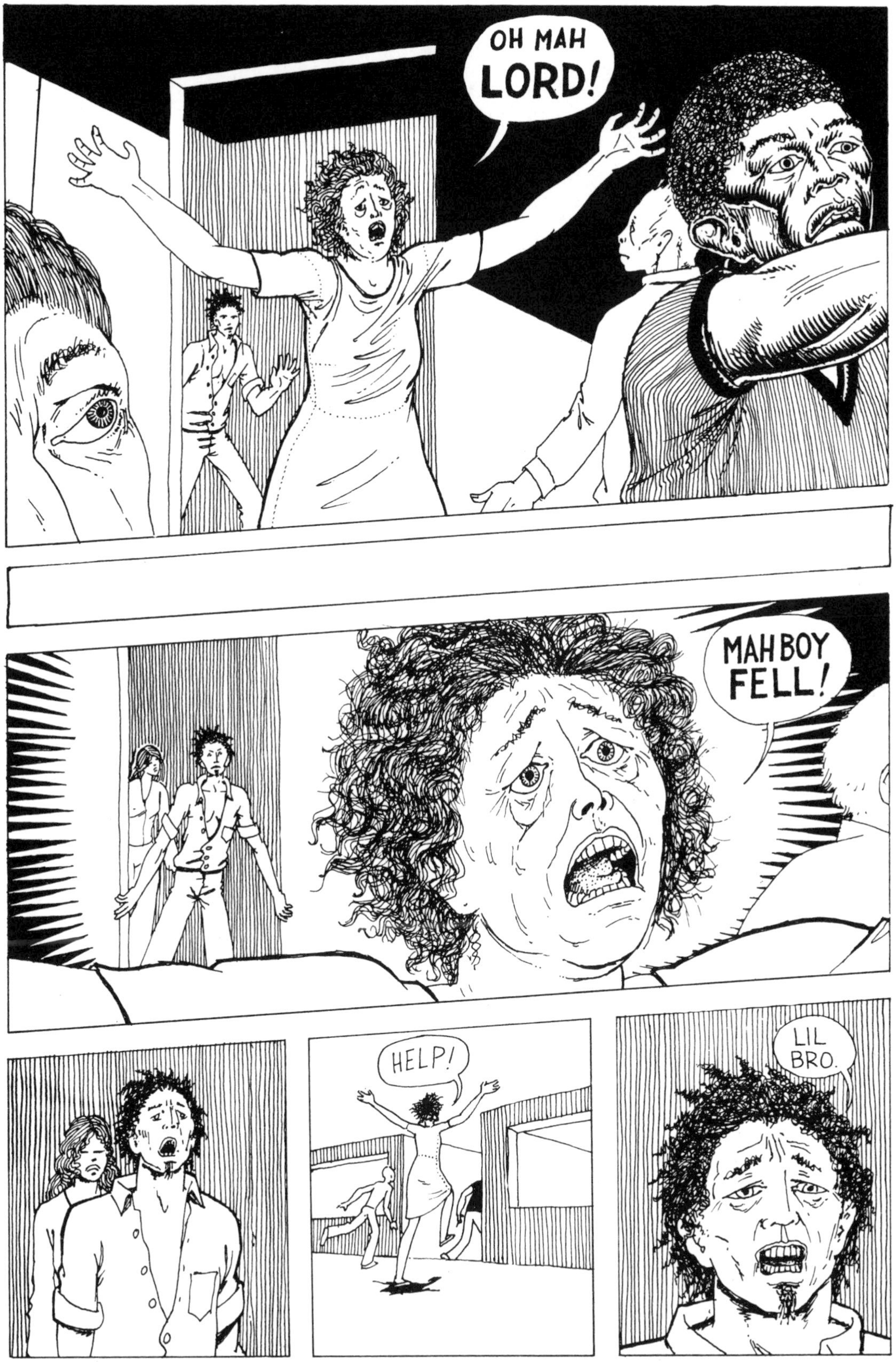
OH MAH LORD!
MAH BOY FELL!
HELP!
LIL BRO.

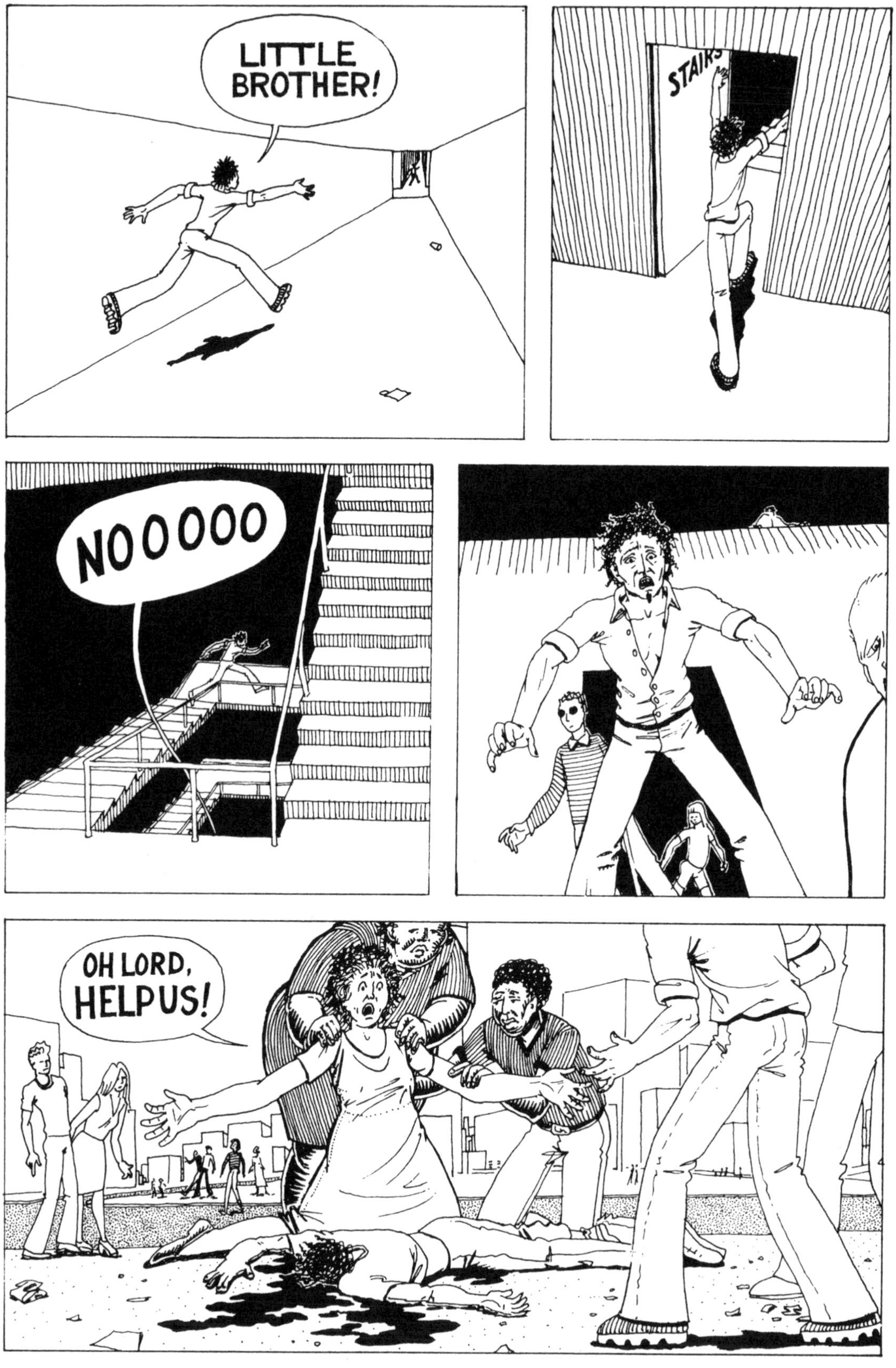
LITTLE BROTHER!
STAIRS
NOOOOO
OH LORD, HELPUS!

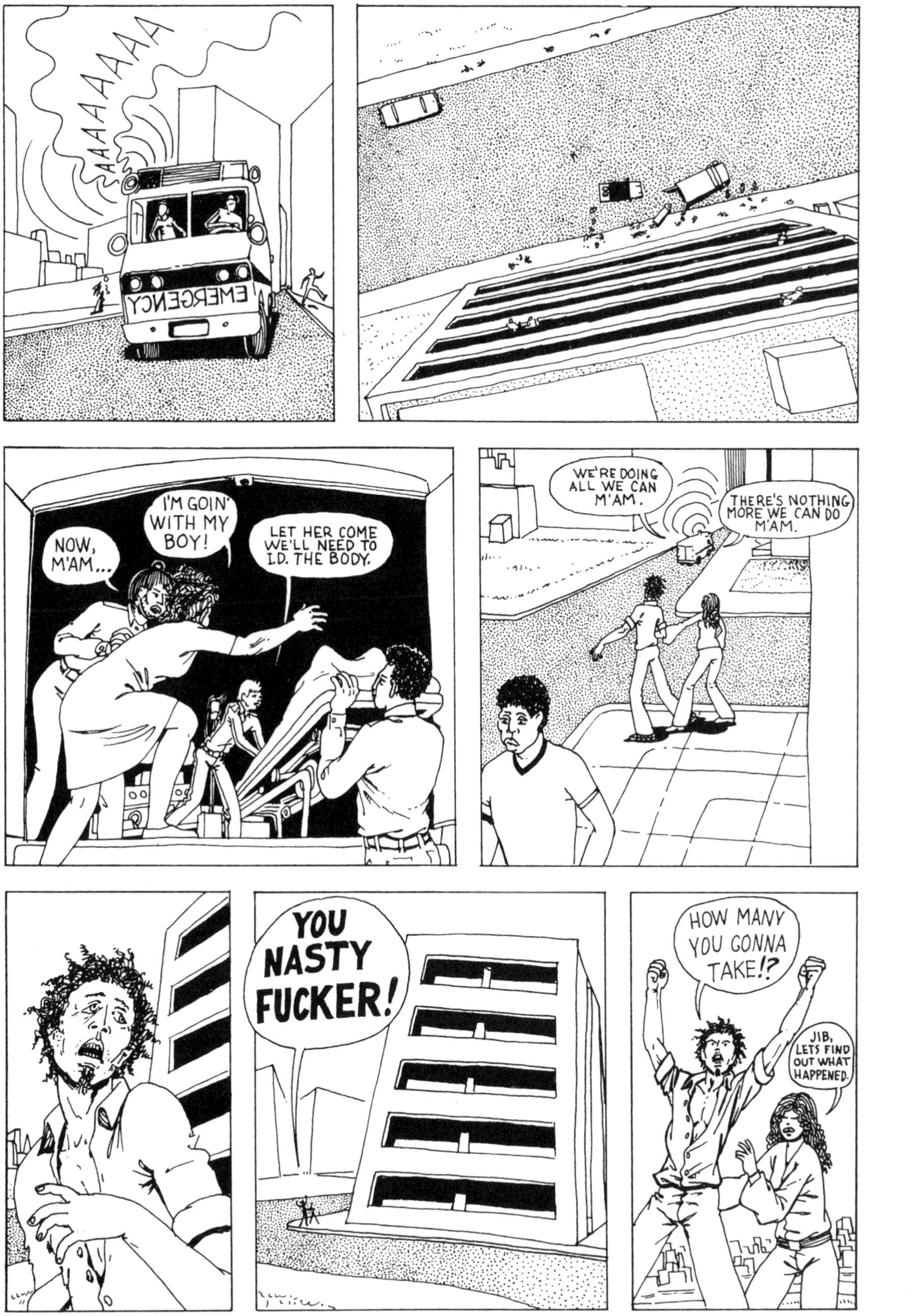
AAAAAAAAA
EMERGENCY
NOW, M'AM...
I'M GOIN' WITH MY BOY!
LET HER COME WE'LL NEED TO I.D. THE BODY.
WE'RE DOING ALL WE CAN M'AM.
THERE'S NOTHING MORE WE CAN DO M'AM.
YOU NASTY FUCKER!
HOW MANY YOU GONNA TAKE!?
JIB, LETS FIND OUT WHAT HAPPENED.

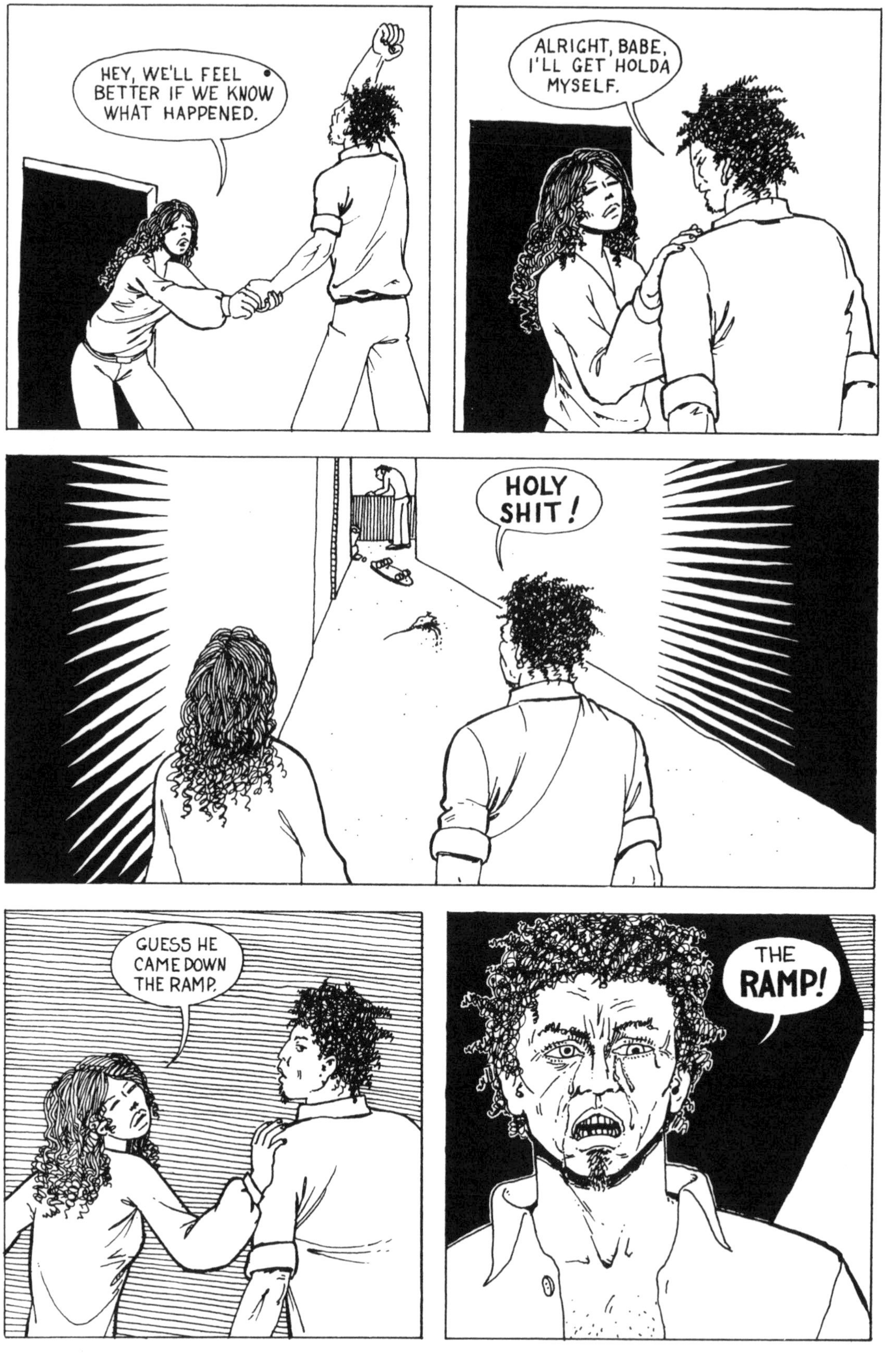
HEY, WE'LL FEEL BETTER IF WE KNOW WHAT HAPPENED.
ALRIGHT, BABE, I'LL GET HOLDA MYSELF.
HOLY SHIT!
GUESS HE CAME DOWN THE RAMP.
THE RAMP!

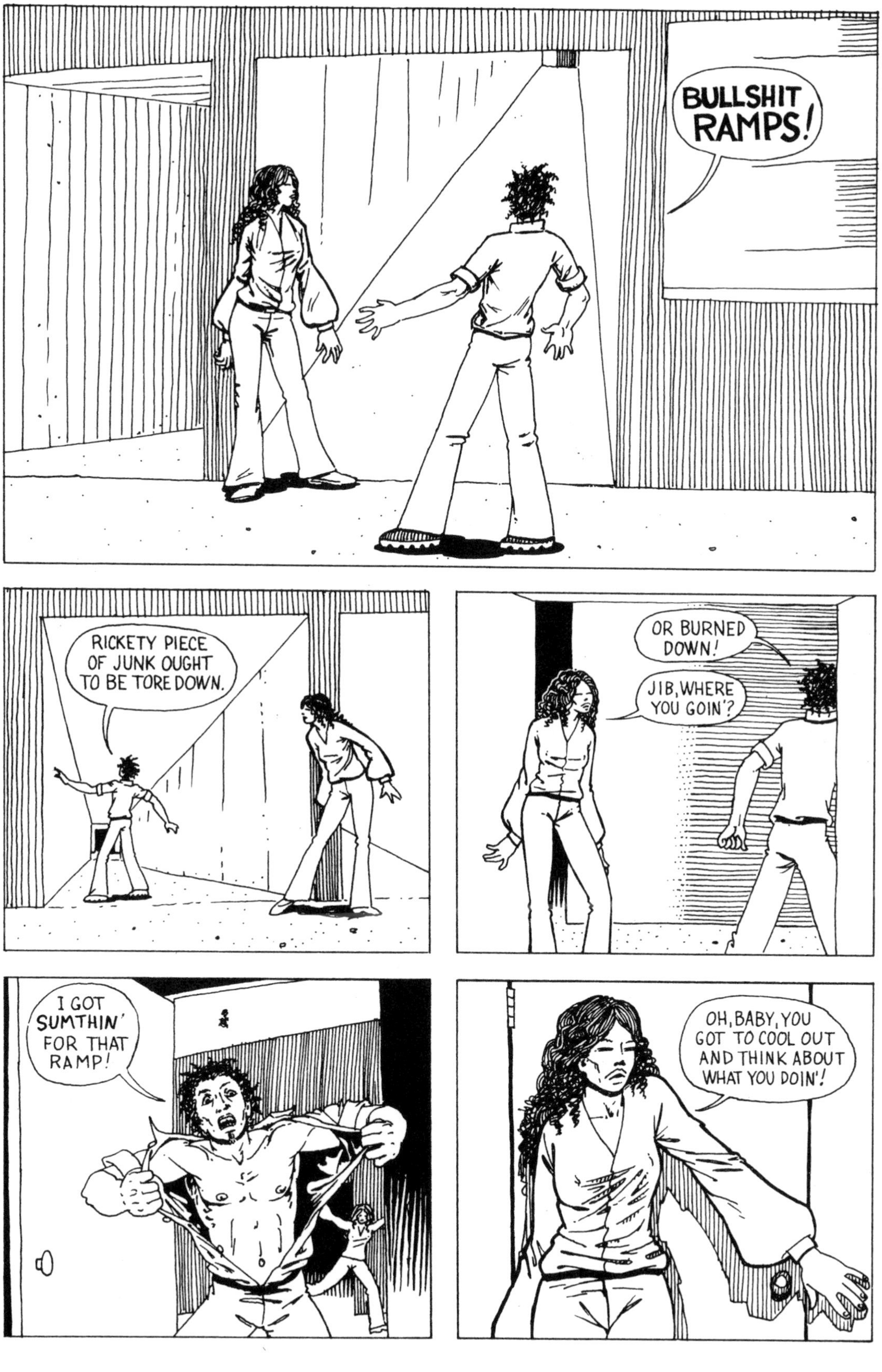
BULLSHIT RAMPS!
RICKETY PIECE OF JUNK OUGHT TO BE TORE DOWN.
OR BURNED DOWN!
JIB, WHERE YOU GOIN'?
I GOT SUMTHIN' FOR THAT RAMP!
OH, BABY, YOU GOT TO COOL OUT AND THINK ABOUT WHAT YOU DOIN'!

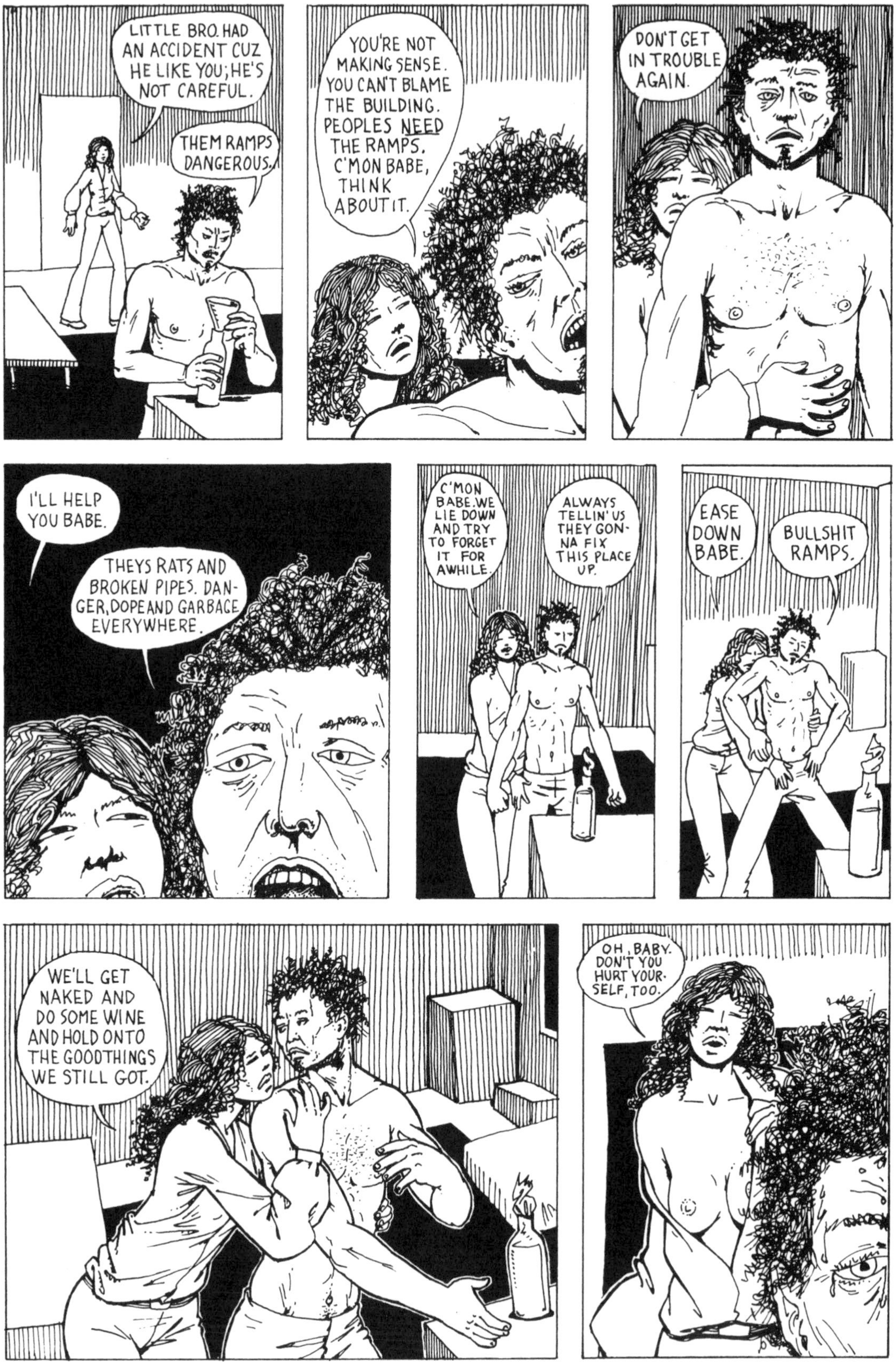

LITTLE BRO. HAD AN ACCIDENT CUZ HE LIKE YOU; HE'S NOT CAREFUL.
THEM RAMPS DANGEROUS.
YOU'RE NOT MAKING SENSE. YOU CAN'T BLAME THE BUILDING. PEOPLES NEED THE RAMPS. C'MON BABE, THINK ABOUT IT.
DON'T GET IN TROUBLE AGAIN.
I'LL HELP YOU BABE.
THEYS RATS AND BROKEN PIPES. DANGER, DOPE AND GARBAGE EVERYWHERE.
C'MON BABE. WE LIE DOWN AND TRY TO FORGET IT FOR AWHILE.
ALWAYS TELLIN' US THEY GONNA FIX THIS PLACE UP.
EASE DOWN BABE.
BULLSHIT RAMPS.
WE'LL GET NAKED AND DO SOME WINE AND HOLD ONTO THE GOODTHINGS WE STILL GOT.
OH, BABY. DON'T YOU HURT YOURSELF, TOO.

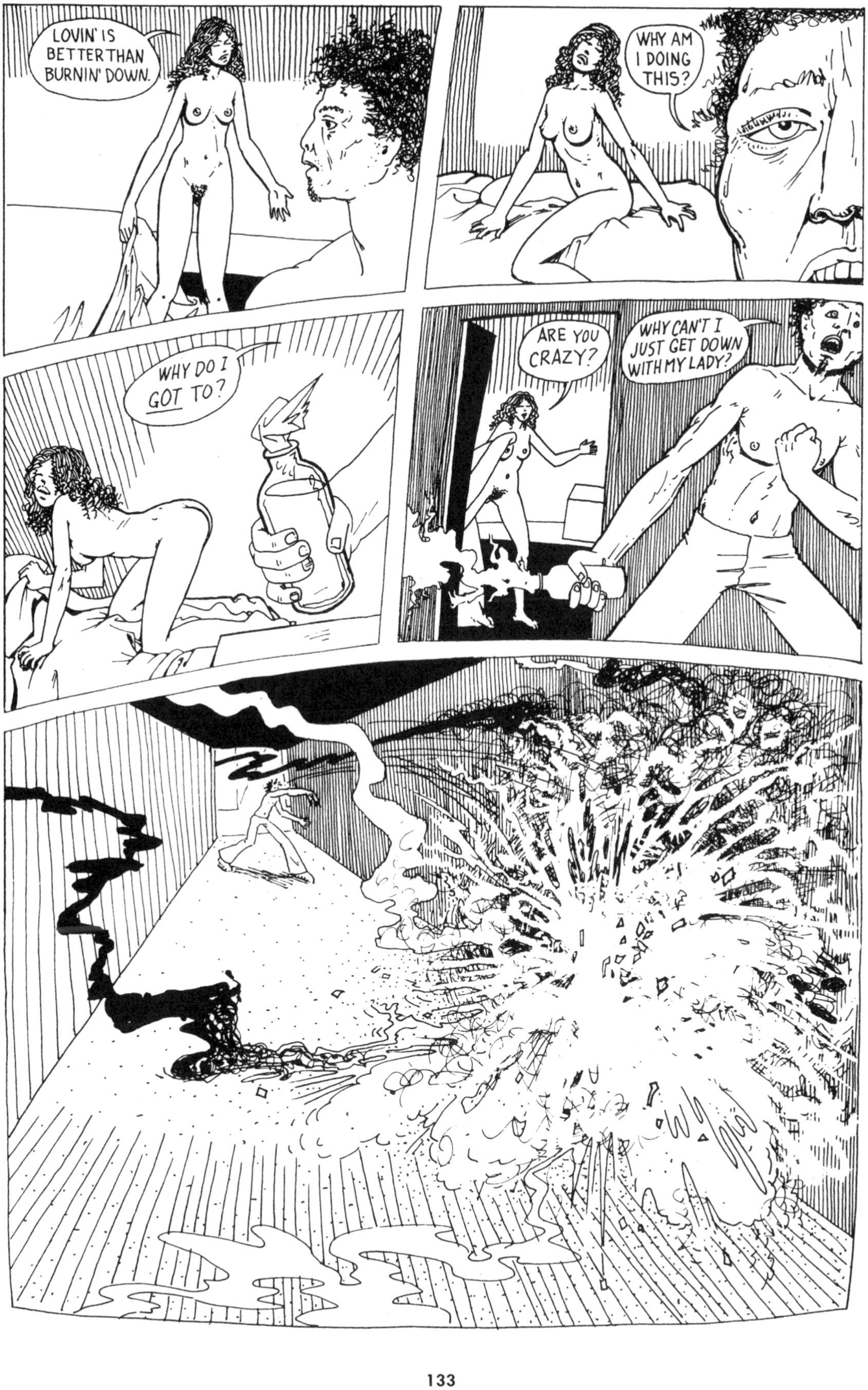
LOVIN' IS BETTER THAN BURNIN' DOWN.
WHY AM I DOING THIS?
WHY DO I GOT TO?
ARE YOU CRAZY?
WHY CAN'T I JUST GET DOWN WITH MY LADY?

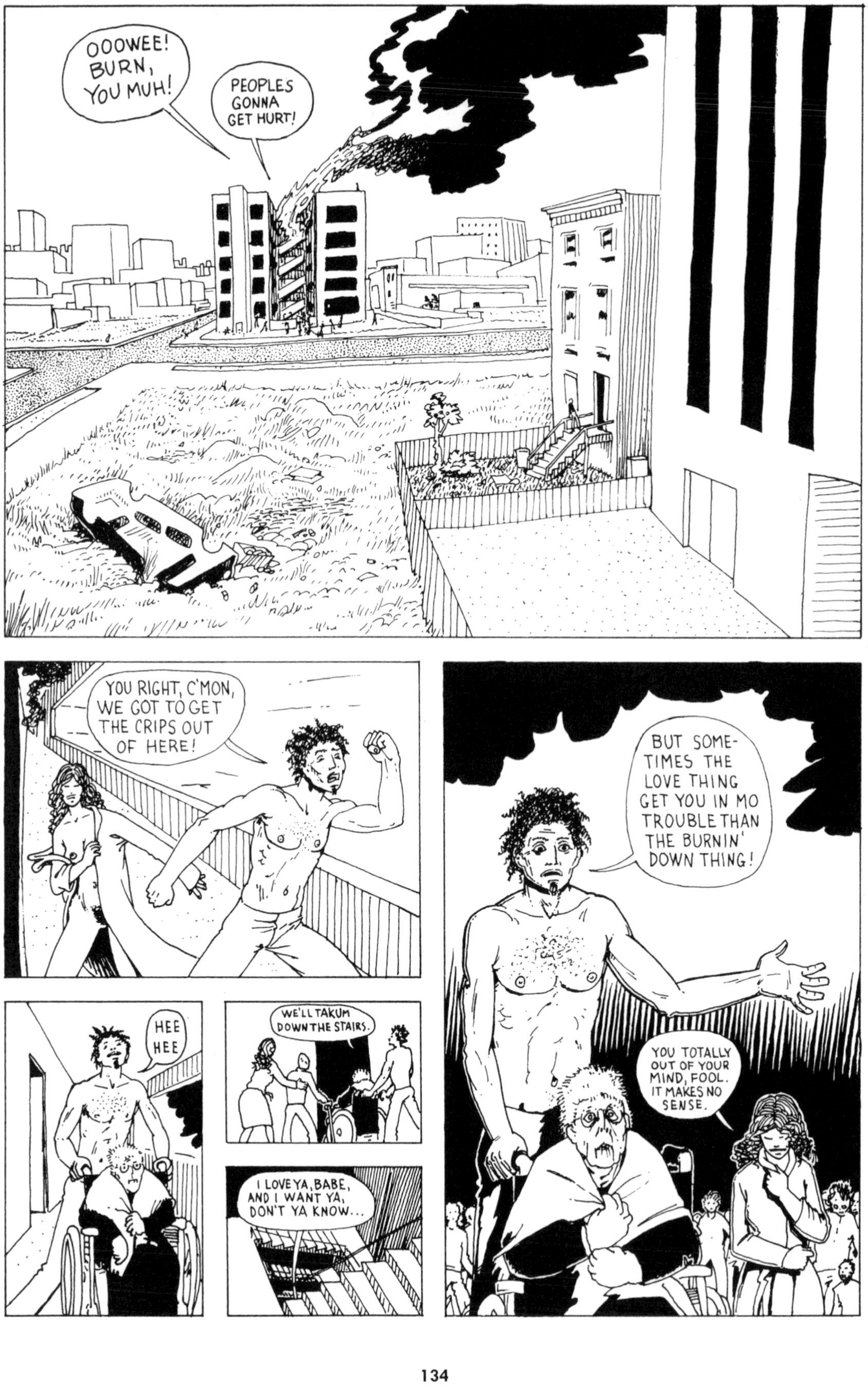
OOOWEE! BURN, YOU MUH!
PEOPLES GONNA GET HURT!
YOU RIGHT, C'MON, WE GOT TO GET THE CRIPS OUT OF HERE!
HEE HEE
WE'LL TAKUM DOWN THE STAIRS.
I LOVE YA, BABE, AND I WANT YA, DON'T YA KNOW...
BUT SOME-TIMES THE LOVE THING GET YOU IN MO TROUBLE THAN THE BURNIN' DOWN THING!
YOU TOTALLY OUT OF YOUR MIND, FOOL. IT MAKES NO SENSE.

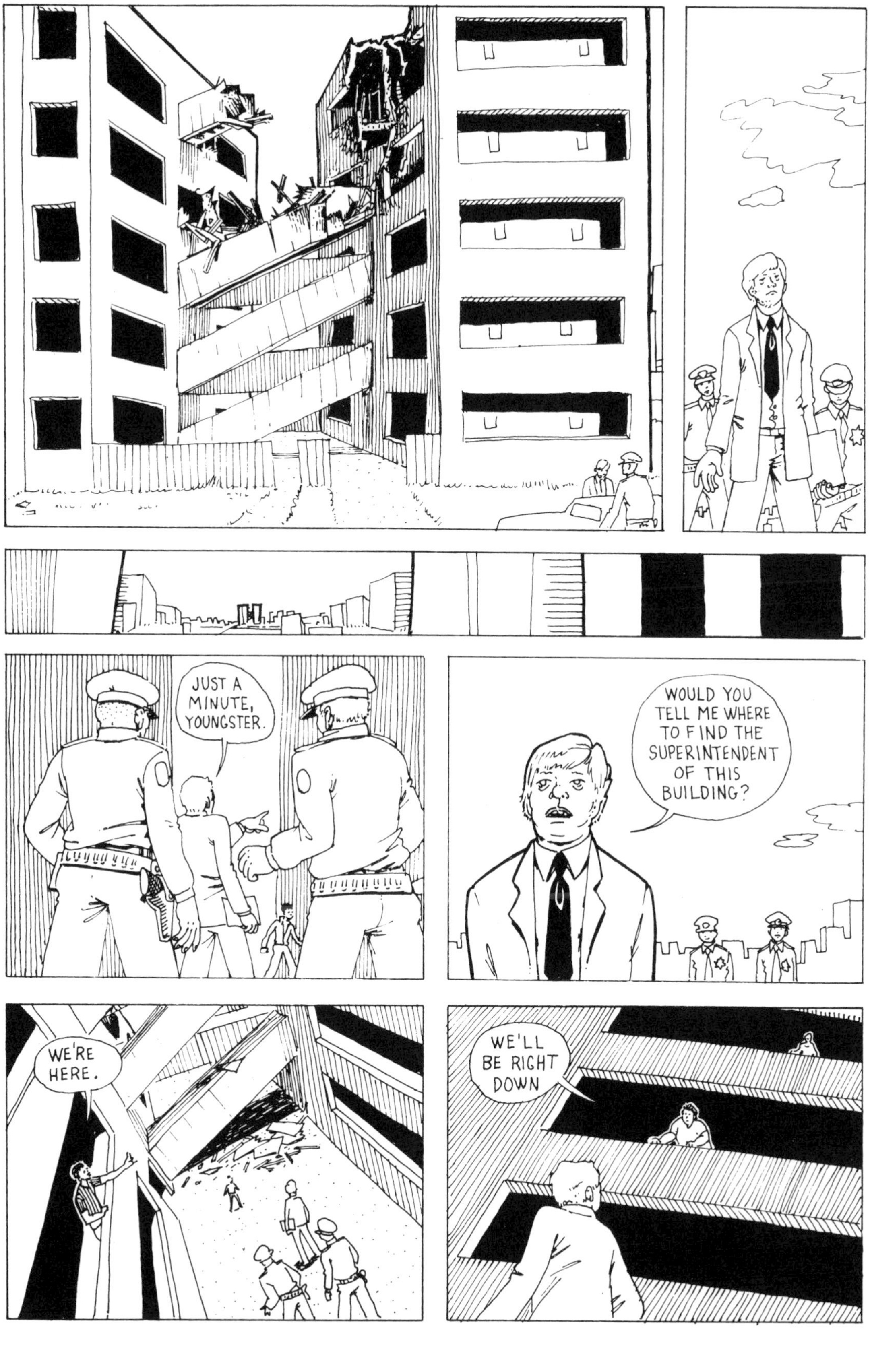
JUST A MINUTE, YOUNGSTER.
WOULD YOU TELL ME WHERE TO FIND THE SUPERINTENDENT OF THIS BUILDING?
WE'RE HERE.
WE'LL BE RIGHT DOWN

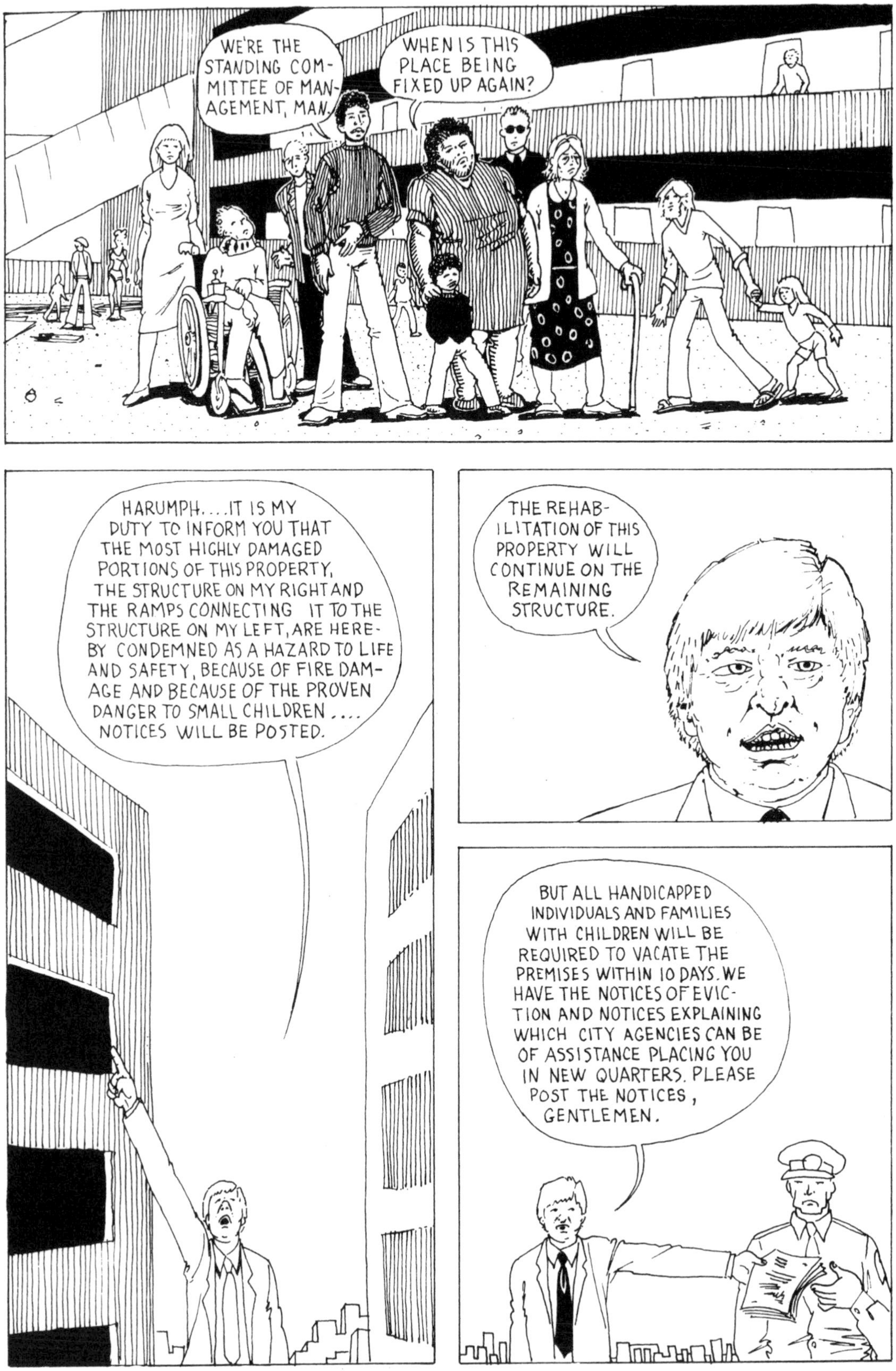
WE'RE THE STANDING COMMITTEE OF MANAGEMENT, MAN.
WHEN IS THIS PLACE BEING FIXED UP AGAIN?
HARUMPH....IT IS MY DUTY TO INFORM YOU THAT THE MOST HIGHLY DAMAGED PORTIONS OF THIS PROPERTY, THE STRUCTURE ON MY RIGHT AND THE RAMPS CONNECTING IT TO THE STRUCTURE ON MY LEFT, ARE HEREBY CONDEMNED AS A HAZARD TO LIFE AND SAFETY, BECAUSE OF FIRE DAMAGE AND BECAUSE OF THE PROVEN DANGER TO SMALL CHILDREN.... NOTICES WILL BE POSTED.
THE REHABILITATION OF THIS PROPERTY WILL CONTINUE ON THE REMAINING STRUCTURE.
BUT ALL HANDICAPPED INDIVIDUALS AND FAMILIES WITH CHILDREN WILL BE REQUIRED TO VACATE THE PREMISES WITHIN 10 DAYS. WE HAVE THE NOTICES OF EVICTION AND NOTICES EXPLAINING WHICH CITY AGENCIES CAN BE OF ASSISTANCE PLACING YOU IN NEW QUARTERS. PLEASE POST THE NOTICES, GENTLEMEN.

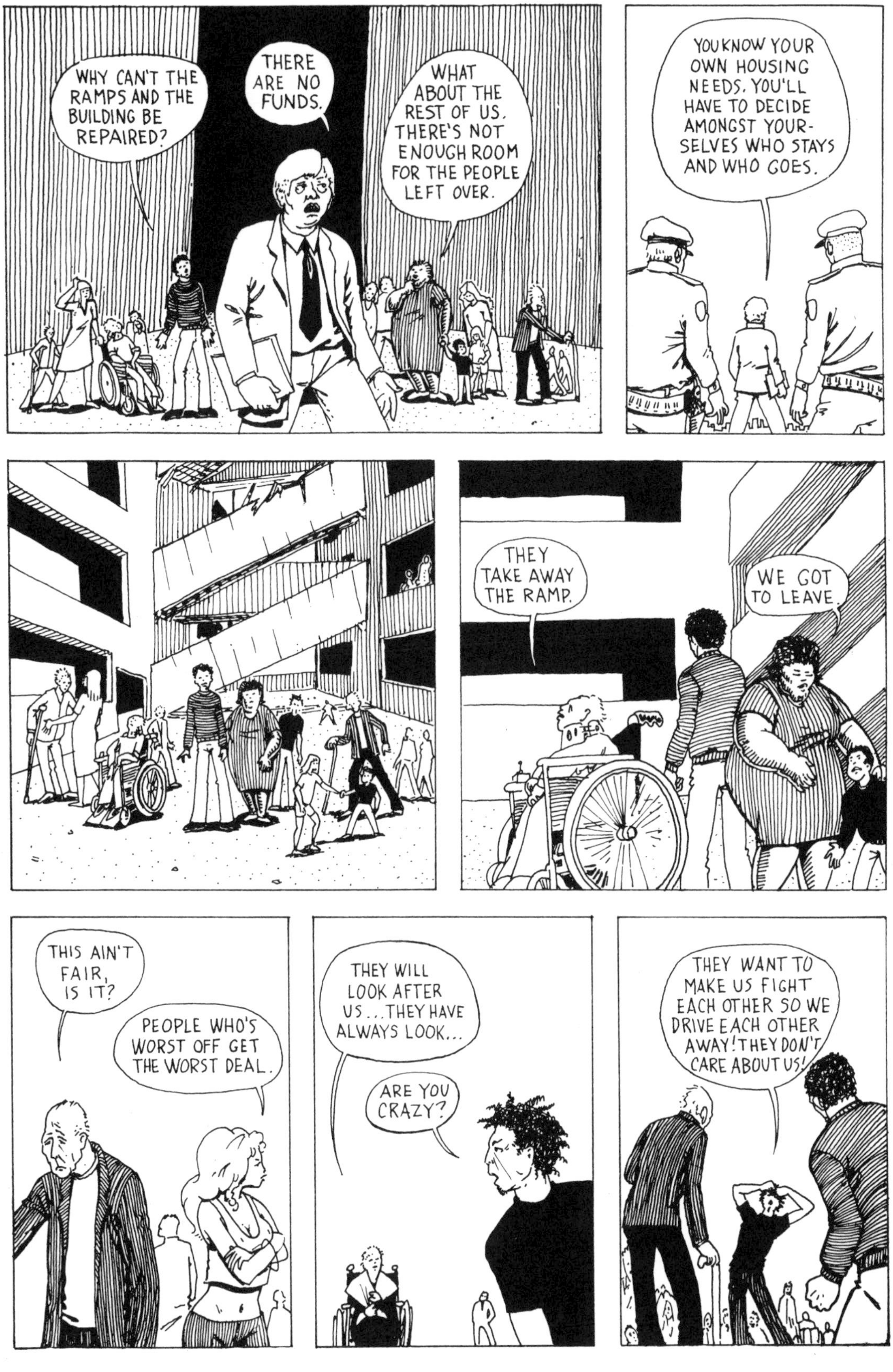
WHY CAN'T THE RAMPS AND THE BUILDING BE REPAIRED?
THERE ARE NO FUNDS.
WHAT ABOUT THE REST OF US. THERE'S NOT ENOUGH ROOM FOR THE PEOPLE LEFT OVER.
YOU KNOW YOUR OWN HOUSING NEEDS. YOU'LL HAVE TO DECIDE AMONGST YOURSELVES WHO STAYS AND WHO GOES.
THEY TAKE AWAY THE RAMP.
WE GOT TO LEAVE.
THIS AIN'T FAIR, IS IT?
PEOPLE WHO'S WORST OFF GET THE WORST DEAL.
THEY WILL LOOK AFTER US... THEY HAVE ALWAYS LOOK...
ARE YOU CRAZY?
THEY WANT TO MAKE US FIGHT EACH OTHER SO WE DRIVE EACH OTHER AWAY! THEY DON'T CARE ABOUT US!

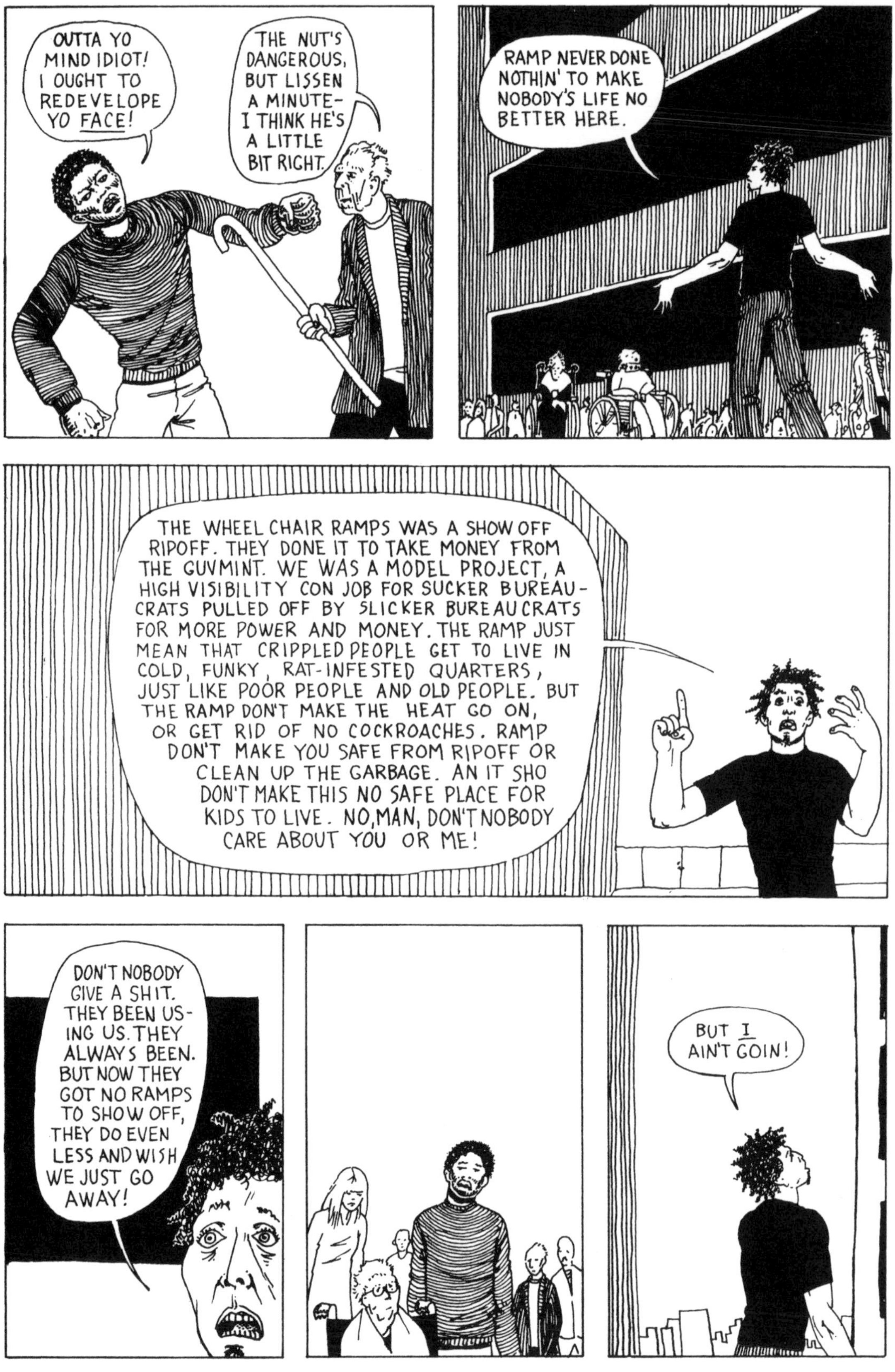
OUTTA YO MIND IDIOT! I OUGHT TO REDEVELOPE YO FACE!
THE NUT'S DANGEROUS, BUT LISSEN A MINUTE- I THINK HE'S A LITTLE BIT RIGHT.
RAMP NEVER DONE NOTHIN' TO MAKE NOBODY'S LIFE NO BETTER HERE.
THE WHEEL CHAIR RAMPS WAS A SHOW OFF RIPOFF. THEY DONE IT TO TAKE MONEY FROM THE GUVMINT. WE WAS A MODEL PROJECT, A HIGH VISIBILITY CON JOB FOR SUCKER BUREAU-CRATS PULLED OFF BY SLICKER BUREAUCRATS FOR MORE POWER AND MONEY. THE RAMP JUST MEAN THAT CRIPPLED PEOPLE GET TO LIVE IN COLD, FUNKY, RAT-INFESTED QUARTERS, JUST LIKE POOR PEOPLE AND OLD PEOPLE. BUT THE RAMP DON'T MAKE THE HEAT GO ON, OR GET RID OF NO COCKROACHES. RAMP DON'T MAKE YOU SAFE FROM RIPOFF OR CLEAN UP THE GARBAGE. AN IT SHO DON'T MAKE THIS NO SAFE PLACE FOR KIDS TO LIVE. NO, MAN, DON'T NOBODY CARE ABOUT YOU OR ME!
DON'T NOBODY GIVE A SHIT. THEY BEEN US-ING US. THEY ALWAYS BEEN. BUT NOW THEY GOT NO RAMPS TO SHOW OFF, THEY DO EVEN LESS AND WISH WE JUST GO AWAY!
BUT I AIN'T GOIN!

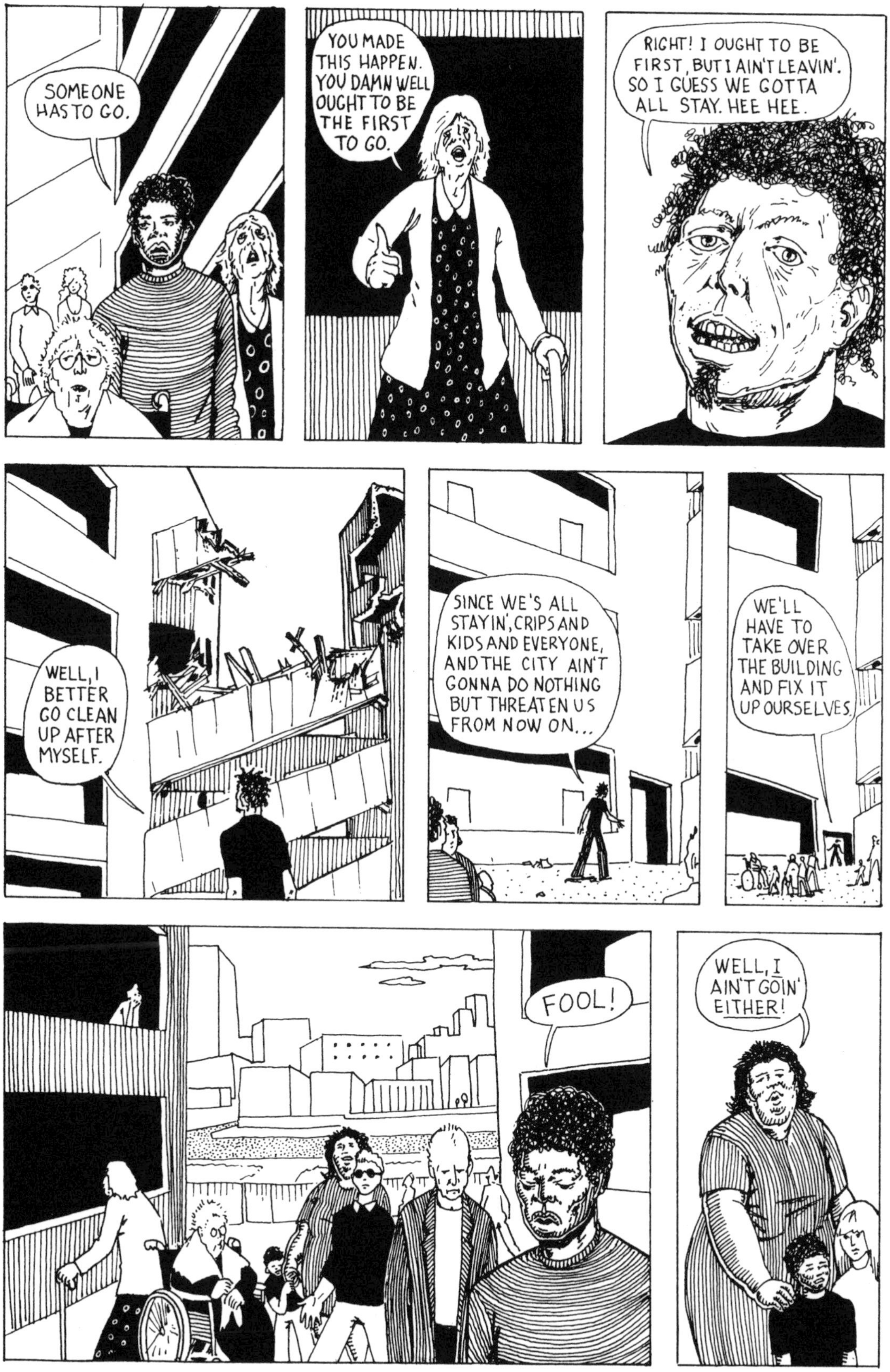
SOMEONE HAS TO GO.
YOU MADE THIS HAPPEN. YOU DAMN WELL OUGHT TO BE THE FIRST TO GO.
RIGHT! I OUGHT TO BE FIRST, BUT I AIN'T LEAVIN'. SO I GUESS WE GOTTA ALL STAY. HEE HEE.
WELL, I BETTER GO CLEAN UP AFTER MYSELF.
SINCE WE'S ALL STAYIN', CRIPS AND KIDS AND EVERYONE, AND THE CITY AIN'T GONNA DO NOTHING BUT THREATEN US FROM NOW ON...
WE'LL HAVE TO TAKE OVER THE BUILDING AND FIX IT UP OURSELVES.
FOOL!
WELL, I AIN'T GOIN' EITHER!

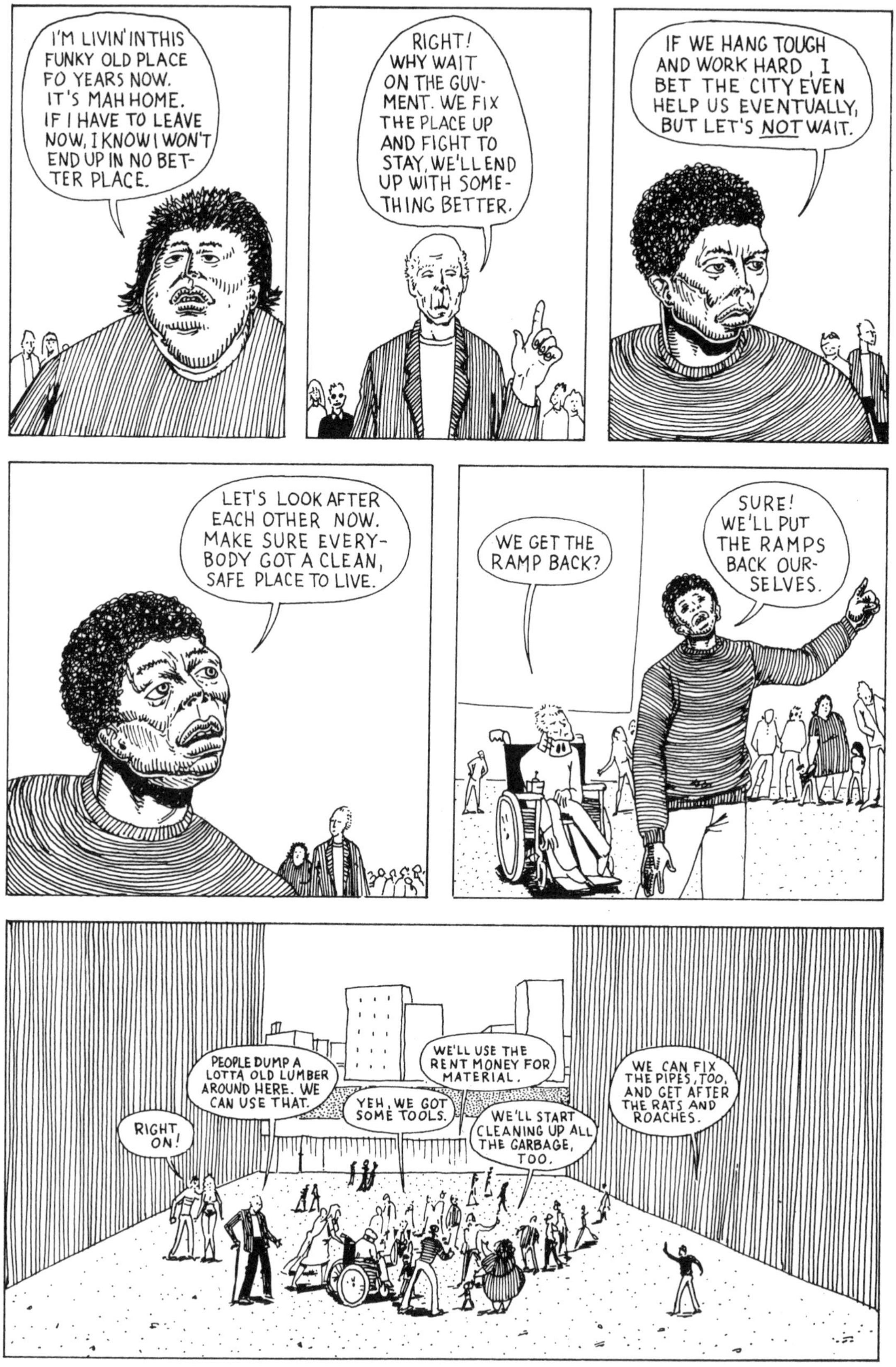
I'M LIVIN' IN THIS FUNKY OLD PLACE FO YEARS NOW. IT'S MAH HOME. IF I HAVE TO LEAVE NOW, I KNOW I WON'T END UP IN NO BETTER PLACE.
RIGHT! WHY WAIT ON THE GUVMENT. WE FIX THE PLACE UP AND FIGHT TO STAY, WE'LL END UP WITH SOMETHING BETTER.
IF WE HANG TOUGH AND WORK HARD, I BET THE CITY EVEN HELP US EVENTUALLY, BUT LET'S NOT WAIT.
LET'S LOOK AFTER EACH OTHER NOW. MAKE SURE EVERYBODY GOT A CLEAN, SAFE PLACE TO LIVE.
WE GET THE RAMP BACK?
SURE! WE'LL PUT THE RAMPS BACK OURSELVES.
RIGHT ON!
PEOPLE DUMP A LOTTA OLD LUMBER AROUND HERE. WE CAN USE THAT.
YEH, WE GOT SOME TOOLS.
WE'LL USE THE RENT MONEY FOR MATERIAL.
WE'LL START CLEANING UP ALL THE GARBAGE, TOO.
WE CAN FIX THE PIPES, TOO, AND GET AFTER THE RATS AND ROACHES.

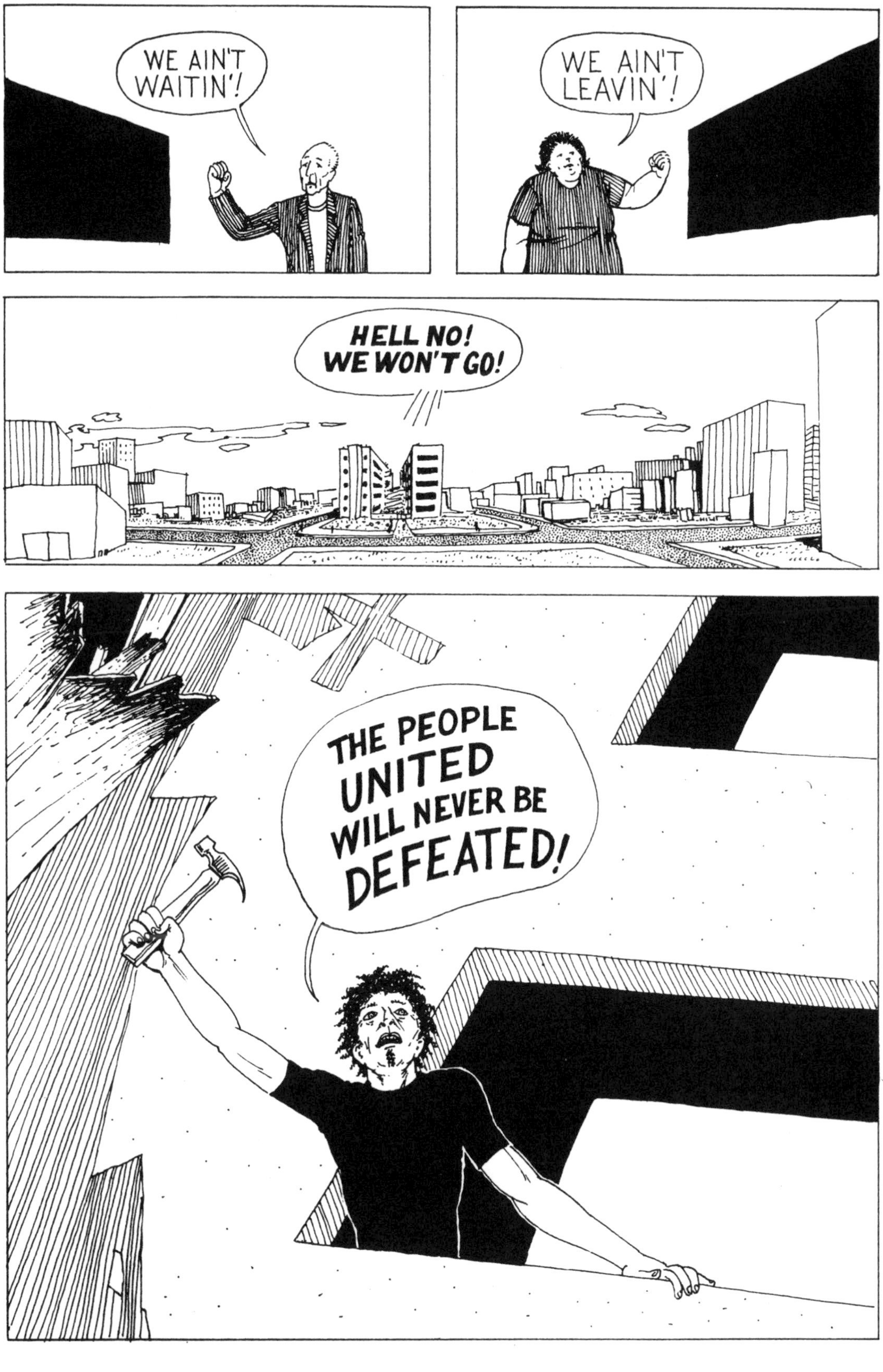
WE AIN'T WAITIN'!
WE AIN'T LEAVIN'!
HELL NO! WE WON'T GO!
THE PEOPLE UNITED WILL NEVER BE DEFEATED!

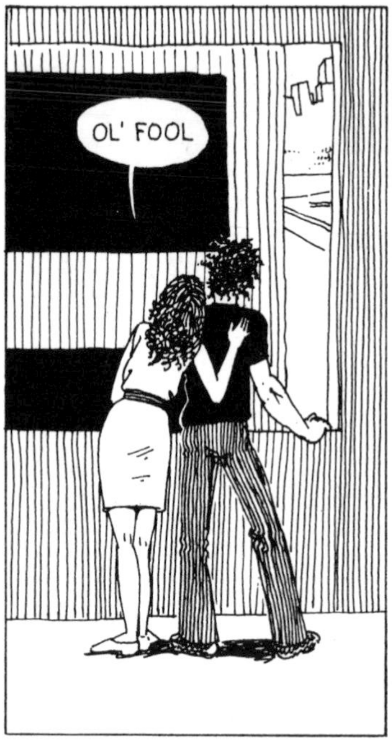
OL' FOOL

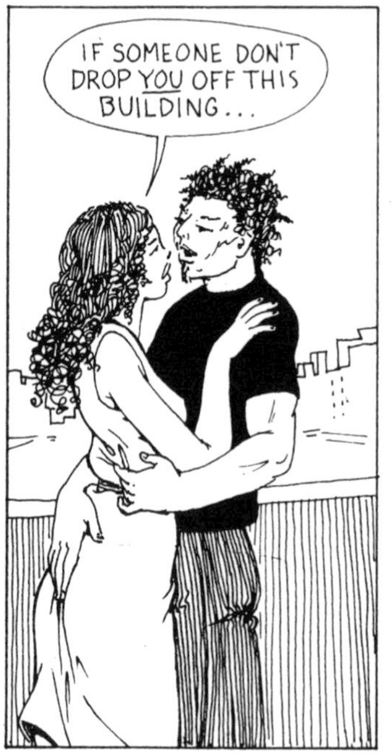
IF SOMEONE DON'T DROP YOU OFF THIS BUILDING...

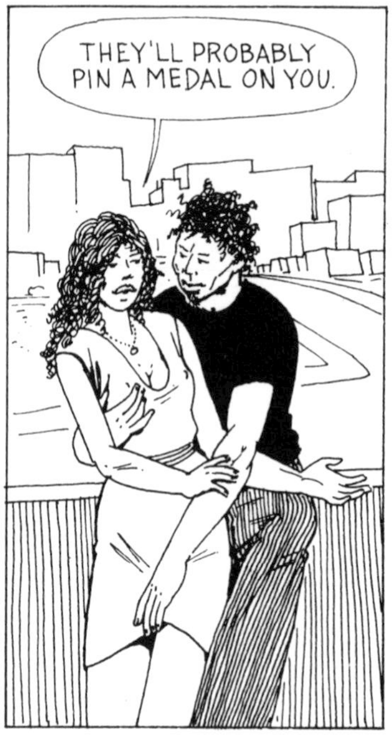
THEY'LL PROBABLY PIN A MEDAL ON YOU.

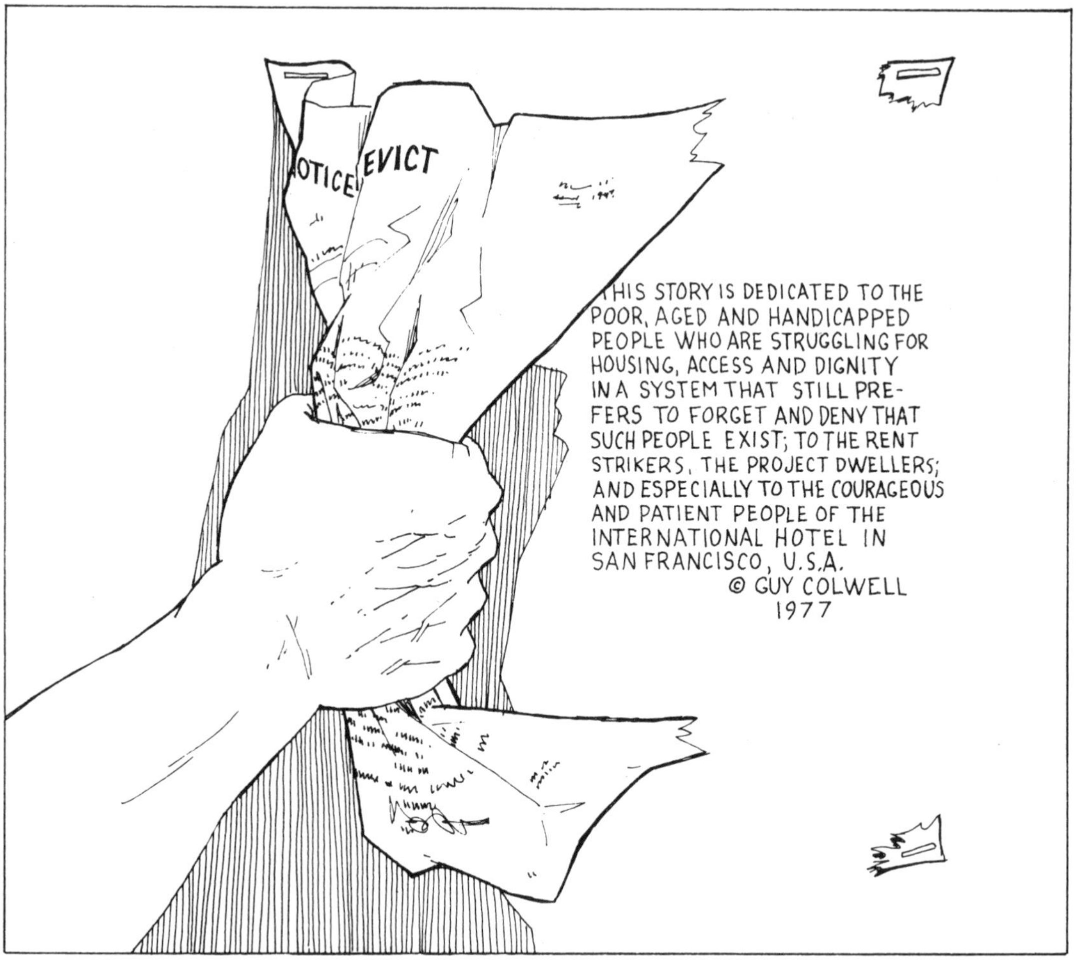
OTICE EVICT
THIS STORY IS DEDICATED TO THE POOR, AGED AND HANDICAPPED PEOPLE WHO ARE STRUGGLING FOR HOUSING, ACCESS AND DIGNITY IN A SYSTEM THAT STILL PREFERS TO FORGET AND DENY THAT SUCH PEOPLE EXIST; TO THE RENT STRIKERS, THE PROJECT DWELLERS; AND ESPECIALLY TO THE COURAGEOUS AND PATIENT PEOPLE OF THE INTERNATIONAL HOTEL IN SAN FRANCISCO, U.S.A.
© GUY COLWELL
1977

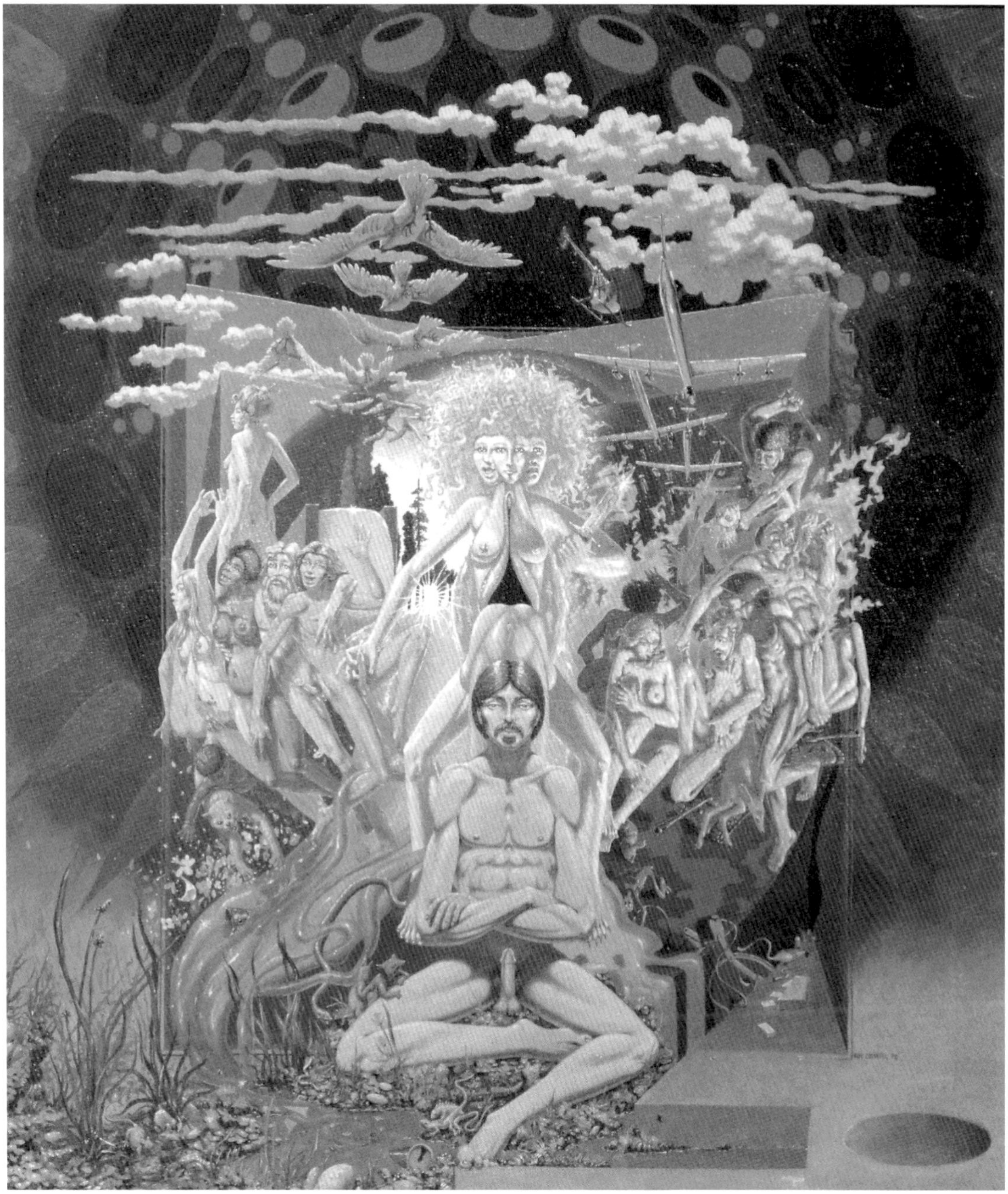

Horny Mandala, oil on canvas, 1975. A satire of spiritual art, *Horny Mandala* deals with philosophical ideas about how sexuality generates not only love, beauty, and pleasure but jealousy, hatred, conflict, and craziness — similar to the themes of the short stories in *Inner City Romance* #5.

INNER CITY ROMANCE #5
(1978)
by Patrick Rosenkranz

"By *Inner City Romance* #5 the Vietnam War was finally over, and I was able to do stories about sex with a minimum of politics. But after that, I had a very different life. The struggles with prison issues were fading into the past, and *Inner City Romance* no longer had the same internal or social well of source material that had made it what it was, so I left it off and stopped thinking I was going to be a cartoonist and got back exclusively to my painting for a decade or so."

Colwell also did graphic design work for Rip Off Press for several years, which in that pre-digital time period included layout, paste-up, copy camera, stripping, color separations, and whatever it took to get a book ready for the printing press.

Weight of History, oil on canvas 1978. Colwell developed this painting while he was living in Paris and visiting many of the great museums around Europe. It became the cover of *Inner City Romance* #5, the last issue in the series.

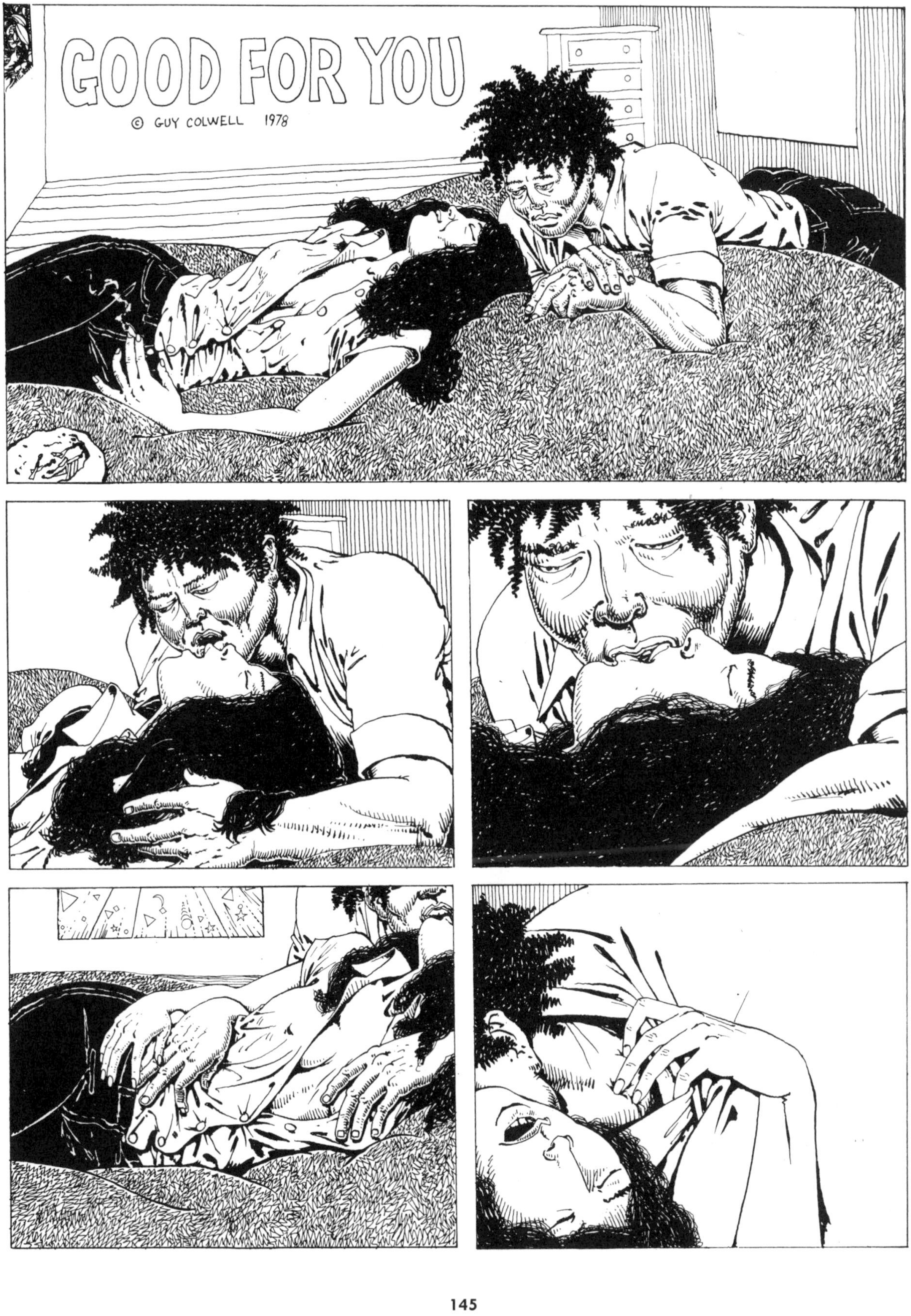
GOOD FOR YOU
© GUY COLWELL 1978

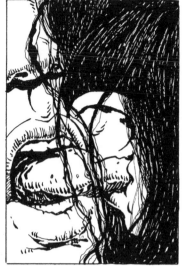

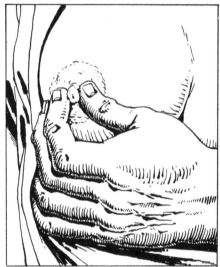

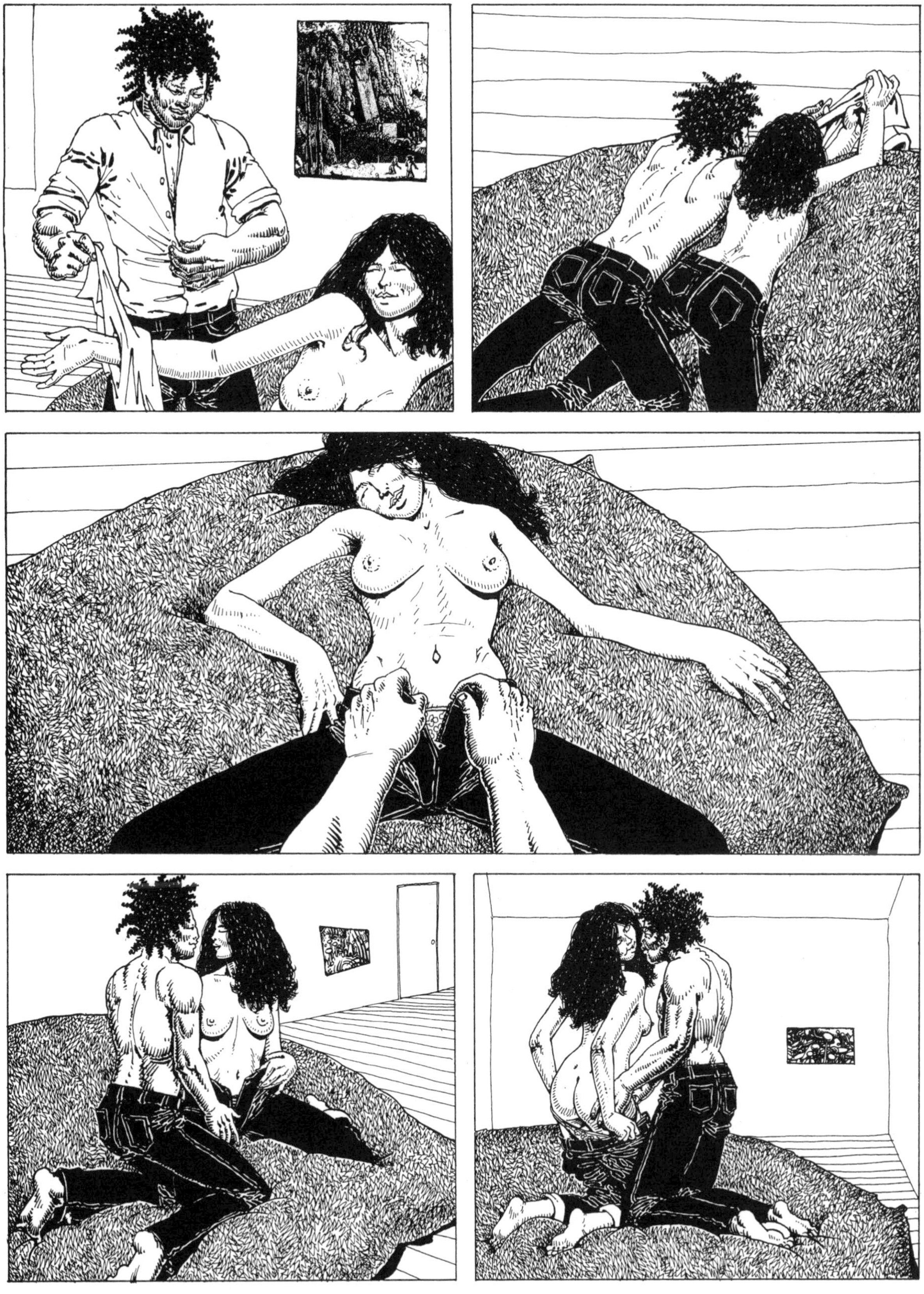

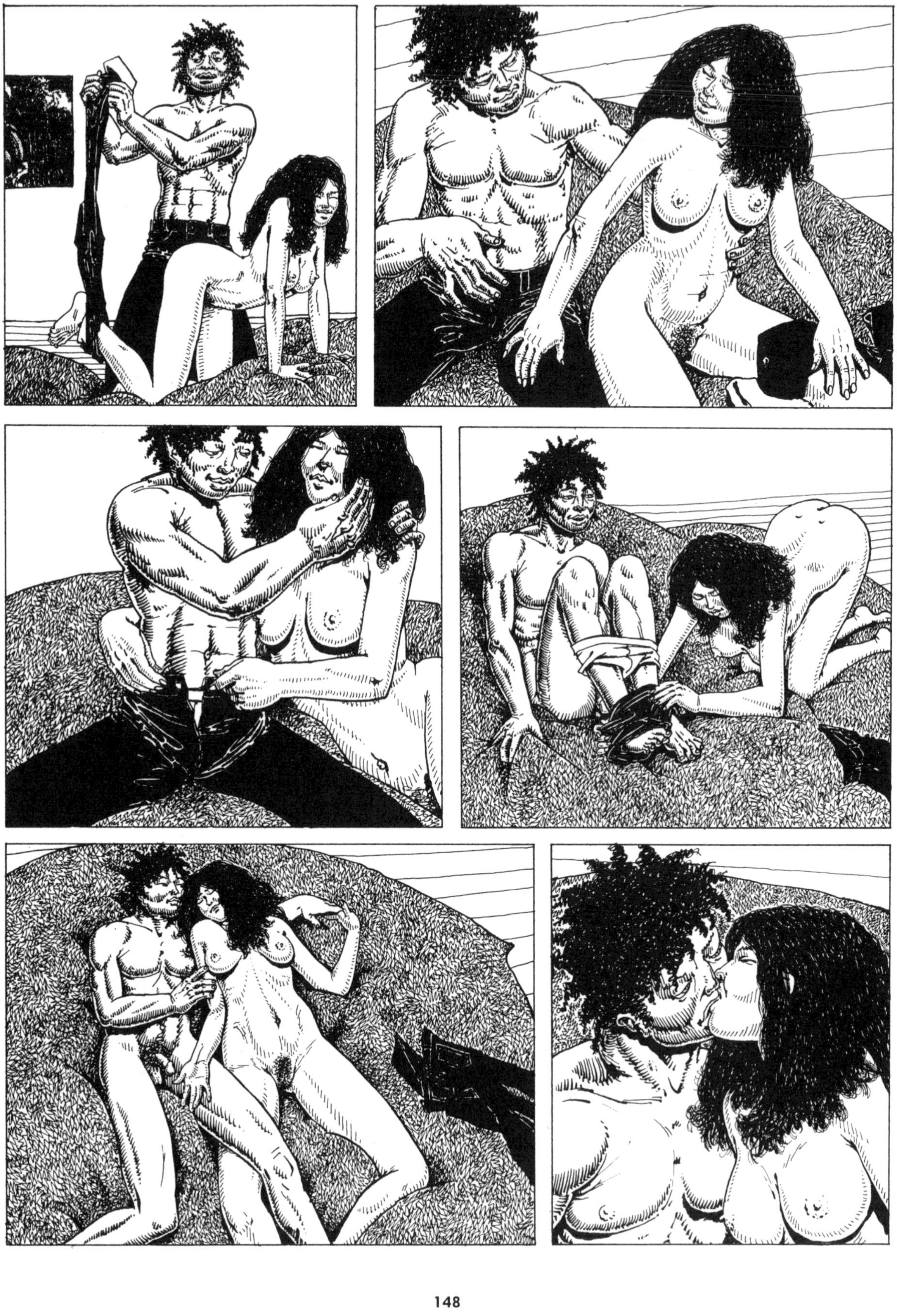

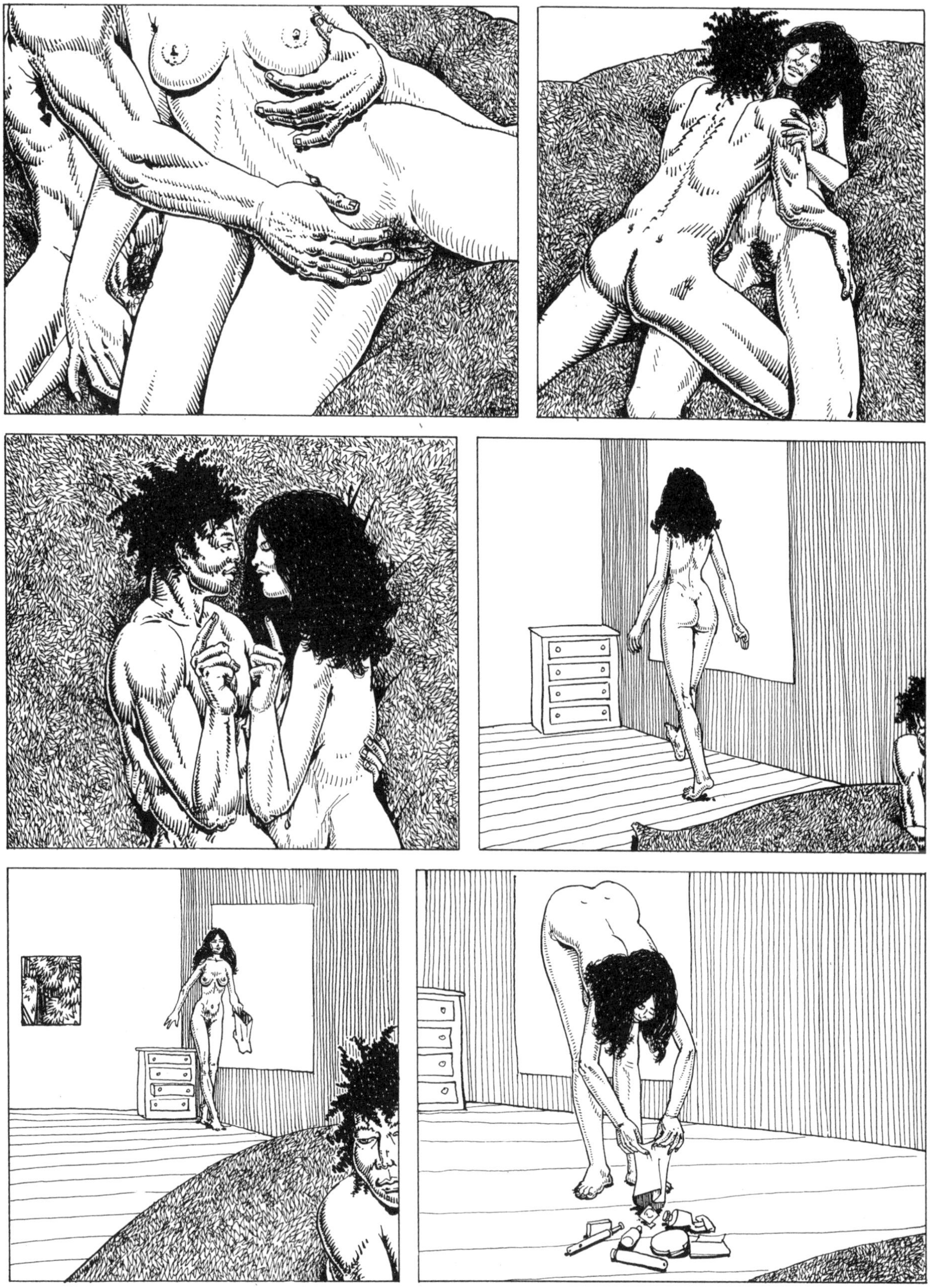

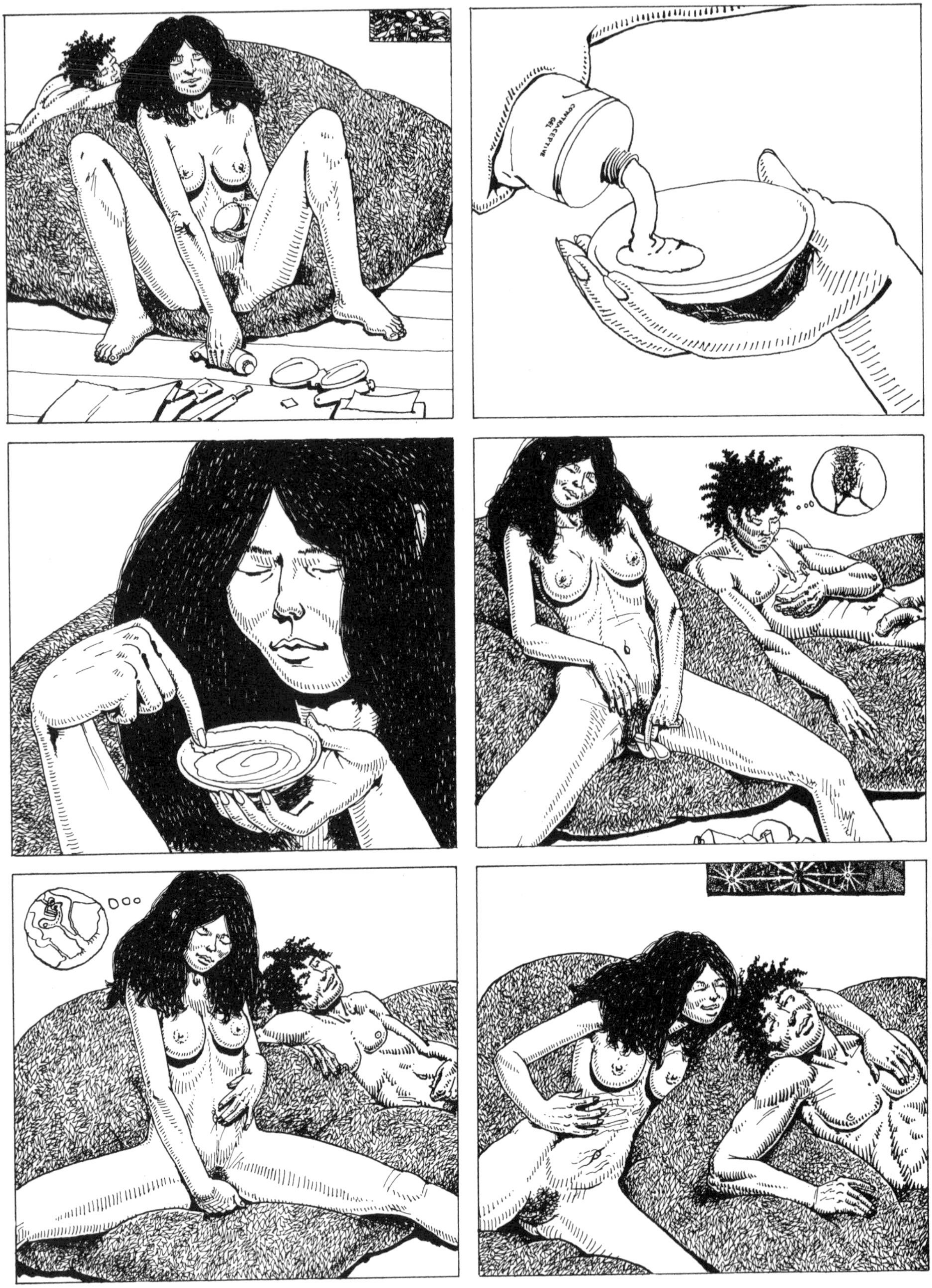
CONTRACEPTIVE GEL

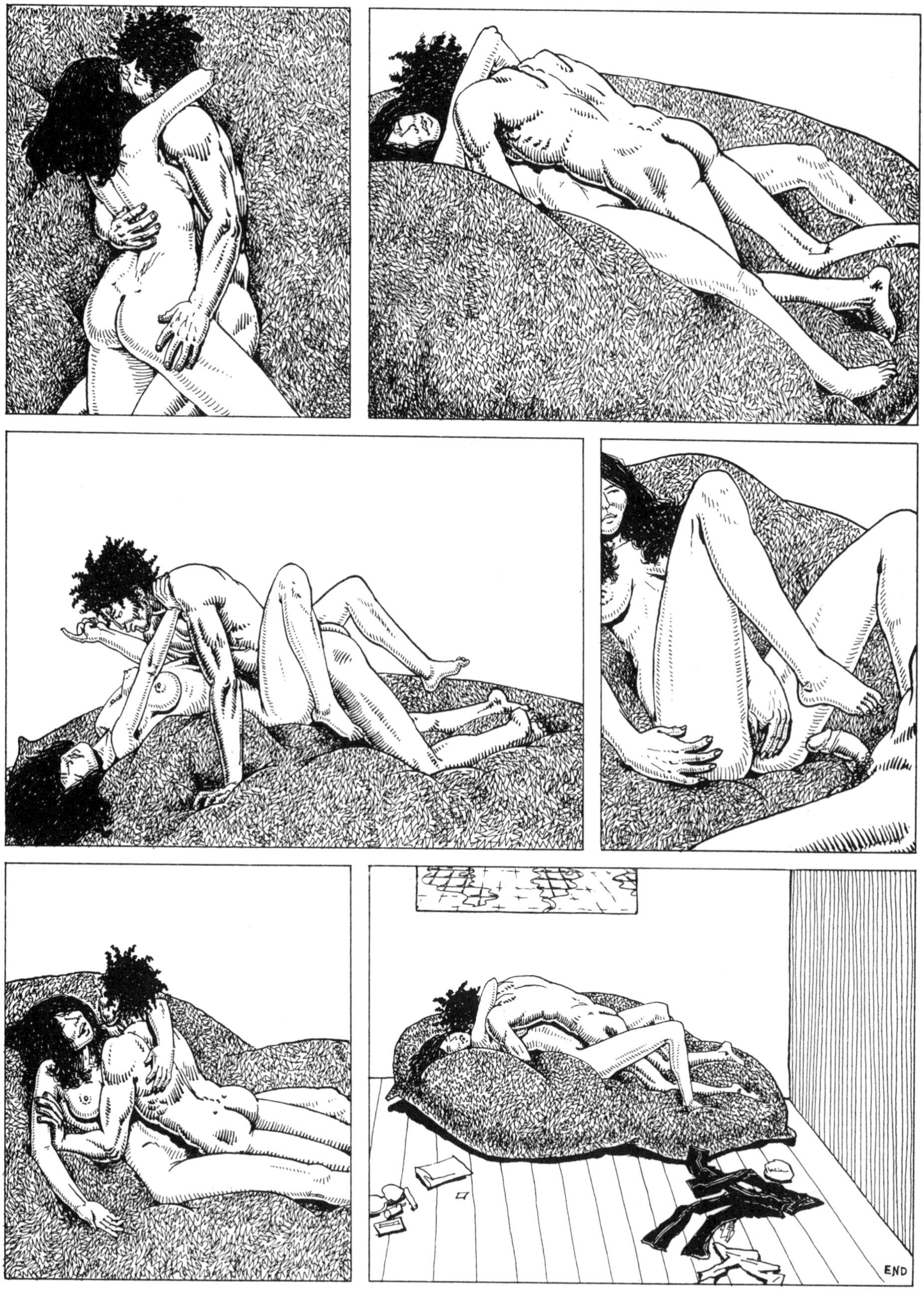
END

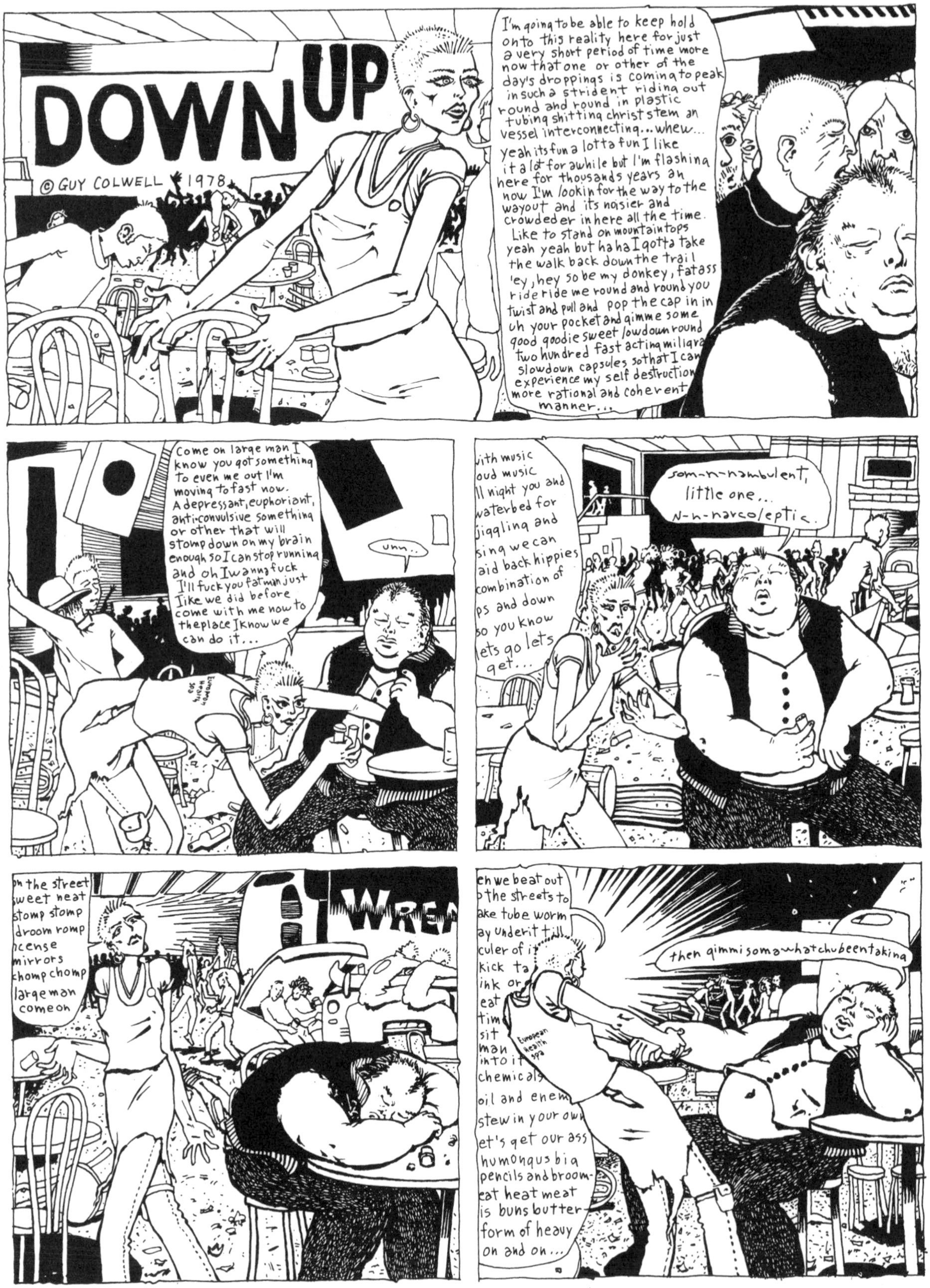
DOWN UP
© GUY COLWELL 1978
I'm going to be able to keep hold onto this reality here for just a very short period of time more now that one or other of the day's droppings is coming to peak in such a strident riding out round and round in plastic tubing shitting christ stem an vessel interconnecting... whew... yeah its fun a lotta fun I like it a lot for awhile but I'm flashing here for thousands years an now I'm lookin for the way to the wayout and its noisier and crowdeder in here all the time. Like to stand on mountaintops yeah yeah but ha ha I gotta take the walk back down the trail 'ey, hey so be my donkey, fatass ride ride me round and round you twist and pull and pop the cap in in uh your pocket and gimme some good goodie sweet lowdown round two hundred fast acting miligra slowdown capsules so that I can experience my self destruction more rational and coherent manner...
Come on large man I know you got something to even me out I'm moving to fast now. A depressant, euphoriant, anti-convulsive something or other that will stomp down on my brain enough so I can stop running and oh I wanna fuck I'll fuck you fat man just like we did before come with me now to the place I know we can do it...
unn..
European Health Spa
with music
oud music
ll night you and
waterbed for
jiggling and
sing we can
aid back hippies
combination of
ps and down
so you know
lets go lets
get...
som-n-nambulent, little one.. n-n-narcoleptic.
n the street
sweet neat
stomp stomp
droom romp
ncense
mirrors
chomp chomp
largeman
come on
WREA
en we beat out
the streets to
ake tube worm
ay under it till
culer of it
kick ta
ink or
eat
tim
sit
man
into it
chemicals
oil and enem
stew in your own
et's get our ass
humongus big
pencils and broom
eat heat meat
is buns butter
form of heavy
on and on...
then gimmi som a whatchu been taking
European Health Spa

Yeah, here man I know whatcha mean and I got just what you need to get you goin again as you might suspect I got dreens all up the butt an whats is yours know the elp you or with whatever I got you need

sweebabe.

Dont see why you don't just eat speed alla time not just lay around boozn eatin, downers dope just space you down and out out I mean you dig the technology is there to burn your self into whatever form you think you to be you...

you fun I like you shit all I wanna fuck so even though you wierd and slow and sad and full of shit you jiggle daddy I like to grease yall up an slide down ha ya oughta maybe dig yoself more.

wachoowannafume fo fat ugly cold gosome weed

but shit uh I don't care you do what want to th your body its your shee then each Donald Duck believe me around th sleepin day or eat it oh, tha horny banana she say walked Dickingh hose and pri

The foa

...get a buzz off stuff in caps yellow purple red said bed dead on her head here to tread around the dread lock black green pink think stink around an around the rink

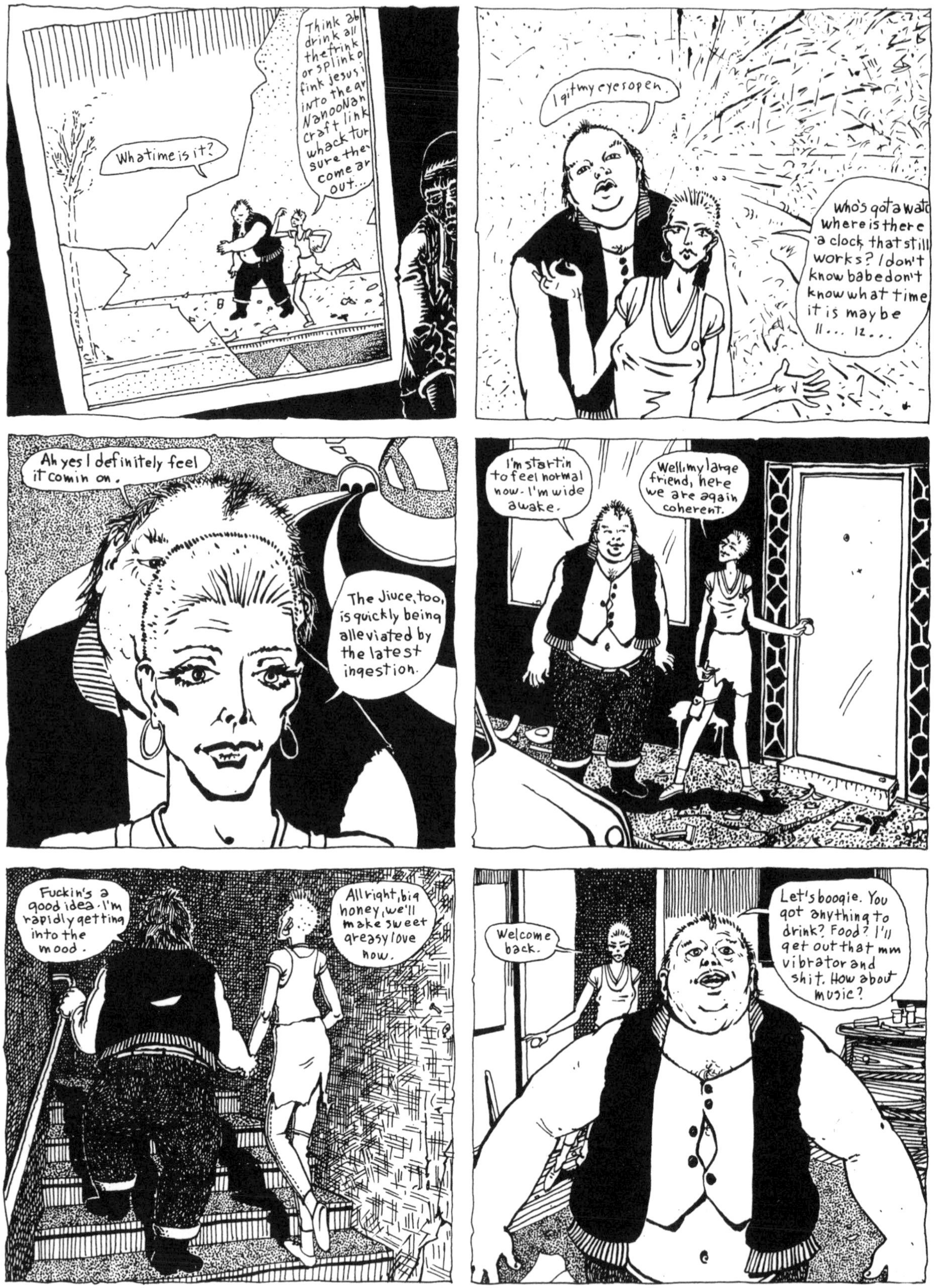
Think ab drink all thefrink or splink o fink jesus i into the ar NanooNan craft link whack tur sure the come ar out...
Whatime is it?
I gitmy eyesopen.
who's gotawatc where is there a clock that still works? I don't know babe don't know what time it is maybe 11... 12...
Ah yes I definitely feel it comin on.
The Jiuce, too, is quickly being alleviated by the latest ingestion.
I'm startin to feel normal now. I'm wide awake.
Well, my large friend, here we are again coherent.
Fuckin's a good idea. I'm rapidly getting into the mood.
Allright, big honey, we'll make sweet greasy love now.
Welcome back.
Let's boogie. You got anything to drink? Food? I'll get out that mm vibrator and shit. How about music?

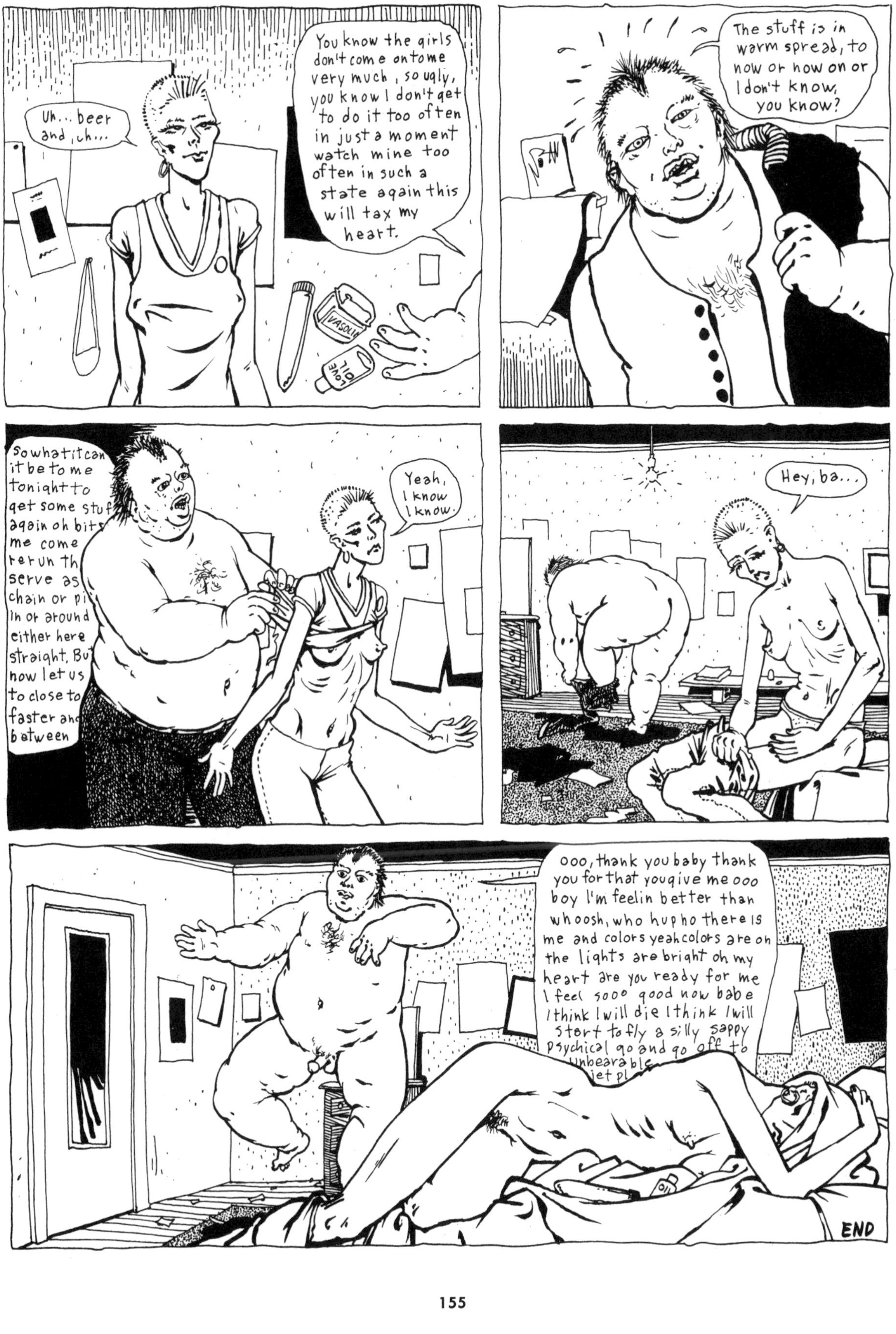
Uh... beer and, uh...
You know the girls don't come on to me very much, so ugly, you know I don't get to do it too often in just a moment watch mine too often in such a state again this will tax my heart.
VASOLIN
LOVE OIL
The stuff is in warm spread, to now or now on or I don't know, you know?
So what it can it be to me tonight to get some stuf again oh bits me come rerun th serve as chain or pi in or around either here straight. But now let us to close to faster and between
Yeah, I know I know.
Hey, ba...
ooo, thank you baby thank you for that you give me ooo boy I'm feelin better than whoosh, who hup ho there is me and colors yeah colors are on the lights are bright oh my heart are you ready for me I feel sooo good now babe I think I will die I think I will start to fly a silly sappy psychical go and go off to unbearable jet pl
END

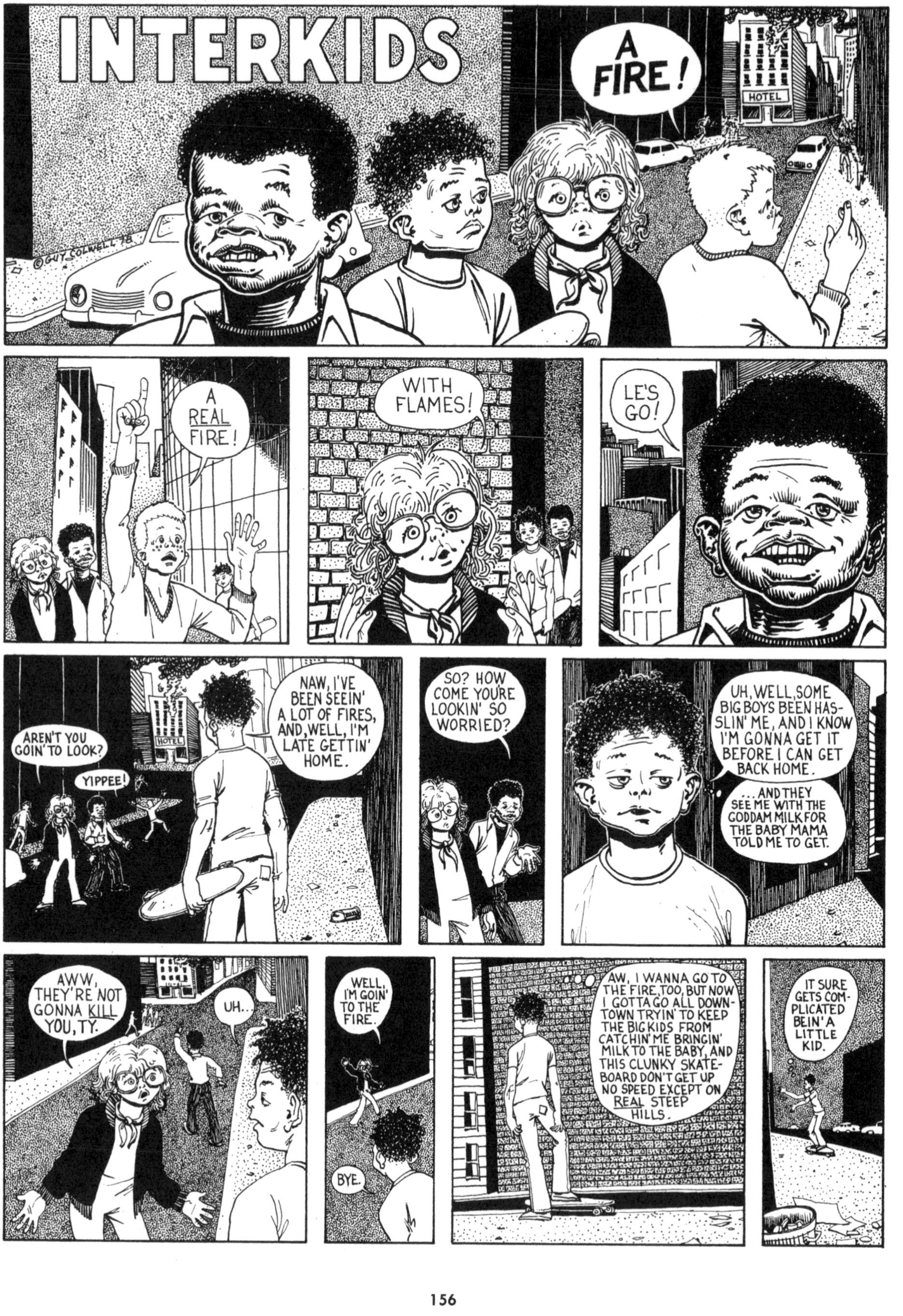
INTERKIDS
©GUY COLWELL '78
A FIRE!
HOTEL
A REAL FIRE!
WITH FLAMES!
LE'S GO!
AREN'T YOU GOIN' TO LOOK?
YIPPEE!
HOTEL
NAW, I'VE BEEN SEEIN' A LOT OF FIRES, AND, WELL, I'M LATE GETTIN' HOME.
SO? HOW COME YOU'RE LOOKIN' SO WORRIED?
UH, WELL, SOME BIG BOYS BEEN HAS-SLIN' ME, AND I KNOW I'M GONNA GET IT BEFORE I CAN GET BACK HOME.
...AND THEY SEE ME WITH THE GODDAM MILK FOR THE BABY MAMA TOLD ME TO GET.
AWW, THEY'RE NOT GONNA KILL YOU, TY.
UH..
WELL, I'M GOIN' TO THE FIRE.
BYE.
AW, I WANNA GO TO THE FIRE, TOO, BUT NOW I GOTTA GO ALL DOWN-TOWN TRYIN' TO KEEP THE BIG KIDS FROM CATCHIN' ME BRINGIN' MILK TO THE BABY, AND THIS CLUNKY SKATE-BOARD DON'T GET UP NO SPEED EXCEPT ON REAL STEEP HILLS.
IT SURE GETS COM-PLICATED BEIN' A LITTLE KID.

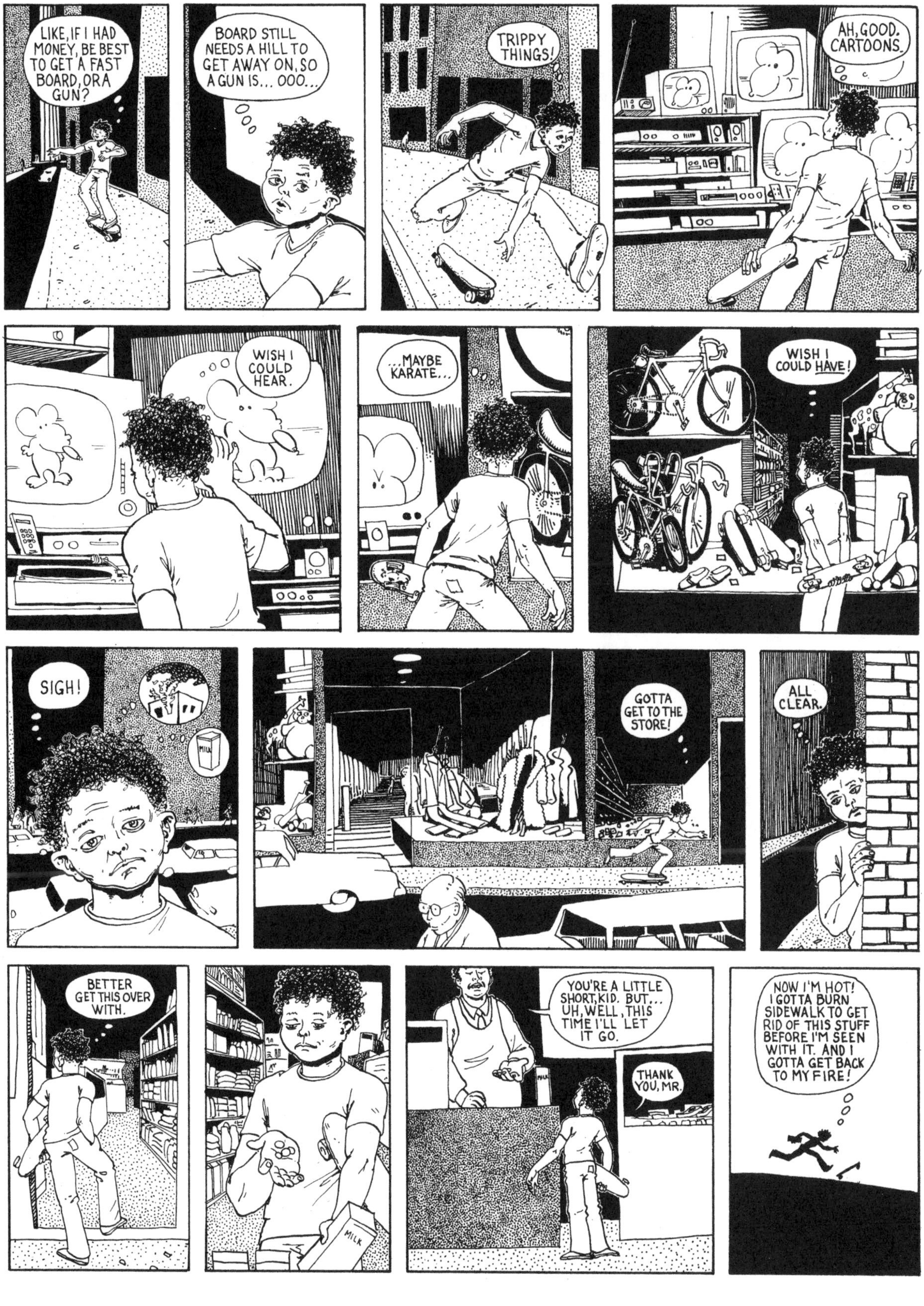
LIKE, IF I HAD MONEY, BE BEST TO GET A FAST BOARD, OR A GUN?
BOARD STILL NEEDS A HILL TO GET AWAY ON, SO A GUN IS... OOO...
TRIPPY THINGS!
AH, GOOD. CARTOONS.
WISH I COULD HEAR.
...MAYBE KARATE...
WISH I COULD HAVE!
SIGH!
MILK
GOTTA GET TO THE STORE!
ALL CLEAR.
BETTER GET THIS OVER WITH.
MILK
YOU'RE A LITTLE SHORT, KID. BUT... UH, WELL, THIS TIME I'LL LET IT GO.
THANK YOU, MR.
NOW I'M HOT! I GOTTA BURN SIDEWALK TO GET RID OF THIS STUFF BEFORE I'M SEEN WITH IT. AND I GOTTA GET BACK TO MY FIRE!

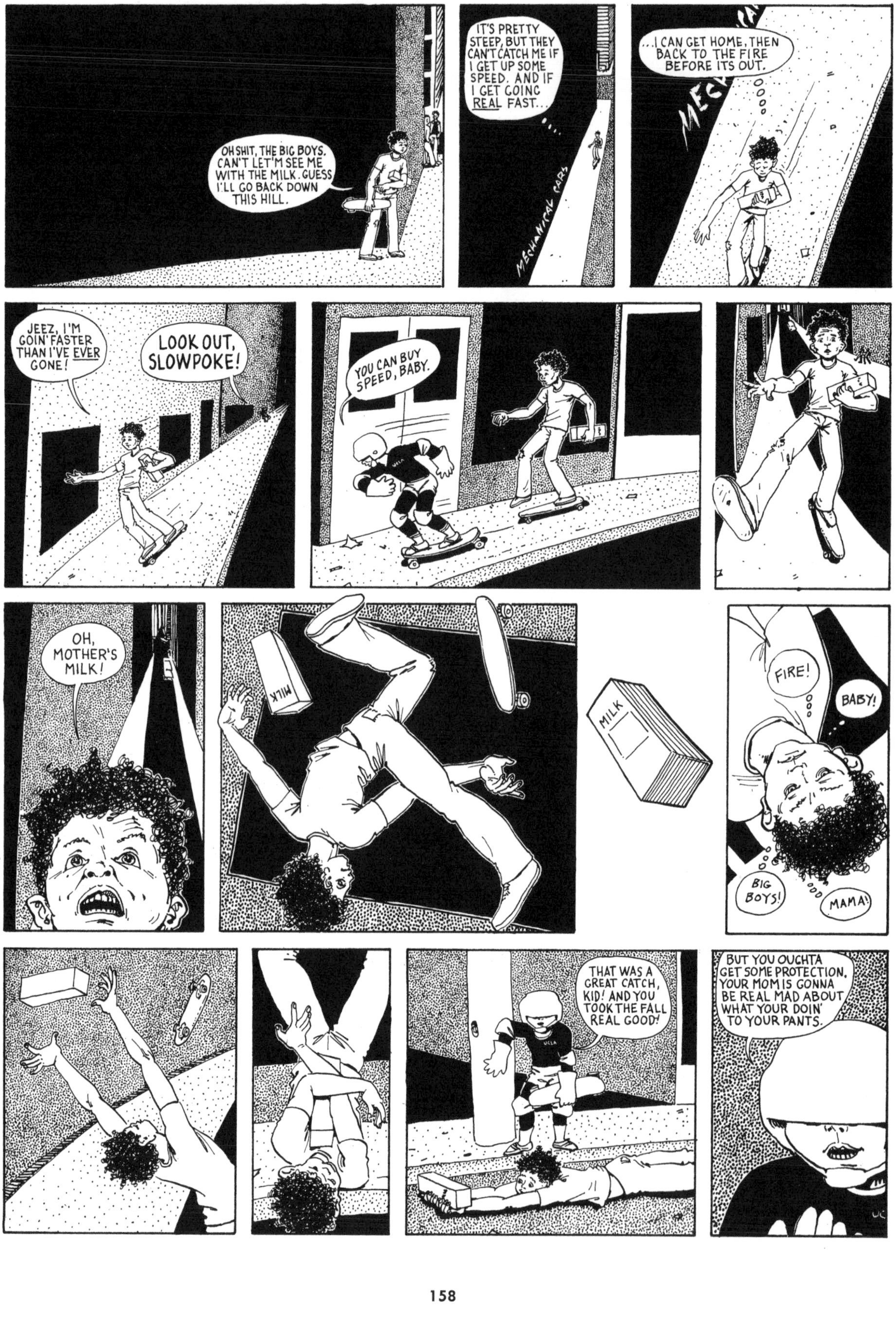
OH SHIT, THE BIG BOYS. CAN'T LET'M SEE ME WITH THE MILK. GUESS I'LL GO BACK DOWN THIS HILL.
IT'S PRETTY STEEP, BUT THEY CAN'T CATCH ME IF I GET UP SOME SPEED. AND IF I GET GOING REAL FAST...
MECHANICAL CARS
...I CAN GET HOME, THEN BACK TO THE FIRE BEFORE ITS OUT.
JEEZ, I'M GOIN' FASTER THAN I'VE EVER GONE!
LOOK OUT, SLOWPOKE!
YOU CAN BUY SPEED, BABY.
OH, MOTHER'S MILK!
MILK
MILK
FIRE!
BABY!
BIG BOYS!
MAMA!
THAT WAS A GREAT CATCH, KID! AND YOU TOOK THE FALL REAL GOOD!
BUT YOU OUCHTA GET SOME PROTECTION. YOUR MOM IS GONNA BE REAL MAD ABOUT WHAT YOUR DOIN' TO YOUR PANTS.

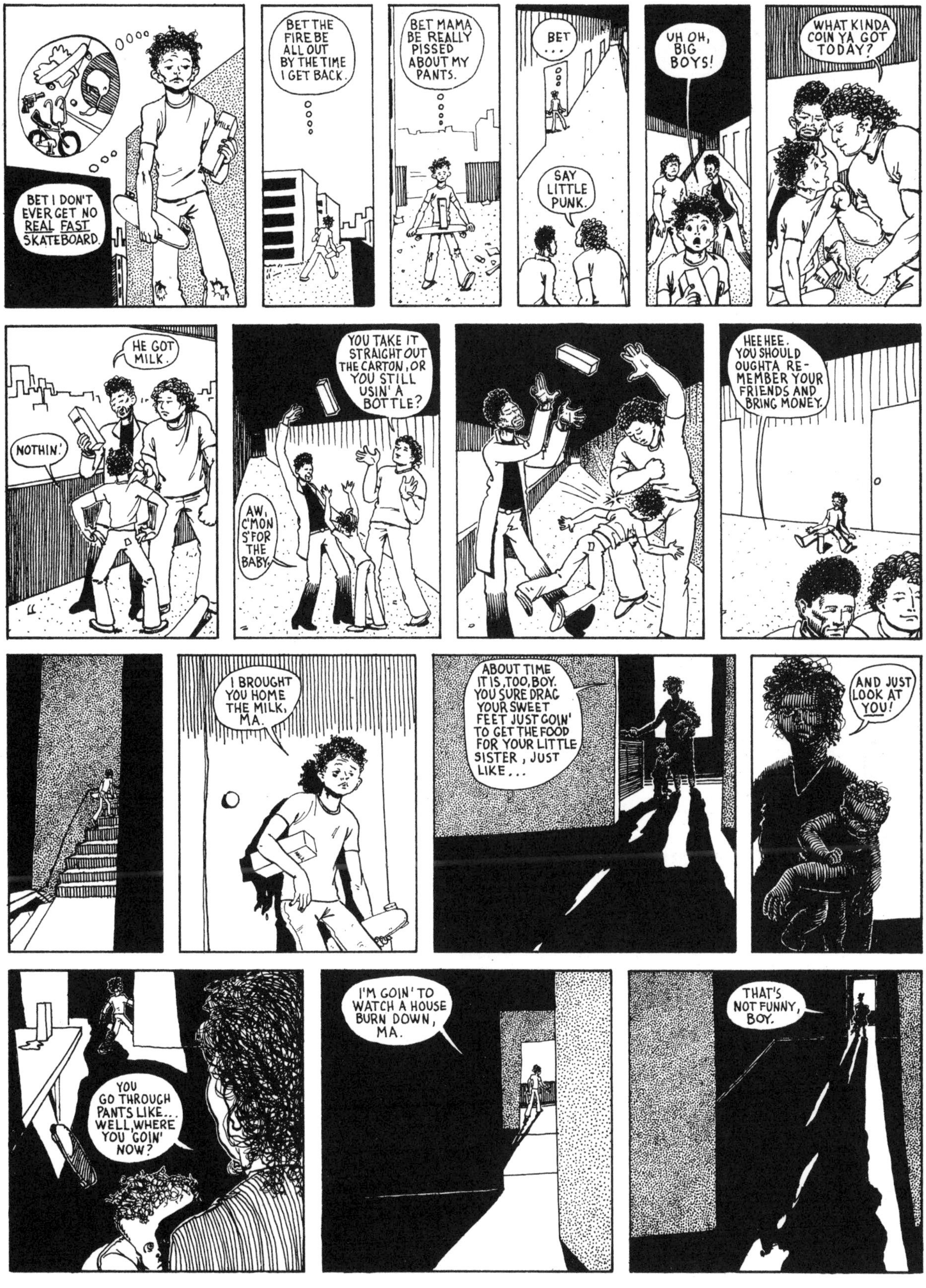
BET I DON'T EVER GET NO REAL FAST SKATEBOARD.
BET THE FIRE BE ALL OUT BY THE TIME I GET BACK.
BET MAMA BE REALLY PISSED ABOUT MY PANTS.
BET ...
SAY LITTLE PUNK.
UH OH, BIG BOYS!
WHAT KINDA COIN YA GOT TODAY?
HE GOT MILK.
NOTHIN'.
YOU TAKE IT STRAIGHT OUT THE CARTON, OR YOU STILL USIN' A BOTTLE?
AW, C'MON S'FOR THE BABY.
HEE HEE. YOU SHOULD OUGHTA RE-MEMBER YOUR FRIENDS AND BRING MONEY.
I BROUGHT YOU HOME THE MILK, MA.
ABOUT TIME IT IS, TOO, BOY. YOU SURE DRAG YOUR SWEET FEET JUST GOIN' TO GET THE FOOD FOR YOUR LITTLE SISTER, JUST LIKE...
AND JUST LOOK AT YOU!
YOU GO THROUGH PANTS LIKE... WELL, WHERE YOU GOIN' NOW?
I'M GOIN' TO WATCH A HOUSE BURN DOWN, MA.
THAT'S NOT FUNNY, BOY.

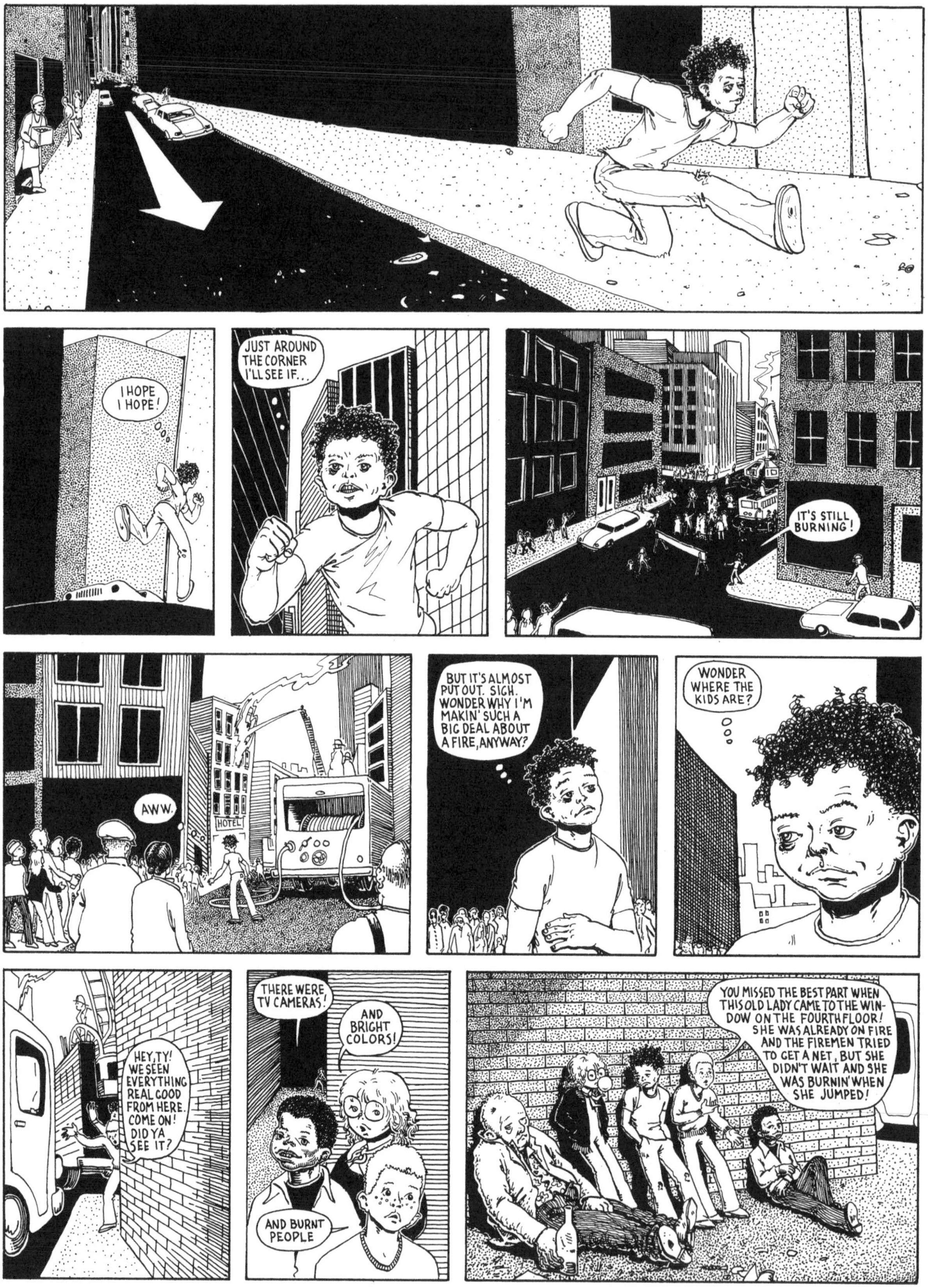
I HOPE I HOPE!
JUST AROUND THE CORNER I'LL SEE IF...
IT'S STILL BURNING!
AWW.
BUT IT'S ALMOST PUT OUT. SIGH. WONDER WHY I'M MAKIN' SUCH A BIG DEAL ABOUT A FIRE, ANYWAY?
WONDER WHERE THE KIDS ARE?
HEY, TY! WE SEEN EVERYTHING REAL GOOD FROM HERE. COME ON! DID YA SEE IT?
THERE WERE TV CAMERAS!
AND BRIGHT COLORS!
AND BURNT PEOPLE
YOU MISSED THE BEST PART WHEN THIS OLD LADY CAME TO THE WINDOW ON THE FOURTH FLOOR! SHE WAS ALREADY ON FIRE AND THE FIREMEN TRIED TO GET A NET, BUT SHE DIDN'T WAIT AND SHE WAS BURNIN' WHEN SHE JUMPED!

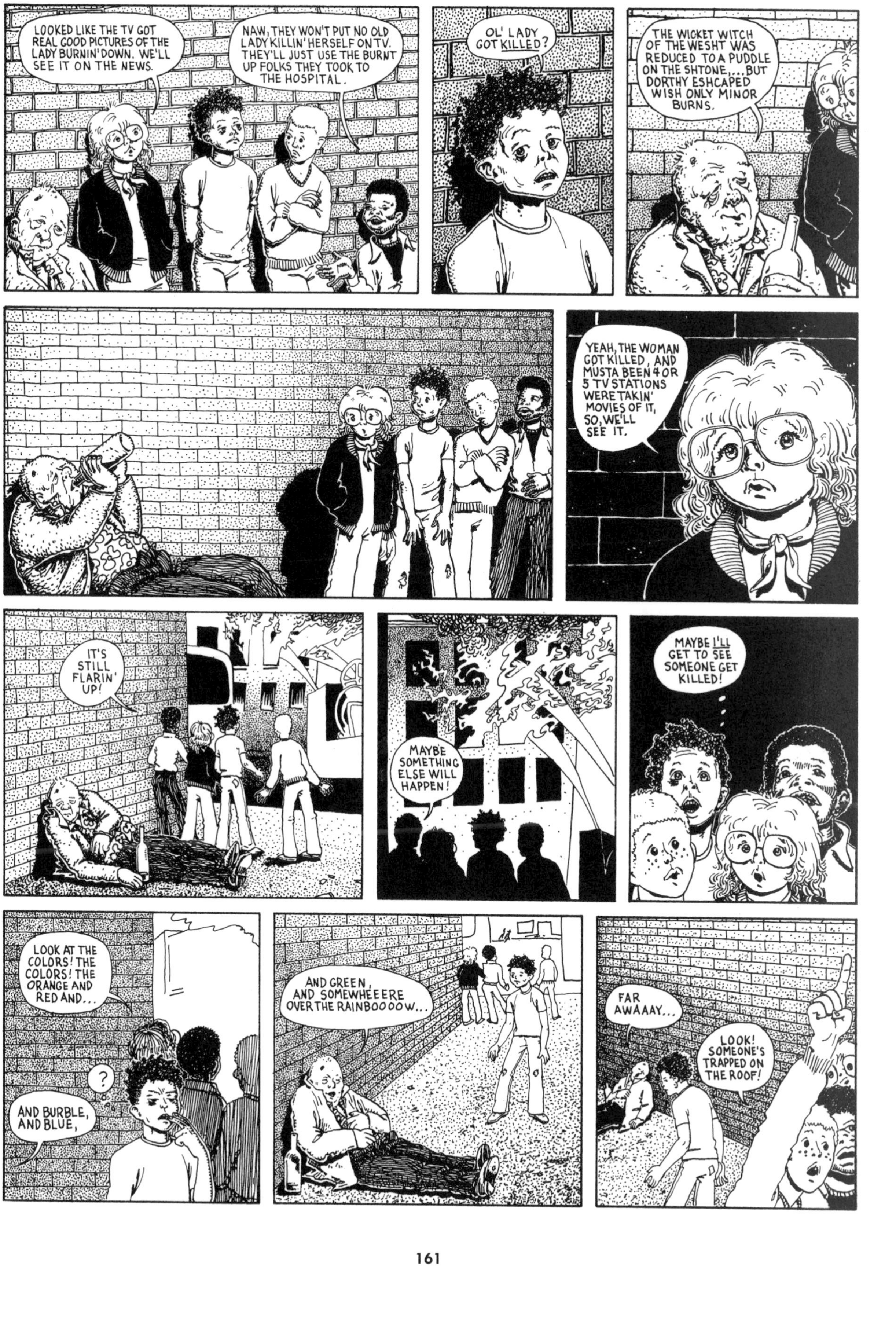
LOOKED LIKE THE TV GOT REAL GOOD PICTURES OF THE LADY BURNIN' DOWN. WE'LL SEE IT ON THE NEWS.
NAW, THEY WON'T PUT NO OLD LADY KILLIN' HERSELF ON TV. THEY'LL JUST USE THE BURNT UP FOLKS THEY TOOK TO THE HOSPITAL.
OL' LADY GOT KILLED?
THE WICKET WITCH OF THE WESHT WAS REDUCED TO A PUDDLE ON THE SHTONE,...BUT DORTHY ESHCAPED WISH ONLY MINOR BURNS.
YEAH, THE WOMAN GOT KILLED, AND MUSTA BEEN 4 OR 5 TV STATIONS WERE TAKIN' MOVIES OF IT, SO, WE'LL SEE IT.
IT'S STILL FLARIN' UP!
MAYBE SOMETHING ELSE WILL HAPPEN!
MAYBE I'LL GET TO SEE SOMEONE GET KILLED!
LOOK AT THE COLORS! THE COLORS! THE ORANGE AND RED AND...
?
AND BURBLE, AND BLUE,
AND GREEN, AND SOMEWHEEERE OVER THE RAINBOOOOW...
FAR AWAAAY...
LOOK! SOMEONE'S TRAPPED ON THE ROOF!

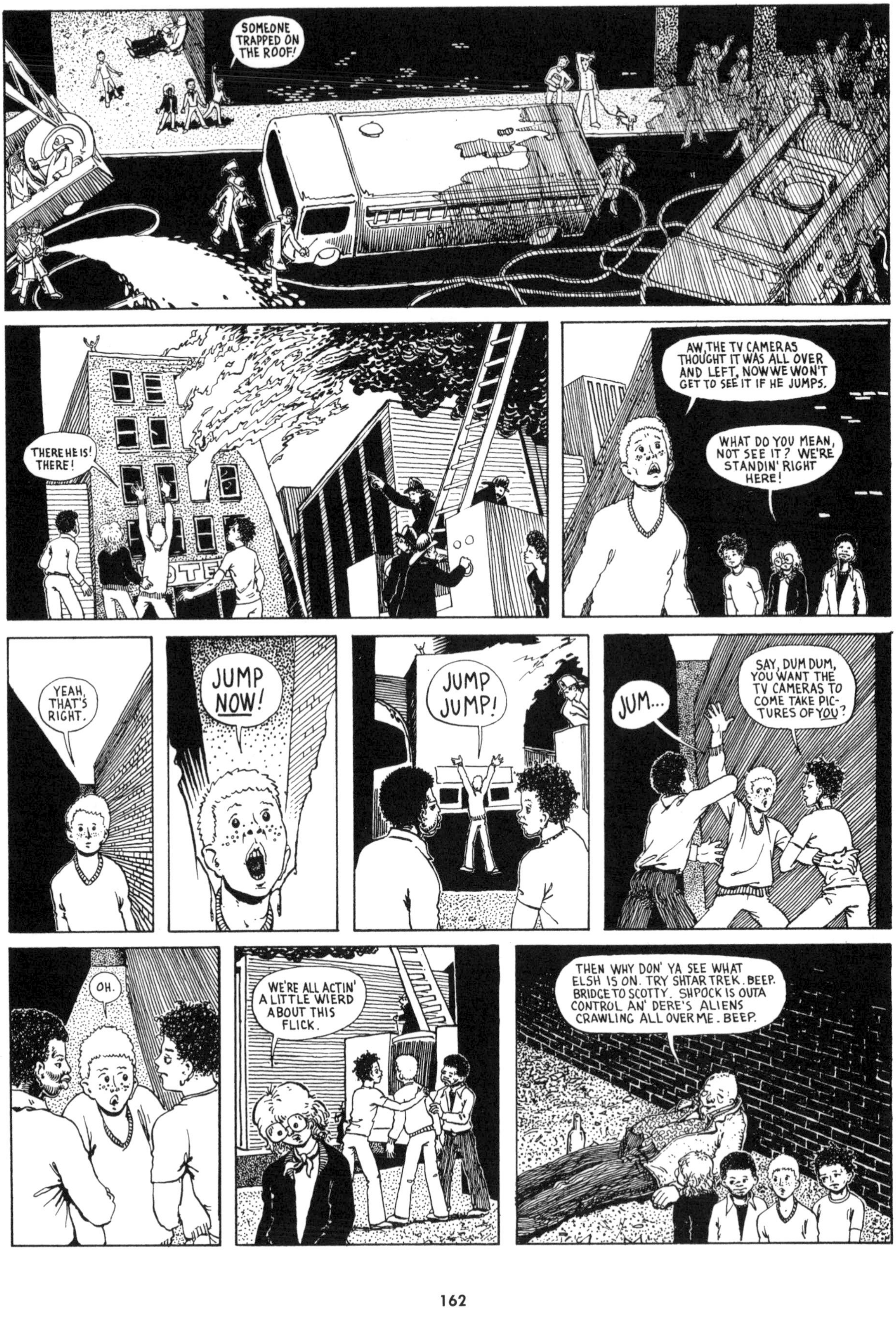
SOMEONE TRAPPED ON THE ROOF!
THERE HE IS! THERE!
AW, THE TV CAMERAS THOUGHT IT WAS ALL OVER AND LEFT, NOW WE WON'T GET TO SEE IT IF HE JUMPS.
WHAT DO YOU MEAN, NOT SEE IT? WE'RE STANDIN' RIGHT HERE!
YEAH, THAT'S RIGHT.
JUMP NOW!
JUMP JUMP!
JUM...
SAY, DUM DUM, YOU WANT THE TV CAMERAS TO COME TAKE PICTURES OF YOU?
OH.
WE'RE ALL ACTIN' A LITTLE WIERD ABOUT THIS FLICK.
THEN WHY DON' YA SEE WHAT ELSH IS ON. TRY SHTAR TREK. BEEP. BRIDGE TO SCOTTY. SHPOCK IS OUTA CONTROL AN' DERE'S ALIENS CRAWLING ALL OVER ME. BEEP.

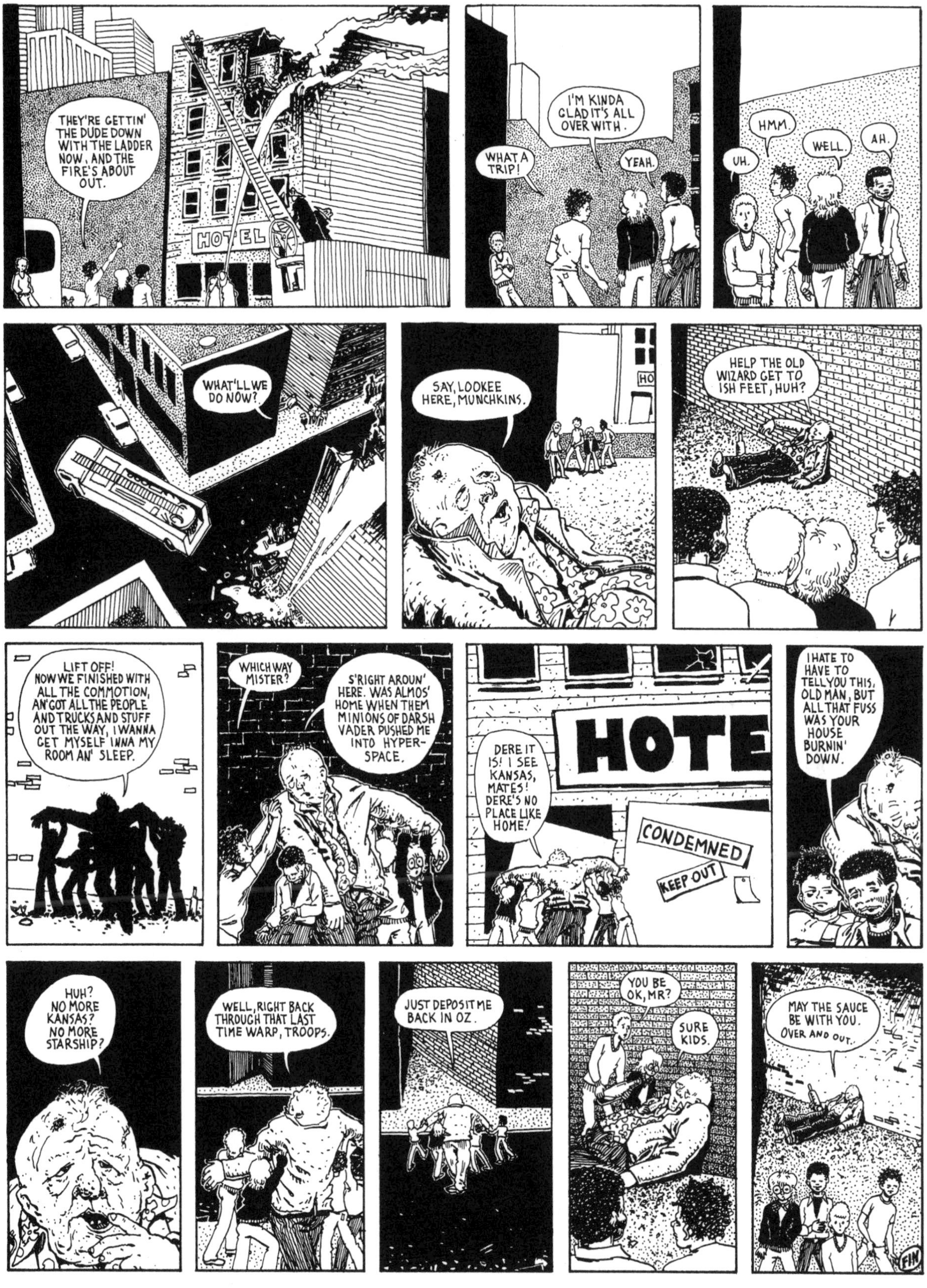
THEY'RE GETTIN' THE DUDE DOWN WITH THE LADDER NOW, AND THE FIRE'S ABOUT OUT.
HOTEL
I'M KINDA GLAD IT'S ALL OVER WITH.
WHAT A TRIP!
YEAH.
HMM.
UH.
WELL.
AH.
WHAT'LL WE DO NOW?
SAY, LOOKEE HERE, MUNCHKINS.
HELP THE OLD WIZARD GET TO ISH FEET, HUH?
LIFT OFF! NOW WE FINISHED WITH ALL THE COMMOTION, AN' GOT ALL THE PEOPLE AND TRUCKS AND STUFF OUT THE WAY, I WANNA GET MYSELF INNA MY ROOM AN' SLEEP.
WHICH WAY MISTER?
S'RIGHT AROUN' HERE. WAS ALMOS' HOME WHEN THEM MINIONS OF DARSH VADER PUSHED ME INTO HYPER-SPACE.
HOTE
DERE IT IS! I SEE KANSAS, MATES! DERE'S NO PLACE LIKE HOME!
CONDEMNED
KEEP OUT
I HATE TO HAVE TO TELL YOU THIS, OLD MAN, BUT ALL THAT FUSS WAS YOUR HOUSE BURNIN' DOWN.
HUH? NO MORE KANSAS? NO MORE STARSHIP?
WELL, RIGHT BACK THROUGH THAT LAST TIME WARP, TROOPS.
JUST DEPOSIT ME BACK IN OZ.
YOU BE OK, MR?
SURE KIDS.
MAY THE SAUCE BE WITH YOU. OVER AND OUT.
FIN

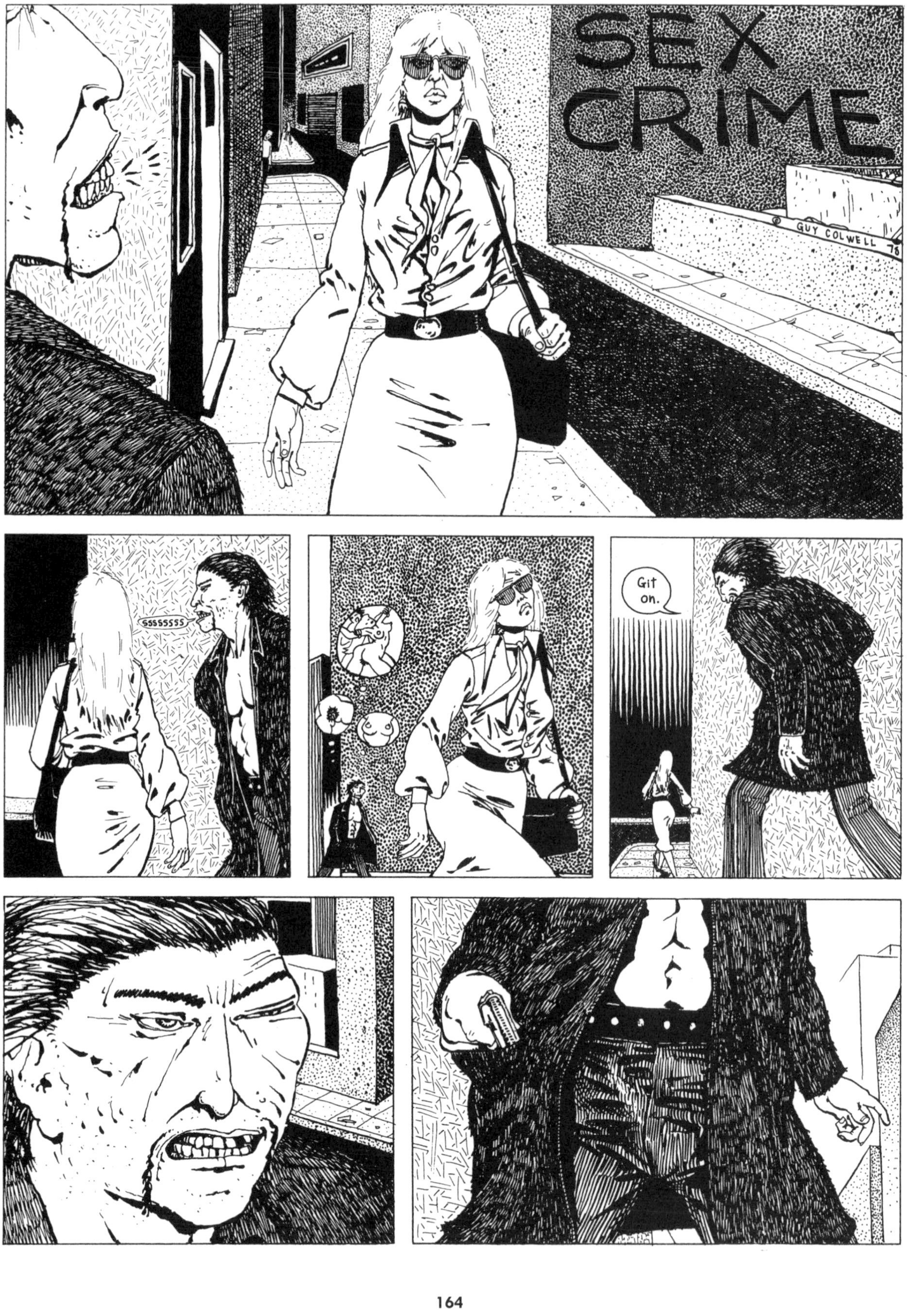
SEX CRIME
© GUY COLWELL 78
SSSSSSSS
Git on.

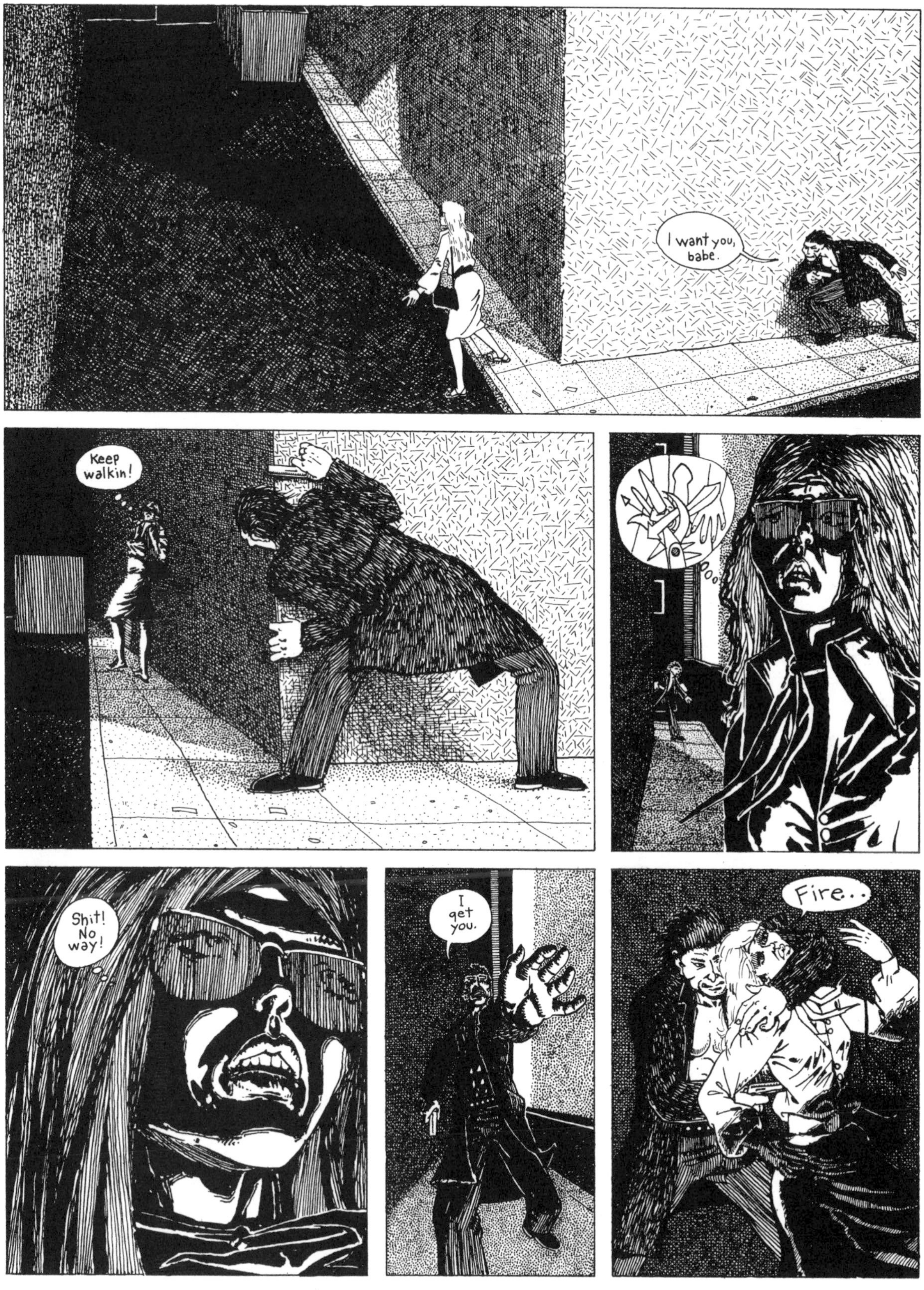
I want you, babe.
Keep walkin!
Shit! No way!
I get you.
Fire...

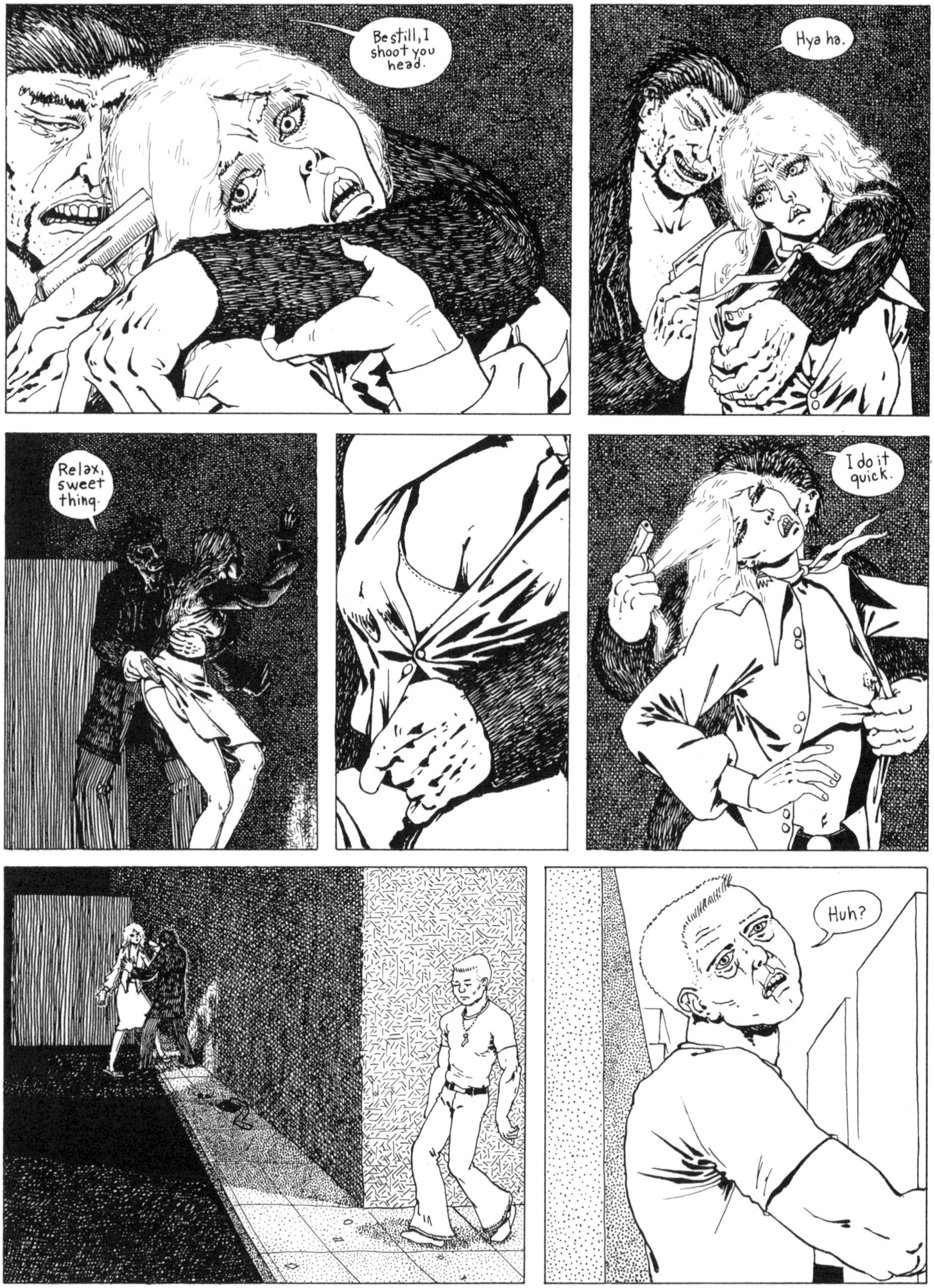
Be still, I shoot you head.
Hya ha.
Relax, sweet thing.
I do it quick.
Huh?

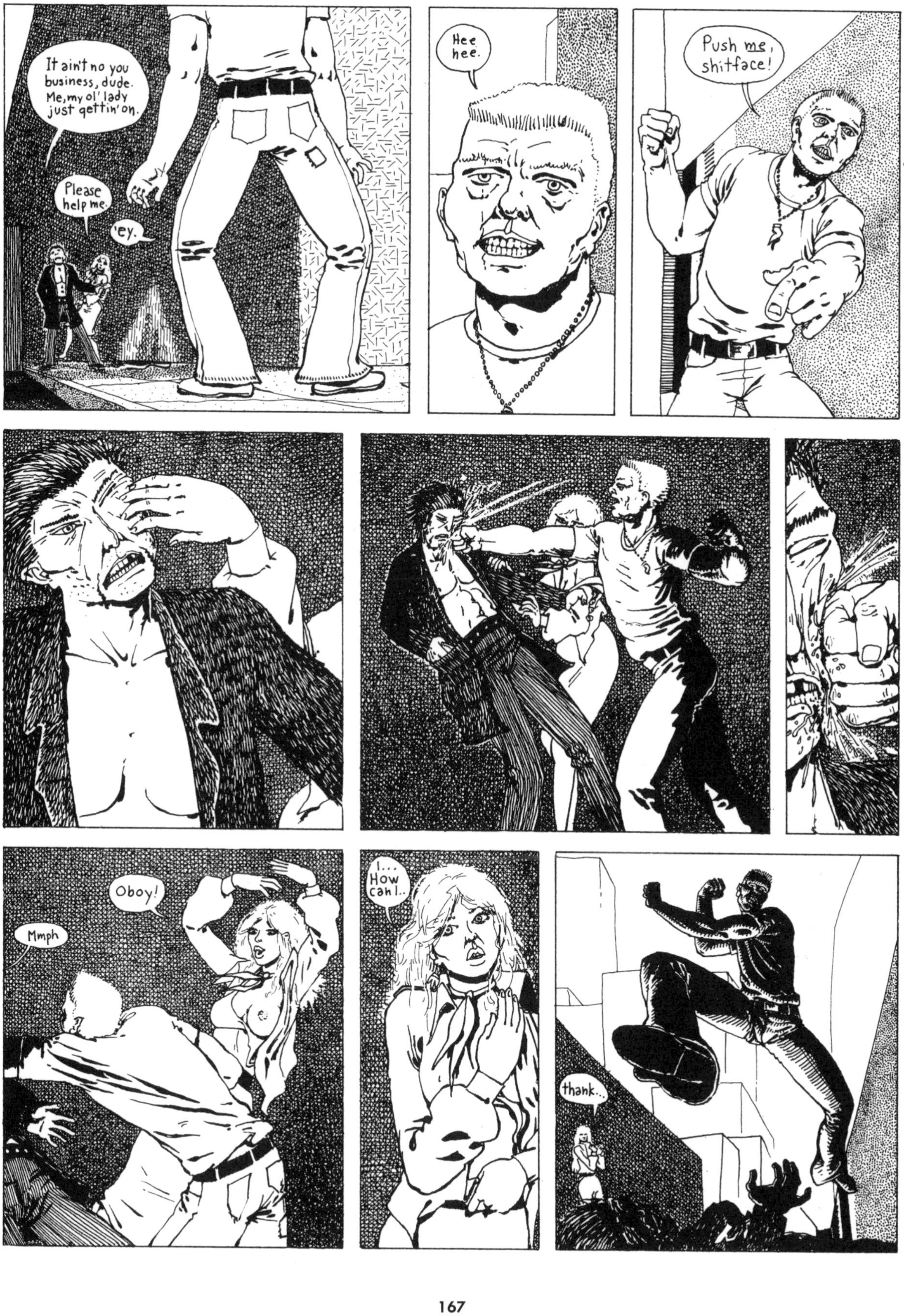
It ain't no you business, dude. Me, my ol' lady just gettin' on.
Please help me.
'ey.
Hee hee.
Push me, shitface!
Oboy!
Mmph
I... How can I..
thank...

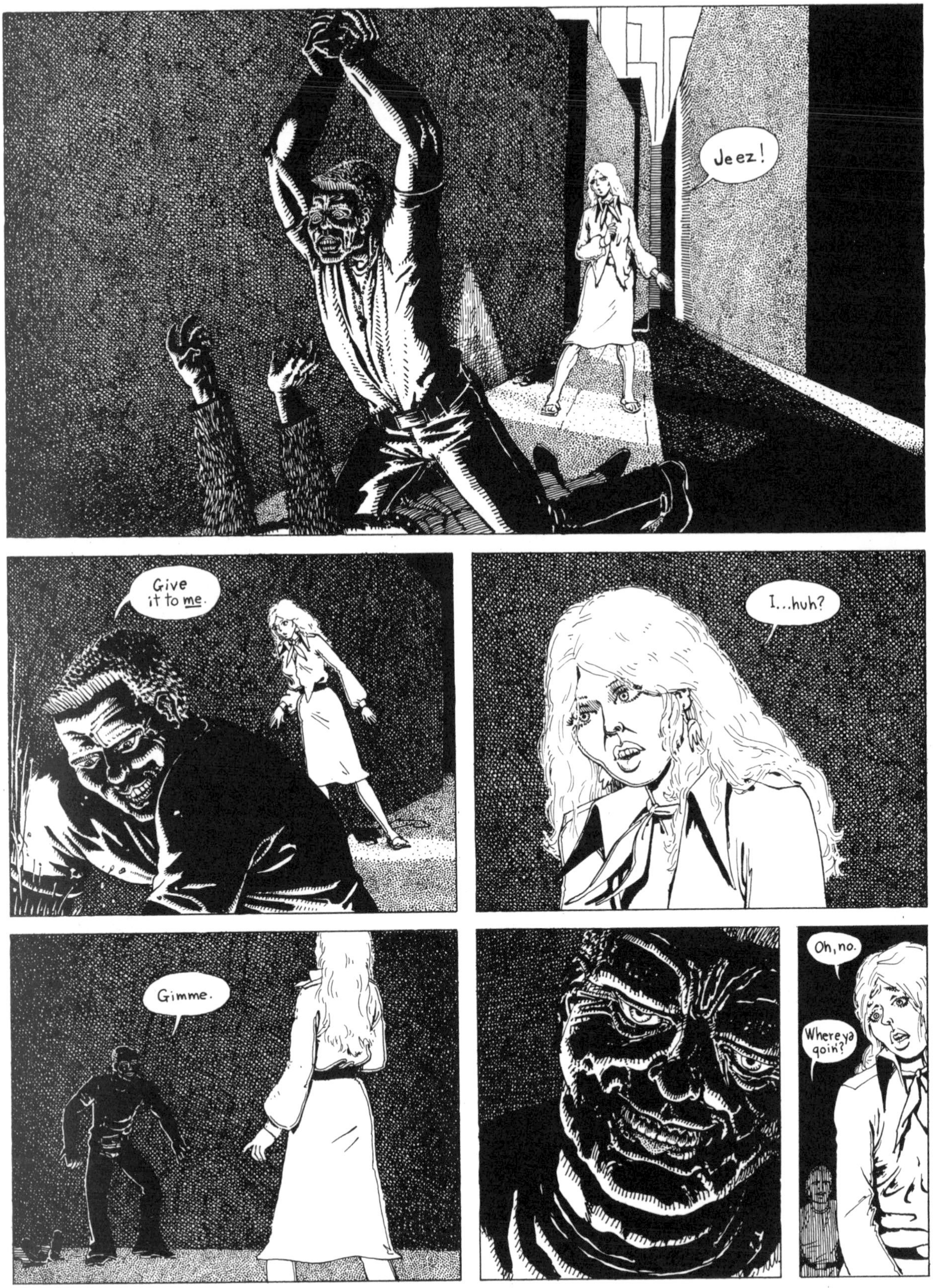
Jeez!
Give it to me.
I...huh?
Gimme.
Oh, no.
Where ya goin?

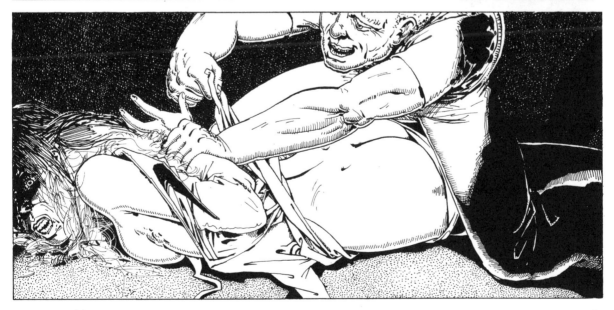

You gun!
BLAM!
BLAM!
You all right, lady?

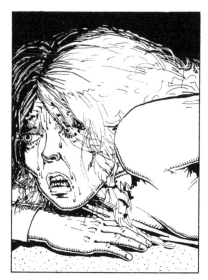

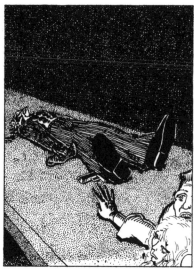

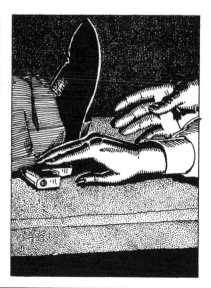

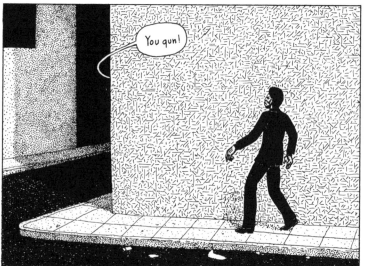

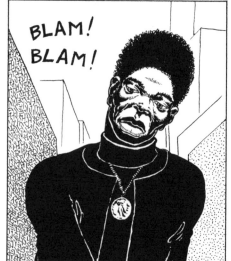

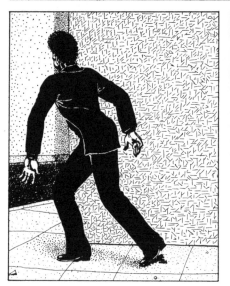

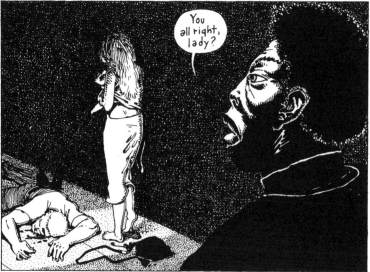

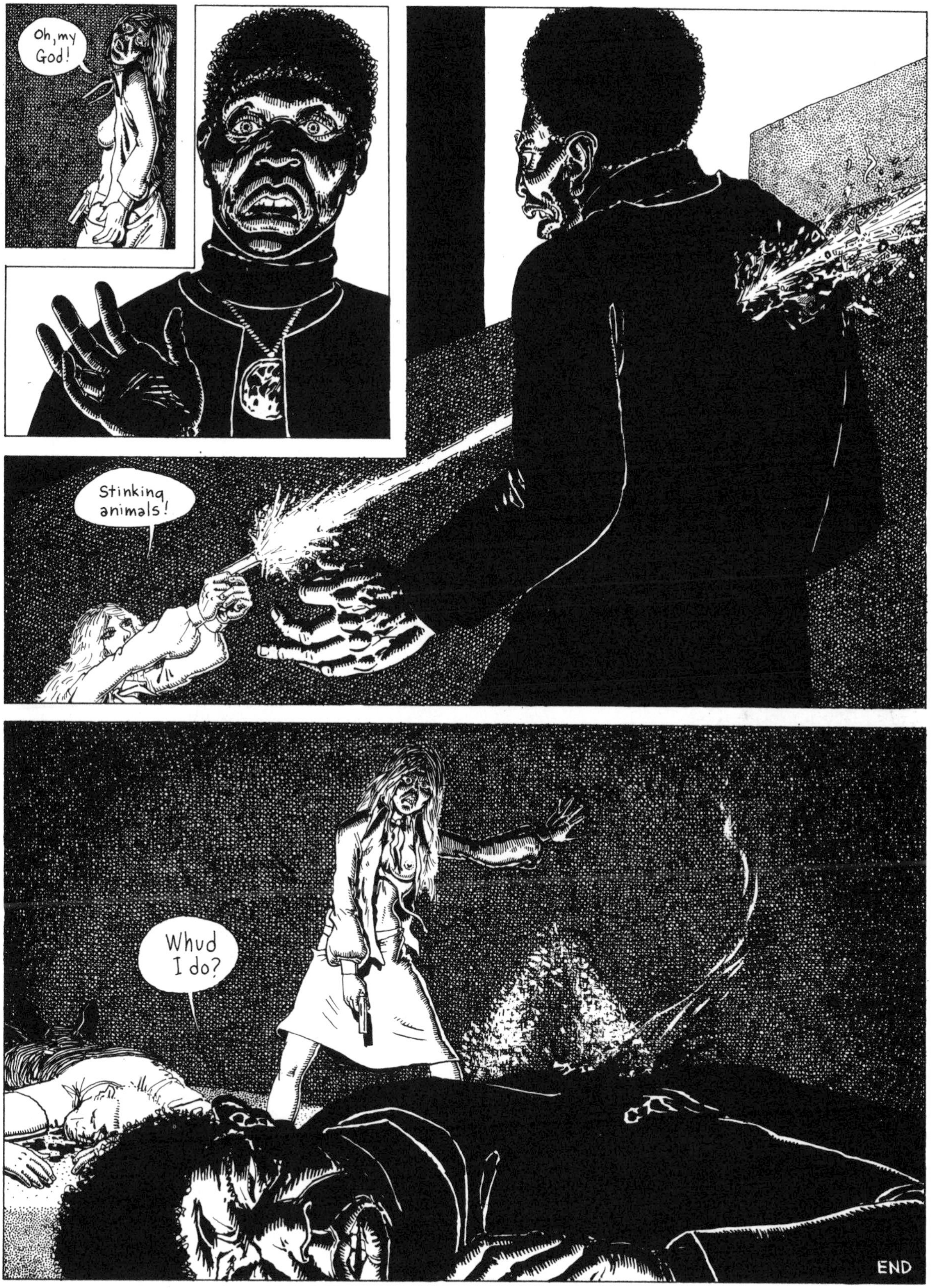
Oh, my God!
Stinking animals!
Whud I do?
END

ALL OVER THE CLOVER

© GUY COLWELL 1978

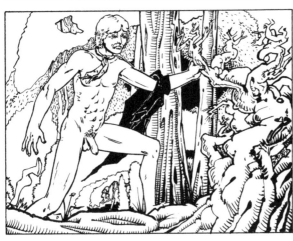

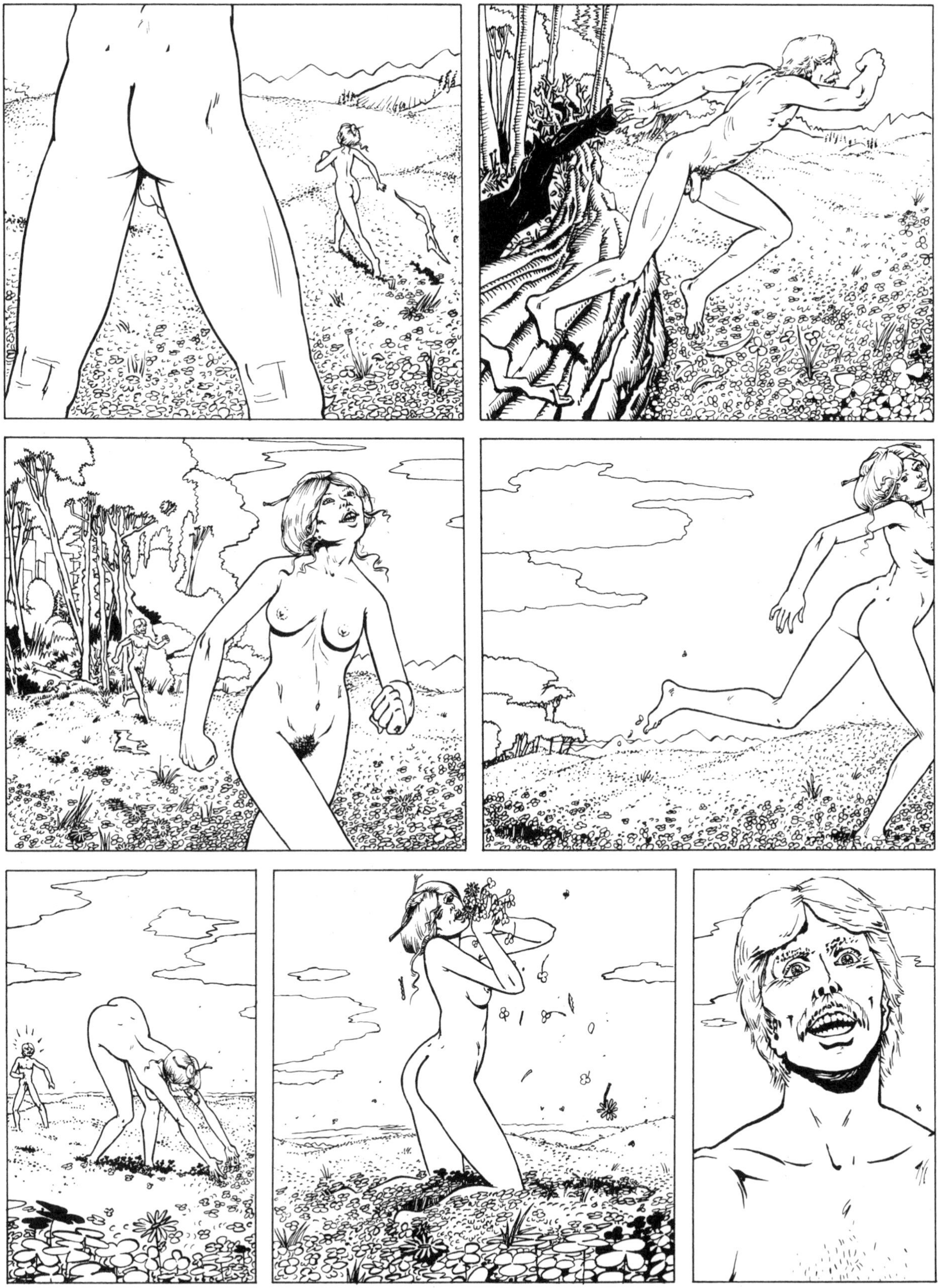

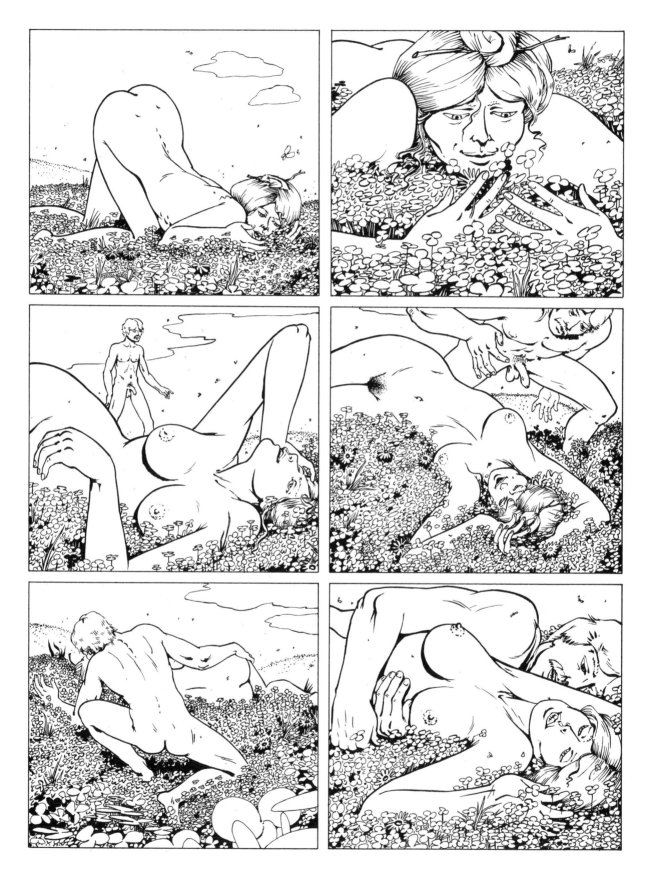

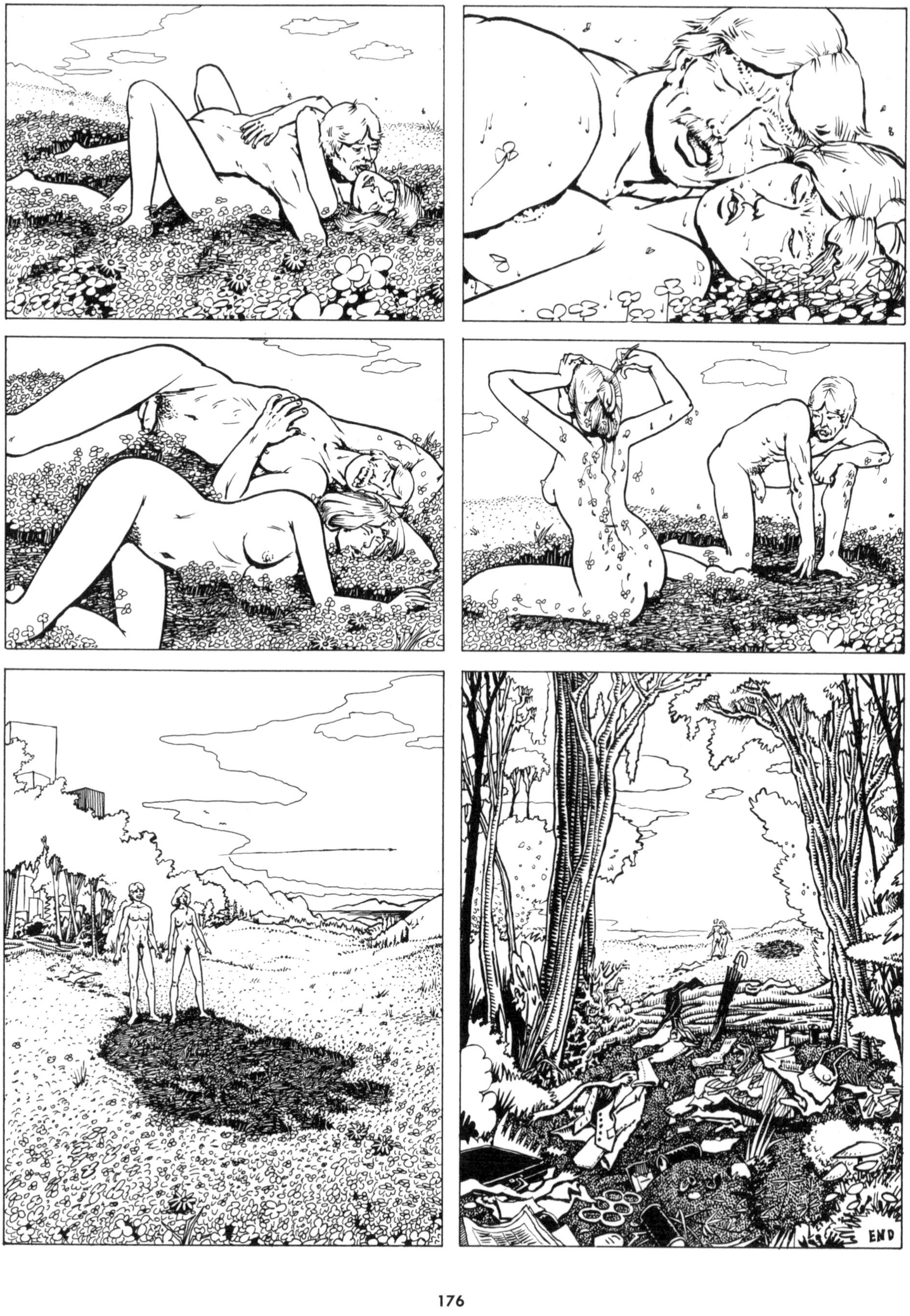
END

EPILOGUE

by Patrick Rosenkranz

Inner City Romance was created during a tumultuous time in our society when cultural and political divisions threatened to bring about another American revolution. It was also a chaotic period for the artist, whose experiences with anti-war protest, incarceration, drug use, sexual liberation, poverty, and radical politics provided the impetus for his art. The social and economic topics addressed in this series represent the viewpoints of the least influential segments of society, and conditions for them have not changed much since that time. Young people are still sent off to fight wars for the interests of the powerful, wealth remains in the hands of an elite oligarchy, freedom of expression is squelched in the interests of national security, and petty lawbreakers spend time behind bars while war criminals and corporate crooks luxuriate in mansions.

"*Inner City Romance* is quite possibly the best, the most artistic of the politically oriented undergrounds. Writer-artist Colwell resists broad caricature more than others working his turf and though he doesn't always succeed in it, his books possess a feeling of humanity that overrides their issues. Colwell is especially good at depicting those tensions and conflicts that arise among those in the poverty life, that threaten to keep the poor powerless and divided, and because of this he's able to show the muddle of motives and emotions that make for real political life. Colwell's leftist sympathies may force him to idealize, but his art is no less real for that."

— Bill Sherman, *The Comics Journal*

"Colwell's art is motivated by two primary sentiments: first, a deep political strain meant to expose and offer commentary on current political, economic, and racial disparities that exist in our society, and second, an awareness of man's uncomfortable relationship with nature and sexuality. Often he presents utopian scenes as if to suggest what could exist. At other times, he highlights racial strife and man's baseness. Both are about asking the viewer to contemplate contemporary society and reflect on rationality and the presumption of social progress during an era of great technological advancement."

— Matt Gonzalez, *Juxtapoz*

Mandala for Post-civilized Pre-pubescents, 1976. This oil-on-canvas mandala composition — a celebration of the hippie mindset, with its vision of a diverse, loving community rejecting the corruption of the urban world and returning to nature — also has a strongly satirical edge. Colwell, a cynical observer of these movements, was never inclined to wholeheartedly embrace flower power or to avoid engagement in the struggle and vitality of modern urban life.

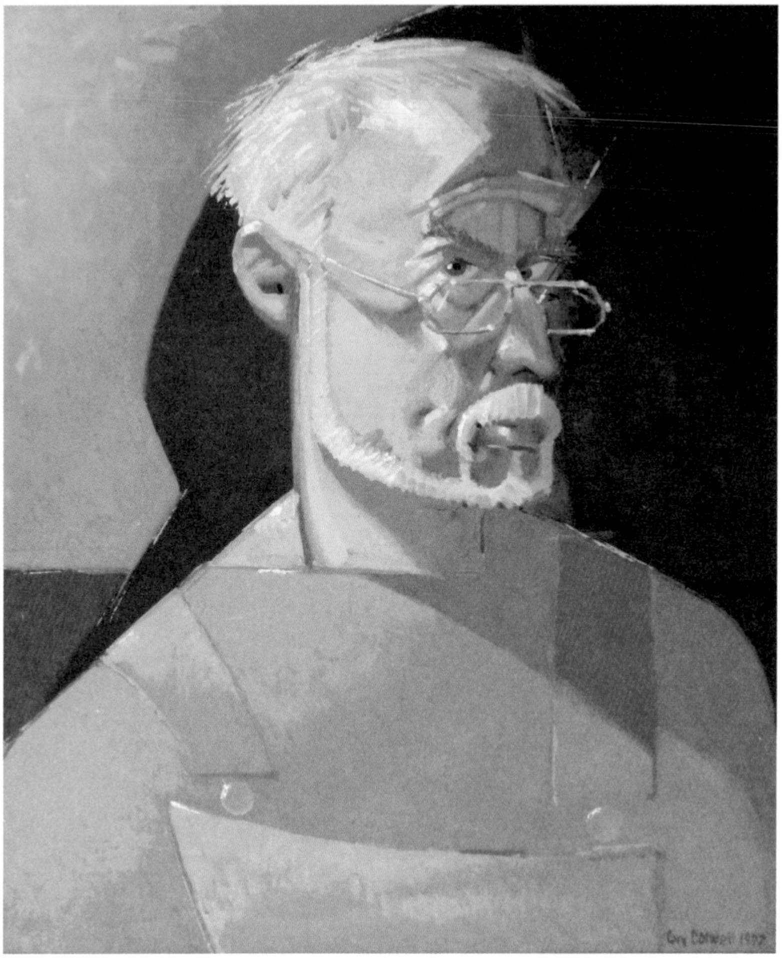
Guy Colwell 1997

Self-Portrait in Green Overalls, oil on canvas, 1997. Colwell looks at his encroaching maturity. Already white-haired, balding, and watching his eyesight deteriorate, he remains confident he still has many productive years ahead.

THE ARTIST

by Patrick Rosenkranz

Guy Colwell was born and raised in the East Bay and still lives and works in Berkeley today. He purposely pursued an artistic career from early childhood and is still productive at age 69 as this book is coming together.

"I have never been a humorous joke writer and I suppose I lack some funny aptitude. I have a kind of serious view of the world and a strong aversion to seeing myself getting into doing things frivolous or trivial."

His single mother, an artist who encouraged his aspirations, raised him and his older brother.

"My father was Claude Arnold Colwell, born 1893 in Alaska, of Scotch-Irish ancestry. He died of cancer in 1946 when I was 11 months old. My mother was Esther Jensen Colwell, born in 1912, the second child of Danish immigrants. She died in 2013 at the age of 101. My brother is Claude Arnold Colwell Jr., known as Arne, born 1943 in St. Paul, Minnesota. I was born March 28, 1945, in Oakland."

Oakland and Berkeley in the post–World War II years were much different than today — "the big city on the edge of wildness," as he describes it in *Central Body: The Art of Guy Colwell.*

"During numerous periods of my life I have tried, as so many people do, to get a little closer to nature. My brother and I spent many days in the wildness of the East Bay

hills and big parks — walking, exploring, often getting off the trails and pushing our way through the forested undergrowth. There was great pleasure in this, but we would often come home with the marks of nature's sharp edges: bee stings, mosquito bites, cuts and bruises, horrendous poison oak. It was fun and beautiful, but the wild places had their claws out. Yet throughout my life I kept going back there and reaching for the joy and beauty. When older, I would take a backpack and tent and go often on solo hikes along seashores or into mountains. It was always calling, but a place to which we cannot return. In my painting there is very often an urban/wild nature blend or a human/wild animal dichotomy. I am always strongly drawn to nature and wildness as a place of constant visual stimulation and for its illusion of quiet, calming peace. But I know there is a chasm between humans and the rest of the natural world and that there is a relentless, remorseless struggle for existence going on there. Humans in modern societies can walk through it, but we have become so good at being able to live long lives without the necessity to kill with our claws and teeth or to flee from predators that we are, in a sense, no longer a part of the natural world. This is a blessing and a sorrow at the same time, and it is a theme that appears in much of my work."

Peace March in Nebraska, watercolor, 1987. This painting commemorates one of the many strange and fascinating interactions between West Coast peaceniks and surprised middle Americans along the route of the 1986 Great Peace March for Global Nuclear Disarmament.

Peace Talks, watercolor, 1987. This painting tries to articulate that some people want to make war and others want to talk peace; and perhaps in this chaos of human aspirations we might even be creeping slowly toward a better, more just, and peaceful world.

Social consciousness is another theme that has permeated Colwell's work for four decades. His life and his art remain inevitably entwined. The issues in his heart are the subjects of his compositions.

"Being more of a hippie peacenik than doctrinaire revolutionary, as we came out of the Vietnam era, my activist focus went more to the anti-nuclear-weapons movement. In the later '70s, I became an organizer for the Bay Area Artists for Nuclear Disarmament, and in the '80s, I helped recruit people for and participated in the Great Peace March for Global Nuclear Disarmament that walked from Los Angeles to Washington, D.C. Throughout all the years since those times, I have tried to keep serious social criticism and activist consciousness as a central part of my artwork."

Sexuality is another constant. His male and female characters, whether old or young, personify the sexual tensions of every conflict and resolution. To couple is to communicate. His best-known erotic comics series, *Doll*, from the 1990s, centers on an astoundingly realistic love mannequin who compels men to fight for her possession. Her passive acceptance of their desires is a weapon of mass destruction that threatens both sexual liberation and Puritanism.

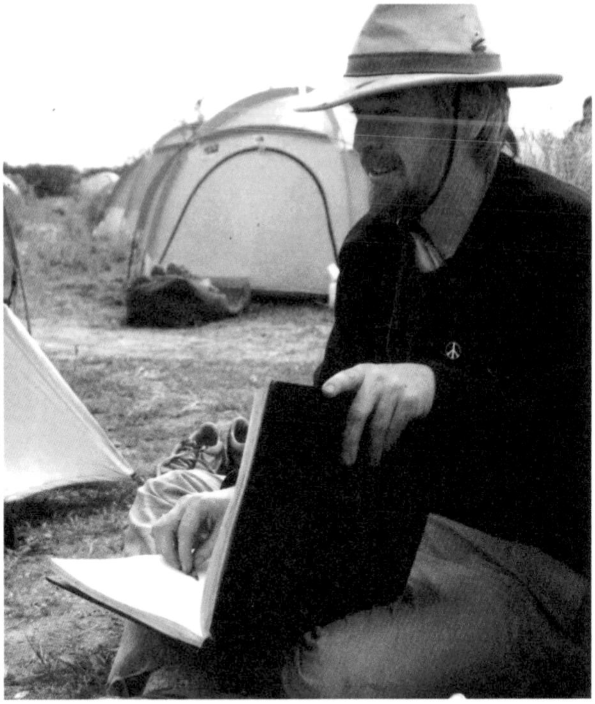

Colwell on the Great Peace March for Global Nuclear Disarmament in 1986. He was still fresh and eager near the beginning of the 3,700-mile journey, which was sometimes on foot and sometimes in vehicles. Fatigue would eventually take its toll, however.

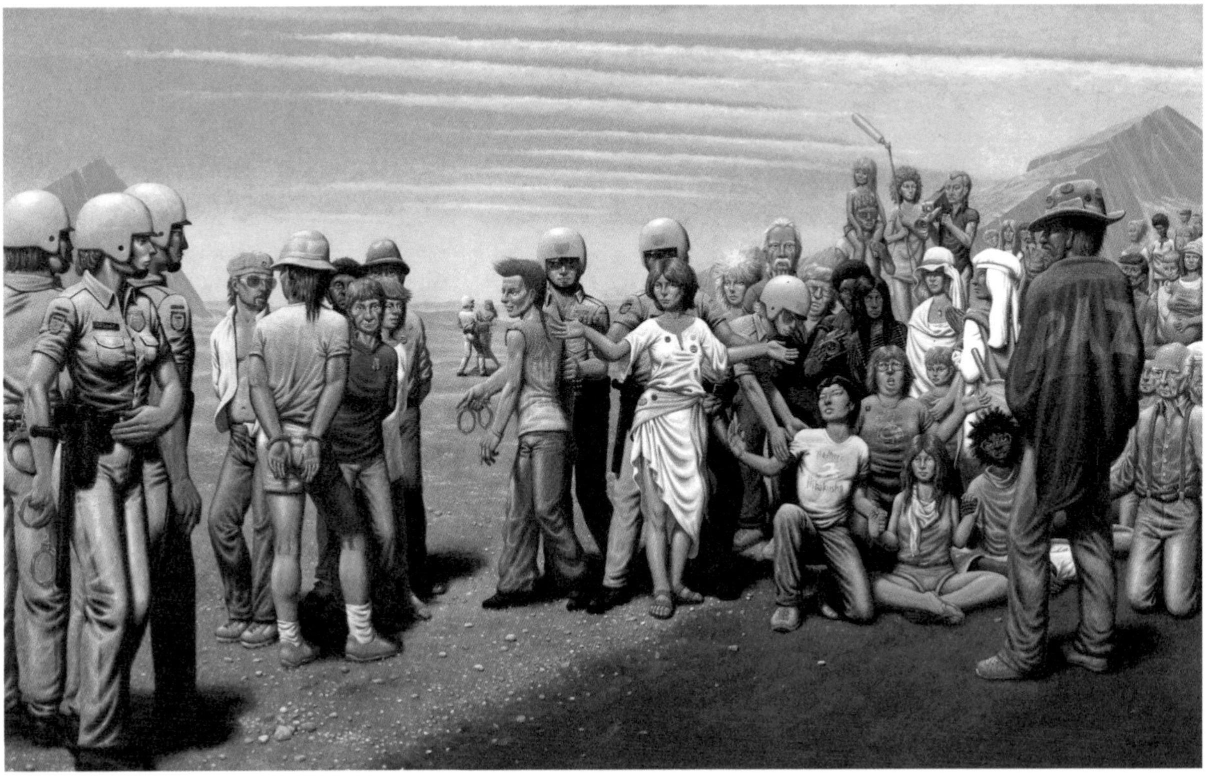

Blockade: Ritual of Non-Violence, oil on canvas, 1989. This ritualized peaceful protest was painted after Colwell took part in an anti-nuclear-weapons demonstration at the Nevada test site.

Colwell in a Zambian village, 1990. One memorable day during a month-long tent-camping journey through Zimbabwe, Zambia, and Malawi, Colwell sketched faces in the village of Cheperan.

artist who did paintings, murals, and prints for at least 20 years before making his first comic book. Black-and-white comics are not what he wants to be remembered for, but he readily admits he really enjoyed drawing them.

"Comics, though in my mind always a secondary pursuit, have given me friends, income, recognition, and travel in a far more accelerated way than would be the case with painting. Doing comics can sometimes be thrilling, engaging, and obsessive. They have a compact and hurried intensity that makes them very exciting to do. A comic book is connected with today and tomorrow, while a painting is something coming out of centuries past and going into centuries future. Comics are rock 'n' roll, paintings are symphonic. Each come out of and answer to a different need. Even if I would prefer to be remembered as a painter, I will never regret that I devoted a big chunk of my time to comics. They not only helped me stay attached to the here and now, they have made it a little richer and happier."

Another comics series, *Stacia Stories*, based on an actual woman of his acquaintance, and numerous nude paintings of men and women in all sizes and shapes demonstrate Colwell's concentrated attention to sexual identity and animal attraction. His subjects remove their clothes to reveal their identities.

His up close and personal firsthand accounts of political action dominate much of his work, showing activists in action and the reactions of the power structure. His paintings also show the impacts of his backpacking adventures in Europe, where he sketched medieval architecture and studied the works of Renaissance masters in England, France, Spain, Italy, and Greece, and the influences of residing in Paris and London. He also chronicles his later trips to both black southern Africa and Islamic northern Africa, where he simultaneously encountered exotic cultures and poverty on a scale unknown in America.

Colwell considers comics such as *Inner City Romance* to be a sideline to his more serious work. He was a pictorial

Gathering Berries on Zomba Plateau, oil on canvas, 1992. The high Zomba Plateau in Malawi is cooled by its elevation above the surrounding savannah. This painting was based on sketches done there in 1990. This natural setting is a stone's throw from a busy complex of government buildings.

GALLERY

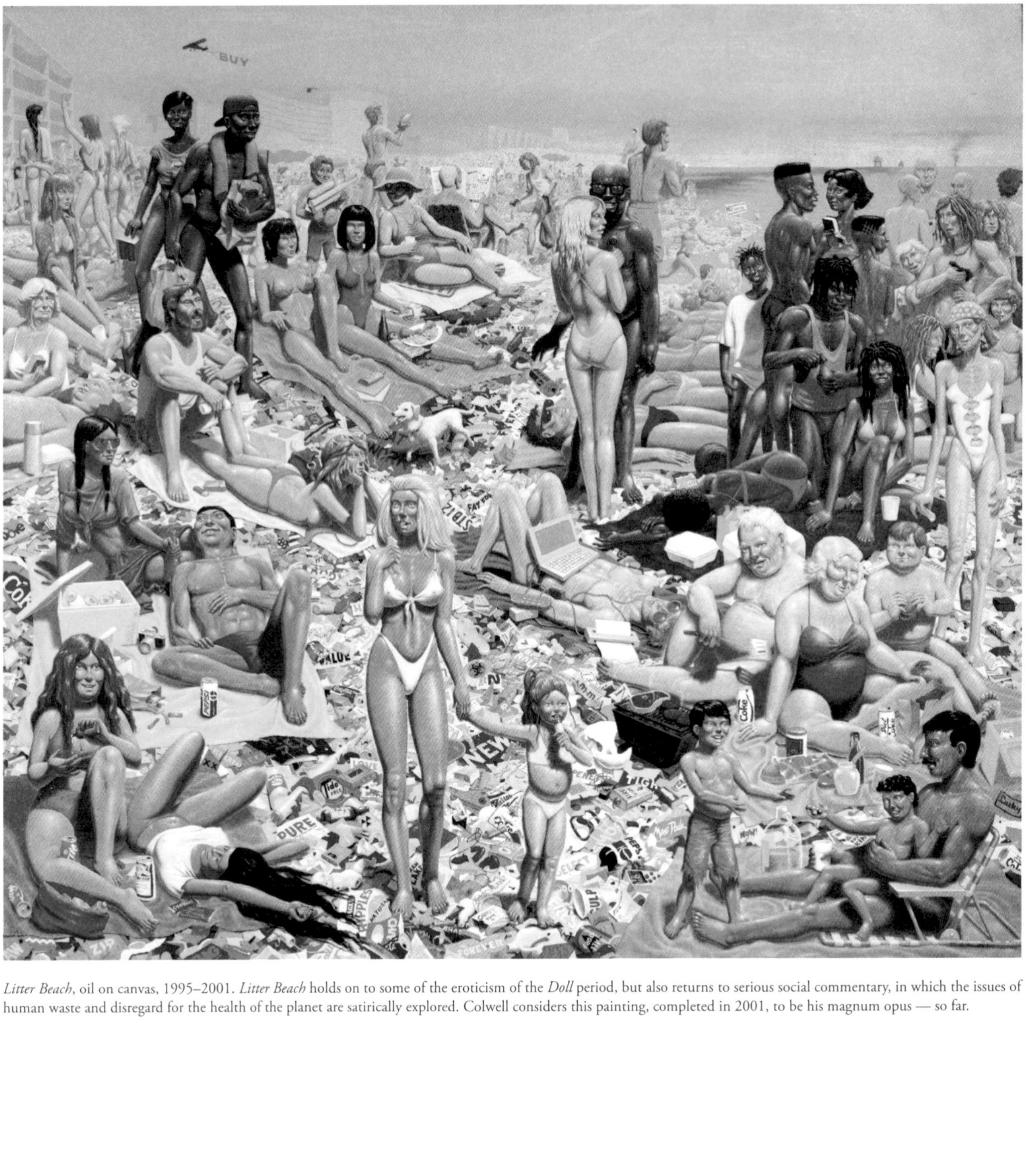
BUY
PURE
ZIP
FOREVER

Litter Beach, oil on canvas, 1995–2001. *Litter Beach* holds on to some of the eroticism of the *Doll* period, but also returns to serious social commentary, in which the issues of human waste and disregard for the health of the planet are satirically explored. Colwell considers this painting, completed in 2001, to be his magnum opus — so far.

Not Exactly Peaceable Kingdom, acrylic on canvas, 2012. This complex composition took a full year to complete. It addresses both the alienation of humans from the natural world and the reality that life in that world is a brutal, ceaseless struggle for survival.

Reception: Self-Portrait With Mop, acrylic on canvas, 2008. Colwell worked for a time as a janitor at the Berkeley Repertory Theater. Rubbing elbows with affluent theater patrons made economic inequality a more prominent theme in his work.

Woman With Melon, acrylic on canvas, 1994. One of the people prepping veggies for the Berkeley chapter of Food Not Bombs was the subject of a sketch that became a painting. One may wonder if, 20 years later, this young woman is still displaying her collection of metallic piercings or if she has settled back into something less overtly renegade.

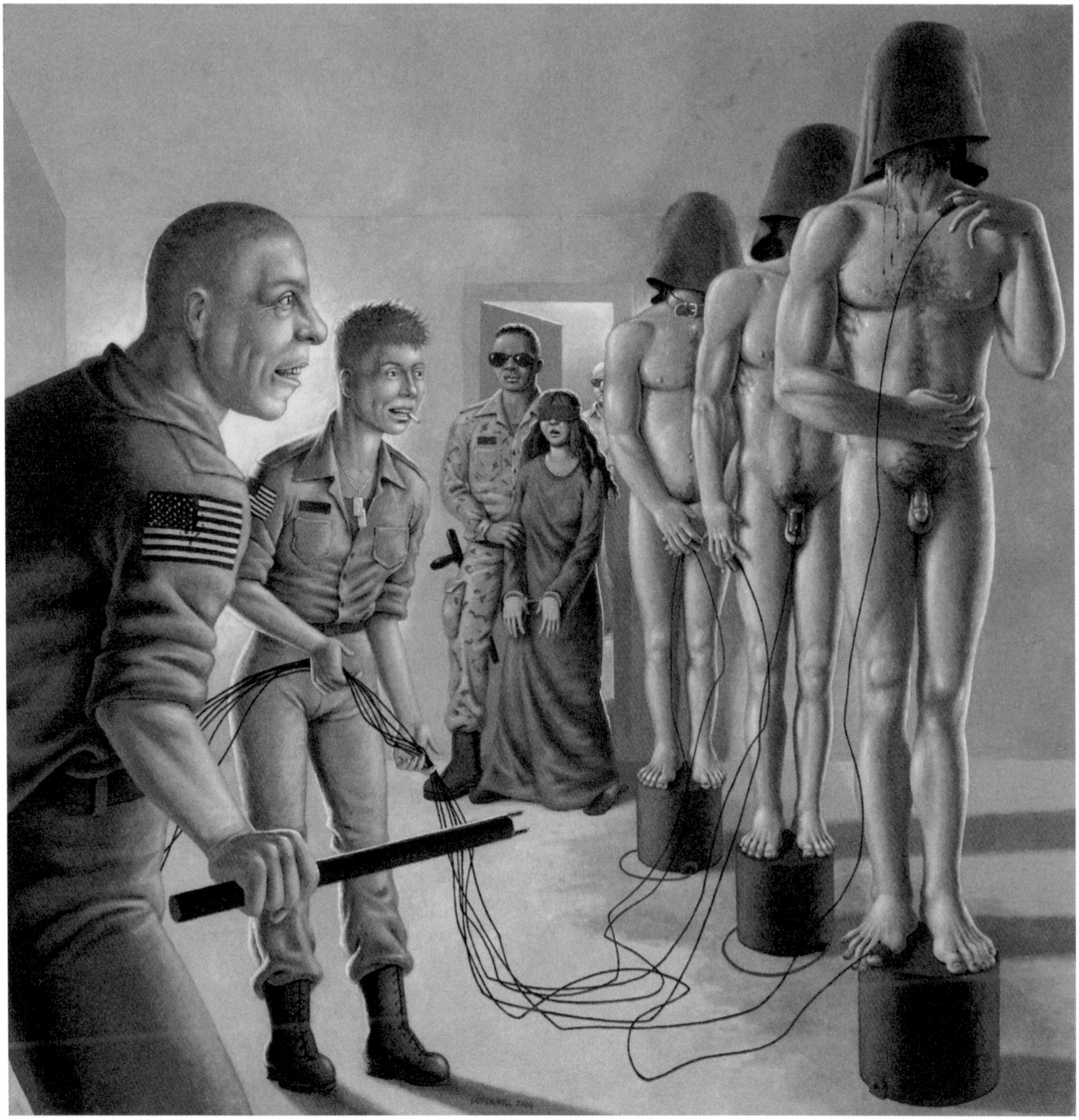

The Abuse, acrylic on canvas, 2004. After 9/11, Colwell felt compelled to be more thoughtful about his subject matter and to revive his political commentary instead of drawing only comics and nudes. This painting of abusive interrogation techniques at the Abu Ghraib prison in Iraq caused an uproar when the gallery displaying it was vandalized and the owner was physically assaulted. The incident, reported internationally, demonstrated the vital power of visual images to impact social discourse — but it also nearly destroyed Colwell's ability to find venues to show his new art.

Institutional Warthog, acrylic on canvas, 2005. It would be shockingly strange to encounter a living wild animal within our clean, sealed, unnatural spaces. Confronting it might frighten us, but we are the products of the same evolutionary wildness as these creatures. The animal truth is within us, and while we may try to hide it from ourselves, the connections are inescapable.

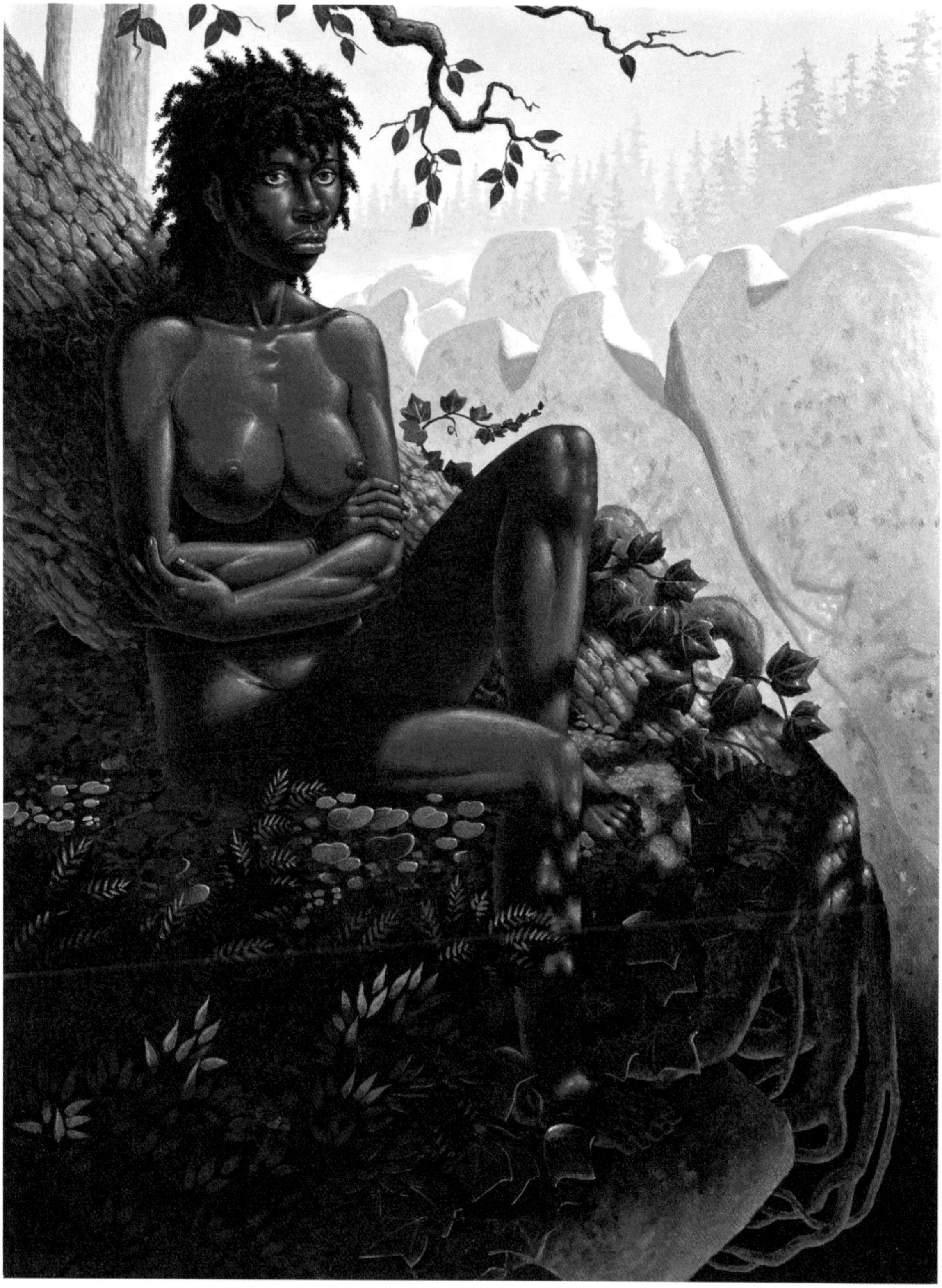

Woman at the Edge, acrylic on canvas, 1993. Colwell drew inspiration for this painting from both his erotic comics work and his travels in Africa. The woman's face is based on a sketch of an ice cream vendor in Victoria Falls, Zimbabwe.

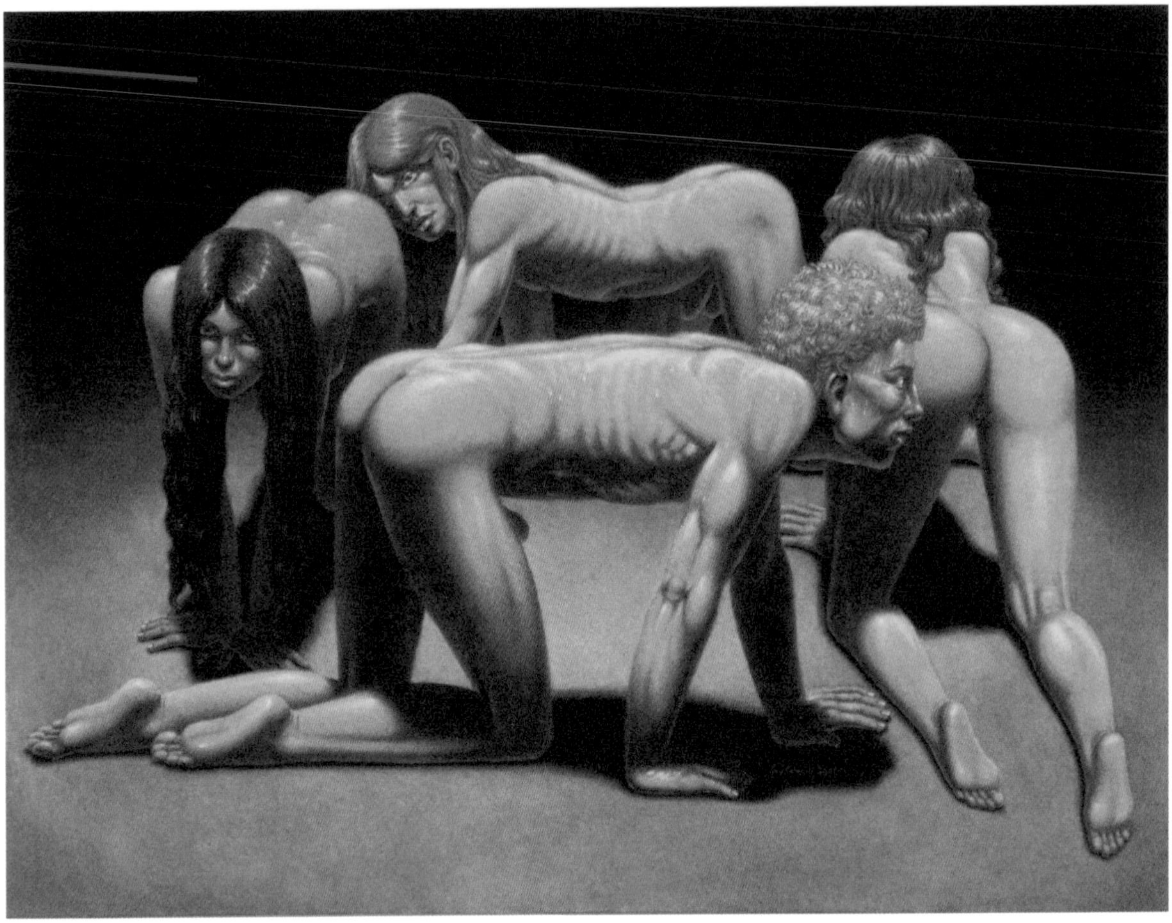

Four Crawlers, oil on canvas, 1989. Good sales of *Doll* comics encouraged more daring erotic imagery. This painting goes a little deeper into the purely sexual realm.

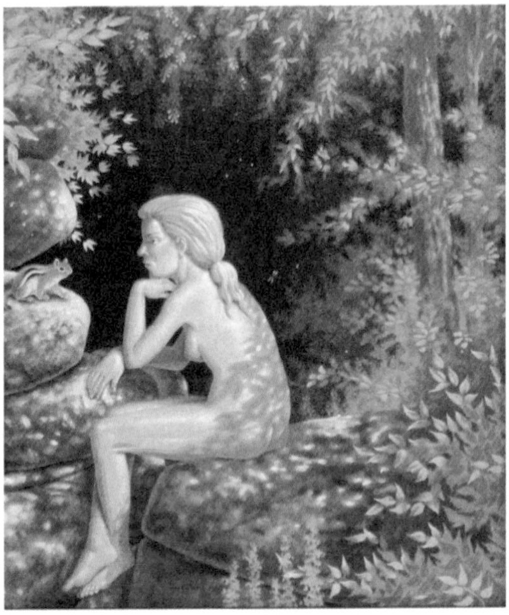

Woman and Ground Squirrel, acrylic on canvas, 1993. The human figure, animals, and natural scenery are all engaging subjects for the painter. Here Colwell puts them all together in an idealistic scene of quiet communion with nature.

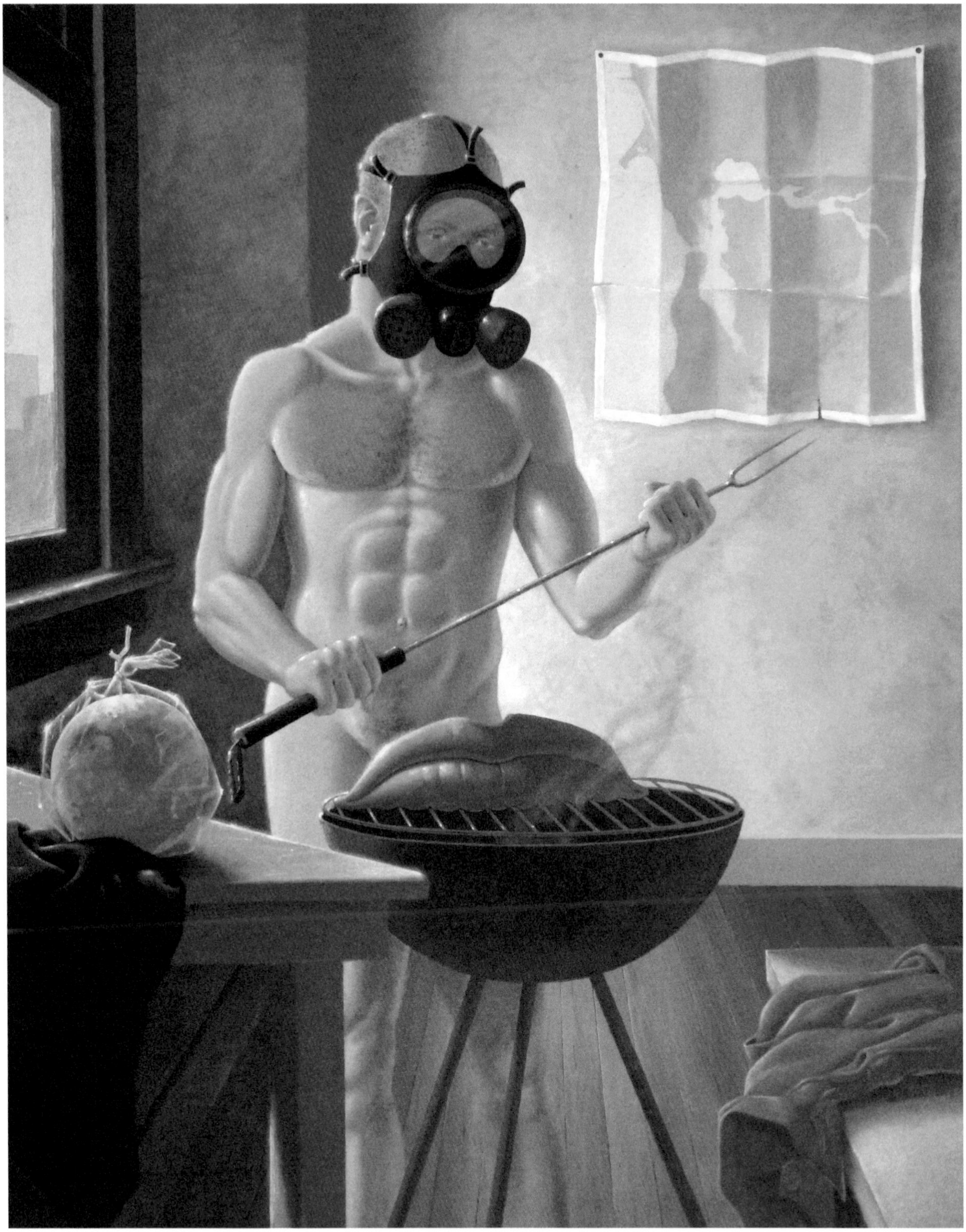

Gasmask, acrylic on canvas, 2001. This painting is from a series of experiments using randomly derived surrealist imagery. Drawn out of a bag full of written words were "gasmask," "twist tie," "barbecue," "Mars," and "lips." And there it is. This painting was also influenced by the lighting in the works of Johannes Vermeer.

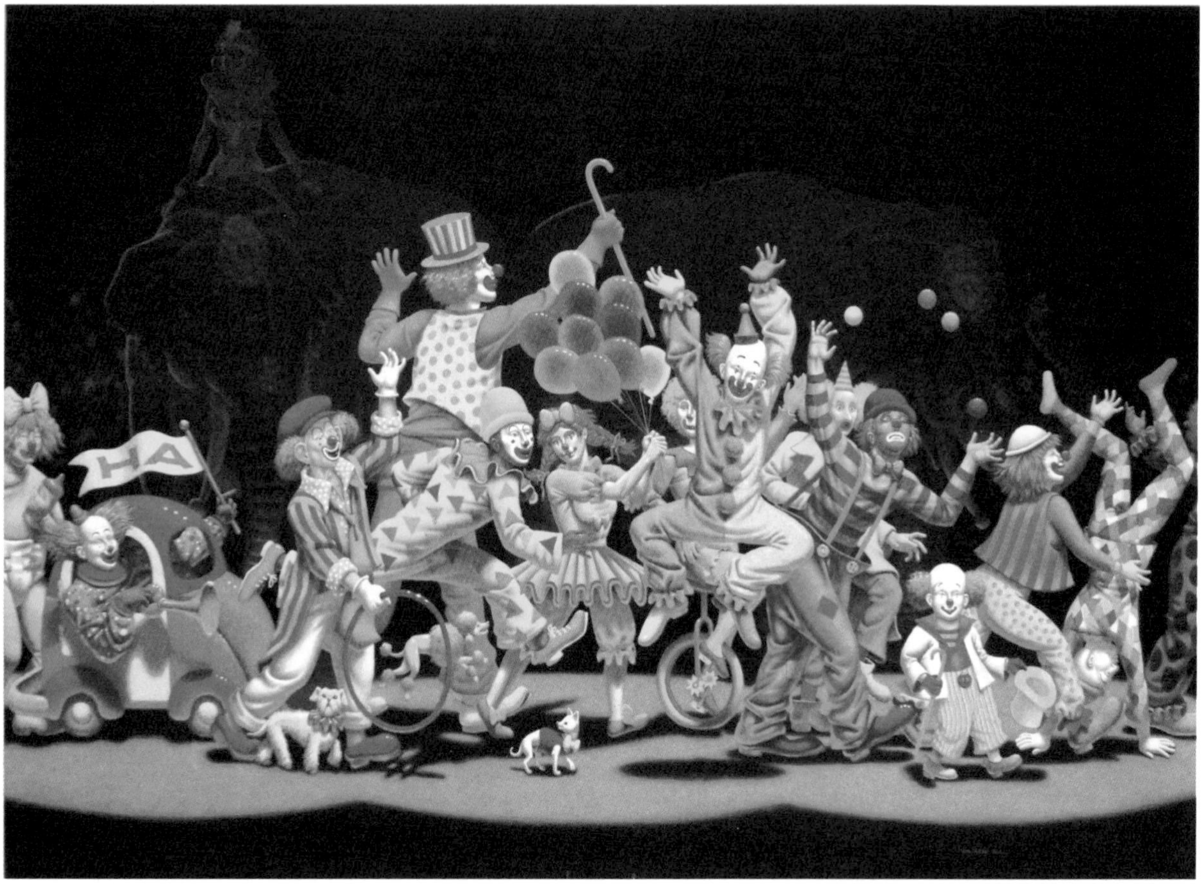
HA

Clowns, acrylic on canvas, 2013. More than just comic relief, this is an allegory of a human lifetime. The figure of a baby enters on the left and the red-and-black representative of death beckons on the right. Throughout our own lifetimes, we do our own little dances from behind our masks, strutting and fretting from beginning to end, trying to make sense of our often-farcical existences.

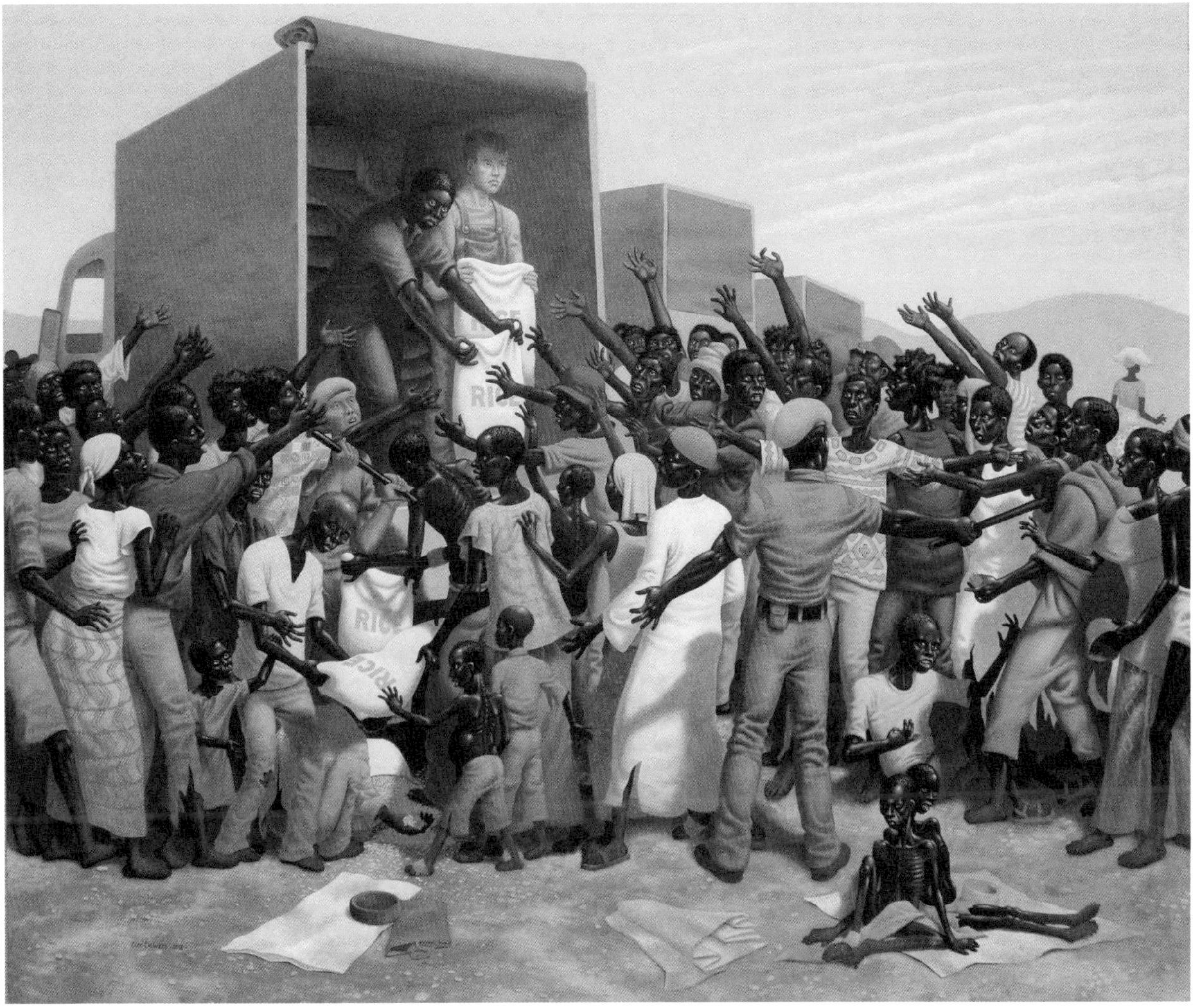
RICE

The Distribution, acrylic on canvas, 2013. This picture focuses on the universal issue of hunger, one of the most unnecessary miseries on our planet, which must be alleviated before there can ever be peace.

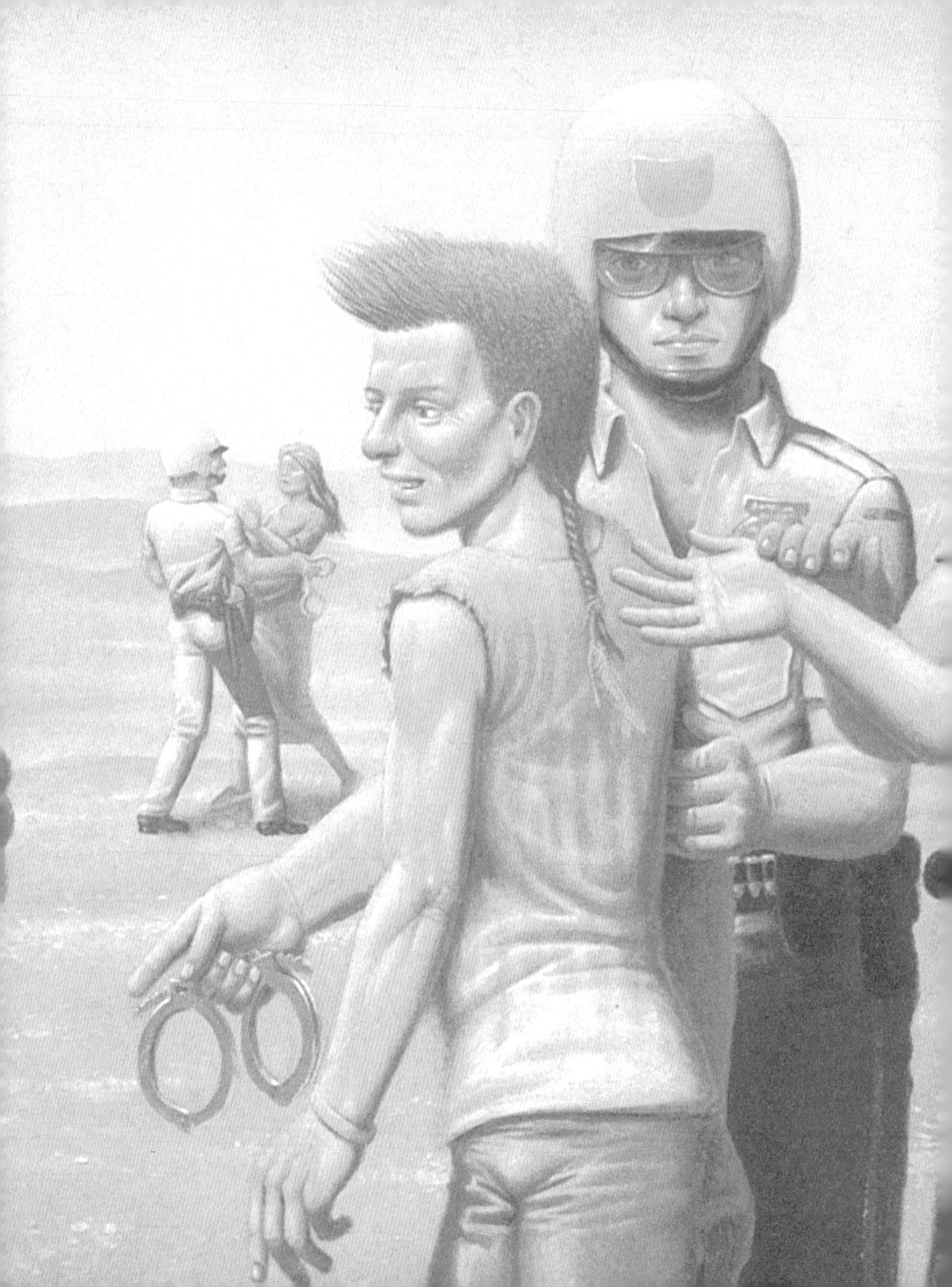